RICHARD HOOKER

Of the Laws of Ecclesiastical Polity

L.E.P.—A

RICHARD HOOKER

Of the Laws of Ecclesiastical Polity

AN ABRIDGED EDITION

Edited by A. S. McGrade

PROFESSOR OF PHILOSOPHY
UNIVERSITY OF CONNECTICUT

and Brian Vickers

PROFESSOR OF ENGLISH LITERATURE
UNIVERSITY OF ZÜRICH

SIDGWICK & JACKSON
LONDON

This edition first published in Great Britain in 1975

ISBN 0 283 97970 4

Printed in Great Britain by A. Wheaton & Company, Exeter
for Sidgwick and Jackson Limited
1 Tavistock Chambers, Bloomsbury Way
London WC1A 2SG

In gratitude for the work of
R. S. Crane, R. P. McKeon

CONTENTS

Preface

Richard Hooker's *Of the Laws of Ecclesiastical Polity* is the first major work in the fields of politics, theology and philosophy to have been written in English. As such it is of particular value to all students of the English sixteenth century, whether their interests be in the history of constitutional theory, the religious controversies of the Reformation, or the expressive and argumentative resources of English prose. The purpose of this edition is to make available to the general reader and to the college or university student a selection of the key phases of Hooker's argument in a modernized readable form, and with two introductions to set the work first in its philosophical-historical, second in its literary contexts.

The first modern edition of Hooker was that prepared by John Keble, published by the Clarendon Press in 1836, and reprinted with corrections and modifications, the last printing being that of 1888 (the seventh) edited by R. W. Church and F. Paget. A new full-scale edition, based on a fresh examination of the text and with appropriate annotation, is now proposed by the Folger Shakespeare Library of Washington, D.C., and is to be published by the Harvard University Press. It will be produced by an international team of authorities on Hooker and the Reformation (including one of our number, A. S. McGrade) and will be spread over six volumes. Inevitably, then, it will take several years to produce and its price will probably be beyond the resources of most students. For these reasons we felt it worth while to issue a one-volume edition at a reasonable cost.

Our policy has been to include complete texts of the three most important parts of Hooker's historical, philosophical and political argument, the Preface, Book I and Book VIII. The old Everyman edition (by R. A. Bayne, 1907: rev. C. Morris, 1954) included only Books I–V, and was without much help to the student. Apart from Keble's edition, Book VIII has only been available (and that in a limited edition long out of print) in the doctoral dissertation of R. A. Houk (New York: Columbia University Press, 1931). So we are glad to be able to make Book VIII accessible again, especially since its discussion of the relationships between King and Church touches one of the key problems in the history of Elizabethan England, much discussed of late.

Due to the limits on the overall size of this edition it was not possible to include the whole of the remaining Books, but we have selected twenty-three of the eighty-one chapters of Book V, and strategically important chapters from the remainder. We always print complete chapters, and since we have included the table of contents for each Book the reader will be able to reconstruct the context for the present selections.

Our treatment of the annotation offered by Hooker and his editors has been guided by the nature of our edition and the audience for which it is intended. From Hooker's own annotations we have retained his Biblical references and those footnotes which add points of substance. Where Hooker gives a Greek or Latin quotation followed by a translation, we print – for reasons of space and cost – his translation only. On the few occasions when Hooker does not offer a translation we have added one in the footnotes (all editorial additions being placed within square brackets). Otherwise we have omitted, in the interests of economy, the Biblical references supplied by Keble, together with the chapter-or-page numbers given to Hooker's secular quotations either by himself or by his editors. We justify this decision for this edition on three grounds: first, Hooker's documentation of his quotations can be taken on trust – there is no juggling with the context such as some other Renaissance writers were given to. Secondly, a flow of references to often obscure patristic or medieval literature is only relevant in a detailed scholarly edition for specialists. Thirdly, such documentation of secondary material does not add to or detract from an understanding of Hooker's argument, and given a limitation on space we would rather include more of Hooker's text than more of his footnotes.

Our text is based on Keble's edition, although in many cases we have restored readings from the earlier editions or from the manuscripts. Our text for Book VIII derives from the manuscript in the library of Trinity College, Dublin, as edited by Keble and Houk. Both editors occasionally departed from the sequence of chapters as given in this manuscript, and Keble even relegated some passages to the appendices and footnotes. The inconsistencies and incoherences throughout the later stages of Book VIII indicate that Hooker did not complete his revision of it, but (with one exception*) we have restored the sequence as found in the Dublin manuscript, which, in the present state of knowledge, seems to be our sole substantive authority for this Book. Because of our departures from Keble's arrangement of Book VIII, our sections 1–8 in Chapter iv correspond with his sections 8 and 1–7, while our sections 10–15 in Chapter vi correspond with Keble's Appendix I and his sections vi. 14 and vi. 10–13.

For permission to base our text on Keble's we are extremely grateful to the delegates of the Clarendon Press. Professors W. Speed Hill and P. G. Stanwood have provided valuable advice and encouragement but are not,

* In Chapter iv the sequence in the Dublin manuscript (fol. 66v–76r) seems awkward, and we agree with Houk in preferring the order as found in the other group of manuscripts. We restore the passage (Dublin ms. 96r–102v) which Keble relegated to an appendix, but we do not follow Houk in rearranging fo. 102–109.

of course, responsible for any deficiencies in this volume. To the staff of Sidgwick & Jackson, especially John Chancellor, and, subsequently, William Armstrong and Jan Widdows, we owe thanks for their stimulus and patience. Christopher Busby will know how much we owe to him. Finally, for help at various stages of preparing the text we are grateful to Gail Lawson, Jonathan Lee and Christian Casparis.

A. S. McGrade, Storrs—Tübingen *February, 1973*
Brian Vickers, Cambridge—Zürich

Note

We are most grateful to the text-editors of the Folger edition of Hooker, Professors Georges Edelen, W. Speed Hill, and P. G. Stanwood, for their extraordinary generosity in permitting us to adopt from their work in progress the following readings (page and line numbers in this volume are followed by a reading adopted and then, in parenthesis, by the reading from Keble it replaces): 74.3 inclinable (men's inclinable), 78.2 suffering (sufferings), 97.4 respect (respects), 97.22 founder (sounder), 156.23 which (that), 156.24 that (which), 164.8 love (law), 168.2 but (both), 169.32 those (these), 193.26 arts (acts), 210.28 thrice (twice), 216.25 be (the), 219.12 to (unto), 220.3 gather from thence (gather), 220.18 cases (causes), 220.21 so animate (animate), 223.27 like (like to), 224.34 altercations (altercation), 234.37 daily read (read), 250.12 him (them), 255.26 even in (in), 265.12 also of (of), 275.34 strong (strong enough), 344.9 so the (the), 344.19 old axiom (axiom), 345.17 in (into), 345.32 seats (states), 345.36 right if (right. If), 349.5 endued (endured), 349.18 they were most tied to law, and so (lawfully reigning they), 349.32 one hand (one), 350.15 or a magistrate, or a (a magistrate, or), 351.10 so (to), 355.6 our (one), 355.18 must (might), 356.2 mash (mast), 362.34 other (other's), 363.22 on any one (in any one), 369.33 societies. It (societies it), 371.37 to (then to), 375.11 but be (be but), 385.18 The (that), 385.40 these (those), 388.32 Christians (Christian), 389.6 Church's (Church), 399.34 reserve (refer), 404.42 did (notwithstanding did), 405.24 his (the), 409.9 commission (dominion), 411.19 service (her vice [service?]). In addition to these readings, we have adopted many changes of type-face and punctuation (especially in Book V) and have used Hooker's table of contents and chapter headings for Book VIII, newly discovered by Professor Stanwood, in place of those devised by Keble.

Introduction 1

HOOKER'S *POLITY* AND THE ESTABLISHMENT OF THE ENGLISH CHURCH

by A. S. McGrade

Richard Hooker's *Of the Laws of Ecclesiastical Polity* is so persuasive an account of Elizabethan Anglicanism that the modern reader often has difficulty understanding the purpose for which it was written. The work itself shows a strain of Stoicism from the beginning: 'Though for no other cause, yet for this; that posterity may know we have not loosely through silence permitted things to pass away as in a dream, there shall be for men's information extant thus much concerning the present state of the Church of God established amongst us, and their careful endeavour which would have upheld the same' (Preface, 1, i, p. 63). Clearly, when he undertook its defence in the 1590s Hooker regarded 'the present state of the Church of God' as a cause easily to be lost. It is an ironic measure of his success that the *Polity* is commonly taken for a serene description of an immemorial, historically necessary institution, the Church of England. To understand Hooker in his own situation or discover what is truly timeless in his work, we must move beyond this monumental interpretation. We must approach Hooker as a man grappling with severe problems, attacking a powerful opposition, and seeking to interpret constructively an establishment that could by no means be taken for granted.

With hindsight we can see that the Anglican cause was in less peril at the end of the sixteenth century than it had been fifty years earlier or was to be fifty years later. At the beginning of Elizabeth's reign, the more zealous English Protestants, especially those exiles returning from Calvin's Geneva, confidently assumed that the reformation begun under Edward VI and reversed under Mary would now be completed to their satisfaction. As time wore on, however, it became evident that the ecclesiastical settlement hastily worked out in 1558–9 and embodied in the Acts of Supremacy and Uniformity would not readily be put aside. The bishops Elizabeth appointed were unsympathetic to further reform. The Queen herself, though not generous in positive support for her bishops, was adamant against all attempts to evict them or alter the forms of worship they strove to enforce. Elizabeth's character and political good fortune gained weight with all sides as the years passed, and mere experience of the established worship also had its effects. Indeed, Anglicanism had many defenders: able men like Hooker's early patron, Bishop Jewel, and, in his own generation, Sutcliffe, Bilson, and Cosins; tenacious men like Whitgift and Bancroft, both of whom became archbishops of Canterbury; wordy men like Dr Bridges, whose work was a fraction as profound as Hooker's but several times as bulky; and men with personal experience of reformed churches on the continent, such as Hooker's friend in later life, the pious Adrian Saravia.[1] We know that by 1593, when the Preface and first four books of the *Polity* appeared, the public was sated with religious works. Hooker needed help from his former student at Oxford, Edwin Sandys, to find a publisher, and the first edition sold slowly. When the first five of the eight books became popular in the early seventeenth century (the surviving portion of Book VI and Books VII and VIII were first published only in 1648 and 1661–2), sympathetic readers must have taken them more as an articulate statement of what England had already accepted than as a polemic against powerful religious alternatives. Within twenty years of its writing, Hooker's work was already being read as a monument.

Were Hooker's fears groundless, then? Quite the reverse. In his preface 'to them that seek (as they term it) the reformation of the laws and orders ecclesiastical in the Church of England,' he addressed himself to active and highly able individual opponents and also to an influential party. When Hooker came to London in 1585 to take up his appointment as Master of the Temple Church, his congregation of lawyers was accustomed to anti-establishment preaching, for the Temple Reader was a leading reformer, Walter Travers. It was Travers who set down in writing 'the Discipline' that Hooker has in mind throughout the *Polity* as the reformers' alternative to Anglicanism.[2] Travers had expected the Mastership for himself and was not disposed to take his subordinate position as a true measure of spiritual authority. For some months, until Archbishop Whitgift removed him, 'the pulpit spake pure Canterbury in the morning and Geneva in the afternoon.'[3] The power of 'Geneva' at this time can be gauged from the fact that Travers hoped to regain his position by appealing against Whitgift's action to the Queen's Privy Council. The appeal was unsuccessful, but its being made and entertained shows that Canterbury could not be sure of acceptance of its own clerical discipline even from the English government.

Along with Travers, Hooker's chief antagonist in the *Polity* was Thomas Cartwright, vigorous defender of reformist 'Admonitions' to Parliament and father of English Presbyterianism. The *Book of Discipline* showed concisely how a properly reformed church should function. 'T.C.' 's successive bouts with Whitgift over the Admonitions had shown exactly why changes were necessary, how the reformers' main positions were grounded in detail in the word of God, and exactly where all arguments for episcopal government and Anglican ceremonies were defective.[4] Cartwright and Travers had been allowed to attack the government and practice of the established Church publicly and repeatedly. They and the other leaders of their cause had numerous followers in the Commons during every Parliament and sympathizers even among the Queen's counsellors. The degree of open hostility towards bishops and their policies which was permitted suggests vividly that the royal government, like Hooker himself, regarded the reformers with respect and foreboding. We need hardly refer in addition to the illegal implementation of reformed practices 'without tarrying for any' effected by Browne and his followers, or to the congregationalist 'prophesyings' and 'classes' harried by Bancroft, the scurrility of Martin Marprelate's anti-episcopal tracts, the execution of the reformers Penry, Barrow, and Greenwood in the same year that Hooker published his preface and first four books,[5] the constant spiritual and military challenge of Roman Catholicism, the general insecurity about the political and ecclesiastical future that marked so much of Elizabeth's reign, or the suppression of Reformation Anglicanism in the Civil War to see that Hooker's melancholy estimate was more than justified. Circumstances and the 'careful endeavour' of its defenders had gained a period of respite for the Anglican settlement. More than silence would be required for it to pass away, and it would not go as in a dream, but the present state of the Church of God was, as Hooker correctly saw, radically uncertain.

Hooker's diagnosis of the problems at hand is given in his preface, which, despite fraternal expressions of personal respect for his opponents and assurances that reasonableness and Christian humility were all that was now required of them, was a thorough-going attempt to discredit their Discipline as haphazard, local to Geneva in its origins, politically subversive in its tendencies. Hooker would have his readers believe that the reformers' attacks on Anglicanism menaced not merely the bishops and their ceremonies, but the whole order of English society (Preface, 8, pp. 90–102). On the surface this seems quite wrong, for Hooker's immediate opponents were as loyal to the Queen as anyone, and their position on political matters was a modest one. Their platform was built on the law of God, that is, on the Bible as it could be plainly interpreted with the aid of the Holy Spirit and without reliance on human authority. Their religious system was thus relatively self-contained. It avoided any preemption of the civil magistrate's authority, and it did not ordinarily call on the civil magistrate to use the force at his disposal for spiritual ends. In regarding church and commonwealth as two distinct orders, two perpetually separate kingdoms, the reformers modelled their thinking more or less consciously on the situation of Christianity in the early Roman empire, a situation in which Christians, seeking the kingdom of heaven, conscientiously respected the secular government that happened to be set over them as a power ordained by God, but ordained primarily for the punishment of wrong-doing, not as a positive spiritual force. To be sure, the reformers' concerns were not exclusively other-worldly, yet the revolution that men like Travers, Cartwright, and the brilliant and energetic Presbyterian organizer, Thomas Field, hoped to achieve in this world was a rebirth of Christian devotion and godly living, not a change in secular politics. Strongly disposed to be exemplary citizens and convinced of the self-sufficiency of ecclesiastical institutions, the reformers had reason to be outraged at any questioning of their loyalty to the Queen and her government. If the political modesty of his opponents' position makes Hooker's discovery of subversive tendencies in their work seem unfair, this very modesty also led to difficulties, for having left the secular sphere outside the normal reach of their principles, the reformers were but poorly prepared for cases which invited or demanded political action from them. To begin with, what were they to do when the proper ecclesiastical discipline was not in effect, but deficient prelates and corrupt ceremonies held sway in its place? Here they concluded readily enough that the Christian magistrate, like Josiah, could appropriately be invoked to step in and purify the Church when it was corrupt; only – and here the difficulty of their position begins to become evident – after rendering this extraordinary service the godly prince must then be required to leave ecclesiastical affairs in the hands of ministers of the gospel. Christ alone should be 'head' of the Church. The magistrate is normally only a member of it, certainly not its supreme governor. What should be done, secondly, if the magistrate himself acts in violation of Christian principles? Once secular officials have come into the Church, whether by taking a hand in its reformation or simply by being Christians, a 'disciplined' Christianity must feel some responsibility for them. The notion that a member of a Christian congregation should be exempt from the discipline which gave the group its identity was hard to accept, and yet the image of a spiritual ecclesiastical body sitting in judgment over secular rulers was also difficult to integrate with reformist ideals as well as with current political reality. Finally, what should be done if the two previous cases occurred together, if corrupt ecclesiastical institutions were not only in effect but were actively supported by the civil ruler, who was thus not merely a sinner in his personal life or in some secular matter but sinned against the Church itself? The reformers might avoid rebellion so long as they could resist identifying crown and bishops with one another, but the fusion of these into one power might prove impossible to bear.

The political problems implicit in his opponents' advocacy of religious reform presented Hooker with his most obvious challenge. The important negative propositions in his own work – for example, his denial in Book II that Scripture provides the only rule of action necessary for this life and his denial in Book III that Scripture necessarily must contain an unalterable form of Church polity – are negations of the disciplinarian principles which led to his opponents' problems. To understand the constructive aspects of Hooker's work, however, we must note the equally severe difficulties inherent in the Anglican position, for the *Polity* is as much a positive effort to overcome these as an attempt to put down enemies. The chief Anglican contention was that ecclesiastical laws and orders established by governmental authority ought to be accepted by all, even though the government did not set itself up as an inspired interpreter of God's word, much less as superior to it. What, then, was the properly religious value of government directives? What religious meaning or status could be claimed for the whole structure of official Christianity? Bilson had contended against Rome, reasonably enough, that there was ample historical precedent for the Christian magistrate's power to 'command for the truth',[6] but this thesis was persuasive only when the magistrate acted to support beliefs or practices whose orthodoxy had already been determined. It was by no means clear what status royal edicts and parliamentary statutes could have as sources of a complete form of ecclesiastical life – and this was the issue. To be sure, no one could accuse Elizabeth of introducing novelties in faith, morals, or the sacraments. Anglican apologists emphasized that the issues between them and the reformers centred on 'things indifferent' (*adiaphora*): matters such as clerical vestments and the balancing of sermons with readings from Scripture as modes of preaching. Until late in Elizabeth's reign, episcopacy itself was defended only as one valid possibility among others for the direction of the Church. The theological modesty of the Anglican position was as much of a problem for the establishment, however, as the reformers' political modesty was for them. Even assuming agreement as to which things were essential to the Church and which variable – and the reformers, of course, did not grant that the choice between the Discipline and episcopacy was in any sense indifferent – why should decisions about the latter come from a secular source? It would seem more pious to conform with usage in the early Church or else leave such matters to the discretion of individuals or the local congregation. Some expression could thus be given in small things – if indeed they were small – to the various gifts of God. It was difficult to see any corresponding religious value in an establishment which could claim no independent theological foundation and which, besides, seemed ineffective in promoting pure devotion or godly living. Hooker's opponents had the spirit of the Reformation behind them. To have refuted them without discovering a *raison d'être* for the Anglican system would have encouraged religious indifference, scepticism, and hypocrisy, all the worst possibilities for a state religion.[7]

Hooker hoped to provide a basis for both the negative and the constructive phases of his task by a systematic examination of 'laws and their several kinds in general' (Book I). While there is universal agreement that this is the high point of the whole work and that Hooker's distinctive contribution to the English Reformation debate consisted of in some way carrying disputed issues back to first principles, it is seldom appreciated how original his scheme of first principles was or exactly how he applied these principles to particular cases. Book I is a remarkable example of Christian and classical learning, as Clement VIII's reported reaction to it suggests: 'There is no learning that this man hath not searcht into; nothing too hard for his understanding: this man indeed deserves the name of an author; his books will get reverence by age, for there is in them such seeds of eternity, that if the rest be like this, they shall last till the last fire shall consume all learning.'[8] Hooker's opponents were also learned men, however, as well as able writers. The first reformers to read the *Polity* grumbled at his excessive use of non-Biblical and non-patristic sources, but they, too, could quote Cicero and, though with less liking, Aristotle. Some of them, in a reaction against pure Calvinism, even took a sympathetic interest in scholastic theology, including that of Thomas Aquinas. We come closer to grasping what is distinctive in Hooker's use of first principles if we turn from the splendid but largely traditional elements included in his survey to the general concept of law in terms of which he ordered those elements. Even here we shall go astray if we assume that Hooker's opponents were against law and order. On the contrary, besides being loyal subjects, they valued law in the Church – God's law – and detested lawlessness in society. Hooker's originality and his practical application of speculative first principles stand out, rather, in his use of law alone as the single master idea in his work and in the concept of law which he employed for this function.

Hooker's is to date the last political theory in the West to be based on a classical and medieval speculative world-view, but the tradition of grounding political wisdom in a comprehensive view of the nature of things had many impressive previous examples, from Pythagoras and Plato through St Augustine and the papalist hierocratic political writers of the middle ages. Typically, however, such thinkers emphasized a distinction of some kind between 'being' or immutable reality on one hand and the world of becoming or process (or flux) on the other. Accordingly, law, in the sense of a rule of action, though based on the higher realm of being, had no application there. The idea applied only on that lower level of reality where things happen. As a result, the need for law was a sign of ontological, if not moral, imperfection. This is changed in Hooker. Instead of using the idea of lawful operation or well-doing as a subordinate idea in a broader speculative system, Hooker set out to fit other concepts and entities – all other entities – into a scheme of lawful operation. This required significant modifications in the narrower traditional legal categories. Thus, Hooker's enumeration of laws includes a 'first eternal law' in accordance with which God Himself acts (I, 2, vi, p. 112), as well as a 'second eternal law' which God has appointed to be kept in general by creatures (I, 3, i, p. 113) and a 'celestial law' governing the activities of angels (I, 4, pp. 117–19). Hooker's conception of a law of nature governing irrational creatures, in contrast with the law of reason proper to man, is also out of the ordinary (I, 3, ii,

p. 113). Although most of what Hooker says in expounding these laws has traditional sources, the application of distinct legal categories to such subjects is his own contribution; it has no basis, for example, in the Thomistic hierarchy of laws which Hooker is often said to have used as the model for his own scheme.[9] (It should be noted in passing that Hooker's distinction between a first and second eternal law may show his appreciation of the important distinction made by Duns Scotus and the nominalists between God's *potentia absoluta* and His *potentia ordinata*.[10] If this were shown to be the case, it would be an especially interesting demonstration that Hooker's scholastic loyalties were not exclusively Thomistic.) As a result of using law as a first principle, Hooker presents an essentially more dynamic cosmos than that of his predecessors. Although God is not literally in motion for Hooker, and it is His 'being' that is a law for His 'working', Hooker talks primarily about working both in God's case and in that of the created world. For all of his love of stability, Hooker was sufficiently a man of the Renaissance to show a positive attitude towards actions and processes at the most basic level of his conceptual scheme. It is regrettable that he found no occasion to work out the metaphysical implications of this shift of first principles systematically, but its influence in giving positive significance to the practical matters discussed in the *Polity* is pervasive. The often quoted encomium of law at the end of Book I (I, 16, viii, pp. 167–8) would have been far less effective if Hooker had been less innovative in his use of tradition at the beginning.

From a speculative standpoint, Hooker's use of law as a basic concept is significant in terms of the ontological distinction between being and becoming. From a practical standpoint, an equally significant distinction is that between laws and men. The 'whole question' calling for discussion in the *Polity*, Hooker tells us, 'concerneth the quality of ecclesiastical laws' (I, 16, i, p. 163; cf. I, 1, iii, p. 109). But does it? He himself suggests a broader set of issues at the beginning of Book II. 'As that which in the title hath been proposed for the matter whereof we treat, is *only* the ecclesiastical law whereby we are governed; so neither is it my purpose to maintain any other thing than that which *therein* truth and reason shall approve. *For concerning the dealings of men* who administer government, and unto whom the execution of that law belongeth; they have their Judge who sitteth in heaven . . . Wherefore, *all these abuses being severed and set apart*, which rise from the corruption of men and not from the laws themselves; come we to those things which in the very whole entire form of our church polity have been (as we persuade ourselves) injuriously blamed . . .' (II, 1, i, p. 169; italics added). In beginning his defence of the established Church with a treatise on law and in making his whole work an account of law rather than men, Hooker 'proposed for the matter' whereof he was to treat a domain of discourse which only partially corresponded with the flesh and blood establishment attacked by the reformers. This choice of subject-matter can be criticized as evasive, since it provided a blanket warrant to avoid answering complaints directed at the concrete performance of the Elizabethan bishops and their clergy and to concentrate instead on the more ideal aspects of the established order embodied in its official norms. It may be said in Hooker's defence, however, that a great deal of the controversy – not, to be sure, the whole of it – did turn on the quality of Anglican laws and orders and that the more exaggerated objections to Anglican personnel undoubtedly deserved to be answered with silence. However the balance of criticism should work out, it is in any case vital to an understanding of Hooker's argument to recognize the specific subject-matter with which it is concerned. The object of Hooker's defence was neither a utopian ideal nor men as they are, but a set of actually promulgated public norms. The ecclesiastical laws and orders Hooker expounded could themselves have been used to criticize the imperfect men officiating in the English Church. They are a normative pattern, an idealization to which ecclesiastical life should conform, even though it often does not. In this respect, Hooker defended not what is, but what ought to be. Yet the 'oughts' he defended were not abstract or unattainable ideals, but laws actually in operation, as public norms, in England at the time of writing. In this respect, Hooker was a realist. He nowhere claimed that the English Church was perfect even in its norms, but because these were the laws and orders of the concrete religious community of which he was part he felt obliged to show what could be urged in their behalf.

If Hooker's decision to write about the *laws* of ecclesiastical polity was both speculatively and polemically significant, the same is true of the general concept of law which he used in carrying out that decision. On this matter, too, his use of traditional materials was both more original and more relevant to the practical disputes of his time than is commonly recognized. The essential point is that Hooker's concept of law was non-authoritative, a peculiarity to which he himself drew discreet attention. 'I am not ignorant,' he says, 'that by "law eternal" the learned for the most part do understand the order, not which God hath eternally purposed himself . . . to observe, but rather that which . . . he hath set down as expedient to be kept by all his creatures . . . They who thus are accustomed to speak apply the name of law unto that only rule of working which superior authority imposeth; whereas we somewhat more enlarging the sense thereof term any kind of rule or canon, whereby actions are framed, a law' (I, 3, i, pp. 112–13). It is remarkable that in spite of this clear indication – or admission – of originality and in spite of the obvious importance of the idea of lawfulness in Hooker's thought, his departure from what 'the learned for the most part' mean by law itself has gone virtually unnoticed.

The reason may be that Hooker himself characteristically failed to emphasize the departure from tradition any more than was necessary for the continuity of his exposition. Yet in this case the difference was by no means a trivial one. In 'somewhat more enlarging' the reference of the term, Hooker omitted from the definition of law what for many thinkers is its most essential property: authoritative or coercive imposition by a superior, limitation of one's person's freedom of action by the command of another. To be sure, the conviction that law is not *only* the will of a superior has great precedents. St Thomas, for example, held law to be the extrinsic principle of action by which God *instructs* men how to achieve the good.[11] Even he, however, specified in his definition of law that it is an ordinance of reason directed to the common good, 'made by one having the care of the community, and promulgated'.[12] Accordingly, on the question of describing God's activity as lawful, although St Thomas emphasized the intelligibility of that activity, he belongs to the majority of the learned who do not apply to it the concept of law, since God has no superior. Hooker's disagreement with the positivist legal tradition, including his contemporary Bodin, is, of course, much greater.[13] Instead of being the command of a sovereign, a limitation of the subject's liberty imposed from above, law for Hooker is any rule relating an action to its appropriate end. 'All things that are have some operation not violent or casual. Neither doth any thing ever begin to exercise the same without some fore-conceived end for which it worketh. And the end which it worketh for is not obtained, unless the work be also fit to obtain it by. For unto every end every operation will not serve. That which doth assign unto each thing the kind, that which doth moderate the force and power, that which doth appoint the form and measure of working, the same we term a law' (I, 2, i, p. 109).

As we have seen, the most immediate consequence of Hooker's non-coercive conception of law was that it allowed him to apply the idea to God. This in itself has the effect of enhancing the attractiveness of law in general. A further consequence of Hooker's idea of law is that it shifts attention away from the conflict of wills always present at least potentially when a superior imposes law upon an inferior and directs attention instead to the activity conforming to law. Strictly speaking, only God can act in accord with a law not made by a superior authority (I, 2, ii, p. 110). In the political sphere in particular, Hooker recognizes authoritative imposition or constraining force as an essential property distinguishing law from counsel or admonition (I, 10, vii–viii, pp. 139–40; cf. VIII, 6, xiii, pp. 389–90), and there is no lack of passages in which he demands obedience to law from his opponents. Despite various remarks on the importance of agreement and consent, however, Hooker gives ambiguous answers at best to those questions about the exact basis of legitimate coercive power which have formed such a large part of political philosophy in the last four hundred years. He was ignored by Hobbes and quoted extensively by Locke, but there have been occasional scholarly suggestions that his position was really the same as Hobbes', differences of style notwithstanding,[14] or, alternatively, that he was far more of a classical conservative than is suggested by Locke.[15] The reason Hooker offers no decisive solution to the problem of legitimacy may well be that he did not regard this as a central issue. As we shall see, the problem he confronted in defending the royal supremacy concerned the nature or quality of political power more than its localization in particular persons. He writes sometimes as if laws made themselves (more often as if whole communities could make laws for themselves without such legislation being an act of one part of the community over and against the others), and as if in obeying them we were acting freely. It is easy enough to accuse him once again of evasion here, but the philosophical difficulties which have increasingly been found in modern theories of legitimacy suggest that the principles underlying earlier political theory may deserve re-examining.

Hooker sought to defend the established regulations of the English Church by placing them in a broader normative context. The various other types of laws examined in Book I of the *Polity* are 'causes' or 'first principles' of the good or bad quality of positive, man-made laws such as the ecclesiastical regulations then in dispute (I, 16, i, p. 163). An accurate assessment of the latter would thus require that they be analysed in terms of these more basic norms. The details of Hooker's complicated scheme of laws eternal, celestial, natural, rational, divine, and positive should be approached with this general relationship of causes and effects in mind. The complexity of the scheme is also a factor deserving comment. Hooker's long discourse in Book I 'serveth but to make manifest, that as the actions of men are of sundry distinct kinds, so the laws thereof must accordingly be distinguished. There are in men operations, some natural, some rational, some supernatural, some politic, some finally ecclesiastical; which if we measure not each by his own proper law, whereas the things themselves are so different, there will be in our understanding and judgment of them confusion' (I, 16, v, p. 165). Even so common an item as the food we eat, Hooker points out, falls under a surprisingly large variety of evaluative principles, ranging from the 'natural' sensory discrimination of what things are food and what are not to religious dietary laws and the Christian eucharist (I, 16, vii, p. 166 f). *A fortiori*, judgments about ecclesiastical laws are vastly more complicated than the less restrained attacks on Anglicanism had allowed. The reformers challenged the arbitrariness of a man-made religious establishment by bringing to bear upon it the law of God, the one incontestably objective source of law available. The first four books of the *Polity* are largely designed to show that the bare appeal to Scripture can also be arbitrary and merely human. If men sincerely wish to get beyond unfounded personal reactions to a particular regulation and reach an objective judgment, it is not enough simply to bring the Bible to bear on the matter. The Bible itself provides ample endorsement of pure, uninspired reasonableness as a basis for action (I, 12, pp. 152–3; II, 1, ii, p. 170), but rationality is in turn a complex matter in both ethics and politics. According to Hooker, for example, an unqualified reference to natural law may be ambiguous. It is necessary to distinguish between primary and secondary laws of nature: norms relevant to man in his original condition as created by God, and principles of equity required by the fall (I, 10, xiii, p. 144). In the same vein, Hooker distinguishes between 'mixedly' and 'merely' human laws: those positive enactments which embody obligations already valid on rational grounds and those which give rise to an obligation where none had previously existed (I, 10, x, p. 142 f). If matters are sifted thoroughly, they come back to the first of Hooker's various first principles and causes, the eternal laws in accordance with which God Himself operates, both in His own free activity and in creation (I, 16, ii, p. 163 f). Questions of lawfulness in an individual's life or in a civil or religious community are thus implicated, for Hooker, in an appreciation of well-doing in everything that exists. The richness of this scheme has both a negative and a positive function in Hooker's argument.

The negative aspect of Hooker's work is nowhere clearer than in his attack, in Books II and III, on the simple appeal to Scripture as an effective method of solving every practical problem. Though he was at pains to defend the sufficiency of Scripture for its intended end of making clear everything essential to salvation (I, 14, pp. 155–9), his attempt to destroy his opponents' self-confidence in bringing all details of ecclesiastical life (indeed, every detail of human life generally) under immediate Biblical direction was aimed at the heart of their position. By his own report, Hooker at one time had taken the reformers' extraordinary zeal and fervour as a sign of the goodness of their cause, but examination of their writings had led to disillusionment (Preface, 1, ii, p. 63 f). 'Sentences out of the word of God ye allege divers: but so, that when the same are discussed, thus it always in a manner falleth out, that what things by virtue thereof ye urge upon us as altogether necessary, are found to be thence collected only by poor and marvellous slight conjecture' (Preface, 4, i, p. 78). It is fair to read Book I of the *Polity* as a presentation of objective grounds for this personal scepticism, which concerned a major theological project of the English Reformation. Hooker's scepticism about simple appeals to Scripture (or to any other single principle) produces, among other things, an appeal to ignorance as a basis for obedience. The causes of goodness or badness in human laws are many and hard to discover. Unless there is manifest or clearly necessary reason to the contrary, therefore, men should accept the laws presently in force, taking it as a sign of their goodness that they have been enacted (I, 8, iii, p. 127; I, 16, ii, p. 163 f). This attitude is reinforced by Hooker's treatment of eternal and natural law. Men do not understand how God works, yet it is certain that there is a purpose in what He does, for otherwise His actions would be 'infinite' even as He Himself is infinite (I, 2, iv, p. 111). Similarly, even with our best efforts of investigation we cannot completely comprehend the causes operative in the natural world, and yet we can appreciate the generally effective functioning of natural agents (I, 3, ii and iv, pp. 113 and 116). Although Hooker does not call attention to the parallels between his accounts of political and theological and scientific ignorance, they must still have an effect on the reader, especially in conjunction with his numerous other suggestions that the grounds of a community's well-being are hidden like the roots of trees or the foundations of houses, or that they require curious, dark, and intricate investigation for their discovery (I, 1, ii, p. 108; I, 16, ii, p. 163; V, 1, i, p. 218 f). The sentiment expressed or implied so often in the *Polity*, that if *some* reason can be found in favour of an existing law it is better not to criticize it except reverently and in due order stems from the sceptical or negative side of Hooker's complex survey in Book I.

Significant as these negative conclusions are in Hooker's thought, the constructive consequences of his speculative exploration of the several kinds of law are still more significant. By considering the operations of God, the angels, and purely natural agents, Hooker hoped to illuminate by analogy the intrinsic goodness of the whole process of reasonably regulated public life. Law, instead of appearing as an irksome and isolated human necessity, is seen in this context as a gift of God and a mark of kinship with the universe, and since Hooker's universe was an admirable one, affiliation with it could only enhance the value of human law. The effect of revealing lawful operation as the norm throughout the cosmos was not so much to bolster the power or authority of human law as to increase its attractiveness. In particular, Hooker hoped to reduce the tension between divine and human law, not by identifying the two, but by relating them to one another as distinct yet non-competing elements of a broader normative scheme. Convinced as they were that their Discipline was Biblically prescribed in every detail, the reformers were often on the verge of having to choose between obeying God and obeying the all too human bishops who, they thought, opposed God. For Hooker the alternatives were not so stark. There is potential religious significance in obeying any legitimate law whatever, since even laws other than directly revealed Biblical injunctions are specifications of the second law eternal, the normative structure that God has built into the fabric of creation, including the natural fabric of human reason (I, 3, i, p. 113). Hence, instead of standing essentially outside the political order and submitting to its authority only from a sense of duty, the zealous Christian is invited to regard life in the community as an integral part of his religious existence. God, the ultimate foundation of all law, is 'very Oneness' (I, 2, ii, p. 110), but human relationships to God arise through the many parts of a complex pattern of values, not exclusively through religion as an isolated phenomenon.

Hooker's use of an affirmative world-view to support an affirmative general assessment of human society deserves particular emphasis given the markedly different tendency of later English political thought. Both Hobbes and Locke, for example, as well as many heirs to the sceptical, conservative side of Hooker's own position, see men building a political world in order to escape from a non-political condition which intolerably frustrates their natural rights and desires. The apparatus of positive law and government is itself purely a mechanism for avoiding bloodshed and protecting individual rights, and in its demands for obedience this mechanism appears as a more or less powerful, more or less controllable, necessary evil. Hooker, following an Aristotelian and Thomistic rather than an Augustinian tradition here, places primary emphasis on the positive value of economic cooperation and human fellowship as a basis for 'politic society' (I, 10, i–ii, pp. 136–7; I, 10, xii, p. 143 f). Accordingly, whereas Hobbes and Locke describe the non-political world in negative terms, as they must, to make political life acceptable by contrast, Hooker's treatment of the non-political is positive. He finds beneficial, law-like operation in every quarter of his speculative survey prior to the discussion of human communities, and therefore lawfulness within the community is metaphysically supported in his scheme by analogy with the non-political, not by contrast. He allows that the present condition of the universe is far from perfect. The matter of the natural world swerves occasionally from the laws governing it, a fact due to divine malediction 'laid for the sin of man upon those creatures which God had made for the use of man' (I, 3, iii, p. 115), nor was Hooker inclined to over-estimate the goodness of human nature itself in its fallen state. Nevertheless, in terms of the scheme of norms which is Hooker's chosen subject-matter in the *Polity*, political life, including humanly regulated ecclesiastical life, is not a lesser evil but potentially one of the best things in an already good world order.

* * *

The problem in understanding Book I of the *Polity* is to see how an apparently serene essay in philosophical theology is geared to the practical crisis of Elizabethan Anglicanism. Once the practical bearing of the first book has been grasped, Hooker's criticism of the reformers' Scripturalism in Books II and III and his general defence of Anglican worship against the charge of superstition in Book IV can be followed readily enough. The difficulty in understanding his massive fifth book lies in the opposite direction. With few exceptions, such as the impressive chapters on the Incarnation and sacraments included in the present volume, every page of Book V shows Hooker embroiled in controversy over Anglican forms of worship or regulations concerning the ministry. The problem is to find general significance. Why, we might ask, did a writer of Hooker's calibre spend so much energy disputing issues which he himself regarded as 'things indifferent'? Does his treatment of these issues lead to anything more constructive than a disorganized collection of defensive claims about Anglican practices that especially offended the reformers? A brief attempt must be made to clarify these matters.

Hooker's opening chapters on the capital importance of religion for the well-being of society provide some enlightenment. In line with a prominent tendency of sixteenth-century English religious writers to interpret particular events in their history as signs of God's pleasure or displeasure with His people, Hooker believed that there was a manifest correlation between the temporal welfare of a society and the state of its religion. He developed this idea later in Book V in his defence of a publicly supported Christian ministry (V, 76, v–viii). Even there, however, he was more circumspect than some more prophetic spirits among the reformers, bringing forward no fewer than eight qualifications which make the observable correlation of prosperity with piety less than perfect (V, 76, v). At the beginning of the book he emphasizes more strongly the moral and psychological effects of religion on the social functioning of individuals, contending that such essential virtues as justice, courage, and temperance depend on piety. If, for example, public officials seek their own gain, 'being not in heart persuaded that justice is God's own work, and themselves his agents in this business . . . formalities of justice do but serve to smother right, and that, which was . . . ordained for the common good, is . . . made the cause of common misery' (V, 1, ii, p. 219). 'If the course of public affairs cannot in any good sort go forward without fit instruments, and that which fitteth them be their virtues, let Polity acknowledge itself indebted to Religion; godliness being the chiefest top and wellspring of all true virtues, even as God is of all good things' (*ibid.*, p. 219). Religion, then, was vitally connected in Hooker's view with the whole range of common life. The motives, habits, and the very concepts of behaviour that sustain society are those expressed and fostered in its religious life. In this respect, as well as in calling forth the blessings of providence amid the chances of history, public religious devotion reflects, celebrates, and helps sustain the positive cosmic order which Hooker had expounded in Book I. This, in the most general terms, is why he was willing to devote so much attention in Book V to 'things (theologically) indifferent'.

His goal was not, however, the social establishment of religion in the abstract. For an adequate understanding of Hooker's treatment of public worship, we must consider more concretely the kind of worship he sought to promote. In contrast with some later Anglican writers, Hooker here laid primary stress neither on orthodoxy, which he took for granted in his disputes with the reformers, nor on ceremonial correctness, but on wholeheartedness. Zeal, along with fear, leads to superstition unless it is rightly guided (V. 3, i, p. 226), but 'the most extreme opposite' to true religion is not superstition but 'affected atheism' (V, 2, pp. 223–6). God has imprinted it in all men's hearts that they should seek and maintain the true religion and shun that which is false, but there are certain sparks of the light of truth mixed in with the errors even of pagan religions (V, 1, iii, p. 221). So far as the world to come is concerned, Christianity alone has good effects (*ibid.*), but in other cases, too, 'religion unfeignedly loved perfecteth men's abilities unto all kinds of virtuous service in the commonwealth' (V, 1, v, p. 222), and without such love the true religion itself yields no benefits. 'They that love the religion which they profess, may have failed in choice, but yet they are sure to reap what benefit the same is able to afford; whereas the best and soundest [religion] professed by them that bear it not the like affection, yieldeth them, retaining it in that sort, no benefit' (V, 1, iv, p. 222). It is this quest for unfeigned affection or wholeheartedness in public worship and Christian life that accounts most fully for Hooker's massive concern with details in Book V, his decision to 'wade through the whole cause' (V, Dedication, iii). If he had been content with the defensive task of showing that Anglican forms of worship were at least no worse from the standpoint of strict orthodoxy than alternatives proposed by the reformers, he could have produced a much briefer treatise. He sought, however, to win for the established Church broad and positive emotional acceptance. To this end constructive interpretation was more in order than efficient rebuttal.

Because Hooker regarded public worship as relevant to the whole range of common life, his interpretation of Anglican practices in Book V is not only conscientious but remarkably, if implicitly, systematic.[16] Thus, for example, in the course of an extended debate with Cartwright over the comparative merits of sermons and scripture readings, he develops subtle and well-grounded views of the limits and potentialities of religious knowledge and language (V, 21–2). In the large block of chapters answering complaints about Anglican forms of prayer (V, 25–49), he takes occasion to examine the structure and dynamics of human desire at a far more basic level than his purely defensive responsibilities required. In discussing such apparently routine or theologically incidental matters as church buildings (V, 11–17) and festival days, he provides the elements for a religious aesthetic, a philosophical theology of space and time. The chapter on festival days is included in the present selections (V, 69, pp. 296–9) as an example of this applied metaphysics. Perhaps the clearest indication that

Hooker had constructive and systematic aims in Book V is the central series of chapters on the Incarnation and the sacraments (V. 50–68). The complaints to be answered in this area were comparatively mild, yet it is just here that Hooker provides one of the most substantial theological treatises to be found in the *Polity* (V, 50–7, pp. 260–87). (Hooker's emphasis on the sacraments is all the more noteworthy, since he was not on the whole a high churchman.) In Book V, then, Hooker canvassed from a devotional viewpoint the main dimensions of human existence: space and time, knowledge and desire, and the immediate presence of God. In each case he emphasized the aspects of Anglican practice that tied it in with the conditions and rhythms of common life. His defence of festival days is again a good illustration. To give but one further example, Hooker's treatment of prayer takes full account of human attachment to the things of this world. No doubt 'in the eye of a perfect judgment' spiritual goods are superior to material ones, but most men are 'better able by sense to discern the wants of this present life than by spiritual capacity to apprehend things above sense, which tend to their happiness in the world to come.' For their sake the Church includes many prayers for earthly things in its services. 'By this means there stealeth upon them a double benefit first because that good affection, which things of smaller account have once set on work, is by so much the more easily raised higher, and secondly, in that the very custom of seeking so particular aid and relief at the hands of God, doth by a secret contradiction withdraw them from endeavouring to help themselves by those wicked shifts which they know can never have his allowance, whose assistance their prayer seeketh. These multiplied petitions of worldly things in prayer have therefore, besides their direct use, a service whereby the Church underhand, through a kind of heavenly fraud, taketh therewith the souls of men as with certain baits' (V, 35, ii, pp. 252–3). Here, as at so many other places, we find in Hooker an observer of human nature, one actively concerned with religion as it affects life. He was the best sort of traditionalist. Instead of taking the past as something essentially lifeless that must for inscrutable reasons be preserved and inflicted on the living, he used the centuries of religious experience with which he had such an impressive scholarly familiarity to discover significances quite likely to be lacking in simple appeals to either contemporary relevance or gospel authenticity.

After Book V of the *Polity* Anglican ceremonial could no longer be regarded as superstitious or, to use the equivalent modern term, meaningless. Indeed, Hooker was so successful in discovering religious meaning in the established laws and orders ecclesiastical that a sympathetic reader could easily forget their political origins. Such a reader might also forget that, according to Hooker, a good case could have been made for practices very different from those presently in force in England. From Hooker's standpoint, it was essential that the relationship between men and God have a channel for theologically correct and also wholehearted expression. He believed, reasonably enough, that uniformity of Christian practice within a single society would facilitate such devotion, but he was quite ready to admit that there might be alternative channels of public religious expression within the scope of orthodox principles which other Christian societies might choose to follow. It would therefore be a mistake to suppose that either the critical or the constructive phases of Hooker's task had been completed with Book V. Even if it were granted that Anglican worship could hold its own when expounded without constant reference to authoritative promulgation, history and theology both demanded an account of the powers actually enforcing that worship.

* * *

Hooker had reserved his discussion of the weightiest questions in dispute, 'Jurisdiction, Dignity, Dominion Ecclesiastical' (VI, 1, i, p. 300), for the final three books of the *Polity*, which were still unpublished when he died in 1600. The research of Sisson, Houk, and Novarr has entirely discredited the tale given in Isaak Walton's life of Hooker, which suggests that enemies of Anglicanism, with the connivance of Hooker's widow, altered his manuscripts immediately after his death.[17] The circumstances of transmission of these manuscripts are obscure, and it is uncertain that more than the beginning of the treatise on penance published in 1648 as Book VI was intended by Hooker as part of his previously announced examination of Presbyterian lay elders.[18] Whatever else he may have written on this subject has unfortunately been lost. There is no question, however, but that Book VII, on episcopacy, and Book VIII, on the crown's 'dominion' in ecclesiastical affairs, are authentic parts of the *Polity*. Most of Book VIII was published in 1648 along with the so-called sixth book. A fragment more appeared in 1661, and the balance, along with Book VII, was published in 1662. Because of these delays, Hooker's discussions of episcopal and royal power had no influence on the historical situation for which they were written. The books deserve attention for their own merits, however, and are logically crucial to the argument of the *Polity*. It is scarcely an exaggeration to say that the moral and intellectual coherence of Hooker's whole work depends on the compatibility of these final books with the ones we have already considered.

Hooker's position on episcopacy has tantalized interpreters of his work ever since Book VII's belated publication. It is so delicately balanced, indeed, that on internal grounds exactly opposite explanations of the delay in publication have been held equally plausibly. Hooker's vindication of episcopacy against the reformers' attacks is so emphatic that the enemies of the established Church could easily be imagined to have repressed the manuscript as a danger to their cause. On the other hand, the endorsement of a divine or apostolic origin for episcopacy is so hypothetical that publication could well have been deferred by high churchmen because Hooker's views fell short of official opinion under the early Stuarts. The first and basic part of Hooker's defence of bishops is a historical survey demonstrating the universal recognition of episcopal authority from very early times (VII, 4–16). Interspersed with this is a more pragmatic, functional justification of the episcopal office as appropriate and effective in meeting the Church's usual governmental needs. Finally, answering the reformers' objections that the saintly bishops of the early Church proved nothing in favour of contemporary bishops, Hooker rejected the ideal of apostolic simplicity of life as a strict requirement for the apostles' successors in Church government, holding instead that a Christian society should honour its spiritual leaders, not impoverish them, and that for the good of society the honours should include wealth and influence (VII, 17–24). Clearly, Hooker regarded the episcopate as much more than an incidental development of the middle ages or a convenience to the English crown, and his statements might have been still more emphatic had he not been reluctant to criticize non-episcopal reformed churches on the continent. The question still remains, however: did he believe that bishops were a theological necessity? Here his position is ambiguous, and perhaps deliberately so. 'If,' he is bold enough to say at one point, 'any thing in the Church's government, surely the first institution of bishops was from heaven, was even of God, the Holy Ghost was the author of it' (VII, 5, x). Understandably enough, high churchmen have read this as an endorsement of their own position. The 'if' at the beginning of Hooker's statement must be taken seriously, however, for he had devoted an entire earlier book of the *Polity* to refuting the claim that some form of Church polity *was* from heaven, in the special sense of being prescribed in the Bible. Perhaps, after writing Book III, Hooker came personally to attach more weight to the possibility that an episcopal form of government was in fact, if not of necessity, set down in Scripture. So far as the argument of Book VII is concerned, however, his response to the reformers was once again oblique. Instead of opposing their unqualified *iure divino* assertions on behalf of presbyterian lay elders with a similarly absolute claim for the legitimacy of bishops, he refuted his opponents' claims (or intended to do so) in Book VI and then based his own episcopal position on principles that were imposing and effective but non-absolute. Book VII suggests that in Hooker's opinion churches which had done away with bishops had made a serious mistake, but we cannot say that he believed this error to be fatal. He did not regard episcopal authority in the Church as ultimate.

Hooker's theory of the royal supremacy is not as ambiguous as his position on episcopacy, but it is at least as complex, combining elements from Greek political philosophy, the Old Testament, and both Roman and English law. From a practical viewpoint, the prerogatives Hooker defended in this controversial and yet too little read eighth book were substantial. The English crown claimed not only the title of supreme head of the Church within its own dominions, but the power to call ecclesiastical assemblies, a veto power in Church legislation, the right to choose bishops, supreme power in ecclesiastical courts, and exemption from excommunication. Even with all this, however, the royal supremacy, as Hooker interpreted it, was limited in both theory and practice. To see clearly whether Hooker's earlier ideas are reiterated, supplemented and developed, or contradicted by his defence of royal ecclesiastical dominion in Book VIII, we must give the subtlety of that defence more attention than it usually receives.

For the reformers, as we have seen, the Church was to be ruled by the word of God, not the power of princes. There was thus an obvious polemical reason for Hooker to emphasize that Scripture itself provided eminent models for royal ecclesiastical power. The New Testament, to be sure, shows the Church in politically ineffective circumstances and at the same time independent of secular control, a situation which had been taken by the reformers as permanently normative for the relations of Church and commonwealth. Since Bishop Gardiner took up the call for a godly prince under Henry VIII,[19] however, Anglican apologists had used such Old Testament rulers as Moses, Josiah, David, and Deborah to justify the ecclesiastical dominance of the English crown, and when it was a matter of securing independence from Rome or supporting their own measures for purifying the Church, reformers, too, had eagerly accepted such analogies. Against this background, Hooker's depiction of the royal supremacy on a Biblical model is natural enough. What is striking is the comparatively small part it plays in his whole account. Apart from passing references in the opening pages of Book VIII, he appeals to the Old Testament only as a defensive measure, to confirm a complicated, essentially philosophical and legal demonstration of the unity of Church and commonwealth and the legitimacy of the English constitution. There is nothing, he concedes, 'for which some colourable reason or other may not be found' (VIII, 3, i, p. 354). It is possible, then, to show 'by experience and practice' the benefits of a royal supremacy in religion? Nothing could serve this purpose better than examples from the Bible. It should be noted, too, that the thesis to be confirmed by these examples concerned the permissibility of lay ecclesiastical power, not its necessity. Hooker's previous argument had been against a perpetual separation of Church and state which would make lay supremacy in the affairs of both legally and theologically impossible. He did not find in the Bible, however, a perpetual positive mandate requiring such supremacy. 'As for supreme power in ecclesiastical affairs, the word of God doth no where appoint that all kings should have it, neither that any should not have it; for which cause it seemeth to stand altogether by human right, that unto Christian kings there is such dominion given' (VIII, 2, i, p. 345). The Bible, as Hooker read it, contains nothing against a royal religious supremacy and even provides occasional examples of its legitimacy and possible benefits, but the positive grounds for such an arrangement had to be sought elsewhere. This reticence in using Biblical resources to give the royal office an essential sacral character was not due to any disillusionment with the current ruler. Hooker had a particularly deep sense of Elizabeth's providential calling as a defender of the English Church, which he had eloquently expressed by suggesting that all churches still standing in the realm could take this inscription, style, or title: 'By the goodness of Almighty God and his servant Elizabeth we are' (V, Dedication, x). The explanation for Hooker's defensive and limited reference to Biblical monarchs lies rather in his conviction that the human community, not its official leaders, was the only generally adequate basis for constructive political theology.

'The word of God doth no where appoint that all kings should have it, neither that any should not have it . . . it seemeth to stand altogether by human right, that unto Christian kings there is such dominion given.' Here in Book VIII, in connection with the last and weightiest question discussed in the *Polity*, we find again the alternatives whose contrasts and tensions had called forth Hooker's whole effort: divine right and human right. The immediate basis for a royal supremacy was, in Hooker's view, human law. His language in the second chapter of Book VIII suggests that a derivation of sovereign power from the people to the prince, on the model of the Roman *lex regia*, was part of the human legal basis he had in mind: although sovereign power naturally or 'originally' resides in the body of a politic society, it can be, and in England for good reason has been, placed by the community in a monarch. Sovereignty continues to reside in the body 'in habit', but resides 'in act' in the prince, except when the royal line fails, in which case the community may make other constitutional provisions (VIII, 2, vii–x, pp. 346–8). The absolutist implications of the *lex regia* are balanced in Hooker, however, by emphasis on the broader legal tradition of English constitutionalism. The crown has 'chiefty of power in the greatest things' in England, which is essential to the best form of monarchy (VIII, 2, xi, p. 349); no person or cause is exempt from the king's power. The king's power is thoroughly limited by law, however, not in its extent, but in its manner of working: 'unto all his proceedings the law itself is a rule' (VIII, 2, xiii, p. 350. See VIII, 2, xvii, pp. 352–3 for specific examples of such limitations), and the crown's own legislative power is mainly the negative one of veto (VIII, 6, viii and xiii, pp. 381 and 390). More generally, 'that people is happiest whose law is their king in the greatest things than that whose king is their law' (VIII, 2, xii, p. 349). Far from its being the case, then, that the will of the prince has the force of law, as in the imperial Roman system, in Hooker's *Polity* law makes the king, and royal actions contrary to law are null (VIII, 2, xiii, p. 350). The moderating effect of these traditional English maxims is reinforced by Hooker's Aristotelian recognition of a variety of possible monarchical regimes as in principle legitimate (VIII, 2, xii, p. 349).[20] The task of a king is not to personify some absolute ideal of kingship, but to bear an office whose nature and limits are largely determined by historical circumstances. The constitutionalism of Book VIII is so pronounced that some scholars have found in it a possible explanation for delay in the book's publication.[21] Whether or not Hooker spent his last years trying to bring his own ideas more closely into line with those of the government he defended, the temperateness of his legal thought is one of its most striking features.

Significant as constitutionalism is in both the argument of the *Polity* and the history of English political thought, it does not by itself solve the chief problem with which Hooker was concerned. In one way, a theory of limited monarchy was quite unnecessary in the circumstances for which Hooker wrote, since Elizabethan reformers had not questioned the legitimacy of the Queen's government or of monarchy in general. In another way, however, any legal rationalization of the crown's supremacy in religious affairs was bound to be futile, for no such account touched the reformers' basic contention that human and divine law were wholly separate things. Hooker had declined to use Old Testament examples to claim a divine basis for royal power in ecclesiastical affairs. He could hardly rest his vindication of the royal supremacy on merely historical human legal acts. Some third element was needed to give constructive religious significance to the human laws in question without at the same time turning them into divine institutions. Hooker found such an element in Greek political philosophy, which he had relied on in his earlier general account of human communities (I, 10, pp. 35–46; cf. III, 1, pp. 193–4), and which he now applied at the beginning of Book VIII to refute his opponents' main theoretical ground for objecting to royal supremacy: the perpetual separation of Church and commonwealth.

Hooker's central philosophical thesis was that the purposes of human association are as comprehensive as man's own potentialities. Since in a religiously conceived universe man has a 'triple estate', 'natural', 'civil', and 'spiritual' (VIII, 1, vi, p. 341; cf. I, 11, i–iv, pp. 146–9), it follows necessarily that a fully-fledged human community will have religious as was as economic, cultural, and moral ends (VIII, 1, ii and iv, pp. 335–6 and 337). Hooker began, of course, with Aristotle's dictum that the purpose of political association is not mere life but the good life.[22] Following medieval tradition, Hooker gave this classical ideal Christian content, thus introducing a much greater emphasis on religion than is found in Aristotle's *Politics*. For Hooker, as we have seen, public worship was both the culmination and the basis of all other communal activity, since God is the first cause and supreme good of the universe, and godliness is the 'top and well-spring' of all other virtues. So far as the structure of his political theory is concerned, however, Hooker found a perfect continuity between classical and Christian civilizations. In pagan society the care of pagan religion was naturally a matter of public concern. In a community of Christians, the care of Christian religion is naturally – just as naturally, naturally in the same sense – a matter of public concern. In both cases, Hooker points out, it has always been found reasonable to assign spiritual and civil functions to distinct persons, but such divisions of function are made within the context of a single concrete community (VIII, 1, iv, pp. 337–9). Hence, despite differences of function and essential nature, when all the citizens are Christians, commonwealth and Church are 'personally' and substantially identical. 'Every body politic hath some religion, but the Church that religion which is only true' (VIII, 1, ii, p. 335). A (national) church, then, is not an aspect of, or something possessed by, or an institution in or alongside of, a state or body politic – a church *is* a politic society. 'As a politic society it doth maintain religion; as a church, that religion which God hath revealed by Jesus Christ' (p. 336). A church, in Hooker's sense of an independent body of Christians, is thus no less political and no more religious than any other self-subsistent human community: no less political, since Christians need civil laws and government as well as spiritual institutions; no more religious, since every such community naturally aims at the good life and hence has religious concerns. A church is set apart from other bodies politic by the adequacy with which these common religious concerns are met. Hooker's dictum that not religion but truth of religion is the distinguishing mark of a church amounts to the claim that, other things being equal, churches are essentially successful political communities. In this sense, England did not have a church. England was a church.

Although Aristotle's concept of the political community had been known in the West since the thirteenth century and was accepted by such influential thinkers as Thomas Aquinas, John of Paris, and Dante in preference to St Augustine's idea of the state as a punishment and remedy for sin,[23] Hooker is unusual, perhaps unique, in utilizing Aristotle's more positive doctrine as a basis for defining churches as political bodies and Christian states as churches. The effect of thus locating religious concerns in the community was to give significant religious status to the English government without making either its legal basis divine or its powers absolute. In Hooker's scheme of things, English constitutional law did not create religious truths, values, or powers. Rather, it localized in the crown (more precisely, in crown, parliament, and convocation) that power to care for religion which is naturally possessed by any independent community. If the power of ecclesiastical dominion was viewed as something originally residing in the body of the community and then merely transferred to its head, the human laws by which this derivation was accomplished could be discussed in a spirit of moderation and prudence. A restrained conception of the crown's power was a natural consequence. Every well-settled community is careful not to 'clean resign up herself' and make over all legislative power to one man (VIII, 6, i, p. 376), and Hooker regarded the fact that royal power was limited by law in England as a mark of practical wisdom in those who had devised the constitution (VIII, 2, xii–xiii, pp. 349–50). Hooker could avoid, or at least greatly reduce, the danger of religious despotism because he had no need to regard government as such as a sacred and therefore absolute power.

From his opponents' standpoint Hooker seemed mistaken in assuming that any body politic could be so Christian as to render unnecessary a basic independence of civil and ecclesiastical institutions. On this point, our current religious pluralism confers on the reformers' opinion an appearance of obvious truth. Certainly, Hooker gives little indication of how the public care of religion should proceed in communities whose members disagree in their fundamental religious beliefs or about the truth and value of religion in general. Indeed, even in his own circumstances, Hooker pays too little heed to the long tradition of secular and spiritual dualism in the Western church. It must be emphasized again, however, that the comprehensive aim Hooker attributed to human association had no effect on the truth or falsity, goodness or badness, of any particular religion. Hooker believed that non-Christian religions in fact contained elements of truth, but this did not in any way depend on their official legal status any more than the truth of Christianity depended on its political standing. Government may legitimately manage the practically important but theologically 'indifferent' details of religion, but princely power can never be a source of religious first principles or make a doctrine true that was previously false (VIII, 6, v, p. 379). Although his aim in writing the *Polity* was to prevent such a situation from arising, Hooker was well aware that disagreement can occur within a community between the adherents of fundamentally different religions. He held it correct to speak in such cases of one civil community along with two or more separate religious communities. The two-kingdom theory of the reformers (which was also developed by Roman Catholic writers) would be valid here (VIII, 1, iii–iv, pp. 337–8). In Hooker's view, however, the normal state of human affairs involved a much closer coincidence of religious and civil association. If the first Christians were a separate people living in an alien land, they set out to convert their neighbours, and their success transformed a pagan empire into a Christian one. According to Hooker, then, the reformers virtually ignored the significant facts that 'whole Rome' had embraced the Christian faith and that substantially the whole population of England was also Christian. They took for a permanent norm what was an important, yet essentially transitional, phase in Western history, and they were led to this historical error by a seriously over-narrow theory of human community. From beginning to end of his own work Hooker sought to establish an alternative to their position which was coherent in both history and theory. We turn now to the question of how far he succeeded.

* * *

In order to see clearly how the major phases of Hooker's argument fit together, we must first note the very different subjects and conclusions of the various segments in which the *Polity* was published. The differences among them have led many critics to conclude that Hooker's argument as a whole is incoherent.[24] In fact, just the reverse is true. The variety of the *Polity*'s parts is not merely compatible with, but essential to, the unity of the whole argument. In the first four books, published in 1593, Hooker was chiefly concerned with necessary or universally valid philosophical and theological first principles. On the basis of his speculative survey of the several kinds of law in Book I he was able to mount a telling attack on certain key principles of the reformers in Books II and III and to elaborate, in Book IV, general criteria for discriminating between wholesome and superstitious religious ceremonies. His detailed treatment of Anglican laws and orders in Book V is dependent on the system of general principles developed in the earlier books, but this dependence is not a matter of logically necessary deduction. Hooker held that good reasons could be given for Anglican practices, but the technical virtuosity with which he marshalled such reasons should not lead us to suppose that he claimed the same permanent validity for Anglican worship and administration as for the normative framework expounded in Book I. If he was critical of what he took to be Bibliolatry on the reformers' side, he did not himself make an idol of the *Book of Common Prayer*. In the last books of the *Polity* there is still another change of subject and attitude. Here Hooker leaves behind the particular contents of established Anglican devotional practices and turns instead to the system of episcopal and royal power that maintained those practices. At the same time, he lays down much more severe conclusions. He does not merely invite the reader to consider a new interpretation of the Prayer Book. Rather, he demands that the English reader obey the law of the land. We are still free to suppose that reasons could be given for practices contrary to those of the Prayer Book, but no alternative of conforming or not conforming is offered in Books VI–VIII. Superficially,

Hooker seems to have returned to the compelling, necessary principles of Book I, but this is not the case. The compulsion in the later books, the need to acknowledge the crown's power of ecclesiastical dominion, is a practical and conditioned necessity, not an eternal speculative truth. If the quality of public worship was to be enhanced and the effectiveness of Christian principles increased (their truth was not in question), then religious affairs needed to be coherently regulated. The English crown's power of ecclesiastical dominion depended for Hooker much more on historical circumstances than on a positive deduction from first principles. Even episcopacy had for him a primarily historical basis and functional significance. Again, therefore, the parts of the *Polity* are interdependent but not identical in content and conclusions. It is easy to imagine arguments more homogeneous than Hooker's. We need only select one major part of his work and revise the other two to match it. For example, beginning with eternally valid metaphysical or religious principles, one could attempt to deduce a uniquely correct set of devotional forms and a uniquely legitimate political constitution. As concerns ecclesiastical matters, this was the project of the English reformers. Much medieval political theory can also be seen as a direct deduction of politics from theology. At the other extreme, one could begin with the practical necessities of politics that Hooker treats in Book VIII and proceed in the other direction, making right and wrong in speculation and worship depend on these purely practical factors. Something like this approach can be found in writers as diverse as Hobbes, Rousseau, and Marx, all of whom held that a society's religious or philosophical beliefs and practices either are, or ought to be, determined by political or social exigencies. Whatever other merits these more homogeneous political and religious positions may have, they do not preserve the specific balance of Hooker's argument. The coherence of that argument depends on combining speculative, devotional, and political considerations in a way that acknowledges the peculiar character of each.

The problems of the English Church which Hooker confronted in the *Polity* were severe. How successful was his complex and massive work in meeting those problems theoretically, and to what extent was the establishment Hooker sought to uphold preserved in fact as well as theory? The half-dozen editions of Books I–V which appeared between 1604 and 1648 suggest that Hooker's criticism of Travers and Cartwright and the extended rationale and justification of established practices he provided in Book V contributed much to the unique flowering of Anglican religious culture under the early Stuarts. While others surpassed Hooker in spirituality or subtle development of particular themes, his work remains the one systematic and intelligible justification of the whole range of Anglican belief and worship. He wrote in trying circumstances, but it is no accident that his work has been so consistently identified with stable and enduring aspects of the Anglican settlement. In important respects, however, even the seventeenth-century English Church fell short of Hooker's hopes. First, Hooker had hoped to win over the reformers and their followers, not merely refute them. This was not only a matter of fraternal charity. The point is, rather, that Hooker's programme in Book V called for a substantially unanimous and wholehearted acceptance of one set of Christian devotional forms by the whole English Christian community. His goal of intelligently guided, socially effective communal piety could hardly be attained if a large segment of the population still felt conscientiously unable to participate in the officially sanctioned worship. Yet this, of course, was increasingly the situation in the early seventeenth century. With the flowering of Anglicanism went the growth of nonconformity.

A second important matter in which the seventeenth-century establishment differed from the state of the Church Hooker sought to preserve was in its attitude towards ecclesiastical government. As we have seen, Hooker provided a complex and subtly balanced basis for the crown's power of ecclesiastical dominion and a theologically modest defence of episcopacy. In both matters he ultimately concluded that the reformers had no justification for disobedience, that, on the contrary, the royal government had the supreme power it claimed. From an immediately practical point of view the early Stuarts seem to have demanded little more. Their underlying theory was different, however, and this ultimately became important in practice, too. The centre of gravity in political thought was shifted. Hooker had grounded the religious authority of royal and episcopal commands in the all-inclusive character of human association; the sacral or potentially sacral character of the community was basic, and consequently law – even human law – functioned to limit governmental power as well as regulate the rest of society. Under the early Stuarts, in contrast, much more weight fell on the sacred character of the offices of king and bishop, less on the community. The significance of law was altered accordingly. Instead of being regarded as a joint product of the community and its rulers or as an impartial and impersonal 'rule of well-doing', as Hooker would have it, it was presented as properly subject to the will of a divinely appointed ruler. Thus, Stuart political theory seriously disturbed Hooker's carefully achieved balance of effective government, a comprehensive world-view, and broadly meaningful devotional practices. As a result, those who had not been won over to Anglicanism were confirmed in their sense that Christian and worldly powers were opposing forces. Like the earliest Christians, Puritans under the Stuarts found themselves in a society whose dominant powers were not merely hostile but, like the emperors of the dying Roman empire, claimed for themselves a unique religious legitimacy. It is not surprising that many who could bear Elizabeth's ecclesiastical settlement became fanatics under her successors. When we recall that Hooker's basic constructive aim was to disclose the intrinsic excellence of laws and orders supported by essentially *non*-sacred authorities, we see that royalist attitudes and theory in the next half-century were in important ways a direct reversal of his thought. The *Polity* has exercised a continuing influence on Anglicanism, but Hooker's ideal of a Christian society has hardly been approximated since the end of his own century, if it was realized – except in passing – even then.

In addition to many powerful forces at work which had no connection with the *Polity*, the absence of Books VII and VIII from early editions may help explain Hooker's failure either to win over the reformers or to inhibit later Anglicans from sacralizing their government. Hooker's own emphasis on law rather than men must also be held responsible to some extent. This emphasis had advantages, and the personal shortcomings of the establishment had been proclaimed and exaggerated by the reformers. Nevertheless, Hooker's tendency to write as if the virtues of an impersonal system of norms were sufficient to insure religious well-being in a society could hardly have won the confidence of his opponents or inspired humility in officials within the system. In spite of their questionable views on ecclesiastical polity, the reformers continued to stir up Christian devotion, while in spite of the excellence of Prayer Book practices, incumbent Anglicans were often ineffective. Such facts as these were difficult even to acknowledge, let alone discuss constructively, given a determination that the whole controversy concerned laws and orders, not men.

A more abstract shortcoming of Hooker's work, but one which in the long term is more serious than exclusive attention to law, is a certain lack of intellectual rigour. Hooker's exposition of Christian cosmology, natural law, and moral theology is extraordinarily eloquent, but it contains little of the hard, formal examination of first principles that was common in the medieval universities and could still be found on the continent during the Reformation. Hooker had reason to avoid appearing a scholastic, yet the strictly rational tenability of his religious world-view was so vital for his purposes in the *Polity* that the comparative absence of precise, systematic argument is an unfortunate omission. Hooker is like Cicero here. Both were convinced of the need for philosophical wisdom as a factor in public affairs and a support for religion; both had personal experience of legal thought and were also familiar with a variety of intellectual traditions poorly appreciated by their compatriots; and both composed eclectic, rhetorically effective pleas on behalf of reason. In each case, however, the result is disappointing from the standpoint of philosophy itself. The *Polity* is technically far less impressive than Hobbes' *Leviathan*. It would obviously be unfair to blame Hooker for the fact that scepticism has been more brilliantly expounded than theism in modern British thought. When we recall, however, the quite different intellectual character of earlier British thinkers such as Scotus Erigena, Grosseteste, Duns Scotus, and Wyclif, we must regret that Hooker was unable to transmit his grasp of earlier tradition more cogently. Too many times he is reduced to the bare assertion that his own premises are natural and self-evident, or to equally bare assertions that his opponents' convictions are mere probabilities or opinions and should be submitted to official correction. Hence, in spite of his own awareness of previous exhaustive analyses and elaborations of such concepts as nature, rationality, self-evidence, and opinion, his position often seems arbitrary at points where understanding is most required. A systematic development of his own ideas, rather than modest reference to them as mere turns of phrase, would also have been valuable, though this, too, would no doubt have been difficult to provide in the polemical context of the *Polity*.

If much of the 'present state of the Church of God' Hooker defended passed away in fact, it remains well established in the *Polity*. The preceding criticisms are themselves testimonies to the stature of his work. Firmer philosophical foundations are required because the argument moves on a high plane. We wish that Hooker had attended to men as well as laws because he had the power to influence men. In spite of its shortcomings, the *Polity* is still the classic expression of what might be called public Christianity. In intellectual matters, Hooker defended objectivity and rational argument against individual inspiration and dogmatism; in his world-view religious ideas are integrated with serious thought about nature, human nature, and society, not left in a purely private realm of personal opinion or imagination. At the same time, with regard to Christian worship, he argued convincingly that the important values and impulses of common life could be taken up in devotional forms embracing a whole community. In politics, accordingly, he held that Christianity was inevitably and properly a subject of official public concern in a society of Christian individuals. In each of these areas – intellectual, devotional, and political – Hooker's 'public' position contradicts assumptions now widely regarded as self-evident, but if this makes the *Polity* more difficult to take for granted, it does not make it less great an achievement or less rewarding to read.

NOTES

1. John Jewel, *An Apology of the Church of England* (1562), ed. J. E. Booty (Ithaca, N.Y., 1963). Matthew Sutcliffe, *Remonstrance to the Demonstration of Discipline* (1590), *De Presbytero* (1591). Thomas Bilson, *Perpetual Government of Christ's Church* (1593). Richard Cosin, *Apology for sundry proceedings by Jurisdiction Ecclesiastical* (1593). John Whitgift, *Works*, ed. J. Ayre (3 vols., Parker Society, London, 1851–53). Richard Bancroft, *A Survey of the Pretended Holy Discipline* (1593); *Daungerous Positions and Proceedings* (1593), partially reprinted in R. G. Usher, *The Presbyterian Movement in the Reign of Queen Elizabeth* (Camden Society, 1905). John Bridges, *A Defence of the Government Established*

(1587). Adrian Saravia, *De Diversis Ministerii Gradibus* (1590). For a useful and readable survey, see Christopher Morris, *Political Thought in England, Tyndale to Hooker* (Oxford, 1953).

2. On Travers and the Book of Discipline, see Patrick Collinson's outstanding study, *The Elizabethan Puritan Movement* (Berkeley, Calif., 1967), pp. 291–302.

3. T. Fuller, *Worthies of England*, p. 264 (quoted by J. Keble in his edition of Hooker's *Works* [Oxford, 1874], vol. I, p. 52 n.).

4. On the admonition controversy, see W. H. Frere and C. E. Douglas, eds, *Puritan Manifestoes* (Church Historical Society, 1907) and D. J. McGinn, *The Admonition Controversy* (New Brunswick, New Jersey, 1949). Cartwright's contributions are partially reprinted in Whitgift's *Works* (London, 1851–53).

5. For this phase of the reform movement, see Collinson, *The Elizabethan Puritan Movement*, pp. 291–447.

6. *The True Difference between Christian Subjection and Unchristian Rebellion* (Oxford, 1585), Part II.

7. For broader treatments of the problems posed by the English crown's supremacy in religious affairs, see Claire Cross, *The Royal Supremacy in the Elizabethan Church* (London and New York, 1969), and W. Haugaard, *Elizabeth and the English Reformation: The Struggle for a Stable Settlement of Religion* (Cambridge, 1968).

8. In his *Life* of Hooker, Isaak Walton reports this, at second hand, as the substance of Pope Clement's reaction on having Book I read to him in Latin.

9. *Summa Theologiae*, IaIIae, qq. 90–108.

10. For the importance of this distinction in late medieval theology, see H. A. Oberman, *The Harvest of Medieval Theology: Gabriel Biel and Late Medieval Nominalism* (Cambridge, Mass., 1963).

11. *Summa Theologiae*, IaIIae, q. 90. The other extrinsic principle of human acts is grace, by which God aids us. The virtues, including faith, hope, and charity, are the inner principles of action.

12. *Ibid.*, article 4, *resp.*

13. For Bodin and other sixteenth-century political writers, as well as an unusually good account of Hooker, see J. W. Allen, *A History of Political Thought in the Sixteenth Century* (London, 1928).

14. H. F. Kearney, 'Richard Hooker: A Reconstruction,' *Cambridge Journal*, V (1952), 300–11.

15. Leo Strauss, *Natural Right and History* (Chicago, 1953).

16. On the systematic character of Book V, see A. S. McGrade, 'The Public and the Religious in Hooker's *Polity*,' *Church History* XXXVII (1968), 404–22.

17. C. J. Sisson, *The Judicious Marriage of Mr. Hooker and the Birth of the Laws of Ecclesiastical Polity* (Cambridge, 1940). R. A. Houk, ed., *Hooker's Ecclesiastical Polity: Book VIII* (New York, 1931). David Novarr, *The Making of Walton's Lives* (Ithaca, N.Y., 1958).

18. The best treatment of this still unsettled matter is W. Speed Hill, 'Hooker's *Polity*: The Problem of the "Three Last Books",' *The Huntington Library Quarterly*, XXXIV (1971), 317–36.

19. Stephen Gardiner, *De Vera Obedientia*, ed. and trans. P. Janelle, *Obedience in Church and State* (Cambridge, 1930).

20. Aristotle, *Politics*, III, 14–15.

21. Peter Munz, *The Place of Hooker in the History of Thought* (London, 1952; New York, 1970), pp. 107 ff.

22. *Politics*, III, 6. On Hooker's relation to Aristotle, see F. S. C. Northrop, *The Meeting of East and West: An Inquiry Concerning World Understanding* (New York, 1946, 1966), pp. 171–181.

23. For the impact of Aristotle's ideas on medieval political thought, see Walter Ullmann, *Principles of Government and Politics in the Middle Ages* (London, 1961), Part III.

24. The *Polity* has been found basically incoherent by H. F. Kearney (note 14 above); Peter Munz (note 21); Gunnar Hillerdal, *Reason and Revelation in Richard Hooker* (Lund, 1962); and others. For a more detailed account of Book VIII and its relation to earlier parts of the *Polity* along the lines of the present essay, see A. S. McGrade, 'The Coherence of Hooker's *Polity*: The Books on Power,' *Journal of the History of Ideas,* XXIV (1963), 163–82. Also see W. J. D. Cargill Thompson's penetrating essay, 'Richard Hooker as a Political Thinker: A Reassessment,' in W. Speed Hill, ed., *Studies in Richard Hooker: Essays Preliminary to an Edition of his Works* (Cleveland and London, 1972), pp. 3–76.

Introduction 2

HOOKER'S PROSE STYLE

by Brian Vickers

Hooker enjoys a high reputation as a prose stylist, but there are surprisingly few studies of his writing, and it is difficult not to feel that his currency value is usually endorsed rather than tested. Actually, the qualities generally attributed to him – moderation, dignity, a stately flow – are not qualities calculated to provoke the reader to see for himself. We can apply to him T. S. Eliot's diagnosis of the status of Ben Jonson in 1919:

> The reputation of Jonson has been of the most deadly kind that can be compelled upon the memory of a great poet. To be universally accepted; to be damned by the praise that quenches all desire to read the book; to be afflicted by the imputation of the virtues which excite the least pleasure; and to be read only by historians and antiquaries – this is the most perfect conspiracy of approval.[1]

Being left to the historians of literature has not benefited Hooker greatly, for his reputation has preceded him, and the traditional comments have been echoed over and over.[2]

Apart from this 'conspiracy of approval' Hooker has suffered the equally unhappy fate of being adapted to a critic's personal interpretation of literature or politics. Thus Coleridge grouped Hooker with Bacon, Milton and Jeremy Taylor and contrasted their 'stately march and difficult evolutions' with the jerky movement of Senecan style: 'The unity in these writers is produced by the unity of the subject, and the perpetual growth and evolution of the thoughts, one generating, and explaining, and justifying, the place of another, – not, as in Seneca, where the thoughts, striking as they are, are merely strung together like beads, without any causation or progression.'[3] Although one may agree with that evaluation of Seneca it is difficult to accept the inter-equation of writers so different in style (and value) as Hooker, Bacon, Milton and Jeremy Taylor. Evidently Coleridge is using Hooker to illustrate his own pre-occupation with 'organicism' at the level of style, and creating a group of exponents of that style as a weapon with which to attack Seneca. Similarly L. C. Knights once used Hooker (amongst others) as a stick with which to beat Bacon, since those representative writers of 'Elizabethan Prose' were said to use metaphors and similes which 'have a life of their own', whereas Bacon used them to illustrate or reinforce an argument.[4] I have shown elsewhere[5] that this is not a valid criterion for the use of metaphor in Renaissance literature, and that it does not fit Bacon. (As we will soon see, it does not fit Hooker either.) But I conclude this brief account of how estimates of Hooker's writing have been subordinated to pre-formulated critical schemes by recording that sometimes these clash between each other: Peter Munz rejected Professor Knight's classification of Hooker as 'Elizabethan' and urged instead that his prose-style is properly labelled 'baroque', since it 'consciously avoids symmetry'.[6] This extraordinary judgment, supported by a footnote which quotes only two sentences by Hooker, is evidently conditioned by the thesis of Professor Munz's book, that in his thought Hooker was incapable of achieving unity, being unable to resolve the tension which he felt between medieval and modern attitudes. Then 'style' is said to parallel 'thought', and the critic can conclude, to his own satisfaction, that 'the complexity of this situation made incongruous and unsymmetrical the style of the thought which had to come to terms with it'. The superficiality of this judgment must be all too evident.

If we are to make a fresh evaluation of Hooker as a writer we must approach him on his own terms, without any pre-formed scheme, and we must – as in all stylistic analysis – relate imagery, or sentence-structure, or whatever aspect we isolate, to the work's overall intention, meaning or function. The *Laws of Ecclesiastical Polity* is a work produced by a controversy; it attacks the Reformers' case, and argues the rationality of the Church of England position by appealing to first principles, to Reason and Revelation, to Natural Law, and to a whole structure of beliefs. It is a work, then, which belongs to the category of oratory known as deliberative, which was traditionally divided into the two opposed categories of praise and blame, *laus* and *vituperatio*.[7] To put the issue in its simplest terms, Hooker has to praise his own party and attack his opponents. If that seems a crassly obvious statement we should note that another tendency in contemporary Hooker criticism is to play down the controversialist side of his work, as if that were a rather shameful activity. Thus C. J. Sisson, whose elucidation of the authenticity of the later books remains a model of bibliographical and historical scholarship,[8] wrote regretfully of the Preface that in it Hooker failed to 'escape the dust of controversy', while in Book VII 'he seems to stumble at times into the rougher paths of abuse and cruel sarcasm which are so sadly familiar in the common run of controversialists of the age'. Happily, this is only a partial deviation from the 'stately dignity and the elaborate measured flow' of the rest of the work.[9] Recently Professor Knights has observed even less of this deplorable controversial manner, and believes that although Hooker could be 'tart' his 'manner and style – the manner and style of reasonableness and courtesy – are in themselves a contribution to the health of political thinking', and that his 'prevailing tone is that of a reasonable persuader, not that of a controversialist'; it is not a style 'based on fear'.[10] Professor Knights prefers Hooker to Milton, whose style is said to be 'highly rhetorical, with a good deal of name-calling, emotionally charged generalities, sweeping assertions', insistent repetitions, this polemical rhetoric being supported by a 'logic [that] is undeviating' (pp. 65, 67).

It is not my business here to decide whether that is a fair and just evaluation of Milton, but I would observe that Hooker's logic is also undeviating, that an unsympathetic reader could refuse many of Hooker's assumptions as question-begging, and that he could point to many 'emotionally charged generalities' in the *Laws of Ecclesiastical Polity*. There is much fear, too, as when Hooker contemplates how the world would be 'clean turned upside down' if the Reformers' policies were accepted (Pref., viii, 5). In a number of places where Hooker considers the possible or actual consequences of individuals or groups opting out of their proper place in the political or ecclesiastical hierarchy his remedy is often a coercive assertion of authority, expressed not without emotion. Is it not, after all, natural that men should experience 'emotion', even 'fear', when considering the most vital issues in politics and religion? Professor Knights may indeed prefer (so do I) that political discussion should be conducted 'in a way that is open, flexible and implicitly *connective*, rather than blinkered, rigid, and narrowly partisan' (p. 53), but perhaps he is setting too high an ideal for political man. Indirectly, it seems to me, he is doing Hooker a disservice in extending the myth of his reasonableness, toleration and piety[11] to the stage at which Hooker becomes a figure who is incredibly 'reasonable', utterly cool and unmoved even by human depravity or the scurrilities of his opponents, who is indeed 'afflicted by the imputation of the virtues which excite the least pleasure', as Eliot said of Jonson. The fact is that Renaissance controversy was an extremely violent genre, as anyone will know who has looked at the literature surrounding Luther or Calvin or Ramus. Hooker may be relatively tolerant – he is less violent than Milton, less caustic than Swift – but he shares those virtues and has others of his own. I deliberately call them 'virtues' because it seems to me that in the defence of one's ideals the polemicist must attack in order to defend; he must discredit the enemy because otherwise in the eyes of the world at large the cause of truth (as he sees it) will be damaged. There are distinctions to be made, of course, between mere abuse and polemical comment, between blundering insult and perceptive irony, and everyone sees by how much Andrew Marvell exceeds Samuel Parker. But the genre is inherently violent; it is properly so; its decorum is not that of 'reasonableness and courtesy'.

Hooker is often dignified, and he never descends to the gutters. But he is not a passionless Stoic expounding pure Reason. He it was who attacked the Stoics for their cult of non-feeling: 'which kind of men hath always accounted . . . commiseration the deadliest sin' (VI, vi, 6).[12] In his attack on the Reformers, since they represent a dangerous evil, he exerts no small emotional energy to discredit them. One effective technique is to summarize or quote from their verbose writings and to follow it with a sharp question or a challenging comment, such as: 'But what did these vain surmises boot?' (Pref., ii, 4; p. 68); 'For why?' (I, x, 7; p. 140); 'our answer is, No' (I, xiii, 2; p. 154); and elsewhere: 'But to what issue doth all this come?'; 'And if so be it were granted them as true, what gain they by it?'; 'But what of all this?'; 'In this they erred'. In these brief jabs we feel ourselves in the middle of a dialogue, as Hooker moves in to attack more forcibly: 'What then?'; 'But what?'; 'No'; 'it cannot be'; 'which is absurd'; 'A shift vain and needless'. Often Hooker places these challenges or rejections at the end of a sequence of summary and argument, so giving his Church the last word: 'Our answer therefore to their reasons is no; to their scoffs nothing' (V, xxx, 4); 'In this sense and construction therefore as they affirm, so we deny, that whatsoever is popish we ought to abrogate' (IV, iii, 1). Sometimes, indeed, Hooker writes as if his opponents were present – in a dispute in the law-courts or in parliament (as, in a sense, given the legal milieu, they are):

> Wherefore to come unto you whose judgment is a lantern of direction for all the rest, you that frame thus the people's hearts . . . on your shoulders is laid the burden of upholding the cause by argument. (Pref., iv, 1: p. 78)

Throughout this chapter (as often in the Preface and elsewhere) the dispute is conducted at a direct, intimate level, which permits him to get closer, to cross-examine: 'Was this a sentence (trow you) of so great force to prove that Scripture is the only rule of all the actions of men?' (II, v, 4). At times the *Laws* reads like a transcript of a trial, for Hooker also invents notional answers by the defendants which are either parodied internally or subjected to sarcasm (e.g. Pref., viii, 1: p. 91f; V, xxix, 7).

If it is a trial, the judge allows counsel for the defence considerable freedom of expression (no more, though, than that claimed by the prosecution). The recent times, in which the Reformers have instituted lay-elders, are summed up as being 'for insolency, pride, and egregious contempt of all good order', the worst that have been (Pref., iv, 5: p. 81). Given the absurdities of the Anabaptists Hooker can indulge his irony:

> When they and their Bibles were alone together, what strange fantastical opinion soever at any time entered into their heads, their use was to think the Spirit taught it them. (Pref., viii, 7: p. 97)

Faced with Machiavellians and others who hold that 'religion and virtue are only as men will account of them' Hooker can only describe this attitude as 'brutishness' (I, x, 1: p. 135). Later those of that opinion are said to have 'a strange kind of madness' and they are disposed of indignantly: 'Wherefore to let go this execrable crew . . .' (V, ii, 4–iii, 1: p. 225 f). Wit returns when he describes the fantasies produced by superstitious men, who 'both darken their eyes and yet sharpen their wits withal' (V. xxii, 7: p. 237). Hooker's most violent polemic is reserved for those who pervert religion: so he appeals to 'that truth which teacheth, that evil ministers of good things are as torches, a light to others, a waste to none but themselves only, and that the foulness of their hands can neither any whit impair the virtue nor stain the glory of the mysteries of Christ' (V, lxii, 10). Those who deny that Church ceremonies have a meaning would perform 'the idle gestures of men whose broken wits are not masters of that they do' (V, lxv, 5). His account of the punishments which God will visit on the wicked is as terrifying as its Old Testament models could have hoped for (V, lxxvi, 4), and his treatment of Tertullian, who, having espoused the Montanist heresy and thus doubted 'the Church's authority and power to remit sin', is suitably violent: 'A sponge steeped in wormwood and gall, a man through too much severity merciless, and neither able to endure nor to be endured of any' (VI, vi, 6).

Today not many readers will be offended on sectarian grounds by Hooker's treatment of the Reformers. Part of his case, though, was to discredit the Catholics, and while the Anglican may feel apologetic on Hooker's behalf, the literary critic can, with studied impartiality, point to the energy with which our author mocks what his church sees as the 'preposterous course, and misordered practice' of papal absolution:

> For against the guiltiness of sin, and the danger of everlasting condemnation thereby incurred, confession and absolution succeeding the same are, as they take it, a remedy sufficient; and therefore what their penitentiaries do think good to enjoin further, whether it be a number of Ave-Maries daily to be scored up, a journey of pilgrimage to be undertaken, some few dishes of ordinary diet to be exchanged, offerings to be made at the shrines of saints, or a little to be scraped off from men's superfluity for relief of poor people, all is in lieu or exchange with God, whose justice, notwithstanding our pardon, yet oweth us still some temporal punishment, either in this or in the life to come, except we quit it ourselves here with works of the former kind, and continued till the balance of God's most strict severity shall find the pains we have taken equivalent with the plagues we should endure, or else that the mercy of the pope relieve us. And at this postern gate cometh in the whole mart of papal indulgences, so infinitely strewed, that the pardon of sin, which heretofore was obtained hardly and by much suit, is with them become now almost impossible to be escaped. (VI. vi. 7)

It was necessary to transcribe the whole of that paragraph to show the control with which Hooker built up to the final irony, justifying the Anglican view of this as 'preposterous' or 'inverted' behaviour. If the paragraph still gives offence, then at least I have made the point clear, that Hooker *is* a 'partisan' writer, and that while he can make connections with philosophies which support his own church's position he is seldom, if ever, prepared to grant the assumptions behind either the Catholics' or the Reformers' beliefs. So we will not be surprised at the violence with which he denounces the 'sacrilege' of those who wish to deprive bishops of their goods (VII, xxiv: pp. 317 ff.), nor the bitter irony with which he satirizes the Reformers' metaphor of that 'two-headed, monstrous being' which, for them, the union of Church and State would represent (VIII, iv, 8: pp. 363 ff.).

I have chosen to start with Hooker as controversialist partly in order to challenge the myth of his impartial sweet reasonableness and partly because it also corrects the received picture of his prose-style as a dignified, stately, Latinate, somewhat remote medium. In the passages already quoted we can see an undignified, uninhibited style; a style which is a weapon. The colloquial element in Hooker's prose has been undervalued, for it appears most often in those passages of controversy from which attention has been deflected. The reader of the Preface will find abundant examples of a flexible, vigorous use of language; and one could pick out such phrases as 'charity cold', 'ifs or ands', 'not left so much as the least pin', 'but a silly argument'. Bellarmine receives two such pungent phrases: it pleased him 'to hoodwink his own knowledge' (VI, vi, 10); and he 'shrunk up the Lutherans' sinews, and cut off our doctrine by the skirts' (VI, vi, 11). More impressive still are those passages in which Hooker appeals for our agreement in his evaluation of a theological controversy with analogies drawn from life at an immediate and general level:

> Now if he that seeketh to reform covetousness or superstition should but labour to induce the contrary, it were but to draw men out of lime into coal-dust. (V, lxv, 20)
>
> What is this else but to deal with the people, as those nurses do with infants, whose mouths they besmear with the backside of the spoon, as though they had fed them, when they themselves devour the food? (VII, xiv, 10)
>
> Such disputes as this do somewhat resemble the wonted practising of well-willers upon their friends in the pangs of death, whose manner is even then to put smoke in their nostrils, and so to fetch them again, although they know it a matter impossible to keep them living. (VIII, iv, 10; p. 371)

I celebrate the energy of such writing.

* * *

Yet, if I have corrected one aspect of the accepted picture of Hooker's prose, there would be many others to consider if a complete account were to be attempted. Among topics which need to be discussed are: his use of inversion and the 'periodic' sentence; his appeal to axioms and general principles; his use of *partitio* or division as an organizing device; his method of word-repetition as a stage in logical deduction; his use of symmetrical syntax and of the traditional figures of rhetoric; his metaphors and analogies. These are all important categories, and to deal with any one of them in full detail would take me far beyond the scope of an introductory essay. I must select, therefore, and on this occasion lean rather towards style than to the issues in his thought which would have to be raised by considering in depth his use of logic, or his appeals to authority through 'axioms' or 'principles', say.

A consequence of our having started from a recognition of the dual structure of the *Laws* (praise and blame) is that we are alerted to the essential principle that details of style are meaningful in connection with their function. Since Hooker is not summarizing in the abstract but evaluating, *pro* and *contra*, then we must decide how these devices of style aid that process, and how successful they are. Take the habits of inverting subject and predicate, and of postponing a verb or another essential syntactical element to the end of a period: these are often linked as 'Latinate' features of his style. At times one must concede that this is indeed merely a case of linguistic influence (not surprising when we consider that the vast majority of serious intellectual works which Hooker read were written in Latin). But often these 'habits' are used purposefully, to evaluate. The two long periods which I quoted earlier attacking papal indulgences withheld their sharpest sting for the tail. Similarly we find periods which reserve judgment, in the form of epithets, to the last: 'erroneous and false' (VIII, iv, 9: p. 371); an ironic account of Ramism ends with the definition of it as an art which 'restraineth the mind of man that it may not wax over-wise' (I, vi, 4: p. 122). The movement of *vituperatio* produces sentences in which (if I may wrench them from their contexts for ease of illustration) the key-words or phrases postponed till last are such as 'gross surmise', 'sword', 'confusion', 'perish', 'baits', 'less than nothing', 'self-deceiving vanity'; conversely, that of *laus* yields such key terms as 'peace', 'mercy', 'piety'.

The suspension of sense is not, as C. S. Lewis argued (*op. cit.*, p. 462), a device for postponing the writer's decision but is often a challenge to us, whether we can make the right evaluation from the preceding terms, and so arrive at the conclusion strengthened by our agreement with Hooker. 'For men to be tied and led by authority, as it were with a kind of captivity of judgment, and though there be reason to the contrary not to listen unto it, but to follow like beasts the first in the herd, they know not nor care not whither' – have we made up our mind how to describe such behaviour? – 'this were brutish'. (II, vii, 6.) 'To raise up falsehoods of old condemned, and to bring that for confirmation of anything doubtful, which hath already been sufficiently proved an error, and is worthily so taken' – thus Hooker has defined, created his target: now he transfixes it: 'this would justly deserve censuring'. (VIII, iv, 9: p. 370) Many other sentences are, as it were, processes of discrimination – not that Hooker is extemporizing, or thinking aloud, but that he shows us the series of evaluations which, taken together, can only yield this or that conclusion. By the contrary process of inversion he can challenge us with a judgment at first view, which the rest of the period will justify: 'Deceived greatly they are therefore . . .' (Pref., iv, 6: p. 81); 'Ways of peaceable conclusion there are . . .' (Pref., vi, 2: p. 85); 'Dangerous it were for the feeble brain of man to wade far into the doings of the Most High . . .' (I, ii, 2: p. 110); 'Impossible it was . . .' (I, iv, 3: p. 118); 'Impossible therefore it is . . .' (II, iv, 4); 'True it is . . .' (III, i, 7: p. 188); 'Obscure it is not . . .' (III, vii, 4).

It is evident from these few examples that with such a device Hooker's argumentative technique is not one of gentle, unemotional exposition, but of a challenging assertion which will be backed up by authority and example. He argues from strength to strength. It is for this reason that he constantly appeals to axioms or maxims which support his case, and calls in question those of his opponents. To give one example out of a hundred, and an exceptionally insistent one, even for him:

So that this we may boldly set down as a principle clear in nature, an axiom which ought not to be called in question, a truth manifest and infallible, that men are eternally bound to honour God with their substance in token of thankful acknowledgement that all they have is from him. (V, lxxix, 1)

On the important issues Hooker is neither deferential nor diffident: he is tough, uncompromising, controlled. If the strength of the whole consists in the interrelation of its parts then *The Laws of Ecclesiastical Polity* derives its strength overall from Hooker's orderly use of *partitio* (in which, as in his use of axioms, he has much in common with Bacon[13]). He divides, distinguishes, sums up; points ahead, predicts where we are going, announces when we have arrived there. To pick only one example of this method I would choose his summing up after he has, in the Preface, set out the plan of the whole work:

Thus have I laid before you the brief of these my travails, and presented unto your view the limbs of that cause litigious between us: the whole entire body whereof being thus compact, it shall be no troublesome thing for any man to find each particular controversy's resting-place, and the coherence it hath with those things, either on which it dependeth, or which depend on it. (Pref. vii, 7: p. 90)

Whereas the vice of Renaissance controversy was that each work became parasitic on the form of the work which it attacked, responding to it blow by blow, Hooker achieved design in the whole by imposing his own order on it.

Design in the part is achieved by a variety of means governing sentence and paragraph structure, which the analysis of any one page will reveal, including syntactical balance, disjunction (that is, the opposition of clauses beginning with such phrases as 'the one . . .'/'the other . . .', 'either'/'or', 'not only'/'but also'), the frequent use of antithesis, and so on. One device which I should like to pick out is the repetition of the key terms in an argument, a repetition which is simultaneously logical (a process of deduction or inference) and rhetorical (a means of adding stress). Such passages are often found most densely at the beginning of sections, when he makes crucial discriminations. The definitions of Law in the first few chapters of Book I, for instance, are a thick tissue of overlapping disjunctions and discriminations (pp. 109 ff.). Chapter two opens with a statement of a general principle, and then deduces each further principle out of the previous one, as we will see if the key elements are italicized:

> All *things* that are, have some *operation* not violent or casual. Neither doth any *thing* ever begin to exercise *the same*, without some fore-conceived *end for which it worketh*. And the *end which it worketh for* is not *obtained*, unless the *work* be also *fit* to *obtain* it by. For unto *every end every operation* will not serve. *That which doth* assign unto each *thing* the *kind*, *that which doth* moderate the force and power, *that which doth* appoint the form and measure of *working*, the same we term a *Law*. So that no certain *end* could ever be *attained*, unless the actions whereby it is *attained* were regular; that is to say, made suitable, *fit* and correspondent unto their *end*, by some canon, rule or *law*. Which *thing* doth first take place in the *works* even of *God himself*. (I, ii, 1: p. 109)

Here the argument proceeds by elimination and deduction: two branches are distinguished, one is rejected as fruitless, the other followed, which in turn gives rise to further branches.

Another, more closely-knit example of this mode of procedure is the preliminary distinction to the section which has to distinguish between matters of discipline and matters of faith and salvation. Since the distinction is a vital one Hooker begins by defining the process of distinction itself:

> The mixture of those things by speech which by nature are divided, is the mother of all error. To take away therefore that error which confusion breedeth, distinction is requisite. Rightly to distinguish is by conceit of mind to sever things different in nature, and to discern wherein they differ. So that if we imagine a difference where there is none, because we distinguish where we should not, it may not be denied that we misdistinguish. The only trial whether we do so, yea or no, dependeth upon comparison between our conceit and the nature of things conceived. (III, iii, 1: p. 194 f.)

The reader will have seen from that passage how the eye and the ear do, in effect, italicize the key-words due to the stress given them by placing and repetition. Reading Hooker is not a process in which the mind can wander or take the occasional holiday: we are kept close to the page, involved in the process of argument. This reasoning process naturally relies on some of the props of logic, at the simplest level in repeated conjunctions marking stages in the argument, such as 'Therefore', 'Wherefore', 'So that', 'Which', and in phrases like 'It followeth'. Some passages resemble arguments in geometry (e.g. I, xi, 4: p. 148 f.) and although Hooker seldom uses the formal syllogism he relies much on the less strict rhetorical version of it, the enthymeme,[14] which was considered by Renaissance theorists to be a more suitable technique for general communication. But he often refers to logical methods, as in mocking the deficiencies of his opponents' logic (Pref., viii, 1: p. 91) or in such a sequence as this: 'The true necessity of baptism a few propositions considered will soon decide. All things which either are known Causes or set Means . . .' are necessary (V, lx, 1). As in the second sentence there, abundant examples of Hooker's use of traditional Aristotelian logic can be found (e.g. VIII, viii, 6: p. 401).

The study of logic and rhetoric are valuable, Bacon noted in 1597, since they make a man 'able to contend'.[15] Both disciplines are put to this use by Hooker, and in rhetoric he fully obeys the traditional injunction that the tropes and schemes be functional, not ornamental.[16] (I shall deal briefly with a few of these rhetorical figures since a knowledge of them offers the modern reader tools to read with, and ways of appreciating Renaissance literature at the level on which it was composed.) In the paragraph on law which I quoted above we can see the cohesive effect of the figure *anaphora*, which repeats the same word(s) at the beginning of successive clauses or sentences: 'That which . . . that which . . . that which . . .' Hooker frequently uses this figure to sustain an argument across a whole paragraph (e.g. Pref., iii, 12: p. 76; Pref., viii, 14: p. 102; I, ii, 5: p. 112; I, iii, 1: p. 113; I, iv, 2: p. 118; etc.). The converse of *anaphora* is *epistrophe*, where the same word is repeated at the end of a series of clauses. This is a much rarer figure, but Hooker handles it well, realizing that the effect of repeating the same word is often to shift the stress back on to the word preceding, as in

a f h q *z*
b e m **r** *z*

where **r** tends to receive most emphasis. So in his placing of this quotation from Ephesians i, 11: 'God worketh all things' not only 'according to his own will', but 'the *Counsel* of his own will' (I, ii, 5: p. 111), where the word which I have italicized is given most stress. To abandon Natural Law, 'to bring things unto the first course they were in, and utterly to take away all kind of public government in the world, were apparently to overturn the whole world' (I, x, 4: p. 139), where, appropriately, the stressed word is 'overturn', the threat of anarchy.

This sense of the functional potential of rhetoric is seen even more clearly in Hooker's frequent use of *antimetabole* (which has come to be known in modern times as *chiasmus*): the form of inversion, AB:BA, as in 'eat to live, not live to eat'. To illustrate the distinction between human will and human appetite Hooker uses the figure twice, the second time glossing the metaphors of the first:

> Appetite is the Will's solicitor,
> and the Will is Appetite's controller;
> What we covet according to the one
> by the other we often reject (I, vii, 3: p. 123).

Antimetabole was called *commutatio* by some rhetoricians, and once Hooker refers explicitly to it, in order to point up the interdependence of the human and the divine in Christ:

> A kind of mutual commutation there is whereby those concrete names, *God* and *Man*, when we speak of Christ, do take interchangeably one another's room, so that for truth of speech it skilleth not whether we say that the Son of God hath created the world, and the Son of Man by his death hath saved it, or else that the Son of Man did create, and the Son of God die to save the world. (V, liii, 4: p. 268)

This figure is useful for the exposition of Hooker's own philosophical and theological beliefs, as in several places in this section of Book V dealing with the interrelationship between God and Christ (V, li–lvii: pp. 262 ff.), or the way in which human consciences are transparent to God, opaque to man: 'To him they seem such as they are, but to us they must be taken for such as they seem' (V, lxviii, 8). But it also works well for polemic, as in his diagnosis of the discord produced by the Reformers' disputes over preaching: 'while they thus labour amongst the people to divide the word, they make the word a mean to divide and distract the people' (V, lxxxi, 11); or in his attack on those 'obstinate hearts' which have rejected 'the mystery of Christ': 'esteeming in the frantic error of their minds the greatest madness in the world to be wisdom, and the highest wisdom foolishness' (III, viii, 9); or in his account of the corruption of the Israelites who worshipped Baal and as a result were condemned as 'a wicked generation of miscreants, which had forsaken the living God, and of him were likewise forsaken' (III, i, 8: p. 189).

Two other rhetorical figures ought to be discussed since they influence, indeed help to create the closely-knit structures of Hooker's argument. *Epanalepsis* is the repetition of the same word at the beginning and end of a clause or sentence. So Hooker uses it in analysing the degrees of freedom which man enjoys, distinguishing between end and means:

necessary that our bodies should be both fed and clothed, howbeit no one kind of food or raiment *necessary*; (II, iv, 4).

To enforce law requires a hierarchy: '*Equals* cannot impose laws and statutes upon their *equals*' (VIII, vi, 1: p. 376). At times the figure can be linked with *ploche* (repeating a word within a clause or sentence), whether to dignify man: 'by virtue of this grace, man is really made God, a *creature* is exalted above the dignity of *all creatures*, and hath *all creatures* else under it' (V, liv, 3: p. 270), or to criticize him: 'even that which we tremble to *do* we *do*, we *ask* those things which we dare not *ask*' (V, xlvii, 4). For a variety of reasons repetition is one of the most characteristic features of Hooker's prose, and it often unites logical with rhetorical methods. This is true of the last of these figures to be discussed, *anadiplosis*, in which the concluding word of one clause or sentence becomes the first word of the succeeding one: 'all things that *are*, *are* good' (I, v, 1: p. 119). There the overlap acts as a link in the argument, and again Hooker seems to be conscious of the form and function of the figure when he discusses the relationship between the existence of the physical body and man's spiritual existence:

These things are linked and as it were chained one to another: we labour to eat, and we eat to live, and we live to do good, and the good which we do is as a seed sown with reference to a future harvest. (I, xi, 1: p. 146)

Within one sentence Hooker embraced the whole rationale of human life, giving it greater point with his rhetoric. This figure, too, is adaptable to polemic, as when he sums up the deficiencies of the Reformers' position: 'So as the form of polity by them set down for perpetuity is three ways faulty: faulty in omitting . . .; faulty in requiring . . .; faulty also in urging . . .' (III, ix, 20) – where *anaphora* sharpens the edge; or in defining at its sharpest the discrepancies in ritual ('Romish rites') used by some Protestant churches: 'Heretics they are, and they are our neighbours' (IV, vi, 2). There the physical contiguity achieved by the hinge-effect opens up the paradox which gives rise to a whole chain of argument against the Reformers. In this example as in so many that I have quoted Hooker displays a sharp eye for detail.

The precision and force of his writing is evident, but to a lesser extent, in metaphor. Classical and Renaissance theorists urged that metaphor should be *used* for conscious purposes (it does not just happen, as in some modern aesthetics), notably to persuade the reader of the validity of the writer's argument by illuminating and evaluating[17]: we are made to see the matter in the light in which he chooses to display it. The major positive metaphor in Hooker is indeed that of light, used according to a long religious tradition as an image of Revelation, and found most commonly as 'the light of nature', or the 'light of reason'. Thus 'Goodness is seen with the eye of the understanding. And the light of that eye, is reason' (I, vii, 2: p. 123); or 'by force of the light of Reason, wherewith God illuminateth every one which cometh into the world', men can distinguish 'truth from falsehood, and good from evil' (I, viii, 3: p. 127). I cannot claim a very high status for Hooker's use of metaphor: the image is often used efficiently but without much force or feeling (he does not rank with Sidney, Donne, Shakespeare or Bacon). His metaphors invite assent, but they seldom stimulate it, or make it unavoidable; he is clear, but cool. Just occasionally the image will be developed in a more imaginative way, as when he bewails man's falling away from God:

> . . . the name of the light of nature is made hateful with men; the 'star of reason and learning', and all other such like helps, beginneth no otherwise to be thought of than if it were an unlucky comet; or as if God had so accursed it, that it should never shine or give light in things concerning our duty any way towards him, but be esteemed as that star in the Revelation called Wormwood, which being fallen from heaven, maketh rivers and waters in which it falleth so bitter, that men tasting them die thereof. (III, viii, 4: p. 197)

That example has the quality which is rare in Hooker (but not in other writers of this period) of being able to make a transition between metaphors, carrying over the feeling from one to the other. Many passages oppose darkness to light (the darkness of human irrationality or perverse swerving from true religion), and most of these are clear but conventional; an exception is the opening of the section on the Cross in baptism: 'In baptism many things of very ancient continuance are now quite and clean abolished, for that the virtue and grace of this sacrament had been therewith overshadowed, as fruit with too great abundance of leaves' (V, lxv, 1).

Perhaps the danger of using the metaphor of light is that it is too familiar, so frequently applied that Hooker did not need to think through it. Of other positive metaphors (that is, those used to support the arguments of his own side) this criticism will not always hold. Many of these are traditional – metaphors of books, of labour and harvest, of fountains or blessings (Christ the well-spring), of voyages (the political metaphor of the ruler as the pilot of the ship), of food for soul and body. Some of these are given individual development – that of the path, say (I, i, 2: p. 108), or that of the book or tables of law (I, xvi, 2: p. 163), or that of the solace of the Eucharist: 'God forbid we should think that the Church doth sin in permitting the wounds of such to be suppled with that oil which this gracious sacrament doth yield, and their bruised minds not only need but beg' (V, lxviii, 12). More original images include this: 'all things which are of God he hath by wonderful art and wisdom sodered as it were together with the glue of mutual assistance . . .' (V, lxxvi, 9), or this: 'these unjust and insolent positions I would not mention, were it not thereby to make the countenance of truth more orient' (VIII, ii, 8: p. 347). When Hooker is particularly moved to praise by his topic the images tend to come in a series, as in this celebration of 'Preaching as the blessed ordinance of God, sermons as keys to the kingdom of heaven, as wings to the soul, as spurs to the good affections of man, unto the sound and healthy as food, as physic unto diseased minds' (V, xxii, 1: p. 233, or in the celebration of Law (I, xvi, 8: p. 167 f.). Most impressive of all are the ecstatic passages praising Christ (V, liv, 5–9: pp. 270 ff.).

Yet, granted the power of such passages, it must be admitted that Hooker displays more imaginative energy in the images attacking his opponents. This is not surprising, since the appeals to the emotions which were systematized by rhetoric are more necessary when confronted with those forces which threaten to destroy the whole hierarchy of religion and society. When Hooker is describing this hierarchy reason is his main tool; when he sees it threatened passion adds its force. The enemy produces a 'sea of . . . gall and bitterness' in which they try to drown Christ (Pref., i, 1: p. 63); they draw their support 'very near the dregs' of the people (Pref., iv, 6: p. 81); their errors will persist 'as long as wit by whetting itself is able to find out any shift, be it never so slight' to escape from contradiction (III, v, 1); they cause sores yet refuse medicine (IV, xii, 7: p. 213). Scoffing atheists have been treated with too much tolerance: 'the fury of this wicked brood hath the reins too much at liberty; their tongues walk at large; the spit-venom of their poisoned hearts breaketh out to the annoyance of others' (V, ii, 2: p. 224). One cause of superstition is zeal, which 'useth the razor many times with such eagerness, that the very life of religion itself is thereby hazarded; through hatred of tares the corn in the field of God is plucked up' (V, iii, 1: p. 226). Heretics are 'monsters', bred both in the East and West (*ibid.* 3: p. 227). And so it goes on: the enemies of the Church of England squirt out poison, imprint evil, clog growth with their weeds, devour life with their grinding jaws, usurp the key of spiritual authority, create festering sores, breed new monsters (in the dark), envelop light in mists of ambiguity, are seedsmen of rebellion.

The violence with which Hooker deals with the enemy is clear evidence of the threat which, he thought, they posed to him and his Church, and his feelings run so high that in many of these passages image merges into image in a strong current of feeling and imagination. But as well as showing them to be dangerous he uses that other tactic, so popular in controversy, of making them seem futile, harmless or ridiculous. Whatever the Anabaptists produced from the 'forge' of their 'possessed' brains would be no serious threat, although it is disconcerting to find that even though their contentions wounded each other 'they had ways to lick one another whole' (Pref., viii, 7: p. 97). The Reformers claim to have created a '"form" of polity', but Hooker adds in a parenthesis: 'if yet we may term that a form of building, when men have laid a few rafters together, and those not all of the soundest neither' (III, xi, 19). They are too often caught up in labyrinths or mazes of their own contriving (V, lxvii, 10, 12: pp. 293 f.), and some critics may be dismissed like dogs, who 'bark . . . idly against that truth' (IV, xi, 12). One need not take the Reformers' objections against Church attire too seriously, since they will collapse of their own accord: 'it booteth them not thus to soder up a broken cause, whereof their first and last discourses will fall asunder do what they can' (V, xxix, 7). They may reply to our exposure of their own contradictions, but the 'answer serveth not to help them out of the briers' (VII, viii, 5). By alternately casting them as monsters or nincompoops Hooker makes his Church's opponents appear frightening or ridiculous: either way we are discouraged from following them.

* * *

Having considered a number of individual devices by which Hooker carries out his twin purposes of praise and blame, it remains only to consider some passages in which he integrates them into a unified movement: figures of rhetoric, images, syntactical structures, as they combine with each other. It is in this area that I would make the highest claims for Hooker. Even the most distinguished Tudor prose finds it difficult to sustain an argument over a long arc: repetitiveness and incoherence are always threatening. To read Hooker's English predecessors in the field of philosophical or religious discourse (More, Elyot, Starkey, Sir Thomas Smith) is to be confronted rather too often with clumsiness and awkwardness. Clearly the triumph of the vernacular and the enormous surge forward in English literature in the 1580s and 90s helped Hooker, but credit must be given him for using the language for difficult, complex argument which still moves with clarity and control. It is not enough to dismiss his style in a few lines (as Mr Carey does) as being merely a pastiche of Ciceronian Latin: Hooker may well have learned control from Cicero but he does more than translate, he re-creates, in English idioms and English structures.

Quotations of such passages are necessarily long, for Hooker works with large units, organizing sentences as if they were (as indeed they are) blocks of stone creating a single building. One might analyse the tremendously vigorous sequence which plots the final positions of the Anabaptists, when all their principles had been turned upside down; in particular the sentence which opens: 'These men, in whose mouths at the first sounded nothing but only mortification of the flesh, were come at the length to think they might lawfully have their six or seven wives apiece . . .' (Pref., viii, 12; p. 100), a paragraph of serious irony worthy of Milton. Or one could consider the highly organized section discussing God's law (I, ii; pp. 109 ff.), or angelic law (I, iv; pp. 117 ff.); or his discussion of the goal of human existence (I, xi; pp. 146 ff.); or the remarkable paragraph defending the practice of the congregation's singing the Psalms (V, xxxix, 4: p. 259 f.). To give some examples. I start with Hooker's insistence on the importance of Church festivals: 'well to celebrate these religious and sacred days is to spend the flower of our time happily. They are the splendour and outward dignity of our religion, forcible witnesses of ancient truth, provocations to the exercise of all piety, shadows of our endless felicity in heaven, on earth everlasting records and memorials, wherein they which cannot be drawn to hearken unto that we teach, may only by looking upon that we do, in a manner read whatsoever we believe' (V, lxxi, 11). In that sequence Hooker began with metaphor and a series of panegyrical phrases in parallel, inverted the structure at '. . . in heaven, on earth', and at the end switched to a series of interconnected verbs, appropriately describing the process of action and reaction which the public celebration of festivals would provoke: 'drawn . . . hearken unto . . . teach . . . looking upon . . . do . . . read . . . believe'.

If we wanted to take a longer sequence for analysis then the great praise of Christ (V, liv: pp. 269 ff.) would be an admirable text. But in the light of my earlier attack on the myth of the 'godly and unmoved' Hooker it might be more fitting to end with a sequence in which he presents his hierarchy as being threatened, under pressure from the forces of anarchy and chaos. In defining the laws of nature Hooker argues that at the creation God made light, separated land from sea, ordered the sun and the rain as by a 'solemn injunction':

> His commanding those things to be which are,
> and to be in such sort as they are,
> to keep that tenure and course which they do,
> importeth the establishment of nature's law.

What then, if this order were upset? To illustrate (or better, dramatize) the consequences Hooker constructs an enormous sentence consisting of a series of parallel clauses listing the levels at which chaos would come; within each clause he intensifies feeling by strong but simple metaphors; and whereas the first six clauses begin with 'if', *anaphora* being used to set out each stage of the operation, the order of the syntax thus being mirrored against the disorder in the sense – in the final stages the 'if' disappears and the instances of chaos come rushing in as disorder takes over altogether:

Now
if nature should intermit her course, and leave altogether
though it were but for a while the observation of her own laws;
if those principal and mother elements of the world,
whereof all things in this lower world are made,
should lose the qualities which now they have;
if the frame of that heavenly arch erected over our
heads should loosen and dissolve itself;
if celestial spheres should forget their wonted motions,
and by irregular volubility turn themselves any way
as it might happen;
if the prince of the lights of heaven, which now
as a giant doth run his unwearied course,
should as it were through a languishing
faintness begin to stand and to rest himself;
if the moon should wander from her beaten way,

the times and seasons of the year blend themselves
by disordered and confused mixture,

the winds breathe out their last gasp,

the clouds yield no rain

the earth be defeated of heavenly influence,

the fruits of the earth pine away as children at the
withered breasts of their mother no longer
able to yield them relief:
What would become of man himself, whom these things now do all serve? See we not plainly that obedience of creatures unto the law of nature is the stay of the whole world? (I, iii, 2: p. 114)

In that extraordinary period the sense alone – deprived, as it were, of all literary resources – would be a compelling argument for not interfering with the natural order; but how much more force is gained by the resources of rhetoric and syntax.[18] The parallel structure first set up an even tempo, then broke it with a faster, accelerating movement up to the climax on the pathetic image of the children dying as their source of life dries up. In the first of the two final interrogatory clauses the key word 'serve' is left to the end, and in the reinforcing question which follows it the key terms are arranged in ascending order of importance, to stress the importance of order: 'obedience – creatures – law – nature – stay – whole world'. This evocation of chaos ranks with the threats of sterility which the Eumenides threaten to unloose at the end of the *Oresteia*, or with the images of disorder in *King Lear, Macbeth, Othello*. Hooker offers us a vision of tragic chaos, but then reassures us with the stability of his final sentence. To be able to sustain such an intense experience over a long period without any strain or confusion is the mark of one of the first great writers of serious prose in English.

NOTES

1. T. S. Eliot, 'Ben Jonson', in *Selected Essays* (London, 1951), p. 147.

2. C. S. Lewis, *English Literature in the Sixteenth Century* (Oxford, 1954), pp. 451–63. Lewis devotes only one page to the style and tends to endorse the accepted view of its 'beauty': 'The style is, for its purpose, perhaps the most perfect in English' (p. 462). However, his account is in every way superior to the facile evaluation by John Carey in *English Poetry and Prose 1540–1674*, ed. C. Ricks (London, 1970) pp. 382–87.

Other studies include G. P. Krapp, *The Rise of English Literary Prose* (New York, 1915), pp. 131–149, the larger part of which is devoted to a summary of content and argument. Mr Krapp is content to describe Hooker as 'an artist in the grand style' (p. 144) with a 'lofty' aim, and 'long rolling cadences' (pp. 145–6), although he criticizes Hooker for lacking 'concrete detail' and for being remote from everyday life. 'He thought in concepts, not in images' (p. 145). Mr Krapp also makes the remarkable claim that symmetrical syntax (antithesis, balance) 'appears scarcely at all in Hooker's writing' (p. 146), a misjudgment that is corrected by Sister M. S. Stueber, C.S.J., 'The Balanced Diction of Hooker's *Polity*', *Publications of the Modern Language Association of America* 71 (1956) pp. 808–826. However, that writer is more concerned to associate Hooker's style with such large (and, be it admitted, vague) concepts as Renaissance Christian humanism, with its 'balanced reason–faith relationship' (p. 808), 'the scholastical-dialectical tradition' (p. 811), and 'the Thomistic emphasis on reason and the intellect' (p. 816). Sister Stueber argues that his style is appropriate to 'his balanced world view' with its teleological design (p. 819 and note), and allows only a few paragraphs in which to analyse Hooker's style; then she compares it with that of the Euphuists, to their discredit. A much closer engagement with the text (mostly Sermon II, 'Of Justification') is offered by W. Speed Hill in 'The Authority of Hooker's Style', *Studies in Philology* 67 (1970) pp. 328–338.

3. *Coleridge on the Seventeenth Century*, ed. R. F. Brinkley (Duke, North Carolina, 1955), pp. 425–6, 414.

4. 'Bacon and the Seventeenth-century Dissociation of Sensibility', in *Explorations* (London, 1946) p. 101.

5. *Francis Bacon and Renaissance Prose* (Cambridge, 1968), chapter 5.

6. Munz, *The Place of Hooker In The History of Thought* (London, 1952), pp. 173–4.

7. For a brief account of this genre, and references to the major sources, see my *Classical Rhetoric in English Poetry* (London, 1970), pp. 68–73. On Renaissance controversy not much has been written, but two useful contributions are R. Pineas, *Thomas More and Tudor Polemics* (Bloomington, Ind., 1970) and T. Kranidas, *The Fierce Equation: A Study of Milton's Decorum* (New York/The Hague, 1966).

8. *The Judicious Marriage of Mr. Hooker and the Birth of 'The Laws of Ecclesiastical Polity'* (Cambridge, 1940). Its conclusions have been substantially endorsed by W. Speed Hill in *Richard Hooker. A Descriptive Bibliography of the Early Editions: 1593–1724* (Cleveland, 1970), which is a trial issue of the *Bibliography* to the forthcoming edition of Hooker sponsored by the Folger Shakespeare Library and to be published by Harvard University Press. On two disputed points Mr Hill disagrees with Sisson: he believes that Hooker *had* completed all

eight books in 1593 (p. 4), and he agrees with Keble that 'Book VI' is the early 'tract of confession' which was not, in fact, intended for the *Laws* (p. 81).
9. Sisson, *op. cit.*, p. 109. Even C. S. Lewis attempts to explain away Hooker's 'sharper, more sarcastic' tone in the later Books by arguing that they are only first drafts: 'the last labour of the file [would have] removed the asperities' (*op. cit.*, p. 453). The 'refutation of the enemy comes in the end to seem a very small thing, a by-product' of Hooker's own philosophical 'model of the universe' (p. 459); 'trouble and passion' are found in other works, not in the 'serenity' of the *Laws* (pp. 461–2).
10. Knights, *Public Voices. Literature and Politics with Special Reference to the Seventeenth Century* (London, 1971) pp. 57–8. Chapter Three is called 'Hooker and Milton: A Contrast of Styles'.
11. It would be interesting to explore the growth of Hooker's reputation (and the reasons for it) which we can trace in the epithets applied to him by his contemporaries, such as 'judicious', 'godly', 'humble', 'venerable', 'reverend'. Cf., e.g., Marvell's wish that Samuel Parker 'had rather imitated the incomparable modesty and candor of Reverend Mr. Hooker in all his writings'. *The Rehearsal Transposed*, ed. D. I. B. Smith (Oxford, 1971) p. 303.
12. All quotations are from the Keble text, by Book, chapter, and section number; where the selection appears in the present volume a page reference is given in addition.
13. I have outlined Renaissance concepts of axioms and of *partitio* in *Francis Bacon and Renaissance Prose*, chapters 3 and 2 respectively.
14. On the rhetorical enthymeme see Aristotle, *Rhetoric* 2.21=1394a21–b23; Quintilian, *Institutes of Oratory* V, 10, 1; VIII, 5, 9; IX, 3, 94; and Puttenham, *The Arte of English Poesie* ed. A. Walker & G. D. Willcock (Cambridge, 1936, 1970) pp. 228–9 (where it is called *aetiologia*). It is significant that in one of the notes which Cranmer wrote in comment on Hooker's MS of Book VI he advised: '. . . in some places, especially where their arguments are weakest, I thinke if you did at the last drawe them into a short enthymeme, it would breed some shame in them and in others a contempt of their kynd of reasoning. As, God hath left in his Church Apostles, teachers, aydes, gouvernements, ergo there must be in every congregation lay elders.' (*Works*, ed. Keble, III, 124).
15. Bacon, *Works*, ed. J. Spedding *et al.* (London, 1857–74), VI, 525 (Essay, 'Of Studies').
16. See my *Classical Rhetoric in English Poetry*, chapter 3. Some examples of Hooker's use of rhetorical figures were given by D. C. Boughner in 'Notes on Hooker's Prose', *Review of English Studies* 15 (1939) pp. 194–200.
17. On metaphor in traditional theory see, e.g., E. R. Curtius, *European Literature and the Latin Middle Ages*, tr. W. R. Trask (New York, 1953) chapters 7, 8; A. D. Leeman, *Orationis Ratio: The Stylistic Theories and Practices of the Orators . . .* (Amsterdam, 1963); R. Tuve, *Elizabethan and Metaphysical Imagery* (Chicago, 1947).
18. Since this introduction was written, George Edelen has published an important essay on 'Hooker's Style' in *Studies in Richard Hooker: Essays preliminary to an edition of his works*, ed. W. Speed Hill (Cleveland and London, 1972), pp. 241–77. Professor Edelen has an illuminating analysis of the 'expressive values' of Hooker's syntax and sentence-structure, including a contrasting analysis of the sentence discussed above: see pp. 258 ff. Whether Hooker used periodic sentences as part of a deliberate policy of suspending judgement (pp. 256 ff.), however, seems questionable: the *Polity* moves from one fixed point to the next, with neither Hooker's opinion nor his church's policies ever in doubt.

Of the Laws of Ecclesiastical Polity

a preface

TO THEM THAT SEEK (AS THEY TERM IT) THE REFORMATION OF THE LAWS AND ORDERS ECCLESIASTICAL, IN THE CHURCH OF ENGLAND

Chapter 1

THE CAUSE AND OCCASION OF HANDLING THESE THINGS, AND WHAT MIGHT BE WISHED IN THEM, FOR WHOSE SAKES SO MUCH PAIN IS TAKEN

THOUGH for no other cause, yet for this; that posterity may know we have not loosely through silence permitted things to pass away as in a dream, there shall be for men's information extant thus much concerning the present state of the Church of God established amongst us, and their careful endeavour which would have upheld the same. At your hands, beloved in our Lord and Saviour Jesus Christ (for in him the love which we bear unto all that would but seem to be born of him, it is not the sea of your gall and bitterness that shall ever drown), I have no great cause to look for other than the selfsame portion and lot, which your manner hath been hitherto to lay on them that concur not in opinion and sentence with you. But our hope is, that the God of peace shall (notwithstanding man's nature too impatient of contumelious malediction) enable us quietly and even gladly to suffer all things, for that work sake which we covet to perform.

[2.] The wonderful zeal and fervour wherewith ye have withstood the received orders of this Church, was the first thing which caused me to enter into consideration, whether (as all your published books and writings peremptorily maintain) every Christian man, fearing God, stand bound to join with you for the furtherance of that which ye term the *Lord's Discipline*. Wherein I must plainly confess unto you, that before I examined your sundry declarations in that behalf, it could not settle in my head to think, but that undoubtedly such numbers of otherwise right well affected and most religiously inclined minds had some marvellous reasonable inducements, which led them with so great earnestness that way. But when once, as near as my slender ability would serve, I had with travail and care performed that part of the Apostle's advice and counsel in such cases, whereby he willeth to "try all things", and was come at the length so far, that there remained only the other clause to be satisfied, wherein he concludeth that "what good is must be held"; there was in my poor understanding no remedy, but to set down this as my final resolute persuasion: "Surely the present form of church-government which the laws of this land have established is such, as no law of God nor reason of man hath hitherto been alleged of force sufficient to prove they do ill, who to the uttermost of their power withstand the alteration thereof." Contrariwise, "The other, which instead of it we are required to accept, is only by error and misconceit named the ordinance of Jesus Christ, no one proof as yet brought forth whereby it may clearly appear to be so in very deed."

[3.] The explication of which two things I have here thought good to offer into your own hands, heartily beseeching you even by the meekness of Jesus Christ, whom I trust ye love; that, as ye tender the peace and quietness of this church, if there be in you that gracious humility which hath ever been the crown and glory of a Christianly-disposed mind, if your own souls, hearts, and consciences (the sound integrity whereof can but hardly stand with the refusal of truth in personal respects) be, as I doubt not but they are, things most dear and precious unto you: let "not the faith which ye have in our Lord Jesus Christ" be blemished "with partialities" [James ii, 1]; regard not who it is which speaketh, but weigh only what is spoken. Think not that ye read the words of one who bendeth himself as an adversary against the truth which ye have already embraced; but the words of one who desireth even to embrace together with you the self-same truth, if it be the truth; and for that cause (for no other, God he knoweth) hath undertaken the burdensome labour of this painful kind of conference. For the plainer access whereunto, let it be lawful for me to rip up to the very bottom, how and by whom your Discipline was planted, at such time as this age we live in began to make first trial thereof.

Chapter 2

THE FIRST ESTABLISHMENT OF NEW DISCIPLINE BY MR. CALVIN'S INDUSTRY IN THE CHURCH OF GENEVA; AND THE BEGINNING OF STRIFE ABOUT IT AMONGST OURSELVES

A founder it had, whom, for mine own part, I think incomparably the wisest man that ever the French Church did enjoy, since the hour it enjoyed him. His bringing up was in the study of the civil law. Divine knowledge he gathered, not by hearing or reading so much, as by teaching others. For, though thousands were debtors to him, as touching knowledge in that kind; yet he to none but only to God, the author of that most blessed fountain, the Book of Life, and of the admirable dexterity of wit, together with the helps of other learning which were his guides: till being occasioned to leave France, he fell at the length upon Geneva; which city the bishop and clergy thereof had a little before (as some do affirm) forsaken, being of likelihood frighted with the people's sudden attempt for abolishment of popish religion: the event of which enterprise they thought it not safe for themselves to wait for in that place. At the coming of Calvin thither, the form of their civil regiment was popular, as it continueth at this day: neither king, nor duke, nor nobleman of any authority or power over them, but officers chosen by the people yearly out of themselves, to order all things with public consent. For spiritual government, they had no laws at all agreed upon, but did what the pastors of their souls by persuasion could win them unto. Calvin, being admitted one of their preachers, and a divinity reader amongst them, considered how dangerous it was that the whole estate of that Church should hang still on so slender a thread as the liking of an ignorant multitude is, if it have power to change whatsoever itself listeth. Wherefore taking unto him two of the other ministers for more countenance of the action (albeit the rest were all against it), they moved, and in the end persuaded with much ado, the people to bind themselves by solemn oath, first never to admit the Papacy amongst them again; and secondly, to live in obedience unto such orders concerning the exercise of their religion, and the form of their ecclesiastical government, as those their true and faithful ministers of God's word had agreeably to scripture set down for that end and purpose.

[2.] When these things began to be put in ure, the people also (what causes moving them thereunto, themselves best know) began to repent them of that they had done, and irefully to champ upon the bit they had taken into their mouths; the rather, for that they grew by means of this innovation into dislike with some Churches near about them, the benefit of whose good friendship their state could not well lack.

It was the manner of those times (whether through men's desire to enjoy alone the glory of their own enterprizes, or else because the quickness of their occasions required present despatch, so it was, that every particular Church did that within itself, which some few of their own thought good, by whom the rest were all directed. Such number of Churches then being, though free within themselves, yet small, common conference beforehand might have eased them of much after trouble. But a greater inconvenience it bred, that every later endeavoured to be certain degrees more removed from conformity with the Church of Rome, than the rest before had been: whereupon grew marvellous great dissimilitudes, and by reason thereof, jealousies, heart-burnings, jars and discords amongst them. Which, notwithstanding, might have easily been prevented, if the orders, which each Church did think fit and convenient for itself, had not so peremptorily been established under that high commanding form, which tendered them unto the people, as things everlastingly required by the law of that Lord of Lords, against whose statutes there is no exception to be taken. For by this mean it came to pass, that one Church could not but accuse and condemn another of disobedience to the will of Christ, in those things where manifest difference was between them; whereas the selfsame orders allowed, but yet established in more wary and suspense manner, as being to stand in force till God should give the opportunity of some general conference what might be best for every of them afterwards to do; this I say had both prevented all occasion of just dislike which others might take, and reserved a greater liberty unto the authors themselves of entering into farther consultation afterwards. Which though never so necessary they could not easily now admit, without some fear of derogation from their credit: and therefore that which once they had done, they became for ever after resolute to maintain.

Calvin therefore and the other two his associates, stiffly refusing to administer the holy Communion to such as would not quietly, without contradiction and murmur, submit themselves unto the orders which their solemn oath had bound them to obey, were in that quarrel banished the town.

[3.] A few years after (such was the levity of that people) the places of one or two of their ministers being fallen void, they were not before so willing to be rid of their learned pastor, as now importunate to obtain him again from them who had given him entertainment, and which were loath to part with him, had not unresistible earnestness been used. One of the town ministers, that saw in what manner the people were bent for the revocation of Calvin, gave him notice of their affection in this sort [Epis. Cal. 24]. "The senate of two hundred being assembled, they all crave Calvin. The next day a general convocation. They cry in like sort again all, We will have Calvin, that good and learned man, Christ's minister. This," saith he, "when I understood, I could not choose but praise God, nor was I able to judge otherwise than that 'this was the Lord's doing, and that it was marvellous in our eyes', and that 'the stone which the builders refused was now made the head of the corner' [Luke xx. 17]." The other two whom they had thrown out (together with Calvin), they were content should enjoy their exile. Many causes might lead them to be more desirous of him. First, his yielding unto them in one thing might happily put them in hope, that time would breed the like easiness of condescending further unto them. For in his absence he had persuaded them, with whom he was able to prevail, that albeit himself did better like of common bread to be used in the Eucharist, yet the other they rather should accept, than cause any trouble in the church about it. Again, they saw that the name of Calvin waxed every day greater abroad, and that together with his fame, their infamy was spread, which had so rashly and childishly ejected him. Besides, it was not unlikely but that his credit in the world might many ways stand the poor town in great stead: as the truth is, their minister's foreign estimation hitherto hath been the best stake in their hedge. But whatsoever secret respects were likely to move them, for contenting of their minds Calvin returned (as it had been another Tully) to his old home.

[4.] He ripely considered how gross a thing it were for men of his quality, wise and grave men, to live with such a multitude, and to be tenants at will under them, as their ministers, both himself and others, had been. For the remedy of which inconvenience, he gave them plainly to understand, that if he did become their teacher again, they must be content to admit a complete form of discipline, which both they and also their pastors should now be solemnly sworn to observe for ever after. Of which discipline the main and principal parts were these: A standing ecclesiastical court to be established; perpetual judges in that court to be their ministers; others of the people to be annually chosen (twice so many in number as they) to be judges together with them in the same court: these two sorts to have the care of all men's manners, power of determining all kind of ecclesiastical causes, and authority to convent, to control, to punish, as far as with excommunication, whomsoever they should think worthy, none either small or great excepted.

This device I see not how the wisest at that time living could have bettered, if we duly consider what the present estate of Geneva did then require. For their bishop and his clergy being (as it is said) departed from them by moonlight, or howsoever, being departed; to choose in his room any other bishop, had been a thing altogether impossible. And for their ministers to seek that themselves alone might have coercive power over the whole church, would perhaps have been hardly construed at that time. But when so frank an offer was made, that for every one minister there should be two of the people to sit and give voice in the ecclesiastical consistory, what inconvenience could they easily find which themselves might not be able always to remedy?

Howbeit (as evermore the simpler sort are, even when they see no apparent cause, jealous notwithstanding over the secret intents and purposes of wiser men) this proposition of his did somewhat trouble them. Of the ministers themselves which had stayed behind in the city when Calvin was gone, some, upon knowledge of the people's earnest intent to recall him to his place again, had beforehand written their letters of submission, and assured him of their allegiance for ever after, if it should like him to hearken unto that public suit. But yet misdoubting what might happen, if this discipline did go forward; they objected against it the example of other reformed churches living quietly and orderly without it. Some of chiefest place and countenance amongst the laity professed with greater stomach their judgments, that such a discipline was little better than Popish tyranny disguised and tendered unto them under a new form. This sort, it may be, had some fear, that the filling up of the seats in the consistory with so great a number of laymen was but to please the minds of the people, to the end they might think their own sway somewhat; but when things came to trial of practice, their pastors' learning would be at all times of force to over-persuade simple men, who knowing the time of their own presidentship to be but short would always stand in fear of their ministers' perpetual authority: and among the ministers themselves, one being so far in estimation above the rest, the voices of the rest were likely to be given for the most part respectively, with a kind of secret dependency and awe: so that in show a marvellous indifferently composed senate ecclesiastical was to govern, but in effect one only man should, as the spirit and soul of the residue, do all in all. But what did these vain surmises boot? Brought they were now to so strait an issue, that of two things they must choose one: namely, whether they would to their endless disgrace, with ridiculous lightness dismiss him whose restitution they had in so impotent manner desired; or else condescend unto that demand, wherein he was resolute either to have it, or to leave them. They thought it better to be somewhat hardly yoked at home, than for ever abroad discredited. Wherefore in the end those orders were on all sides assented unto: with no less alacrity of mind than cities unable to hold out longer are wont to shew, when they take conditions such as it liketh him to offer them which hath them in the narrow straits of advantage.

[5.] Not many years were over-passed, before these twice-sworn men adventured to give their last and hottest assault to the fortress of the same discipline, childishly granting by common consent of their whole Senate, and that under their town seal, a relaxation to one Bertelier, whom the Eldership had excommunicated; further also decreeing, with strange absurdity, that to the same Senate it should belong to give final judgment in matter of excommunication, and to absolve whom it pleased them: clean contrary to their own former deeds and oaths. The report of which decree being forthwith brought unto Calvin; "Before," saith he, "this decree take place, either my blood or banishment shall sign it." Again, two days before the communion should be celebrated, his speech was publickly to like effect: "Kill me if ever this hand do reach forth the things that are holy to them whom THE CHURCH hath judged despisers." Whereupon, for fear of tumult, the forenamed Bertelier was by his friends advised for that time not to use the liberty granted him by the Senate, nor to present himself in the church, till they saw somewhat further what would ensue. After the communion quietly ministered, and some likelihood of peaceable ending these troubles without any more ado, that very day in the afternoon, besides all men's expectation, concluding his ordinary sermon, he telleth them, that because he neither had learned nor taught to strive with such as are in authority, "therefore," saith he, "the case so standing as now it doth, let me use these words of the apostle unto you, 'I commend you unto God and the word of his grace' "; and so bade them heartily all 'adieu'.

[6.] It sometimes cometh to pass, that the readiest way which a wise man hath to conquer is to fly. This voluntary and unexpected mention of sudden departure caused presently the Senate (for according to their wonted manner they still continued only constant in unconstancy) to gather themselves together, and for a time to suspend their own decree, leaving things to proceed as before till they had heard the judgment of four Helvetian cities concerning the matter which was in strife. This to have done at the first before they gave assent unto any order had shewed some wit and discretion in them: but now to do it was as much as to say in effect, that they would play their parts on a stage. Calvin therefore dispatcheth with all expedition his letters unto some principal pastor in every of those cities, craving earnestly at their hands, to respect this cause as a thing whereupon the whole state of religion and piety in that church did so much depend, that God and all good men were now inevitably certain to be trampled under foot, unless those four cities by their good means might be brought to give sentence with the ministers of Geneva, when the cause should be brought before them: yea so to give it, that two things it might effectually contain; the one an absolute approbation of the discipline of Geneva as consonant unto the word of God, without any cautions, qualifications, ifs or ands; the other an earnest admonition not to innovate or change the same. His vehement request herein as touching both points was satisfied. For albeit the said Helvetian Churches did never as yet observe that discipline, nevertheless, the Senate of Geneva having required their judgment concerning these three questions: First, "After what manner, by God's commandment, according to the scripture and unspotted religion, excommunication is to be exercised:" Secondly, "Whether it may not be exercised some other way than by the Consistory:" Thirdly, "What the use of their Churches was to do in this case: [Ep. 166]" answer was returned from the said Churches, "That they had heard already of those consistorial laws, and did acknowledge them to be *godly* ordinances *drawing towards* the prescript of the word of God; for which cause they did not think it good for *the Church of Geneva* by innovation to change the same, but rather to keep them as they were." Which answer, although not answering unto the former demands, but respecting what Master Calvin had judged requisite for them to answer, was notwithstanding accepted without any further reply: in as much as they plainly saw, that when stomach doth strive with wit, the match is not equal. And so the heat of their former contentions began to slake.

[7.] The present inhabitants of Geneva, I hope, will not take it in evil part, that the faultiness of their people heretofore is by us so far forth laid open, as their own learned guides and pastors have thought necessary to discover it unto the world. For out of their books and writings it is that I have collected this whole narration, to the end it might thereby appear in what sort amongst them that discipline was planted, for which so much contention is raised amongst ourselves. The reason which moved Calvin herein to be so earnest, was, as Beza himself testifieth, "For that he saw how needful these bridles were, to be put in the jaws of that city." That which by wisdom he saw to be requisite for that people, was by as great wisdom compassed.

But wise men are men, and the truth is truth. That which Calvin did for establishment of his discipline, seemeth more commendable than that which he taught for the countenancing of it established. Nature worketh in us all a love to our own counsels. The contradiction of others is a fan to inflame that love. Our love set on fire to maintain that which once we have done, sharpeneth the wit to dispute, to argue, and by all means to reason for it. Wherefore a marvel it were if a man of so great capacity, having such incitements to make him desirous of all kind of furtherances unto his cause, could espy in the whole Scripture of God nothing which might breed at the least a probable opinion of likelihood, that divine authority itself was the same way somewhat inclinable. And all which the wit even of Calvin was able from thence to draw, by sifting the very utmost sentence and syllable, is no more than that certain speeches there are which to him did seem to intimate that all Christian churches ought to have their Elderships endued with power of excommunication, and that a part of those Elderships every where should be chosen out from amongst the laity, after that form which himself had framed Geneva unto. But what argument are ye able to shew, whereby it was ever proved by Calvin, that any one sentence of Scripture doth necessarily enforce these things, or the rest wherein your opinion concurreth with his against the orders of your own church?

[8.] We should be injurious unto virtue itself, if we did derogate from them whom their industry hath made great. Two things of principal moment there are which have deservedly procured him honour throughout the world: the one his exceeding pains in composing the Institutions of Christian religion; the other his no less industrious travails for exposition of holy Scripture according unto the same Institutions. In which two things whosoever they were that after him bestowed their labour, he gained the advantage of prejudice against them, if they gainsayed; and of glory above them, if they consented. His writings published after the question about that discipline was once begun omit not any the least occasion of extolling the use and singular necessity thereof. Of what account the Master of Sentences was in the church of Rome, the same and more amongst the preachers of reformed churches Calvin had purchased; so that the perfectest divines were judged they, which were skilfullest in Calvin's writings. His books almost the very canon to judge both doctrine and discipline by. French churches, both under others abroad and at home in their own country, all cast according to that mould which Calvin had made. The Church of Scotland in erecting the fabric of their reformation took the self-same pattern. Till at length the discipline, which was at the first so weak, that without the staff of their approbation, who were not subject unto it themselves, it had not brought others under subjection, began now to challenge universal obedience, and to enter into open conflict with those very Churches, which in desperate extremity had been relievers of it.

[9.] To one of those churches which lived in most peaceable sort, and abounded as well with men for their learning in other professions singular, as also with divines whose equals were not elsewhere to be found, a church ordered by Gualter's discipline, and not by that which Geneva adoreth; unto this church, the Church of Heidelberg, there cometh one who craving leave to dispute publicly defendeth with open disdain of their government, that "to a minister with his Eldership power is given by the law of God to excommunicate whomsoever, yea even kings and princes themselves." Here were the seeds sown of that controversy which sprang up between Beza and Erastus about the matter of excommunication, whether there ought to be in all churches an Eldership having power to excommunicate, and a part of that Eldership to be of necessity certain chosen out from amongst the laity for that purpose. In which disputation they have, as to me it seemeth, divided very equally the truth between them; Beza most truly maintaining the necessity of excommunication, Erastus as truly the non-necessity of lay elders to be ministers thereof.

[10.] Amongst ourselves, there was in King Edward's days some question moved by reason of a few men's scrupulosity touching certain things. And beyond seas, of them which fled in the days of Queen Mary, some contenting themselves abroad with the use of their own service-book at home authorized before their departure out of the realm, others liking better the Common Prayer-book of the Church of Geneva translated, those smaller contentions before begun were by this mean somewhat increased. Under the happy reign of her Majesty which now is, the greatest matter a while contended for was the wearing of the cap and surplice, till there came Admonitions directed unto the high court of Parliament, by men who concealing their names thought it glory enough to discover their minds and affections, which now were universally bent even against all the orders and laws, wherein this church is found unconformable to the platform of Geneva. Concerning the Defender of which Admonitions, all that I mean to say is but this: *there will come a time when three words uttered with charity and meekness shall receive a far more blessed reward than three thousand volumes written with disdainful sharpness of wit.* But the manner of men's writing must not alienate our hearts from the truth, if it appear they have the truth: as the followers of the same defender do think he hath, and in that persuasion they follow him, no otherwise than himself doth Calvin, Beza, and others, with the like persuasion that they in this cause had the truth. We being as fully persuaded otherwise, it resteth that some kind of trial be used to find out which part is in error.

Chapter 3

BY WHAT MEANS SO MANY OF THE PEOPLE ARE TRAINED INTO THE LIKING OF THAT DISCIPLINE

The first mean whereby nature teacheth men to judge good from evil, as well in laws as in other things, is the force of their own discretion. Hereunto therefore St. Paul referreth oftentimes his own speech to be considered of by them that heard him. "I speak as to them which have understanding, judge ye what I say." [1 Cor. x. 15] Again afterward, "Judge in yourselves, is it comely that a woman pray uncovered?" [1 Cor. xi. 13] The exercise of this kind of judgment our Saviour requireth in the Jews [Luke xii. 56f.]. In them of Berea the Scripture commendeth it [Acts xvii. 11]. Finally, whatsoever we do, if our own secret judgment consent not unto it as fit and good to be done, the doing of it to us is sin, although the thing itself be allowable. St. Paul's rule therefore generally is, "Let every man in his own mind be fully persuaded of that thing which he either alloweth or doth." [Rom. xiv. 5]

[2.] Some things are so familiar and plain, that truth from falsehood, and good from evil, is most easily discerned in them, even by men of no deep capacity. And of that nature, for the most part, are things absolutely unto all men's salvation necessary, either to be held or denied, either to be done or avoided. For which cause St. Augustine acknowledgeth, that they are not only set down, but also plainly set down in Scripture; so that he which heareth or readeth may without any great difficulty understand. Other things also there are belonging (though in a lower degree of importance) unto the offices of Christian men: which, because they are more obscure, more intricate and hard to be judged of, therefore God hath appointed some to spend their whole time principally in the study of things divine, to the end that in these more doubtful cases their understanding might be a light to direct others. "If the understanding power or faculty of the soul be" (saith the grand physician) "like unto bodily sight, not of equal sharpness in all, what can be more convenient than that, even as the dark-sighted man is directed by the clear about things visible; so likewise in matters of deeper discourse the wise in heart do shew the simple where his way lieth?" [Galen] In our doubtful cases of law, what man is there who seeth not how requisite it is that professors of skill in that faculty be our directors? So it is in all other kinds of knowledge. And even in this kind likewise the Lord hath himself appointed, that "the priest's lips should preserve knowledge, and that other men should seek the truth at his mouth, because he is the messenger of the Lord of hosts." [Mal. ii. 7]) Gregory Nazianzen, offended at the people's too great presumption in controlling the judgment of them to whom in such cases they should have rather submitted their own, seeketh by earnest entreaty to stay them within their bounds: "Presume not ye that are sheep to make yourselves guides of them that should guide you; neither seek ye to overskip the fold which they about you have pitched. It sufficeth for your part, if ye can well frame yourselves to be ordered. Take not upon you to judge your judges, nor to make them subject to your laws who should be a law to you; for God is not a God of sedition and confusion, but of order and of peace."

[3.] But ye will say that if the guides of the people be blind, the common sort of men must not close up their own eyes and be led by the conduct of such [Matt. xv. 14]: if the priest be "partial in the law," [Mal. ii. 9] the flock must not therefore depart from the ways of sincere truth, and in simplicity yield to be followers of him for his place sake and office over them. Which thing, though in itself most true, is in your defence notwithstanding weak; because the matter wherein ye think that ye see, and imagine that your ways are sincere, is of far deeper consideration than any one amongst five hundred of you conceiveth. Let the vulgar sort amongst you know, that there is not the least branch of the cause wherein they are so resolute, but to the trial of it a great deal more appertaineth than their conceit doth reach unto. I write not this in disgrace of the simplest that way given, but I would gladly they knew the nature of that cause wherein they think themselves thoroughly instructed and are not; by means whereof they daily run themselves, without feeling their own hazard, upon the dint of the Apostle's sentence against "evil-speakers as touching things wherein they are ignorant". [Jude 10; 2 Pet. ii. 12]

[4.] If it be granted a thing unlawful for private men, not called unto public consultation, to dispute which is the best state of Civil polity (with a desire of bringing in some other kind than that under which they already live, for of such disputes I take it his meaning was); if it be a thing confessed, that of such questions they cannot determine without rashness, inasmuch as a great part of them consisteth in special circumstances, and for one kind as many reasons may be brought as for another; is there any reason in the world, why they should better judge what kind of regiment ecclesiastical is the fittest? For in the civil state more insight, and in those affairs more experience a great deal must needs be granted them, than in this they can possibly have. When they which write in defence of your discipline and commend it unto the Highest not in the least cunning manner, are forced notwithstanding to acknowledge, "that with whom the truth is they know not," they are not certain; what certainty or knowledge can the multitude have thereof?

[5.] Weigh what doth move the common sort so much to favour this innovation, and it shall soon appear unto you, that the force of particular reasons which for your several opinions are alleged is a thing whereof the multitude never did nor could so consider as to be therewith wholly carried;

but certain general inducements are used to make saleable your cause in gross; and when once men have cast a fancy towards it, any slight declaration of specialties will serve to lead forward inclinable and prepared minds.

[6.] The method of winning the people's affection unto a general liking of "the cause" (for so ye term it) hath been this. First, in the hearing of the multitude, the faults especially of higher callings are ripped up with marvellous exceeding severity and sharpness of reproof; which being oftentimes done begetteth a great good opinion of integrity, zeal, and holiness, to such constant reprovers of sin, as by likelihood would never be so much offended at that which is evil, unless themselves were singularly good.

[7.] The next thing hereunto is, to impute all faults and corruptions, wherewith the world aboundeth, unto the kind of ecclesiastical government established. Wherein, as before by reproving faults they purchased unto themselves with the multitude a name to be virtuous; so by finding out this kind of cause they obtain to be judged wise above others: whereas in truth unto the form even of Jewish government, which the Lord himself (they all confess) did establish, with like shew of reason they might impute those faults which the prophets condemn in the governors of that commonwealth, as to the English kind of regiment ecclesiastical (whereof also God himself though in other sort is author) the stains and blemishes found in our state; which springing from the root of human frailty and corruption, not only are, but have been always more or less, yea and (for any thing we know to the contrary) will be till the world's end complained of, what form of government soever take place.

[8.] Having gotten thus much sway in the hearts of men, a third step is to propose their own form of church government, as the only sovereign remedy of all evils; and to adorn it with all the glorious titles that may be. And the nature, as of men that have sick bodies, so likewise of the people in the crazedness of their minds possessed with dislike and discontentment at things present, is to imagine that any thing (the virtue whereof they hear commended) would help them; but that most, which they least have tried.

[9.] The fourth degree of inducement is by fashioning the very notions and conceits of men's minds in such sort, that when they read the scripture, they may think that every thing soundeth towards the advancement of that discipline, and to the utter disgrace of the contrary. Pythagoras, by bringing up his scholars in the speculative knowledge of numbers, made their conceits therein so strong, that when they came to the contemplation of things natural, they imagined that in every particular thing they even beheld as it were with their eyes, how the elements of number gave essence and being to the works of nature. A thing in reason impossible; which notwithstanding, through their misfashioned preconceit, appeared unto them no less certain, than if nature had written it in the very foreheads of all the creatures of God [Arist. *Metaph.* lib. i. cap. 5]. When they of the "Family of Love" have it once in their heads, that "Christ" doth not signify any one person, but a quality whereof many are partakers; that to be "raised" is nothing else but to be regenerated, or endued with the said quality; and that when separation of them which have it from them which have it not is here made, this is "judgment": how plainly do they imagine that the Scripture every where speaketh in the favour of that sect? And assuredly, the very cause which maketh the simple and ignorant to think they even see how the word of God runneth currently on your side, is, that their minds are forestalled and their conceits perverted beforehand, by being taught, that an "Elder" doth signify a layman admitted only to the office or rule of government in the Church; a "Doctor," one which may only teach, and neither preach nor administer the Sacraments; a "Deacon," one which hath charge of the alms-box, and of nothing else: that the "Sceptre," the "rod," the "throne" and "kingdom" of Christ, are a form of regiment, only by Pastors, Elders, Doctors, and Deacons; that by mystical resemblance Mount Sion and Jerusalem are the churches which admit, Samaria and Babylon the churches which oppugn the said form of regiment. And in like sort they are taught to apply all things spoken of repairing the walls and decayed parts of the city and temple of God, by Esdras, Nehemias, and the rest, as if purposely the Holy Ghost had therein meant to foresignify, what the authors of Admonitions to the Parliament, of Supplications to the Council, of Petitions to her Majesty, and of such other like writs, should either do or suffer in behalf of this their cause.

[10.] From hence they proceed to an higher point, which is the persuading of men credulous and over-capable of such pleasing errors, that it is the special illumination of the Holy Ghost, whereby they discern those things in the word, which others reading yet discern them not. "Dearly beloved," saith St. John, "give not credit unto every spirit." [1 John iv. 1] There are but two ways whereby the Spirit leadeth men into all truth: the one extraordinary, the other common; the one belonging but unto some few, the other extending itself unto all that are of God; the one, that which we call by a special divine excellency "Revelation", the other "Reason". If the Spirit hath led them by, forasmuch as persuasions grounded upon reason discipline out of Scripture, they must profess themselves to be all (even men, women, and children) Prophets. Or if reason be the hand which the Spirit hath led them by, forasmuch as persuasions grounded upon reason are either weaker or stronger according to the force of those reasons whereupon the same are grounded, they must every of them from the greatest to the least be able for every several article to shew some special reason as strong as their persuasion therein is earnest. Otherwise how can it be but that some other sinews there are from which that overplus of strength in persuasion doth arise? Most sure it is, that when men's affections do frame their opinions, they are in defence of error more earnest a great deal, than (for the most part) sound believers in the maintenance of truth apprehended according to the nature of that evidence which scripture yieldeth: which being in some things plain, as in the principles of Christian doctrine; in some things, as in these matters of discipline, more dark and doubtful; frameth correspondently that inward assent which God's most gracious Spirit worketh by it as by his effectual instrument. It is not therefore the fervent earnestness of their persuasion, but the soundness of those reasons whereupon the same is built, which must declare their opinions in these things to have been wrought by the Holy Ghost, and not by the fraud of that evil spirit, which is even in his illusions strong [2 Thess. ii. 11].

[11.] After that the fancy of the common sort hath once thoroughly apprehended the Spirit to be author of their persuasion concerning discipline; then is instilled into their hearts, that the same Spirit leading men into this opinion doth thereby seal them to be God's children; and that, as the state of the times now standeth, the most special token to know them that are God's own from others is an earnest affection that way. This hath bred high terms of separation between such and the rest of the world; whereby the one sort are named "The" brethren, "The" godly, and so forth; the other, worldlings, time-servers, pleasers of men not of God, with such like.

[12.] From hence, they are easily drawn on to think it exceeding necessary, for fear of quenching that good Spirit, to use all means whereby the same may be both strengthened in themselves, and made manifest unto others. This maketh them diligent hearers of such as are known that way to incline; this maketh them eager to take and to seek all occasions of secret conference with such; this maketh them glad to use such as counsellors and directors in all their dealings which are of weight, as contracts, testaments, and the like; this maketh them, through an unweariable desire of receiving instruction from the masters of that company, to cast off the care of those very affairs which do most concern their estate, and to think that then they are like unto Mary, commendable for making choice of the better part. Finally, this is it which maketh them willing to charge, yea, oftentimes even to overcharge themselves, for such men's sustenance and relief, lest their zeal to the cause should any way be unwitnessed. For what is it which poor beguiled souls will not do through so powerful incitements?

[13.] In which respect it is also noted, that most labour hath been bestowed to win and retain towards this cause them whose judgments are commonly weakest by reason of their sex. And although not "women loden with sins," [2 Tim. iii. 6] as the apostle Saint Paul speaketh, but (as we verily esteem of them for the most part) women propense and inclinable to holiness be otherwise edified in good things, rather than carried away as captives into any kind of sin and evil by such as enter into their houses, with purpose to plant there a zeal and a love towards this kind of discipline: yet some occasion is hereby ministered for men to think, that if the cause which is thus furthered did gain by the soundness of proof whereupon it doth build itself, it would not most busily endeavour to prevail where least ability of judgment is: and therefore, that this so eminent industry in making proselytes more of that sex than of the other groweth, for that they are deemed apter to serve as instruments and helps in the cause. Apter they are through the eagerness of their affection, that maketh them, which way soever they take, diligent in drawing their husbands, children, servants, friends and allies the same way; apter through that natural inclination unto pity, which breedeth in them a greater readiness than in men to be bountiful towards their preachers who suffer want; apter through sundry opportunities, which they especially have, to procure encouragements for their brethren; finally, apter through a singular delight which they take in giving very large and particular intelligence, how all near about them stand affected as concerning the same cause.

[14.] But be they women or be they men, if once they have tasted of that cup, let any man of contrary opinion open his mouth to persuade them, they close up their ears, his reasons they weigh not, all is answered with rehearsal of the words of John, "We are of God; he that knoweth God heareth us:' [1 John iv. 6] as for the rest, ye are of the world, for this world's pomp and vanity it is that ye speak, and the world, whose ye are, heareth you." Which cloak sitteth no less fit on the back of their cause, than of the Anabaptists, when the dignity, authority and honour of God's magistrate is upheld against them. Shew these eagerly-affected men their inability to judge of such matters; their answer is, "God hath chosen the simple." [1 Cor. i. 27] Convince them of folly, and that so plainly, that very children upbraid them with it; they have their bucklers of like defence: "Christ's own apostle was accounted mad: the best men evermore by the sentence of the world have been judged to be out of their right minds." [Acts xxvi. 24; Sap. v. 4]

[15.] When instruction doth them no good, let them feel but the least degree of most mercifully-tempered severity, they fasten on the head of the Lord's vicegerents here on earth whatsoever they any where find uttered against the cruelty of bloodthirsty men, and to themselves they draw all the sentences which scripture hath in the favour of innocency persecuted for the truth; yea, they are of their due and deserved sufferings no less proud, than those ancient disturbers to whom Saint Augustine writeth, saying: "Martyrs rightly so named are they not which suffer for their disorder, and for the ungodly breach they have made of Christian unity, but which for righteousness' sake are persecuted. For Agar also suffered persecution at the hands of Sara, wherein, she which did impose was holy, and she unrighteous which did bear the burden. In like sort, with thieves was the Lord himself crucified; but they, who were matched in the pain which they suffered, were in the cause of their suffering disjoined. . . . If that must needs be the true church which doth endure persecution, and not that which persecuteth, let them ask of the apostle what church Sara did represent, when she held her maid in affliction. For even our mother which is free, the heavenly Jerusalem, that is to say, the true Church of God, was, as he doth affirm, prefigured in that very woman by whom the bondmaid was so sharply handled. Although, if all things be thoroughly scanned, she did in truth more persecute Sara by proud resistance, than Sara her by severity of punishment."

[16.] These are the paths wherein ye have walked that are of the ordinary sort of men; these are the very steps ye have trodden, and the manifest degrees whereby ye are of your guides and directors trained up in that school: a custom of inuring your ears with reproof of faults especially in your governors; an use to attribute those faults to the kind of spiritual regiment under which ye live; boldness in warranting the force of their discipline for the cure of all such evils; a slight of framing your conceits to imagine that Scripture every where favoureth that discipline; persuasion that the cause why ye find it in Scripture is the illumination of the Spirit, that the same Spirit is a seal unto you of your nearness unto God, that ye are by all means to nourish and witness it in yourselves, and to strengthen on every side your minds against whatsoever might be of force to withdraw you from it.

Chapter 4

WHAT HATH CAUSED SO MANY OF THE LEARNEDER SORT TO APPROVE THE SAME DISCIPLINE

Wherefore to come unto you whose judgment is a lantern of direction for all the rest, you that frame thus the people's hearts, not altogether (as I willingly persuade myself) of a politic intent or purpose, but yourselves being first overborne with the weight of greater men's judgments: on your shoulders is laid the burden of upholding the cause by argument. For which purpose sentences out of the word of God ye allege divers: but so, that when the same are discussed, thus it always in a manner falleth out, that what things by virtue thereof ye urge upon us as altogether necessary, are found to be thence collected only by poor and marvellous slight conjectures. I need not give instance in any one sentence so alleged, for that I think the instance in any alleged otherwise a thing not easy to be given. A very strange thing sure it were, that such a discipline as ye speak of should be taught by Christ and his apostles in the word of God, and no church ever have found it out, nor received it till this present time; contrariwise, the government against which ye bend yourselves be observed every where throughout all generations and ages of the Christian world, no church ever perceiving the word of God to be against it. We require you to find out but one church upon the face of the whole earth, that hath been ordered by your discipline, or hath not been ordered by ours, that is to say, by episcopal regiment, sithence the time that the blessed Apostles were here conversant.

[2.] Many things out of antiquity ye bring, as if the purest times of the Church had observed the selfsame orders which you require; and as though your desire were that the churches of old should be patterns for us to follow, and even glasses, wherein we might see the practice of that which by you is gathered out of Scripture. But the truth is, ye mean nothing less. All this is done for fashion's sake only: for ye complain of it as of an injury, that men should be willed to seek for examples and patterns of government in any of those times that have been before. Ye plainly hold, that from the very Apostles' time till this present age, wherein yourselves imagine ye have found out a right pattern of sound discipline, there never was any time safe to be followed. Which thing ye thus endeavour to prove. "Out of Egesippus" ye say that "Eusebius writeth", how although "as long as the Apostles lived the Church did remain a pure virgin, yet after the death of the Apostles, and after they were once gone whom God vouchsafed to make hearers of the divine wisdom with their own ears, the placing of wicked error began to come into the Church. Clement also in a certain place, to confirm that there was corruption of doctrine immediately after the Apostles' time, allegeth the proverb, that 'There are few sons like their fathers'. Socrates saith of the churches of Rome and Alexandria, the most famous churches in the Apostles' times, that about the year 430, the Roman and Alexandrian bishops, leaving the sacred function, were degenerate to a secular rule or dominion." Hereupon ye conclude, that it is not safe to fetch our government from any other than the Apostles' times.

[3.] Wherein by the way it may be noted, that in proposing the Apostles' times as a pattern for the Church to follow, though the desire of you all be one, the drift and purpose of you all is not one. The chiefest thing which lay-reformers yawn for is, that the clergy may through conformity in state and condition be apostolical, poor as the Apostles of Christ were poor. In which one circumstance if they imagine so great perfection, they must think that Church which hath such store of mendicant Friars, a church in that respect most happy. Were it for the glory of God and the good of his Church indeed that the clergy should be left even as bare as the Apostles when they had neither staff nor scrip, that God, which should lay upon them the condition of his Apostles, would I hope endue them with the selfsame affection which was in that holy Apostle, whose words concerning his own right virtuous contentment of heart, "as well how to want, as how to abound" [Phil. iv. 12], are a most fit episcopal emprese. The Church of Christ is a body mystical. A body cannot stand, unless the parts thereof be proportionable. Let it therefore be required on both parts, at the hands of the clergy, to be in meanness of state like the Apostles; at the hands of the laity, to be as they were who lived under the Apostles: and in this reformation there will be, though little wisdom, yet some indifferency.

[4.] But your reformation which are of the clergy (if yet it displease you not that I should say ye are of the clergy) seemeth to aim at a broader mark. Ye think that he which will perfectly reform must bring the form of church-discipline unto the state which then it was at. A thing neither possible, nor certain, nor absolutely convenient.

Concerning the first, what was used in the Apostles' times, the Scripture fully declareth not; so that making their times the rule and canon of church-polity, ye make a rule, which being not possible to be fully known, is as impossible to be kept.

Again, sith the later even of the Apostles' own times had that which in the former was not thought upon; in this general proposing of the apostolical times, there is no certainty which should be followed: especially seeing that ye give us great cause to doubt how far ye allow those times. For albeit "the loover of antichristian building were not," ye say, as then "set up, yet the foundations thereof were secretly and under the ground laid in the Apostles' times:" so that all other times ye plainly reject, and the Apostles' own times ye approve with marvellous great suspicion, leaving it intricate and doubtful, wherein we are to keep ourselves unto the pattern of their times.

Thirdly, whereas it is the error of the common multitude to consider only what hath been of old, and if the same were well, to see whether still it continue; if not, to condemn that presently which is, and never to search upon what ground or consideration the change might grow: such rudeness cannot be in you so well borne with, whom learning and judgment hath enabled much more soundly to discern how far the times of the Church and the orders thereof may alter without offence. True it is, the ancienter, the better ceremonies of religion are; howbeit, not absolutely true and without exception: but true only so far forth as those different ages do agree in the state of those things, for which at the first those rites, orders, and ceremonies, were instituted. In the Apostles' times that was harmless, which being now revived would be scandalous; as their *oscula sancta* [Rom. xvi. 16; 2 Cor. xiii. 12]. Those feasts of charity [Epist. Jud. 12], which being instituted by the Apostles, were retained in the Church long after, are not now thought any where needful. What man is there of understanding, unto whom it is not manifest how the way of providing for the clergy by tithes, the device of almshouses for the poor, the sorting out of the people into their several parishes together with sundry other things which the Apostles' times could not have (being now established) are much more convenient and fit for the Church of Christ, than if the same should be taken away for conformity's sake with the ancientest and first times?

[5.] The orders therefore, which were observed in the Apostles' times, are not to be urged as a rule universally either sufficient or necessary. If they be, nevertheless on your part it still remaineth to be better proved, that the form of discipline, which ye entitle apostolical, was in the Apostles' times exercised. For of this very thing ye fail even touching that which ye make most account of, as being matter of substance in discipline, I mean the power of your lay-elders, and the difference of your Doctors from the Pastors in all churches. So that in sum, we may be bold to conclude, that besides these last times, which for insolency, pride, and egregious contempt of all good order, are the worst, there are none wherein ye can truly affirm, that the complete form of your discipline, or the substance thereof, was practised.

[6.] The evidence therefore of antiquity failing you, ye fly to the judgments of such learned men, as seem by their writings to be of opinion, that all Christian churches should receive your discipline, and abandon ours. Wherein, as ye heap up the names of a number of men not unworthy to be had in honour; so there are a number whom when ye mention, although it serve you to purpose with the ignorant and vulgar sort, who measure by tale and not by weight, yet surely they who know what quality and value the men are of, will think ye draw very near the dregs. But were they all of as great account as the best and chiefest amongst them, with us notwithstanding neither are they, neither ought they to be of such reckoning, that their opinion or conjecture should cause the laws of the Church of England to give place. Much less when they neither do all agree in that opinion, and of them which are at agreement, the most part through a courteous inducement have followed one man as their guide, finally that one therein not unlikely to have swerved. If any chance to say it is probable that in the Apostles' times there were lay-elders, or not to mislike the continuance of them in the Church, or to affirm that Bishops at the first were a name but not a power distinct from presbyters, or to speak any thing in praise of those Churches which are without episcopal regiment, or to reprove the fault of such as abuse that calling; all these ye register for men persuaded as you are, that every Christian Church standeth bound by the law of God to put down Bishops, and in their rooms to elect an Eldership so authorized as you would have it for the government of each parish. Deceived greatly they are therefore, who think that all they whose names are cited amongst the favourers of this cause, are on any such verdict agreed.

[7.] Yet touching some material points of your discipline, a kind of agreement we grant there is amongst many divines of reformed Churches abroad. For, first, to do as the Church of Geneva did, the learned in some other Churches must needs be the more willing, who having used in like manner not the slow and tedious help of proceeding by public authority, but the people's more quick endeavour for alteration, in such an exigent I see not well how they could have stayed to deliberate about any other regiment than that which already was devised to their hands, that which in like case had been taken, that which was easiest to be established without delay, that which was likeliest to content the people by reason of some kind of sway which it giveth them. When therefore the example of one Church was thus at the first almost through a kind of constraint or necessity followed by many, their concurrence in persuasion about some material points belonging to the same polity is not strange. For we are not to marvel greatly, if they which have all done the same thing, do easily embrace the same opinion as concerning their own doings.

[8.] Besides, mark I beseech you that which Galen in matter of philosophy noteth; for the like falleth out even in questions of higher knowledge. It fareth many times with men's opinions as with rumours and reports. "That which a credible person telleth is easily thought probable by such as are well persuaded of him. But if two, or three, or four, agree all in the same tale, they judge it then to be out of controversy, and so are many times overtaken for want of due consideration; either some common cause leading them all into error, or one man's oversight deceiving many through their too much credulity and easiness of belief." Though ten persons be brought to give testimony in any cause, yet if the knowledge they have of the thing whereunto they come as witnesses, appear to have grown from some one amongst them, and to have spread itself from hand to hand, they all are in force but as one testimony. Nor is it otherwise here where the daughter churches do speak their mother's dialect; here where so many sing one song, by reason that he is the guide of the choir, concerning whose deserved authority amongst even the gravest divines we have already spoken at large. Will ye ask what should move those many learned to be followers of one man's judgment, no necessity of argument forcing them thereunto? Your demand is answered by yourselves. Loth ye are to think that they, whom ye judge to have attained as sound knowledge in all points of doctrine as any since the Apostles' time, should mistake in discipline. Such is naturally our affection, that whom in great things we mightily admire, in them we are not persuaded willingly that any thing should be amiss. The reason whereof is, "for that as dead flies putrify the ointment of the apothecary, so doth a little folly him that is in estimation for wisdom". [Eccles. x. 1] This in every profession hath too much authorized the judgments of a few. This with Germans hath caused Luther, and with many other Churches Calvin, to prevail in all things. Yet are we not able to define, whether the wisdom of that God (who setteth before us in holy Scripture so many admirable patterns of virtue, and no one of them without somewhat noted wherein they were culpable, to the end that to Him alone it might always be acknowledged, "Thou only art holy, thou only art just;") might not permit those worthy vessels of his glory to be in some things blemished with the stain of human frailty, even for this cause, lest we should esteem of any man above that which behoveth.

Chapter 5

THEIR CALLING FOR TRIAL BY DISPUTATION

Notwithstanding, as though ye were able to say a great deal more than hitherto your books have revealed to the world, earnest challengers ye are of trial by some public disputation. Wherein if the thing ye crave be no more than only leave to dispute openly about those matters that are in question, the schools in universities (for any thing I know) are open unto you. They have their yearly Acts and Commencements, besides other disputations both ordinary and upon occasion, wherein the several parts of our own ecclesiastical discipline are oftentimes offered unto that kind of examination; the learnedest of you have been of late years noted seldom or never absent from thence at the time of those greater assemblies; and the favour of proposing there in convenient sort whatsoever ye can object (which thing myself have known them to grant of scholastical courtesy unto strangers) neither hath (as I think) nor ever will (I presume) be denied you.

[2.] If your suit be to have some great extraordinary confluence, in expectation whereof the laws that already are should sleep and have no power over you, till in the hearing of thousands ye all did acknowledge your error and renounce the further prosecution of your cause: haply they whose authority is required unto the satisfying of your demand do think it both dangerous to admit such concourse of divided minds, and unmeet that laws, which being once solemnly established are to exact obedience of all men and to constrain thereunto, should so far stoop as to hold themselves in suspense from taking any effect upon you till some disputer can persuade you to be obedient. A law is the deed of the whole body politic, whereof if ye judge yourselves to be any part, then is the law even your deed also. And were it reason in things of this quality to give men audience, pleading for the overthrow of that which their own very deed hath ratified? Laws that have been approved may be (no man doubteth) again repealed, and to that end also disputed against, by the authors thereof themselves. But this is when the whole doth deliberate what laws each part shall observe, and not when a part refuseth the laws which the whole hath orderly agreed upon.

[3.] Notwithstanding, forasmuch as the cause we maintain is (God be thanked) such as needeth not to shun any trial, might it please them on whose approbation the matter dependeth to condescend so far unto you in this behalf, I wish heartily that proof were made even by solemn conference in orderly and quiet sort, whether you would yourselves be satisfied, or else could by satisfying others draw them to your part. Provided always, first, inasmuch as ye go about to destroy a thing which is in force, and to draw in that which hath not as yet been received; to impose on us that which we think not ourselves bound unto, and to overthrow those things whereof we are possessed; that therefore ye are not to claim in any such conference other than the plaintiff's or opponent's part, which must consist altogether in proof and confirmation of two things: the one, that our orders by you condemned we ought to abolish, the other, that yours we are bound to accept in the stead thereof: secondly, because the questions in controversy between us are many, if once we descend unto particularities, that for the easier and more orderly proceeding therein the most general be first discussed, nor any question left off, nor in each question the prosecution of any one argument given over and another taken in hand, till the issue whereunto by replies and answers both parts are come, be collected, read, and acknowledged as well on the one side as on the other to be the plain conclusion which they are grown unto: thirdly, for avoiding of the manifold inconveniences whereunto ordinary and extemporal disputers are subject, as also because if ye should singly dispute one by one as every man's own wit did best serve, it might be conceived by the rest that haply some other would have done more; the chiefest of you do all agree in this action, that whom ye shall then choose your speaker, by him that which is publickly brought into disputation be acknowledged by all your consents not to be his allegation but yours, such as ye all are agreed upon, and have required him to deliver in all your names; the true copy whereof being taken by a notary, that a reasonable time be allowed for return of answer unto you in the like form. Fourthly, whereas a number of conferences have been had in other causes with the less effectual success, by reason of partial and untrue reports published afterwards unto the world; that to prevent this evil, there be at the first a solemn declaration made on both parts, of their agreement to have that very book and no other set abroad, wherein their present authorized notaries do write those things fully and only, which being written and there read, are by their own open testimony acknowledged to be their own. Other circumstances hereunto belonging, whether for the choice of time, place, and language, or for prevention of impertinent and needless speech, or to any end and purpose else, they may be thought on when occasion serveth.

In this sort to broach my private conceit for the ordering of a public action I should be loth (albeit I do it not otherwise than under correction of them whose gravity and wisdom ought in such cases to overrule), but that so venturous boldness I see is a thing now general; and am thereby of good hope, that where all men are licensed to offend, no man will shew himself a sharp accuser.

Chapter 6

NO END OF CONTENTION, WITHOUT SUBMISSION OF BOTH PARTS UNTO SOME DEFINITIVE SENTENCE

What success God may give unto any such kind of conference or disputation, we cannot tell. But of this we are right sure, that nature, Scripture, and experience itself, have all taught the world to seek for the ending of contentions by submitting itself unto some judicial and definitive sentence, whereunto neither part that contendeth may under any pretence or colour refuse to stand. This must needs be effectual and strong. As for other means without this, they seldom prevail. I would therefore know, whether for the ending of these irksome strifes wherein you and your followers do stand thus formally divided against the authorized guides of this church, and the rest of the people subject unto their charge; whether, I say, ye be content to refer your cause to any other higher judgment than your own, or else intend to persist and proceed as ye have begun, till yourselves can be persuaded to condemn yourselves. If your determination be this, we can be but sorry that ye should deserve to be reckoned with such, of whom God himself pronounceth, "The way of peace they have not known." [Rom. iii. 17]

[2.] Ways of peaceable conclusion there are, but these two certain: the one, a sentence of judicial decision given by authority thereto appointed within ourselves; the other, the like kind of sentence given by a more universal authority. The former of which two ways God himself in the Law prescribeth, and his Spirit it was which directed the very first Christian churches in the world to use the latter.

The ordinance of God in the Law was this. "If there arise a matter too hard for thee in judgment, between blood and blood, between plea, &c. then shalt thou arise, and go up unto the place which the Lord thy God shall choose; and thou shalt come unto the Priests of the Levites, and unto the Judge that shall be in those days, and ask, and they shall shew thee the sentence of judgment, and thou shalt do according to that thing, which they of that place which the Lord hath chosen shew thee, and thou shalt observe to do according to all that they inform thee; according to the law which they shall teach thee, and according to the judgment which they shall tell thee, shalt thou do; thou shalt not decline from the thing which they shall shew thee to the right hand nor to the left. And that man that will do presumptuously, not hearkening unto the Priest (that standeth before the Lord thy God to minister there) or unto the Judge, that man shall die, and thou shalt take away evil from Israel." [Deut. xvii. 8]

When there grew in the Church of Christ a question, Whether the Gentiles believing might be saved, although they were not circumcised after the manner of Moses, nor did observe the rest of those legal rites and ceremonies whereunto the Jews were bound; after great dissension and disputation about it, their conclusion in the end was to have it determined by sentence at Jerusalem; which was accordingly done in a council there assembled for the same purpose [Acts xv]. Are ye able to allege any just and sufficient cause wherefore absolutely ye should not condescend in this controversy to have your judgments overruled by some such definitive sentence, whether it fall out to be given with or against you; that so these tedious contentions may cease?

[3.] Ye will perhaps make answer, that being persuaded already as touching the truth of your cause, ye are not to hearken unto any sentence, no not though Angels should define otherwise, as the blessed Apostle's own example teacheth: again, that men, yea councils, may err; and that, unless the judgment given do satisfy your minds, unless it be such as ye can by no further argument oppugn, in a word, unless you perceive and acknowledge it yourselves consonant with God's word; to stand unto it not allowing it were to sin against your own consciences.

But consider I beseech you first as touching the Apostle, how that wherein he was so resolute and peremptory, our Lord Jesus Christ made manifest unto him even by intuitive revelation, wherein there was no possibility of error. That which you are persuaded of, ye have it no otherwise than by your own only probable collection, and therefore such bold asseverations as in him were admirable, should in your mouths but argue rashness. God was not ignorant that the priests and judges, whose sentence in matters of controversy he ordained should stand, both might and oftentimes would be deceived in their judgment. Howbeit, better it was in the eye of His understanding, that sometime an erroneous sentence definitive should prevail, till the same authority perceiving such oversight, might afterwards correct or reverse it, than that strifes should have respite to grow, and not come speedily unto some end.

Neither wish we that men should do any thing which in their hearts they are persuaded they ought not to do, but this persuasion ought (we say) to be fully settled in their hearts; that in litigious and controversed causes of such quality, the will of God is to have them do whatsoever the doubt many times the sentence amongst the Jews did seem unto one part in their private opinion to swerve utterly from that which is right: as no sentence of judicial and final decision shall determine, yea, though it seem or other contending, and yet in this case, God did then allow them to do that which in their private judgment it seemed, yea and perhaps truly seemed, that the law did disallow. For if God be not the author of confusion but of peace, then can he not be the author of our refusal, but of our contentment, to stand unto some definitive sentence; without which almost impossible it is that either we should avoid confusion, or ever hope to attain peace. To small purpose had the Council of Jerusalem been assembled, if once their determination being set down, men might afterwards have defended their former opinions. When therefore they had given their definitive sentence, all controversy was at an end. Things were disputed before they came to be determined; men afterwards were not to dispute any longer, but to obey. The sentence of judgment finished their strife, which their disputes before judgment could not do. This was ground sufficient for any reasonable man's conscience to build the duty of obedience upon, whatsoever his own opinion were as touching the matter before in question. So full of wilfulness and self-liking is our nature, that without some definitive sentence, which being given may stand, and a necessity of silence on both sides afterward imposed, small hope there is that strifes thus far prosecuted will in short time quietly end.

[4.] Now it were in vain to ask you, whether ye could be content that the sentence of any court already erected should be so far authorized, as that among the Jews established by God himself, for the determining of all controversies: "That man which will do presumptuously, not hearkening unto the Priest that standeth before the Lord to minister there, nor unto the Judge, let him die." Ye have given us already to understand, what your opinion is in part concerning her sacred Majesty's Court of High Commission; the nature whereof is the same with that amongst the Jews, albeit the power be not so great. The other way haply may like you better, because Master Beza, in his last book save one written about these matters, professeth himself to be now weary of such combats and encounters, whether by word or writing, inasmuch as he findeth that "controversies thereby are made but brawls"; and therefore wisheth "that in some common lawful assembly of churches all these strifes may at once be decided."

[5.] Shall there be then in the meanwhile no "doings"? Yes. There are the weightier matters of the law, "judgment, and mercy, and fidelity." [Matt. xxiii. 23] These things we ought to do; and these things, while we contend about less, we leave undone. Happier are they whom the Lord when he cometh shall find "doing" in these things, than disputing about "Doctors, Elders, and Deacons." Or if there be no remedy but somewhat needs ye must do which may tend to the setting forward of your discipline; do that which wise men, who think some statute of the realm more fit to be repealed than to stand in force, are accustomed to do before they come to parliament where the place of enacting is; that is to say, spend the time in re-examining more duly your cause, and in more thoroughly considering of that which ye labour to overthrow. As for the orders which are established, sith equity and reason, the law of nature, God and man, do all favour that which is in being, till orderly judgment of decision be given against it; it is but justice to exact of you, and perverseness in you it should be to deny thereunto your willing obedience.

[6.] Not that I judge it a thing allowable for men to observe those laws which in their hearts they are steadfastly persuaded to be against the law of God: but your persuasion in this case ye are all bound for the time to suspend; and in otherwise doing, ye offend against God by troubling his Church without any just or necessary cause. Be it that there are some reasons inducing you to think hardly of our laws. Are those reasons demonstrative, are they necessary, or but mere probabilities only? An argument necessary and demonstrative is such, as being proposed unto any man and understood, the mind cannot choose but inwardly assent. Any one such reason dischargeth, I grant, the conscience, and setteth it at full liberty. For the public approbation given by the body of this whole church unto those things which are established, doth make it but probable that they are good. And therefore unto a necessary proof that they are not good it must give place. But if the skilfullest amongst you can shew that all the books ye have hitherto written be able to afford any one argument of this nature, let the instance be given. As for probabilities, what thing was there ever set down so agreeable with sound reason, but some probable shew against it might be made? Is it meet that when publicly things are received, and have taken place, general obedience thereunto should cease to be exacted, in case this or that private person, led with some probable conceit, should make open protestation, "I Peter or John disallow them, and pronounce them nought?" In which case your answer will be, that concerning the laws of our church, they are not only condemned in the opinion of "a private man, but of thousands," yea and even "of those amongst which divers are in public charge and authority." As though when public consent of the whole hath established any thing, every man's judgment being thereunto compared were not private, howsoever his calling be to some kind of public charge. So that of peace and quietness there is not any way possible, unless the probable voice of every entire society or body politic overrule all private of like nature in the same body. Which thing effectually proveth, that God, being author of peace and not of confusion in the church, must needs be author of those men's peaceable resolutions, who concerning these things have determined with themselves to think and do as the church they are of decreeth, till they see necessary cause enforcing them to the contrary.

Chapter 7

THE MATTER CONTAINED IN THESE EIGHT BOOKS

Nor is mine own intent any other in these several books of discourse, than to make it appear unto you, that for the ecclesiastical laws of this land, we are led by great reason to observe them, and ye by no necessity bound to impugn them. It is no part of my secret meaning to draw you hereby into hatred, or to set upon the face of this cause any fairer glass than the naked truth doth afford; but my whole endeavour is to resolve the conscience, and to shew as near as I can what in this controversy the heart is to think, if it will follow the light of sound and sincere judgment, without either cloud of prejudice, or mist of passionate affection.

[2.] Wherefore seeing that laws and ordinances in particular, whether such as we observe, or such as yourselves would have established; when the mind doth sift and examine them, it must needs have often recourse to a number of doubts and questions about the nature, kinds, and qualities of laws in general; whereof unless it be thoroughly informed, there will appear no certainty to stay our persuasion upon: I have for that cause set down in the first place an introduction on both sides needful to be considered: declaring therein what law is, how different kinds of laws there are, and what force they are of according unto each kind.

[3.] This done, because ye suppose the laws for which ye strive are found in Scripture, but those not, against which ye strive; and upon this surmise are drawn to hold it as the very main pillar of your whole cause, "That Scripture ought to be the only rule of all our actions," and consequently that the church-orders which we observe being not commanded in Scripture, are offensive and displeasant unto God: I have spent the second Book in sifting of this point, which standeth with you for the first and chiefest principle whereon ye build.

[4.] Whereunto the next in degree is, That as God will have always a Church upon earth, while the world doth continue, and that Church stand in need of government; of which government it behoveth Himself to be both the Author and Teacher: so it cannot stand with duty that man should ever presume in any wise to change and alter the same; and therefore "that in Scripture there must of necessity be found some particular form of Polity Ecclesiastical, the Laws whereof admit not any kind of alteration."

[5.] The first three Books being thus ended, the fourth proceedeth from the general grounds and foundations of your cause unto your general accusations against us, as having in the orders of our Church (for so you pretend) "corrupted the right form of church-polity with manifold popish rites and ceremonies, which certain reformed Churches have banished from amongst them, and have thereby given us such example as" (you think) "we ought to follow." This your assertion hath herein drawn us to make search, whether these be just exceptions against the customs of our Church, when ye plead that they are the same which the Church of Rome hath, or that they are not the same which some other reformed Churches have devised.

[6.] Of those four Books which remain and are bestowed about the specialties of that cause which lieth in controversy, the first examineth the causes by you alleged, wherefore the public duties of Christian religion, as our prayers, our Sacraments, and the rest, should not be ordered in such sort as with us they are; nor that power, whereby the persons of men are consecrated unto the ministry, be disposed of in such manner as the laws of this church do allow. The second and third are concerning the power of jurisdiction: the one, whether laymen, such as your governing Elders are, ought in all congregations for ever to be invested with that power; the other, whether Bishops may have that power over other Pastors, and therewithal that honour, which with us they have? And because besides the power of order which all consecrated persons have, and the power of jurisdiction which neither they all nor they only have, there is a third power, a power of Ecclesiastical Dominion, communicable, as we think, unto persons not ecclesiastical, and most fit to be restrained unto the Prince or Sovereign commander over the whole body politic: the eighth book we have allotted unto this question, and have sifted therein your objections against those preeminences royal which thereunto appertain.

[7.] Thus have I laid before you the brief of these my travails, and presented under your view the limbs of that cause litigious between us: the whole entire body whereof being thus compact, it shall be no troublesome thing for any man to find each particular controversy's resting-place, and the coherence it hath with those things, either on which it dependeth, or which depend on it.

Chapter 8

HOW JUST CAUSE THERE IS TO FEAR THE MANIFOLD DANGEROUS EVENTS LIKELY TO ENSUE UPON THIS INTENDED REFORMATION, IF IT DID TAKE PLACE

The case so standing therefore, my brethren, as it doth, the wisdom of governors ye must not blame, in that they further also forecasting the manifold strange and dangerous innovations which are more than likely to follow, if your discipline should take place, have for that cause thought it hitherto a part of their duty to withstand your endeavours that way. The rather, for that they have seen already some small beginnings of the fruits thereof, in them who concurring with you in judgment about the necessity of that discipline, have adventured without more ado to separate themselves from the rest of the Church, and to put your speculations in execution. These men's hastiness the warier sort of you doth not commend; ye wish they had held themselves longer in, and not so dangerously flown abroad before the feathers of the cause had been grown; their error with merciful terms ye reprove, naming them, in great commiseration of mind, your "poor brethren." They on the contrary side more bitterly accuse you as their "false brethren;" and against you they plead, saying: "From your breasts it is that we have sucked those things, which when ye delivered unto us ye termed that heavenly, sincere, and wholesome milk of God's word [1 Pet. ii. 2], howsoever ye now abhor as poison that which the virtue thereof hath wrought and brought forth in us. You sometime our companions, guides and familiars, with whom we have had most sweet consultations [Ps. lv. 13], are now become our professed adversaries, because we think the statute-congregations in England to be no true Christian churches; because we have severed ourselves from them; and because without their leave and license that are in civil authority, we have secretly framed our own churches according to the platform of the word of God. For of that point between you and us there is no controversy. Alas! what would ye have us to do? As such time as ye were content to accept us in the number of your own, your teachings we heard, we read your writings: and though we would, yet able we are not to forget with what zeal ye have ever professed, that in the English congregations (for so many of them as be ordered according unto their own laws) the very public service of God is fraught as touching matter with heaps of intolerable pollutions, and as concerning form, borrowed from the shop of Antichrist; hateful both ways in the eyes of the Most Holy; the kind of their government by Bishops and Archbishops Antichristian; that discipline which Christ hath 'essentially tied,' that is to say, so united unto his Church, that we cannot account it really to be his Church which hath not in it the same discipline, that very discipline no less there despised, than in the highest throne of Antichrist; all such parts of the word of God as do any way concern that discipline no less unsoundly taught and interpreted by all authorized English pastors, than by Antichrist's factors themselves; at baptism crossing, at the supper of the Lord kneeling, at both, a number of other the most notorious badges of Antichristian recognizance usual. Being moved with these and the like your effectual discourses, whereunto we gave most attentive ear, till they entered even into our souls, and were as fire within our bosoms; we thought we might hereof be bold to conclude, that sith no such Antichristian synagogue may be accounted a true church of Christ, you by accusing all congregations ordered according to the laws of England as Antichristian, did mean to condemn those congregations, as not being any of them worthy the name of a true Christian church. Ye tell us now it is not your meaning. But what meant your often threatenings of them, who professing themselves the inhabitants of Mount Sion, were too loth to depart wholly as they should out of Babylon? Whereat our hearts being fearfully troubled, we durst not, we durst not continue longer so near her confines, lest her plagues might suddenly overtake us, before we did cease to be partakers with her sins: for so we could not choose but acknowledge with grief that we were, when, they doing evil, we by our presence in their assemblies seemed to like thereof, or at leastwise not so earnestly to dislike, as became men heartily zealous of God's glory. For adventuring to erect the discipline of Christ without the leave of the Christian magistrate, haply ye may condemn us as fools, in that we hazard thereby our estates and persons further than you which are that way more wise think necessary; but of any offence or sin therein committed against God, with what conscience can you accuse us, when your own positions are, that the things we observe should every of them be dearer unto us than ten thousand lives; that they are the peremptory commandments of God; that no mortal man can dispense with them, and that the magistrate grievously sinneth in not constraining thereunto? Will ye blame any man for doing that of his own accord, which all men should be compelled to do that are not willing of themselves? When God commandeth, shall we answer that we will obey, if so be Cæsar will grant us leave? Is discipline an ecclesiastical matter or a civil? If an ecclesiastical, it must of necessity belong to the duty of the minister. And the minister (you say) holdeth all his authority of doing whatsoever belongeth unto the spiritual charge of the house of God even immediately from God himself, without dependency upon any magistrate. Whereupon it followeth, as we suppose, that the hearts of the people being willing to be under the sceptre of Christ, the minister of God, into whose hands the Lord himself hath put that sceptre, is without all excuse if thereby he guide them not. Nor do we find that hitherto greatly ye have disliked those churches abroad, where the people with direction of their godly ministers have even against the will of the magistrate brought in either the doctrine or discipline of Jesus Christ. For which cause we must now think the very same thing of you, which our Saviour did sometime utter concerning false-hearted Scribes and Pharisees, 'they say, and do not.'" [Matt. xxiii. 3] Thus the foolish Barrowist deriveth his schism by way of conclusion, as to him it seemeth, directly and plainly out of your principles. Him therefore we leave to be satisfied by you from whom he hath sprung.

[2.] And if such by your own acknowledgement be persons dangerous, although as yet the alterations which they have made are of small and tender growth; the changes likely to ensue throughout all states and vocations within this land, in case your desire should take place, must be thought upon.

First concerning the supreme power of the Highest, they are no small prerogatives, which now thereunto belonging the form of your discipline will constrain it to resign; as in the last book of this treatise we have shewed at large.

Again it may justly be feared whether our English nobility, when the matter came in trial, would contentedly suffer themselves to be always at the call, and to stand to the sentence of a number of mean persons assisted with the presence of their poor teacher, a man (as sometimes it happeneth) though better able to speak, yet little or no whit apter to judge, than the rest: from whom, be their dealings never so absurd, (unless it be by way of complaint to a synod) no appeal may be made unto any one of higher power, inasmuch as the order of your discipline admitteth no standing inequality of courts, no spiritual judge to have any ordinary superior on earth, but as many supremacies as there are parishes and several congregations.

[3.] Neither is it altogether without cause that so many do fear the overthrow of all learning as a threatened sequel of this your intended discipline. For if "the world's preservation" depend upon "the multitude of the wise;" [Sap. vi. 24] and of that sort the number hereafter be not likely to wax over-great, "when" (that wherewith the son of Sirach professeth himself at the heart grieved) "men of understanding are" already so "little set by:" [Ecclus. xxvi. 28] how should their minds whom the love of so precious a jewel filleth with secret jealousy even in regard of the least things which may any way hinder the flourishing estate thereof, choose but misdoubt lest this discipline, which always you match with divine doctrine as her natural and true sister, be found unto all kinds of knowledge a step-mother; seeing that the greatest worldly hopes, which are proposed unto the chiefest kind of learning, ye seek utterly to extirpate as weeds, and have grounded your platform on such propositions as do after a sort undermine those most renowned habitations, where through the goodness of Almighty God all commendable arts and sciences are with exceeding great industry hitherto (and so may they for ever continue) studied, proceeded in, and professed? To charge you as purposely bent to the overthrow of that, wherein so many of you have attained no small perfection, were injurious. Only therefore I wish that yourselves did well consider, how opposite certain your positions are unto the state of collegiate societies, whereon the two universities consist. Those degrees which their statutes bind them to take are by your laws taken away; yourselves who have sought them ye so excuse, as that ye would have men to think ye judge them not allowable, but tolerable only, and to be borne with, for some help which ye find in them unto the furtherance of your purposes, till the corrupt estate of the Church may be better reformed. Your laws forbidding ecclesiastical persons utterly the exercise of civil power must needs deprive the Heads and Masters in the same colleges of all such authority as now they exercise, either at home, by punishing the faults of those, who not as children to their parents by the law of nature, but altogether by civil authority are subject unto them: or abroad by keeping courts amongst their tenants. Your laws making permanent inequality amongst ministers, a thing repugnant to the word of God, enforce those colleges, the seniors whereof are all or any part of them ministers under the government of a master in the same vocation, to choose as oft as they meet together a new president. For if ye judge it necessary to do in synods, for the avoiding of permanent inequality amongst ministers, the same cause must needs even in these collegiate assemblies enforce the like. Except peradventure ye mean to avoid all such absurdities, by dissolving those corporations, and by bringing the universities unto the form of the School of Geneva. Which thing men the rather are inclined to look for, inasmuch as the ministry, whereinto their founders with singular providence have by the same statutes appointed them necessarily to enter at a certain time, your laws bind them much more necessarily to forbear, till some parish abroad call for them.

[4.] Your opinion concerning the law civil is that the knowledge thereof might be spared, as a thing which this land doth not need. Professors in that kind being few, ye are the bolder to spurn at them, and not to dissemble your minds as concerning their removal: in whose studies although myself have not much been conversant, nevertheless exceeding great cause I see there is to wish that thereunto more encouragement were given; as well for the singular treasures of wisdom therein contained, as also for the great use we have thereof, both in decision of certain kinds of causes arising daily within ourselves, and especially for commerce with nations abroad, whereunto that knowledge is most requisite. The reasons wherewith ye would persuade that Scripture is the only rule to frame all our actions by, are in every respect as effectual for proof that the same is the only law whereby to determine all our civil controversies. And then what doth let, but that as those men may have their desire, who frankly broach it already that the work of reformation will never be perfect, till the law of Jesus Christ be received alone; so pleaders and counsellors may bring their books of the common law, and bestow them as the students of curious and needless arts [Acts xix. 19] did theirs in the Apostles' time? I leave them to scan how far those words of yours may reach, wherein ye declare that, whereas now many houses lie waste through inordinate suits of law, "this one thing will shew the excellency of discipline for the wealth of the realm, and quiet of subjects; that the Church is to censure such a party who is apparently troublesome and contentious, and without REASONABLE CAUSE upon a mere will and stomach doth vex and molest his brother, and trouble the country." For mine own part I do not see but that it might very well agree with your principles, if your discipline were fully planted, even to send out your writs of surcease unto all courts of England besides, for the most things handled in them.

[5.] A great deal further I might proceed and descend lower. But forasmuch as against all these and the like difficulties your answer is, that we ought to search what things are consonant to God's will, not which be most for our own ease; and therefore that your discipline being (for such is your error) the absolute commandment of Almighty God, it must be received although the world by receiving it should be clean turned upside down; herein lieth the greatest danger of all. For whereas the name of divine authority is used to countenance these things, which are not the commandments of God, but your own erroneous collections; on him ye must father whatsoever ye shall afterwards be led, either to do in withstanding the adversaries of your cause, or to think in maintenance of your doings. And what this may be, God doth know. In such kinds of error the mind once imagining itself to seek the execution of God's will, laboureth forthwith to remove both things and persons which any way hinder it from taking place; and in such cases if any strange or new thing seem requisite to be done, a strange and new opinion concerning the lawfulness thereof is withal received and broached under countenance of divine authority.

[6.] One example herein may serve for many, to shew that false opinions, touching the will of God to have things done, are wont to bring forth mighty and violent practices against the hindrances of them; and those practices new opinions more pernicious than the first, yea most extremely sometimes opposite to that which the first did seem to intend. Where the people took upon them the reformation of the Church by casting out popish superstition, they, having received from their pastors a general instruction "that whatsoever the heavenly Father hath not planted must be rooted out," [Matt. xv. 13] proceeded in some foreign places so far that down went oratories and the very temples of God themselves. For as they chanced to take the compass of their commission stricter or larger, so their dealings were accordingly more or less moderate. Amongst others there sprang up presently one kind of men, with whose zeal and forwardness the rest being compared were thought to be marvellous cold and dull. These, grounding themselves on rules more general; that whatsoever the law of Christ commandeth not, thereof Antichrist is the author: and that whatsoever Antichrist or his adherents did in the world, the true professors of Christ are to undo; found out many things more than others had done, the extirpation whereof was in their conceit as necessary as of any thing before removed. Hereupon they secretly made their doleful complaints every where as they went, that albeit the world did begin to profess some dislike of that which was evil in the kingdom of darkness, yet fruits worthy of a true repentance were not seen; and that if men did repent as they ought, they must endeavour to purge the earth of all manner evil, to the end there might follow a new world afterward, wherein righteousness only should dwell. Private repentance they said must appear by every man's fashioning his own life contrary unto the customs and orders of this present world, both in greater things and in less. To this purpose they had always in their mouths those greater things, charity, faith, the true fear of God, the cross, the mortification of the flesh. All their exhortations were to set light of the things in this world, to count riches and honours vanity, and in token thereof not only to seek neither, but if men were possessors of both, even to cast away the one and resign the other, that all men might see their unfeigned conversion unto Christ. They were solicitors of men to fasts, to often meditations of heavenly things, and as it were conferences in secret with God by prayers, not framed according to the frozen manner of the world, but expressing such fervent desires as might even force God to hearken unto them. Where they found men in diet, attire, furniture of house, or any other way, observers of civility and decent order, such they reproved as being carnally and earthly minded. Every word otherwise than severely and sadly uttered seemed to pierce like a sword through them. If any man were pleasant, their manner was presently with deep sighs to repeat those words of our Saviour Christ, "Woe be to you which now laugh, for ye shall lament." [Luke vi. 25] So great was their delight to be always in trouble, that such as did quietly lead their lives, they judged of all other men to be in most dangerous case. They so much affected to cross the ordinary custom in every thing, that when other men's use was to put on better attire, they would be sure to shew themselves openly abroad in worse; the ordinary names of the days in the week they thought it a kind of profaneness to use, and therefore accustomed themselves to make no other distinction than by numbers, the First, Second, Third day.

[7.] From this they proceeded unto public reformation, first ecclesiastical, and then civil. Touching the former, they boldly avouched that themselves only had the truth, which thing upon peril of their lives they would at all times defend; and that since the apostles lived, the same was never before in all points sincerely taught. Wherefore that things might again be brought to that ancient integrity which Jesus Christ by his word requireth, they began to control the ministers of the gospel for attributing so much force and virtue unto the scriptures of God read, whereas the truth was, that when the word is said to engender faith in the heart, and to convert the soul of man, or to work any such spiritual divine effect, these speeches are not thereunto appliable as it is read or preached, but as it is ingrafted in us by the power of the Holy Ghost opening the eyes of our understanding, and so revealing the mysteries of God, according to that which Jeremy promised before should be, saying, "I will put my law in their inward parts, and I will write it in their hearts." [Jer. xxxi. 33] The Book of God they notwithstanding for the most part so admired, that other disputation against their opinions than only by allegation of Scripture they would not hear; besides it they thought no other writings in the world should be studied; insomuch as one of their great prophets exhorting them to cast away all respect unto human writings, so far to his motion they condescended, that as many as had any books save the Holy Bible in their custody, they brought and set them publicly on fire. When they and their Bibles were alone together, what strange fantastical opinion soever at any time entered into their heads, their use was to think the Spirit taught it them. Their phrensies concerning our Saviour's incarnation, the state of souls departed, and suchlike, are things needless to be rehearsed. And forasmuch as they were of the same suit with those of whom the apostle speaketh, saying, "They are still learning, but never attain to the knowledge of truth," [2 Tim. iii. 7] it was no marvel to see them every day broach some new thing, not heard of before. Which restless levity they did interpret to be their growing to spiritual perfection, and a proceeding from faith to faith. The differences amongst them grew by this mean in a manner infinite, so that scarcely was there found any one of them, the forge of whose brain was not possessed with some special mystery. Whereupon, although their mutual contentions were most fiercely prosecuted amongst themselves, yet when they came to defend the cause common to them all against the adversaries of their faction, they had ways to lick one another whole; the founder in his own persuasion excusing THE DEAR BRETHREN, which were not so far enlightened, and professing a charitable hope of the mercy of God towards them notwithstanding their swerving from him in some things. Their own ministers they highly magnified as men whose vocation was from God; the rest their manner was to term disdainfully Scribes and Pharisees, to account their calling an human creature, and to detain the people as much as might be from hearing them. As touching Sacraments, Baptism administered in the Church of Rome they judged to be but an execrable mockery and no baptism; both because the ministers thereof in the Papacy are wicked idolaters, lewd persons, thieves and murderers, cursed creatures, ignorant beasts; and also for that to baptize is a proper action belonging unto none but the Church of Christ, whereas Rome is Antichrist's synagogue.The custom of using godfathers and godmothers at christenings they scorned. Baptizing of infants, although confessed by themselves to have been continued ever sithence the very Apostles' own times, yet they altogether condemned; partly because sundry errors are of no less antiquity; and partly for that there is no commandment in the gospel of Christ which saith, "Baptize infants", but he contrariwise in saying, "Go preach and baptize," doth appoint that the minister of baptism shall in that action first administer doctrine, and then baptism; as also in saying, "Whosoever doth believe and is baptized," he appointeth that the party to whom baptism is administered shall first believe and then be baptized;

to the end that believing may go before this sacrament in the receiver, no otherwise than preaching in the giver; sith equally in both, the law of Christ declareth not only what things are required, but also in what order they are required. The Eucharist they received (pretending our Lord and Saviour's example) after supper; and for avoiding all those impieties which have been grounded upon the mystical words of Christ, "This is my body, this is my blood," they thought it not safe to mention either body or blood in that sacrament, but rather to abrogate both, and to use no words but these, "Take, eat, declare the death of our Lord: drink, shew forth our Lord's death." In rites and ceremonies their profession was hatred of all conformity with the Church of Rome: for which cause they would rather endure any torment than observe the solemn festivals which others did, inasmuch as Antichrist (they said) was the first inventor of them.

[8.] The pretended end of their civil reformation was that Christ might have dominion over all; that all crowns and sceptres might be thrown down at his feet; that no other might reign over Christian men but he, no regiment keep them in awe but his discipline, amongst them no sword at all be carried besides his, the sword of spiritual excommunication. For this cause they laboured with all their might in overturning the seats of magistracy, because Christ hath said, "Kings of nations;" [Luke xxii. 25] in abolishing the execution of justice, because Christ hath said, "Resist not evil;" in forbidding oaths, the necessary means of judicial trial, because Christ hath said, "Swear not at all:" finally, in bringing in community of goods, because Christ by his apostles hath given the world such example, to the end that men might excel one another not in wealth, the pillar of secular authority, but in virtue.

[9.] These men at the first were only pitied in their error, and not much withstood by any; the great humility, zeal, and devotion, which appeared to be in them, was in all men's opinion a pledge of their harmless meaning. The hardest that men of sound understanding conceived of them was but this, "O quam honesta voluntate miseri errant! With how good a meaning these poor souls do evil!" Luther made request unto Frederick duke of Saxony, that within his dominion they might be favourably dealt with and spared, for that (their error excepted) they seemed otherwise right good men. By means of which merciful toleration they gathered strength, much more than was safe for the state of the commonwealth wherein they lived. They had their secret corner-meetings and assemblies in the night, the people flocked unto them by thousands.

[10.] The means whereby they both allured and retained so great multitudes were most effectual: first, a wonderful show of zeal towards God, wherewith they seemed to be even rapt in every thing they spake: secondly, an hatred of sin, and a singular love of integrity, which men did think to be much more than ordinary in them, by reason of the custom which they had to fill the ears of the people with invectives against their authorized guides, as well spiritual as civil: thirdly, the bountiful relief wherewith they eased the broken estate of such needy creatures, as were in that respect the more apt to be drawn away: fourthly, a tender compassion which they were thought to take upon the miseries of the common sort, over whose heads their manner was even to pour down showers of tears, in complaining that no respect was had unto them, that their goods were devoured by wicked cormorants, their persons had in contempt, all liberty both temporal and spiritual taken from them, that it was high time for God now to hear their groans, and to send them deliverance: lastly, a cunning sleight which they had to stroke and smooth up the minds of their followers, as well by appropriating unto them all the favourable titles, the good words, and the gracious promises in Scripture, as also by casting the contrary always on the heads of such as were severed from that retinue. Whereupon the people's common acclamation unto such deceivers was, "These are verily the men of God, these are his true and sincere prophets." If any such prophet or man of God did suffer by order of law condign and deserved punishment, were it for felony, rebellion, murder, or what else, the people (so strangely were their hearts enchanted), as though blessed Saint Stephen had been again martyred, did lament that God took away his most dear servants from them.

[11.] In all these things being fully persuaded, that what they did, it was obedience to the will of God, and that all men should do the like; there remained, after speculation, practice, whereby the whole world thereunto (if it were possible) might be framed. This they saw could not be done but with mighty opposition and resistance; against which to strengthen themselves, they secretly entered into league of association. And peradventure considering, that although they were many, yet long wars would in time waste them out; they began to think whether it might not be that God would have them do, for their speedy and mighty increase, the same which sometime God's own chosen people, the people of Israel, did. Glad and fain they were to have it so, which very desire was itself apt to breed both an opinion of possibility, and a willingness to gather arguments of likelihood, that so God himself would have it. Nothing more clear unto their seeming, than that a new Jerusalem being often spoken of in Scripture, they undoubtedly were themselves that new Jerusalem, and the old did by way of a certain figurative resemblance signify what they should both be and do. Here they drew in a sea of matter, by applying all things unto their own company, which are any where spoken concerning divine favours and benefits bestowed upon the old commonwealth of Israel: concluding that as Israel was delivered out of Egypt, so they spiritually out of the Egypt of this world's servile thraldom unto sin and superstition; as Israel was to root out the idolatrous nations, and to plant instead of them a people which feared God; so the same Lord's good will and pleasure was now, that these new Israelites should, under the conduct of other Joshuas, Samsons, and Gideons, perform a work no less miraculous in casting out violently the wicked from the earth, and establishing the kingdom of Christ with perfect liberty: and therefore, as the cause why the children of Israel took unto one man many wives, might be lest the casualties of war should any way hinder the promise of God concerning their multitude from taking effect in them; so it was not unlike that for the necessary propagation of Christ's kingdom under the Gospel the Lord was content to allow as much.

[12.] Now whatsoever they did in such sort collect out of Scripture, when they came to justify or persuade it unto others, all was the heavenly Father's appointment, his commandment, his will and charge. Which thing is the very point, in regard whereof I have gathered this declaration. For my purpose herein is to shew, that when the minds of men are once erroneously persuaded that it is the will of God to have those things done which they fancy, their opinions are as thorns in their sides, never suffering them to take rest till they have brought their speculations into practice. The lets and impediments of which practice their restless desire and study to remove leadeth them every day forth by the hand into other more dangerous opinions, sometimes quite and clean contrary to their first pretended meanings: so as what will grow out of such errors as go masked under the cloak of divine authority, impossible it is that ever the wit of man should imagine, till time have brought forth the fruits of them: for which cause it behoveth wisdom to fear the sequels thereof, even beyond all apparent cause of fear. These men, in whose mouths at the first sounded nothing but only mortification of the flesh, were come at the length to think they might lawfully have their six or seven wives apiece; they which at the first thought judgment and justice itself to be merciless cruelty, accounted at the length their own hands sanctified with being imbrued in Christian blood; they who at the first were wont to beat down all dominion, and to urge against poor constables, "Kings of nations;" had at length both consuls and kings of their own erection amongst themselves; finally, they which could not brook at the first that any man should seek, no not by law, the recovery of goods injuriously taken or withheld from him, were grown at the last to think they could not offer unto God more acceptable sacrifice, than by turning their adversaries clean out of house and home, and by enriching themselves with all kind of spoil and pillage; which thing being laid to their charge, they had in a readiness their answer, that now the time was come, when according to our Saviour's promise, "the meek ones must inherit the earth;" [Matt. v. 5] and that their title hereunto was the same which the righteous Israelites had unto the goods of the wicked Egyptians [Exod. xi. 2].

[13.] Wherefore sith the world hath had in these men so fresh experience, how dangerous such active errors are, it must not offend you, though, touching the sequel of your present mispersuasions, much more be doubted, than your own intents and purposes do haply aim at. And yet your words already are somewhat, when ye affirm, that your Pastors, Doctors, Elders, and Deacons, ought to be in this Church of England, "whether her Majesty and our state will or no;" when for the animating of your confederates ye publish the musters which ye have made of your own bands, and proclaim them to amount I know not to how many thousands; when ye threaten, that sith neither your suits to the parliament, nor supplications to our convocation-house, neither your defences by writing, nor challenges of disputation in behalf of that cause are able to prevail, we must blame ourselves, if to bring in discipline some such means hereafter be used as shall cause all our hearts to ache. "That things doubtful are to be construed in the better part," is a principle not safe to be followed in matters concerning the public state of a commonweal. But howsoever these and the like speeches be accounted as arrows idly shot at random, without either eye had to any mark, or regard to their lighting-place; hath not your longing desire for the practice of your discipline brought the matter already unto this demurrer amongst you, whether the people and their godly pastors that way affected ought not to make separation from the rest, and to begin the exercise of discipline without the license of civil powers, which license they have sought for, and are not heard? Upon which question as ye have now divided yourselves, the warier sort of you taking the one part, and the forwarder in zeal the other; so in case these earnest ones should prevail, what other sequel can any wise man imagine but this, that having first resolved that attempts for discipline without superiors are lawful, it will follow in the next place to be disputed what may be attempted against superiors which will not have the sceptre of that discipline to rule over them? Yea even by you which have stayed yourselves from running headlong with the other sort, somewhat notwithstanding there hath been done without the leave or liking of your lawful superiors, for the exercise of a part of your discipline amongst the clergy thereunto addicted. And lest examination of principal parties therein should bring those things to light, which might hinder and let your proceedings; behold, for a bar against that impediment, one opinion ye have newly added unto the rest even upon this occasion, an opinion to exempt you from taking oaths which may turn to the molestation of your brethren in that cause. The next neighbour opinion whereunto, when occasion requireth, may follow for dispensation with oaths already taken, if they afterwards be found to import a necessity of detecting ought which may bring such good men into trouble or damage, whatsoever the cause be. O merciful God, what man's wit is there able to sound the depth of these dangerous and fearful evils, whereinto our weak and impotent nature is inclinable to sink itself, rather than to shew an acknowledgment of error in that which once we have unadvisedly taken upon us to defend, against the stream as it were of a contrary public resolution!

[14.] Wherefore if we any thing respect their error, who being persuaded even as you are, have gone further upon that persuasion than you allow; if we regard the present state of the highest governor placed over us, if the quality and disposition of our nobles, if the orders and laws of our famous universities, if the profession of the civil or the practice of the common law amongst us, if the mischiefs whereinto even before our eyes so many others have fallen headlong from no less plausible and fair beginnings than yours are: there is in every of these considerations most just cause to fear lest our hastiness to embrace a thing of so perilous consequence should cause posterity to feel those evils, which as yet are more easy for us to prevent than they would be for them to remedy.

Chapter 9

THE CONCLUSION OF ALL

The best and safest way for you therefore, my dear brethren, is, to call your deeds past to a new reckoning, to reexamine the cause ye have taken in hand, and to try it even point by point, argument by argument, with all the diligent exactness ye can; to lay aside the gall of that bitterness wherein your minds have hitherto over-abounded, and with meekness to search the truth. Think ye are men, deem it not impossible for you to err; sift unpartially your own hearts, whether it be force of reason or vehemency of affection, which hath bred and still doth feed these opinions in you. If truth do any where manifest itself, seek not to smother it with glosing delusions, acknowledge the greatness thereof, and think it your best victory when the same doth prevail over you.

[2.] That ye have been earnest in speaking or writing again and again the contrary way, shall be no blemish or discredit at all unto you. Amongst so many so huge volumes as the infinite pains of St. Augustine have brought forth, what one hath gotten him greater love, commendation and honour, than the book wherein he carefully collecteth his own oversights, and sincerely condemneth them? Many speeches there are of Job's whereby his wisdom and other virtues may appear; but the glory of an ingenuous mind he hath purchased by these words only, "Behold, I will lay mine hand on my mouth: I have spoken once, yet will I not therefore maintain argument; yea twice, howbeit for that cause further I will not proceed." [Job xl, 4, 5]

[3.] Far more comfort it were for us (so small is the joy we take in these strifes) to labour under the same yoke, as men that look for the same eternal reward of their labours, to be joined with you in bands of indissoluble love and amity, to live as if our persons being many our souls were but one, rather than in such dismembered sort to spend our few and wretched days in a tedious prosecuting of wearisome contentions: the end whereof, if they have not some speedy end, will be heavy even on both sides. Brought already we are even to that estate which Gregory Nazianzen mournfully describeth, saying, "My mind leadeth me" (sith there is no other remedy) "to fly and to convey myself into some corner out of sight, where I may scape from this cloudy tempest of maliciousness, whereby all parts are entered into a deadly war amongst themselves, and that little remnant of love which was, is now consumed to nothing. The only godliness we glory in, is to find out somewhat whereby we may judge others to be ungodly. Each other's faults we observe as matter of exprobation and not of grief. By these means we are grown hateful in the eyes of the heathens themselves, and (which woundeth us the more deeply) able we are not to deny but that we have deserved their hatred. With the better sort of our own our fame and credit is clean lost. The less we are to marvel if they judge vilely of us, who although we did well would hardly allow thereof. On our backs they also build that are lewd, and what we object one against another, the same they use to the utter scorn and disgrace of us all. This we have gained by our mutual home-dissensions. This we are worthily rewarded with, which are more forward to strive than becometh men of virtuous and mild disposition."

[4.] But our trust in the Almighty is, that with us contentions are now at their highest float, and that the day will come (for what cause of despair is there?) when the passions of former enmity being allayed, we shall with ten times' redoubled tokens of our unfeignedly reconciled love, shew ourselves each towards other the same which Joseph and the brethren of Joseph were at the time of their interview in Egypt. Our comfortable expectation and most thirsty desire whereof what man soever amongst you shall any way help to satisfy, (as we truly hope there is no one amongst you but some way or other will,) the blessings of the God of peace, both in this world and in the world to come, be upon him more than the stars of the firmament in number.

What Things are handled in the Books following:

The *first* Book, concerning laws in general.

The *second*, of the use of divine law contained in scripture; whether that be the only law which ought to serve for our direction in all things without exception.

The *third*, of Laws concerning Ecclesiastical Polity; whether the form thereof be in Scripture so set down, that no addition or change is lawful.

The *fourth*, of general exceptions taken against the laws of our polity, as being popish, and banished out of certain reformed Churches.

The *fifth*, of our Laws that concern the public religious duties of the Church, and the manner of bestowing that power of order, which enableth men in sundry degrees and callings to execute the same.

The *sixth*, of the power of jurisdiction, which the reformed platform claimeth unto lay-elders, with others.

The *seventh*, of the power of jurisdiction, and the honour which is annexed thereunto in Bishops.

The *eighth*, of the power of ecclesiastical dominion or supreme authority, which with us the highest governor or Prince hath, as well in regard of domestical Jurisdictions, as of that other foreignly claimed by the Bishop of Rome.

the first book

CONCERNING LAWS AND THEIR SEVERAL KINDS IN GENERAL

The matter contained in this first book

Chapter 1

THE CAUSE OF WRITING THIS GENERAL DISCOURSE

HE THAT goeth about to persuade a multitude, that they are not so well governed as they ought to be, shall never want attentive and favourable hearers; because they know the manifold defects whereunto every kind of regiment is subject, but the secret lets and difficulties, which in public proceedings are innumerable and inevitable, they have not ordinarily the judgment to consider. And because such as openly reprove supposed disorders of state are taken for principal friends to the common benefit of all, and for men that carry singular freedom of mind; under this fair and plausible colour whatsoever they utter passeth for good and current. That which wanteth in the weight of their speech, is supplied by the aptness of men's minds to accept and believe it. Whereas on the other side, if we maintain things that are established, we have not only to strive with a number of heavy prejudices deeply rooted in the hearts of men, who think that herein we serve the time, and speak in favour of the present state, because thereby we either hold or seek preferment; but also to bear such exceptions as minds so averted beforehand usually take against that which they are loth should be poured into them.

[2.] Albeit therefore much of that we are to speak in this present cause may seem to a number perhaps tedious, perhaps obscure, dark, and intricate; (for many talk of the truth, which never sounded the depth from whence it springeth; and therefore when they are led thereunto they are soon weary, as men drawn from those beaten paths wherewith they have been inured;) yet this may not so far prevail as to cut off that which the matter itself requireth, howsoever the nice humour of some be therewith pleased or no. They unto whom we shall seem tedious are in no wise injuried by us, because it is in their own hands to spare that labour which they are not willing to endure. And if any complain of obscurity, they must consider, that in these matters it cometh no otherwise to pass than in sundry the works both of art and also of nature, where that which hath greatest force in the very things we see is notwithstanding itself oftentimes not seen. The stateliness of houses, the goodliness of trees, when we behold them delighteth the eye; but that foundation which beareth up the one, that root which ministereth unto the other nourishment and life, is in the bosom of the earth concealed; and if there be at any time occasion to search into it, such labour is then more necessary than pleasant, both to them which undertake it and for the lookers-on. In like manner, the use and benefit of good laws all that live under them may enjoy with delight and comfort, albeit the grounds and first original causes from whence they have sprung be unknown, as to the greatest part of men they are. But when they who withdraw their obedience pretend that the laws which they should obey are corrupt and vicious; for better examination of their quality, it behoveth the very foundation and root, the highest well-spring and fountain of them to be discovered. Which because we are not oftentimes accustomed to do, when we do it the pains we take are more needful a great deal than acceptable, and the matters which we handle seem by reason of newness (till the mind grow better acquainted with them) dark, intricate, and unfamiliar. For as much help whereof as may be in this case, I have endeavoured throughout the body of this whole discourse, that every former part might give strength unto all that follow, and every later bring some light unto all before. So that if the judgments of men do but hold themselves in suspense as touching these first more general meditations, till in order they have perused the rest that ensue; what may seem dark at the first will afterwards be found more plain, even as the later particular decisions will appear, I doubt not, more strong, when the other have been read before.

[3.] The Laws of the Church, whereby for so many ages together we have been guided in the exercise of Christian religion and the service of the true God, our rites, customs, and orders of ecclesiastical government, are called in question: we are accused as men that will not have Christ Jesus to rule over them, but have wilfully cast his statutes behind their backs, hating to be reformed and made subject unto the sceptre of his discipline. Behold therefore we offer the laws whereby we live unto the general trial and judgment of the whole world; heartily beseeching Almighty God, whom we desire to serve according to his own will, that both we and others (all kind of partial affection being clean laid aside) may have eyes to see and hearts to embrace the things that in his sight are most acceptable.

And because the point about which we strive is the quality of our laws, our first entrance hereinto cannot better be made, than with consideration of the nature of law in general, and of that law which giveth life unto all the rest, which are commendable, just, and good; namely the law whereby the Eternal himself doth work. Proceeding from hence to the law, first of Nature, then of Scripture, we shall have the easier access unto those things which come after to be debated, concerning the particular cause and question which we have in hand.

Chapter 2

OF THAT LAW WHICH GOD FROM BEFORE THE BEGINNING HATH SET FOR HIMSELF TO DO ALL THINGS BY

All things that are, have some operation not violent or casual. Neither doth any thing ever begin to exercise the same, without some fore-conceived end for which it worketh. And the end which it worketh for is not obtained, unless the work be also fit to obtain it by. For unto every end every operation will not serve. That which doth assign unto each thing the kind, that which doth moderate the force and power, that which doth appoint the form and measure of working, the same we term a *Law*. So that no certain end could ever be attained, unless the actions whereby it is attained were regular; that is to say, made suitable, fit and correspondent unto their end, by some canon, rule or law. Which thing doth first take place in the works even of God himself.

[2.] All things therefore do work after a sort, according to law: all other things according to a law, whereof some superior, unto whom they are subject, is author; only the works and operations of God have Him both for their worker, and for the law whereby they are wrought. The being of God is a kind of law to his working: for that perfection which God is, giveth perfection to that he doth. Those natural, necessary, and internal operations of God, the *generation* of the Son, the *proceeding* of the Spirit, are without the compass of my present intent: which is to touch only such operations as have their beginning and being by a voluntary purpose, wherewith God hath eternally decreed when and how they should be. Which eternal decree is that we term an eternal law.

Dangerous it were for the feeble brain of man to wade far into the doings of the Most High; whom although to know be life, and joy to make mention of his name; yet our soundest knowledge is to know that we know him not as indeed he is, neither can know him: and our safest eloquence concerning him is our silence, when we confess without confession that his glory is inexplicable, his greatness above our capacity and reach. He is above, and we upon earth; therefore it behoveth our words to be wary and few.

Our God is one, or rather very *Oneness*, and mere unity, having nothing but itself in itself, and not consisting (as all things do besides God) of many things. In which essential Unity of God a Trinity personal nevertheless subsisteth, after a manner far exceeding the possibility of man's conceit. The works which outwardly are of God, they are in such sort of Him being one, that each Person hath in them somewhat peculiar and proper. For being Three, and they all subsisting in the essence of one Deity; from the Father, by the Son, through the Spirit, all things are. That which the Son doth hear of the Father, and which the Spirit doth receive of the Father and the Son, the same we have at the hands of the Spirit as being the last, and therefore the nearest unto us in order, although in power the same with the second and the first. [John xvi. 13–15]

[3.] The wise and learned among the very heathens themselves have all acknowledged some First Cause, whereupon originally the being of all things dependeth. Neither have they otherwise spoken of that cause than as an Agent, which knowing *what* and *why* it worketh, observeth in working a most exact *order* or *law*. Thus much is signified by that which Homer mentioneth, "Jupiter's *Counsel* was accomplished" [*Il.* 1. 5]. Thus much acknowledged by Mercurius Trismegistus, "The creator made the whole world not with hands, but by *Reason*". Thus much confest by Anaxagoras and Plato, terming the maker of the world an *Intellectual* worker. Finally the Stoics, although imagining the first cause of all things to be fire, held nevertheless that the same fire, having art, did "Proceed by a certain and a set *Way* in the making of the world". They all confess therefore in the working of that first cause, that *counsel* is used, *reason* followed, a *way* observed; that is to say, constant *order* and *law* is kept; whereof itself must needs be author unto itself. Otherwise it should have some worthier and higher to direct it, and so could not itself be the first. Being the first, it can have no other than itself to be the author of that law which it willingly worketh by.

God therefore is a law both to himself, and to all other things besides. To himself he is a law in all those things, whereof our Saviour speaketh, saying, "My Father worketh as yet, so I." [John v. 17] God worketh nothing without cause. All those things which are done by him have some end for which they are done; and the end for which they are done is a reason of his will to do them. His will had not inclined to create woman, but that he saw it could not be well if she were not created. *Non est bonum*, "It is not good man should be alone; therefore let us make a helper for him." [Gen. ii. 18] That and nothing else is done by God, which to leave undone were not so good.

If therefore it be demanded, why God having power and ability infinite, the effects notwithstanding of that power are all so limited as we see they are: the reason hereof is the end which he hath proposed, and the law whereby his wisdom hath stinted the effects of his power in such sort, that it doth not work infinitely, but correspondently unto that end for which it worketh, even "all things in most decent and comely sort", all things in "measure, number, and weight." [Sap. viii. 1; xi. 20]

[4.] The general end of God's external working is the exercise of his most glorious and most abundant virtue. Which abundance doth shew itself in variety, and for that cause this variety is oftentimes in Scripture exprest by the name of *riches* [Ephes. i. 7; Phil. iv. 19; Col. ii. 3]. "The Lord hath made all things for his own sake." [Prov. xvi. 4] Not that any thing is made to be beneficial unto him, but all things for him to shew beneficence and grace in them.

The particular drift of every act proceeding externally from God we are not able to discern, and therefore cannot always give the proper and certain reason of his works. Howbeit undoubtedly a proper and certain reason there is of every finite work of God, inasmuch as there is a law imposed upon it; which if there were not, it should be infinite, even as the worker himself is.

[5.] They err therefore who think that of the will of God to do this or that there is no reason besides his will. Many times no reason known to us; but that there is no reason thereof I judge it most unreasonable to imagine, inasmuch as he worketh all things not only according to his own will, but "the Counsel of his own will". [Ephes. i. 11] And whatsoever is done with counsel or wise resolution hath of necessity some reason why it should be done, albeit that reason be to us in some things so secret, that it forceth the wit of man to stand, as the blessed Apostle himself doth, amazed thereat: "O the depth of the riches both of the wisdom and knowledge of

God! how unsearchable are his judgments," &c. [Rom. xi. 33]. That law eternal which God himself hath made to himself, and thereby worketh all things whereof he is the cause and author; that law in the admirable frame whereof shineth with most perfect beauty the countenance of that wisdom which hath testified concerning herself, "The Lord possessed me in the beginning of his way, even before his works of old I was set up;" [Prov. viii. 22] that law, which hath been the pattern to make, and is the card to guide the world by; that law which hath been of God and with God everlastingly; that law, the author and observer whereof is one only God to be blessed for ever: how should either men or angels be able perfectly to behold? The book of this law we are neither able nor worthy to open and look into. That little thereof which we darkly apprehend we admire, the rest with religious ignorance we humbly and meekly adore.

[6.] Seeing therefore that according to this law He worketh, "of whom, through whom, and for whom, are all things;" [Rom. xi. 36] although there seem unto us confusion and disorder in the affairs of this present world: "let no man doubt but that every thing is well done, because the world is ruled by so good a guide," [Boeth. *Cons. Phil.* 4. 5] as transgresseth not His own law, than which nothing can be more absolute, perfect, and just.

The law whereby He worketh is eternal, and therefore can have no show or colour of mutability: for which cause, a part of that law being opened in the promises which God hath made (because his promises are nothing else but declarations what God will do for the good of men) touching those promises the Apostle hath witnessed, that God may as possibly "deny himself" [2 Tim. ii. 13] and not be God, as fail to perform them. And concerning the counsel of God, he termeth it likewise a thing "unchangeable;" [Heb. vi. 17] the counsel of God, and that law of God whereof now we speak, being one.

Nor is the freedom of the will of God any whit abated, let or hindered, by means of this; because the imposition of this law upon himself is his own free and voluntary act.

This law therefore we may name eternal, being *that order which God before all ages hath set down with himself, for himself to do all things by.*

Chapter 3

THE LAW WHICH NATURAL AGENTS HAVE GIVEN THEM TO OBSERVE, AND THEIR NECESSARY MANNER OF KEEPING IT

I am not ignorant that by "law eternal" the learned for the most part do understand the order, not which God hath eternally purposed himself in all his works to observe, but rather that which with himself he hath set down as expedient to be kept by all his creatures, according to the several condition wherewith he hath endued them. They who thus are accustomed to speak apply the name of Law unto that only rule of working which superior authority imposeth; whereas we, somewhat more enlarging the sense thereof, term any kind of rule or canon, whereby actions are framed, a law. Now that law which, as it is laid up in the bosom of God, they call *Eternal*, receiveth according unto the different kinds of things which are subject unto it different and sundry kinds of names. That part of it which ordereth natural agents we call usually *Nature's* law; that which Angels do clearly behold and without any swerving observe is a law *Celestial* and heavenly; the law of *Reason*, that which bindeth creatures reasonable in this world, and with which by reason they may most plainly perceive themselves bound; that which bindeth them, and is not known but by special revelation from God, *Divine* law; *Human* law, that which out of the law either of reason or of God men probably gathering to be expedient, they make it a law. All things therefore, which are as they ought to be, are conformed unto *this second law eternal*; and even those things which to this eternal law are not conformable are notwithstanding in some sort ordered by *the first eternal law*. For what good or evil is there under the sun, what action correspondent or repugnant unto the law which God hath imposed upon his creatures, but in or upon it God doth work according to the law which himself hath eternally purposed to keep; that is to say, the *first law eternal*? So that a twofold law eternal being thus made, it is not hard to conceive how they both take place in all things [Aquinas, *Summa*, IaIIae, q. 93, art. 4, 5, 6].

[2.] Wherefore to come to the law of nature: albeit thereby we sometimes mean that manner of working which God hath set for each created thing to keep; yet forasmuch as those things are termed most properly natural agents, which keep the law of their kind unwittingly, as the heavens and elements of the world, which can do no otherwise than they do; and forasmuch as we give unto intellectual natures the name of *Voluntary* agents, that so we may distinguish them from the other; expedient it will be, that we sever the law of nature observed by the one from that which the other is tied unto. Touching the former, their strict keeping of one tenure, statute, and law, is spoken of by all, but hath in it more than men have as yet attained to know, or perhaps ever shall attain, seeing the travail of wading herein is given of God to the sons of men, that perceiving how much the least thing in the world hath in it more than the wisest are able to reach unto, they may by this means learn humility. Moses, in describing the work of creation, attributeth speech unto God: "God said, Let there be light: let there be a firmament: let the waters under the heaven be gathered together into one place: let the earth bring forth: let there be lights in the firmament of heaven." Was this only the intent of Moses, to signify the infinite greatness of God's power by the easiness of his accomplishing such effects, without travail, pain, or labour? Surely it seemeth that Moses had herein besides this a further purpose, namely, first to teach that God did not work as a necessary but a voluntary agent, intending beforehand and decreeing with himself that which did outwardly proceed from him: secondly, to shew that God did then institute a law natural to be observed by creatures, and therefore according to the manner of laws, the institution thereof is described, as being established by solemn injunction. His commanding those things to be which are, and to be in such sort as they are, to keep that tenure and course which they do, importeth the establishment of nature's law. This world's first creation, and the preservation since of things created, what is it but only so far forth a manifestation by execution, what the eternal law of God is concerning things natural? And as it cometh to pass in a kingdom rightly ordered, that after a law is once published, it presently takes effect far and wide, all states framing themselves thereunto; even so let us think it fareth in the natural course of the world: since the time that God did first proclaim the edicts of his law upon it, heaven and earth have hearkened unto his voice, and their labour hath been to do his will: He "made a law for the rain;" He gave his "decree unto the sea, that the waters should not pass his commandment." Now if nature should intermit her course, and leave altogether, though it were but for a while, the observation of her own laws; if those principal and mother elements of the world, whereof all things in this lower world are made, should lose the qualities which now they have; if the frame of that heavenly arch erected over our heads should loosen and dissolve itself; if celestial spheres should forget their wonted motions, and by irregular volubility turn themselves any way as it might happen; if the prince of the lights of heaven, which now as a giant doth run his unwearied course [Ps. xix. 5], should as it were through a languishing faintness begin to stand and to rest himself; if the moon should wander from her beaten way, the times and seasons of the year blend themselves by disordered and confused mixture, the winds breathe out their last gasp, the clouds yield no rain, the earth be defeated of heavenly influence, the fruits of the earth pine away as children at the withered breasts of their mother no longer able to yield them relief: what would become of man himself, whom these things now do all serve? See we not plainly that obedience of creatures unto the law of nature is the stay of the whole world?

[3.] Notwithstanding with nature it cometh sometimes to pass as with art. Let Phidias have rude and obstinate stuff to carve, though his art do that it should, his work will lack that beauty which otherwise in fitter matter it might have had. He that striketh an instrument with skill may cause notwithstanding a very unpleasant sound, if the string whereon he striketh chance to be uncapable of harmony. In the matter whereof things natural consist, that of Theophrastus taketh place: "Much of it is oftentimes such as will by no means yield to receive that impression which were best and most perfect." Which defect in the matter of things natural, they who gave themselves unto the contemplation of nature amongst the heathen observed often: but the true original cause thereof, divine malediction, laid for the sin of man upon these creatures which God had made for the use of man, this being an article of that saving truth which God hath revealed unto his Church, was above the reach of their merely natural capacity and understanding. But howsoever these swervings are now and then incident into the course of nature, nevertheless so constantly the laws of nature are by natural agents observed, that no man denieth but those things which nature worketh are wrought, either always or for the most part, after one and the same manner.

[4.] If here it be demanded what that is which keepeth nature in obedience to her own law, we must have recourse to that higher law whereof we have already spoken, and because all other laws do thereon depend, from thence we must borrow so much as shall need for brief resolution in this point. Although we are not of opinion therefore, as some are, that nature in working hath before her certain exemplary draughts or patterns, which subsisting in the bosom of the Highest, and being thence discovered, she fixeth her eye upon them, as travellers by sea upon the pole-star of the world, and that according thereunto she guideth her hand to work by imitation: although we rather embrace the oracle of Hippocrates, that "each thing both in small and in great fulfilleth the task which destiny hath set down;" and concerning the manner of executing and fulfilling the same, "what they do they know not, yet is it in show and appearance as though they did know what they do; and the truth is they do not discern the things which they look on:" nevertheless, forasmuch as the works of nature are no less exact, than if she did both behold and study how to express some absolute shape or mirror always present before her; yea, such her dexterity and skill appeareth, that no intellectual creature in the world were able by capacity to do that which nature doth without capacity and knowledge; it cannot be but nature hath some director of infinite knowledge to guide her in all her ways. Who the guide of nature, but only the God of nature? "In him we live, move, and are." [Acts xvii. 28] Those things which nature is said to do, are by divine art performed, using nature as an instrument; nor is there any such art or knowledge divine in nature herself working, but in the Guide of nature's work.

Whereas therefore things natural which are not in the number of voluntary agents, (for of such only we now speak, and of no other,) do so necessarily observe their certain laws, that as long as they keep those forms*

* Form in other creatures is a thing proportionable unto the soul in living creatures. Sensible it is not, nor otherwise discernible than only by effects. According to the diversity of inward forms, things of the world are distinguished into their kinds.

which give them their being, they cannot possibly be apt or inclinable to do otherwise than they do; seeing the kinds of their operations are both constantly and exactly framed according to the several ends for which they serve, they themselves in the meanwhile, though doing that which is fit, yet knowing neither what they do, nor why: it followeth that all which they do in this sort proceedeth originally from some such agent, as knoweth, appointeth, holdeth up, and even actually frameth the same.

The manner of this divine efficiency, being far above us, we are no more able to conceive by our reason than creatures unreasonable by their sense are able to apprehend after what manner we dispose and order the course of our affairs. Only thus much is discerned, that the natural generation and process of all things receiveth order of proceeding from the settled stability of divine understanding. This appointeth unto them their kinds of working; the disposition whereof in the purity of God's own knowledge and will is rightly termed by the name of *Providence*. The same being referred unto the things themselves here disposed by it, was wont by the ancient to be called *natural Destiny*. That law, the performance whereof we behold in things natural, is as it were an authentical or an original draught written in the bosom of God himself; whose Spirit being to execute the same useth every particular nature, every mere natural agent, only as an instrument created at the beginning, and ever since the beginning used, to work his own will and pleasure withal. Nature therefore is nothing else but God's instrument: in the course whereof Dionysius perceiving some sudden disturbance is said to have cried out, "either God doth suffer impediment, and is by a greater than himself hindered; or if that be impossible, then hath he determined to make a present dissolution of the world; the execution of that law beginning now to stand still, without which the world cannot stand."

This workman, whose servitor nature is, being in truth but only one, the heathens imagining to be more, gave him in the sky the name of Jupiter, in the air the name of Juno, in the water the name of Neptune, in the earth the name of Vesta and sometimes of Ceres, the name of Apollo in the sun, in the moon the name of Diana, the name of Æolus and divers other in the winds; and to conclude, even so many guides of nature they dreamed of, as they saw there were kinds of things natural in the world. These they honoured, as having power to work or cease accordingly as men deserved of them. But unto us there is one only Guide of all agents natural, and he both the Creator and the Worker of all in all, alone to be blessed, adored and honoured by all for ever.

[5.] That which hitherto hath been spoken concerneth natural agents considered in themselves. But we must further remember also, (which thing to touch in a word shall suffice,) that as in this respect they have their law, which law directeth them in the means whereby they tend to their own perfection: so likewise another law there is, which toucheth them as they are sociable parts united into one body; a law which bindeth them each to serve unto other's good, and all to prefer the good of the whole before whatsoever their own particular; as we plainly see they do, when things natural in that regard forget their ordinary natural wont; that which is heavy mounting sometime upwards of its own accord, and forsaking the centre of the earth which to itself is most natural, even as if it did hear itself commanded to let go the good it privately wisheth, and to relieve the present distress of nature in common.

Chapter 4

THE LAW WHICH ANGELS DO WORK BY

But now that we may lift up our eyes (as it were) from the footstool to the throne of God, and leaving these natural, consider a little the state of heavenly and divine creatures: touching Angels, which are spirits [Ps. civ. 4; Heb. i. 7; Ephes. iii. 10] immaterial and intellectual, the glorious inhabitants of those sacred palaces, where nothing but light and blessed immortality, no shadow of matter for tears, discontentments, griefs, and uncomfortable passions to work upon, but all joy, tranquillity, and peace, even for ever and ever doth dwell: as in number and order they are huge, mighty, and royal armies [Dan. vii. 10; Matt. xxvi. 53; Heb. xii. 22; Luke ii. 13], so likewise in perfection of obedience unto that law, which the Highest, whom they adore, love, and imitate, hath imposed upon them, such observants they are thereof, that our Saviour himself being to set down the perfect *idea* of that which we are to pray and wish for on earth, did not teach to pray or wish for more than only that here it might be with us, as with them it is in heaven [Matt. vi. 10]. God which moveth mere natural agents as an efficient only, doth otherwise move intellectual creatures, and especially his holy angels: for beholding the face of God [Matt. xviii. 10], in admiration of so great excellency they all adore him; and being rapt with the love of his beauty, they cleave inseparably for ever unto him. Desire to resemble him in goodness maketh them unweariable and even unsatiable in their longing to do by all means all manner good unto all the creatures of God, but especially unto the children of men [Ps. xci. 11, 12; Luke xv. 7; Heb. i. 14; Acts x. 3]: in the countenance of whose nature, looking downward, they behold themselves beneath themselves; even as upward, in God, beneath whom themselves are, they see that character which is no where but in themselves and us resembled. Thus far even the paynims have approached; thus far they have seen into the doings of the angels of God; Orpheus confessing, that "the fiery throne of God is attended on by those most industrious angels, careful how all things are performed amongst men"; and the Mirror of human wisdom plainly teaching, that God moveth angels, even as that thing doth stir man's heart, which is thereunto presented amiable. Angelical actions may therefore be reduced unto these three general kinds: first, most delectable love arising from the visible apprehension of the purity, glory, and beauty of God, invisible saving only unto spirits that are pure [Job xxxviii. 7; Matt. xviii. 10]; secondly, adoration grounded upon the evidence of the greatness of God, on whom they see how all things depend [Ps. cxlviii. 2; Heb. i. 6; Isa. vi. 3]; thirdly, imitation*, bred by the presence of his exemplary goodness, who ceaseth not before them daily to fill heaven and earth with the rich treasures of most free and undeserved grace.

[2.] Of angels, we are not to consider only what they are and do in regard of their own being, but that also which concerneth them as they are linked into a kind of corporation amongst themselves, and of society or fellowship with men. Consider angels each of them severally in himself, and their law is that which the prophet David mentioneth, "All ye his angels praise him." [Ps. cxlviii. 2] Consider the angels of God associated, and their law is that which disposeth them as an army, one in order and degree above another [Luke ii. 13; Matt. xxvi. 53]. Consider finally the angels as having with us that communion which the apostle to the Hebrews noteth, and in regard whereof angels have not disdained to profess themselves our "fellow-servants;" from hence there springeth up a third law, which bindeth them to works of ministerial employment [Heb. xii. 22; Apoc. xxii. 9]. Every of which their several functions are by them performed with joy.

[3.] A part of the angels of God notwithstanding (we know) have fallen [2 Pet. ii. 4; Jude 6], and that their fall hath been through the voluntary breach of that law, which did require at their hands continuance in the exercise of their high and admirable virtue. Impossible it was that ever their will should change or incline to remit any part of their duty, without some object having force to avert their conceit from God, and to draw it another way; and that before they attained that high perfection of bliss, wherein now the elect angels are without possibility of falling. Of any thing more than of God they could not by any means like, as long as whatsoever they knew besides God they apprehended it not in itself without dependency upon God; because so long God must needs seem infinitely better than any thing which they so could apprehend. Things beneath them could not in such sort be presented unto their eyes, but that therein they must needs see always how those things did depend on God. It seemeth therefore that there was no other way for angels to sin, but by reflex of their understanding upon themselves; when being held with admiration of

* This is intimated wheresoever we find them termed "the sons of God," as Job i. 6, and xxxviii. 7.

their own sublimity and honour, the memory of their subordination unto God and their dependency on him was drowned in this conceit; whereupon their adoration, love, and imitation of God could not choose but be also interrupted. The fall of angels therefore was pride. Since their fall, their practices have been the clean contrary unto those before mentioned [John viii. 44; 1 Pet. v. 8]. For being dispersed, some in the air, some on the earth, some in the water, some among the minerals, dens, and caves, that are under the earth; they have by all means laboured to effect an universal rebellion against the laws, and as far as in them lieth utter destruction of the works of God. These wicked spirits the heathens honoured instead of gods, both generally under the name of *Dii inferi*, "gods infernal;" and particularly, some in oracles, some in idols, some as household gods, some as nymphs: in a word, no foul and wicked spirit which was not one way or other honoured of men as God, till such time as light appeared in the world and dissolved the works of the devil. Thus much therefore may suffice for angels, the next unto whom in degree are men.

Chapter 5

THE LAW WHEREBY MAN IS IN HIS ACTIONS DIRECTED TO THE IMITATION OF GOD

God alone excepted, who actually and everlastingly is whatsoever he may be, and which cannot hereafter be that which now he is not; all other things besides are somewhat in possibility, which as yet they are not in act. And for this cause there is in all things an appetite or desire, whereby they incline to something which they may be; and when they are it, they shall be perfecter than now they are. All which perfections are contained under the general name of *Goodness*. And because there is not in the world any thing whereby another may not some way be made the perfecter, therefore all things that are, are good.

[2.] Again, sith there can be no goodness desired which proceedeth not from God himself, as from the supreme cause of all things; and every effect doth after a sort contain, at leastwise resemble, the cause from which it proceedeth: all things in the world are said in some sort to seek the highest, and to covet more or less the participation of God himself. Yet this doth no where so much appear as it doth in man, because there are so many kinds of perfections which man seeketh. The first degree of goodness is that general perfection which all things do seek, in desiring the continuance of their being. All things therefore coveting as much as may be to be like unto God in being ever, that which cannot hereunto attain personally doth seek to continue itself another way, that is by offspring and propagation. The next degree of goodness is that which each thing coveteth by affecting resemblance with God in the constancy and excellency of those operations which belong unto their kind. The immutability of God they strive unto, by working either always or for the most part after one and the same manner; his absolute exactness they imitate, by tending unto that which is most exquisite in every particular. Hence have risen a number of axioms in philosophy, showing how "the works of nature do always aim at that which cannot be bettered."

[3.] These two kinds of goodness rehearsed are so nearly united to the things themselves which desire them, that we scarcely perceive the appetite to stir in reaching forth her hand towards them. But the desire of those perfections which grow externally is more apparent; especially of such as are not expressly desired unless they be first known, or such as are not for any other cause than for knowledge itself desired. Concerning perfections in this kind, that by proceeding in the knowledge of truth, and by growing in the exercise of virtue, man amongst the creatures of this inferior world aspireth to the greatest conformity with God, this is not only known unto us, whom he himself hath so instructed [Matt. v. 48; Sap. vii. 27], but even they do acknowledge, who amongst men are not judged the nearest unto him. With Plato what one thing more usual, than to excite men unto the love of wisdom, by shewing how much wise men are thereby exalted above men; how knowledge doth raise them up into heaven; how it maketh them, though not gods, yet as gods, high, admirable, and divine? And Mercurius Trismegistus speaking of the virtues of a righteous soul, "Such spirits" (saith he) "are never cloyed with praising and speaking well of all men, with doing good unto every one by word and deed, because they study to frame themselves according to THE PATTERN of the Father of spirits."

Chapter 6

MEN'S FIRST BEGINNING TO GROW TO THE KNOWLEDGE OF THAT LAW WHICH THEY ARE TO OBSERVE

In the matter of knowledge, there is between the angels of God and the children of men this difference: angels already have full and complete knowledge in the highest degree that can be imparted unto them; men, if we view them in their spring, are at the first without understanding or knowledge at all [see Isa. vii. 16]. Nevertheless from this utter vacuity they grow by degrees, till they come at length to be even as the angels themselves are. That which agreeth to the one now, the other shall attain unto in the end; they are not so far disjoined and severed, but that they come at length to meet. The soul of man being therefore at the first as a book, wherein nothing is and yet all things may be imprinted; we are to search by what steps and degrees it riseth unto perfection of knowledge.

[2.] Unto that which hath been already set down concerning natural agents this we must add, that albeit therein we have comprised as well creatures living as void of life, if they be in degree of nature beneath men; nevertheless a difference we must observe between those natural agents that work altogether unwittingly, and those which have, though weak, yet some understanding what they do, as fishes, fowls, and beasts have. Beasts are in sensible capacity as ripe even as men themselves, perhaps more ripe. For as stones, though in dignity of nature inferior unto plants, yet exceed them in firmness of strength or durability of being; and plants, though beneath the excellency of creatures endued with sense, yet exceed them in the faculty of vegetation and of fertility: so beasts, though otherwise behind men, may notwithstanding in actions of sense and fancy go beyond them; because the endeavours of nature, when it hath a higher perfection to seek, are in lower the more remiss, not esteeming thereof so much as those things do, which have no better proposed unto them.

[3.] The soul of man therefore being capable of a more divine perfection, hath (besides the faculties of growing unto sensible knowledge which is common unto us with beasts) a further ability, whereof in them there is no show at all, the ability of reaching higher than unto sensible things. Till we grow to some ripeness of years, the soul of man doth only store itself with conceits of things of inferior and more open quality, which afterwards do serve as instruments unto that which is greater; in the meanwhile above the reach of meaner creatures it ascendeth not. When once it comprehendeth any thing above this, as the differences of time, affirmations, negations, and contradictions in speech, we then count it to have some use of natural reason. Whereunto if afterwards there might be added the right helps of true art and learning (which helps, I must plainly confess, this age of the world, carrying the name of a learned age, doth neither much know nor greatly regard), there would undoubtedly be almost as great difference in maturity of judgment between men therewith inured, and that which now men are, as between men that are now and innocents. Which speech if any condemn, as being over hyperbolical, let them consider but this one thing. No art is at the first finding out so perfect as industry may after make it. Yet the very first man that to any purpose knew the way we speak of [Aristotelical Demonstration] and followed it, hath alone thereby performed more very near in all parts of natural knowledge, than sithence in any one part thereof the whole world besides hath done.

[4.] In the poverty of that other new devised aid [Ramistry] two things there are notwithstanding singular. Of marvellous quick despatch it is, and doth shew them that have it as much almost in three days, as if it dwell threescore years with them. Again, because the curiosity of man's wit doth many times with peril wade farther in the search of things than were convenient; the same is thereby restrained unto such generalities as every where offering themselves are apparent unto men of the weakest conceit that need be. So as following the rules and precepts thereof, we may define it to be, an Art which teacheth the way of speedy discourse, and restraineth the mind of man that it may not wax over-wise.

[5.] Education and instruction are the means, the one by use, the other by precept, to make our natural faculty of reason both the better and the sooner able to judge rightly between truth and error, good and evil. But at what time a man may be said to have attained so far forth the use of reason, as sufficeth to make him capable of those Laws, whereby he is then bound to guide his actions; this is a great deal more easy for common sense to discern, than for any man by skill and learning to determine; even as it is not in philosophers, who best know the nature both of fire and of gold, to teach what degree of the one will serve to purify the other, so well as the artisan, who doth this by fire, discerneth by sense when the fire hath that degree of heat which sufficeth for his purpose.

Chapter 7

OF MAN'S WILL, WHICH IS THE THING THAT LAWS OF ACTION ARE MADE TO GUIDE

By reason man attaineth unto the knowledge of things that are and are not sensible. It resteth therefore that we search how man attaineth unto the knowledge of such things unsensible as are to be known that they may be done. Seeing then that nothing can move unless there be some end, the desire whereof provoketh unto motion; how should that divine power of the soul, that "spirit of our mind," [Eph. iv. 23] as the apostle termeth it, ever stir itself unto action, unless it have also the like spur? The end for which we are moved to work, is sometimes the goodness which we conceive of the very working itself, without any further respect at all; and the cause that procureth action is the mere desire of action, no other good besides being thereby intended. Of certain turbulent wits it is said, "Illis quieta movere magna merces videbatur:" they thought the very disturbance of things established an hire sufficient to set them on work [Sallust]. Sometimes that which we do is referred to a further end, without the desire whereof we would leave the same undone; as in their actions that gave alms to purchase thereby the praise of men [Matt. vi. 2].

[2.] Man in perfection of nature being made according to the likeness of his Maker resembleth him also in the manner of working: so that whatsoever we work as men, the same we do wittingly work and freely; neither are we according to the manner of natural agents any way so tied, but that it is in our power to leave the things we do undone. The good which either is gotten by doing, or which consisteth in the very doing itself, causeth not action, unless apprehending it as good we so like and desire it: that we do unto any such end, the same we choose and prefer before the leaving of it undone. Choice there is not, unless the thing which we take be so in our power that we might have refused and left it. If fire consume the stubble, it chooseth not so to do, because the nature thereof is such that it can do no other. To choose is to will one thing before another. And to will is to bend our souls to the having or doing of that which they see to be good. Goodness is seen with the eye of the understanding. And the light of that eye, is reason. So that two principal fountains there are of human action, *Knowledge* and *Will*; which Will, in things tending towards any end, is termed *Choice*. Concerning Knowledge, "Behold, (saith Moses,) I have set before you this day good and evil, life and death." [Deut. xxx. 19] Concerning Will, he addeth immediately, "Choose life;" that is to say, the things that tend unto life, them choose.

[3.] But of one thing we must have special care, as being a matter of no small moment; and that is, how the Will, properly and strictly taken, as it is of things which are referred unto the end that man desireth, differeth greatly from that inferior natural desire which we call Appetite. The object of Appetite is whatsoever sensible good may be wished for; the object of Will is that good which Reason doth lead us to seek. Affections, as joy, and grief, and fear, and anger, with such like, being as it were the sundry fashions and forms of Appetite, can neither rise at the conceit of a thing indifferent, nor yet choose but rise at the sight of some things. Wherefore it is not altogether in our power, whether we will be stirred with affections or no: whereas actions which issue from the disposition of the Will are in the power thereof to be performed or stayed. Finally, Appetite is the Will's solicitor, and the Will is Appetite's controller; what we covet according to the one, by the other we often reject; neither is any other desire termed properly Will, but that where Reason and Understanding, or the show of Reason, prescribeth the thing desired.

It may be therefore a question, whether those operations of men are to be counted voluntary, wherein that good which is sensible provoketh Appetite, and Appetite causeth action, Reason being never called to counsel; as when we eat or drink, or betake ourselves unto rest, and such like. The truth is, that such actions in men having attained to the use of Reason are voluntary. For as the authority of higher powers hath force even in those things, which are done without their privity, and are of so mean reckoning that to acquaint them therewith it needeth not; in like sort, voluntarily we are said to do that also, which the Will if it listed might hinder from being done, although about the doing thereof we do not expressly use our reason or understanding, and so immediately apply our wills thereunto. In cases therefore of such facility, the Will doth yield her assent as it were with a kind of silence, by not dissenting; in which respect her force is not so apparent as in express mandates or prohibitions, especially upon advice and consultation going before.

[4.] Where understanding therefore needeth, in those things Reason is the director of man's Will by discovering in action what is good. For the Laws of well-doing are the dictates of right Reason. Children, which are not as yet come unto those years whereat they may have; again, innocents, which are excluded by natural defect from ever having; thirdly, madmen, which for the present cannot possibly have the use of right Reason to guide themselves, have for their guide the Reason that guideth other men, which are tutors over them to seek and to procure their good for them. In the rest there is that light of Reason, whereby good may be known from evil, and which discovering the same rightly is termed right.

[5.] The Will notwithstanding doth not incline to have or do that which Reason teacheth to be good, unless the same do also teach it to be possible. For albeit the Appetite, being more general, may wish any thing which seemeth good, be it never so impossible; yet for such things the reasonable Will of man doth never seek. Let Reason teach impossibility in any thing, and the Will of man doth let it go; a thing impossible it doth not affect, the impossibility thereof being manifest.

[6.] There is in the Will of man naturally that freedom, whereby it is apt to take or refuse any particular object whatsoever being presented unto it. Whereupon it followeth, that there is no particular object so good, but it may have the shew of some difficulty or unpleasant quality annexed to it, in respect whereof the Will may shrink and decline it; contrariwise (for so things are blended) there is no particular evil which hath not some appearance of goodness whereby to insinuate itself. For evil as evil cannot be desired: if that be desired which is evil, the cause is the goodness which is or seemeth to be joined with it. Goodness doth not move by being, but by being apparent; and therefore many things are neglected which are most precious, only because the value of them lieth hid. Sensible Goodness is most apparent, near, and present; which causeth the Appetite to be therewith strongly provoked. Now pursuit and refusal in the Will do follow, the one the affirmation the other the negation of goodness, which the understanding apprehendeth, grounding itself upon sense, unless some higher Reason do chance to teach the contrary. And if Reason have taught it rightly to be good, yet not so apparently that the mind receiveth it with utter impossibility of being otherwise, still there is place left for the Will to take or leave. Whereas therefore amongst so many things as are to be done, there are so few, the goodness whereof Reason in such sort doth or easily can discover, we are not to marvel at the choice of evil, even then when the contrary is probably known. Hereby it cometh to pass that custom inuring the mind by long practice, and so leaving there a sensible impression, prevaileth more than reasonable persuasion what way soever. Reason therefore may rightly discern the thing which is good, and yet the Will of man not incline itself thereunto, as oft as the prejudice of sensible experience doth oversway.

[7.] Nor let any man think that this doth make any thing for the just excuse of iniquity. For there was never sin committed, wherein a less good was not preferred before a greater, and that wilfully; which cannot be done without the singular disgrace of Nature, and the utter disturbance of that divine order, whereby the preeminence of chiefest acceptation is by the best things worthily challenged. There is not that good which concerneth us, but it hath evidence enough for itself, if Reason were diligent to search it out. Through neglect thereof, abused we are with the show of that which is not; sometimes the subtilty of Satan inveigling us as it did Eve [2 Cor. xi. 3], sometimes the hastiness of our Wills preventing the more considerate advice of sound Reason, as in the Apostles [Luke ix. 54], when they no sooner saw what they liked not, but they forthwith were desirous of fire from heaven; sometimes the very custom of evil making the heart obdurate against whatsoever instructions to the contrary, as in them over whom our Saviour spake weeping, "O Jerusalem, how often, and thou wouldest not!" [Matt. xxiii. 37] Still therefore that wherewith we stand blameable, and can no way excuse it, is, In doing evil, we prefer a less good before a greater, the greatness whereof is by reason investigable and may be known. The search of knowledge is a thing painful; and the painfulness of knowledge is that which maketh the Will so hardly inclinable thereunto. The root hereof, divine malediction; whereby the instruments* being weakened wherewithal the soul (especially in reasoning) doth work, it preferreth rest in ignorance before wearisome labour to know. For a spur of diligence therefore we have a natural thirst after knowledge ingrafted in us. But by reason of that original weakness in the instruments, without which the understanding part is not able in this world by discourse to work, the very conceit of painfulness is as a bridle to stay us. For which cause the Apostle, who knew right well that the weariness of the flesh is an heavy clog to the Will, striketh mightily upon this key, "Awake thou that sleepest; Cast off all which presseth down; Watch; Labour; Strive to go forward, and to grow in knowledge" [Eph. v. 14; Heb. xii. 1, 12; 1 Cor. xvi. 13; Prov. ii. 4; Luke xiii. 24].

Neo Platonic

* "A corruptible body is heavy unto the soul, and the earthly mansion keepeth down the mind that is full of cares. And hardly can we discern the things that are upon earth, and with great labour find we out the things which are before us. Who can then seek out the things that are in heaven?" Sap. ix. 15, 16.

Chapter 8

OF THE NATURAL WAY OF FINDING OUT LAWS BY REASON TO GUIDE THE WILL UNTO THAT WHICH IS GOOD

Wherefore to return to our former intent of discovering the natural way, whereby rules have been found out concerning that goodness wherewith the Will of man ought to be moved in human actions; as every thing naturally and necessarily doth desire the utmost good and greatest perfection whereof Nature hath made it capable, even so man. Our felicity therefore being the object and accomplishment of our desire, we cannot choose but wish and covet it. All particular things which are subject unto action, the Will doth so far forth incline unto, as Reason judgeth them the better for us, and consequently the more available to our bliss. If Reason err, we fall into evil, and are so far forth deprived of the general perfection we seek. Seeing therefore that for the framing of men's actions the knowledge of good from evil is necessary, it only resteth that we search how this may be had. Neither must we suppose that there needeth one rule to know the good and another the evil by. For he that knoweth what is straight doth even thereby discern what is crooked, because the absence of straightness in bodies capable thereof is crookedness. Goodness in actions is like unto straightness; wherefore that which is done well we term *right*. For as the straight way is most acceptable to him that travelleth, because by it he cometh soonest to his journey's end; so in action, that which doth lie the evenest between us and the end we desire must needs be the fittest for our use. Besides which fitness for use, there is also in rectitude, beauty; as contrariwise in obliquity, deformity. And that which is good in the actions of men, doth not only delight as profitable, but as amiable also. In which consideration the Grecians most divinely have given to the active perfection of men a name expressing both beauty and goodness [Καλοκἀγαθία] because goodness in ordinary speech is for the most part applied only to that which is beneficial. But we in the name of goodness do here imply both.

[2.] And of discerning goodness there are but these two ways; the one the knowledge of the causes whereby it is made such; the other the observation of those signs and tokens, which being annexed always unto goodness argue that where they are found, there also goodness is, although we know not the cause by force whereof it is there. The former of these is the most sure and infallible way, but so hard that all shun it, and had rather walk as men do in the dark by haphazard, than tread so long and intricate mazes for knowledge' sake. As therefore physicians are many times forced to leave such methods of curing as themselves know to be the fittest, and being overruled by their patients' impatiency are fain to try the best they can, in taking that way of cure which the cured will yield unto; in like sort, considering how the case doth stand with this present age full of tongue and weak of brain, behold we yield to the stream thereof; into the causes of goodness we will not make any curious or deep inquiry; to touch them now and then it shall be sufficient, when they are so near at hand that easily they may be conceived without any far-removed discourse: that way we are contented to prove, which being the worse in itself, is notwithstanding now by reason of common imbecility the fitter and likelier to be brooked.

[3.] Signs and tokens to know good by are of sundry kinds; some more certain and some less. The most certain token of evident goodness is, if the general persuasion of all men do so account it. And therefore a common received error is never utterly overthrown, till such time as we go from signs unto causes, and shew some manifest root or fountain thereof common unto all, whereby it may clearly appear how it hath come to pass that so many have been overseen. In which case surmises and slight probabilities will not serve, because the universal consent of men is the perfectest and strongest in this kind, which comprehendeth only the signs and tokens of goodness. Things casual do vary, and that which a man doth but chance to think well of cannot still have the like hap. Wherefore although we know not the cause, yet thus much we may know; that some necessary cause there is, whensoever the judgments of all men generally or for the most part run one and the same way, especially in matters of natural discourse. For of things necessarily and naturally done there is no more affirmed but this, "They keep either always or for the most part one tenure." The general and perpetual voice of men is as the sentence of God himself. For that which all men have at all times learned, Nature herself must needs have taught; and God being the author of Nature, her voice is but his instrument. By her from Him we receive whatsoever in such sort we learn. Infinite duties there are, the goodness whereof is by this rule sufficiently manifested, although we had no other warrant besides to approve them. The Apostle St. Paul having speech concerning the heathen saith of them, "They are a law unto themselves". [Rom. ii. 14] His meaning is, that by force of the light of Reason, wherewith God illuminateth every one which cometh into the world, men being enabled to know truth from falsehood, and good from evil, do thereby learn in many things what the will of God is; which will himself not revealing by any extraordinary means unto them, but they by natural discourse attaining the knowledge thereof, seem the makers of those Laws which indeed are his, and they but only the finders of them out.

[4.] A law therefore generally taken, is a directive rule unto goodness of operation. The rule of divine operations outward, is the definitive appointment of God's own wisdom set down within himself. The rule of natural agents that work by simple necessity, is the determination of the wisdom of God, known to God himself the principal director of them, but not unto them that are directed to execute the same. The rule of natural agents which work after a sort of their own accord, as the beasts do, is the judgment of common sense or fancy concerning the sensible goodness of those objects wherewith they are moved. The rule of ghostly or immaterial natures, as spirits and angels, is their intuitive intellectual judgment concerning the amiable beauty and high goodness of that object, which with unspeakable joy and delight doth set them on work. The rule of voluntary agents on earth is the sentence that Reason giveth concerning the goodness of those things which they are to do. And the sentences which Reason giveth are some more some less general, before it come to define in particular actions what is good.

[5.] The main principles of Reason are in themselves apparent. For to make nothing evident of itself unto man's understanding were to take away all possibility of knowing anything. And herein that of Theophrastus is true, "They that seek a reason of all things do utterly overthrow Reason." In every kind of knowledge some such grounds there are, as that being proposed the mind doth presently embrace them as free from all possibility of error, clear and manifest without proof. In which kind axioms or principles more general are such as this, "that the greater good is to be chosen before the less." If therefore it should be demanded what reason there is, why the Will of Man, which doth necessarily shun harm and covet whatsoever is pleasant and sweet, should be commanded to count the pleasures of sin gall, and notwithstanding the bitter accidents wherewith virtuous actions are compassed, yet still to rejoice and delight in them: surely this could never stand with Reason, but that wisdom thus prescribing groundeth her laws upon an infallible rule of comparison, which is, "That small difficulties, when exceeding great good is sure to ensue, and on the other side momentary benefits, when the hurt which they draw after them is unspeakable, are not at all to be respected." This rule is the ground whereupon the wisdom of the Apostle buildeth a law, enjoining patience unto himself: "The present lightness of our affliction worketh unto us even with abundance upon abundance an eternal weight of glory; while we look not on the things which are seen, but on the things which are not seen: for the things which are seen are temporal, but the things which are not seen are eternal" [2 Cor. iv. 17]: therefore Christianity to be embraced, whatsoever calamities in those times it was accompanied withal. Upon the same ground our Saviour proveth the law most reasonable, that doth forbid those crimes which men for gain's sake fall into. "For a man to win the world if it be with the loss of his soul, what benefit or good is it?" [Matt. xvi. 26] Axioms less general, yet so manifest that they need no further proof, are such as these, "God to be worshipped;" "parents to be honoured;" others to be used by us as we ourselves would by them." Such things, as soon as they are alleged, all men acknowledge to be good; they require no proof or further discourse to be assured of their goodness.

Notwithstanding whatsoever such principle there is, it was at the first found out by discourse, and drawn from out of the very bowels of heaven and earth. For we are to note, that things in the world are to us discernible, not only so far forth as serveth for our vital preservation, but further also in a twofold higher respect. For first, if all other uses were utterly taken away, yet the mind of man being by nature speculative and delighted with contemplation in itself, they were to be known even for mere knowledge and understanding's sake. Yea further, besides this, the knowledge of every the least thing in the whole world hath in it a second peculiar benefit unto us, inasmuch as it serveth to minister rules, canons, and laws, for men to direct those actions by, which we properly term human. This did the very heathens themselves obscurely insinuate, by making *Themis*, which we call *Jus*, or Right, to be the daughter of heaven and earth.

[6.] We know things either as they are in themselves, or as they are in mutual relation one to another. The knowledge of that which man is in reference unto himself, and other things in relation unto man, I may justly term the mother of all those principles, which are as it were edicts, statutes, and decrees, in that Law of Nature, whereby human actions are framed. First, therefore, having observed that the best things, where they are not hindered, do still produce the best operations, (for which cause, where many things are to concur unto one effect, the best is in all congruity of reason to guide the residue, that it prevailing most, the work principally done by it may have greatest perfection): when hereupon we come to observe in ourselves, of what excellency our souls are in comparison of our bodies, and the diviner part in relation unto the baser of our souls; seeing that all these concur in producing human actions, it cannot be well unless the chiefest do command and direct the rest. The soul then ought to conduct the body, and the spirit of our minds the soul. This is therefore the first Law, whereby the highest power of the mind requireth general obedience at the hands of all the rest concurring with it unto action.

[7.] Touching the several grand mandates, which being imposed by the understanding faculty of the mind must be obeyed by the Will of Man, they are by the same method found out, whether they import our duty towards God or towards man.

Touching the one, I may not here stand to open, by what degrees of discourse the minds even of mere natural men have attained to know, not only that there is a God, but also what power, force, wisdom, and other properties that God hath, and how all things depend on him. This being therefore presupposed, from that known relation which God hath unto us as unto children, and unto all good things as unto effects whereof himself is the principal cause, these axioms and laws natural concerning our duty have arisen, "that in all things we go about his aid is by prayer to be craved:" "that he cannot have sufficient honour done unto him, but the utmost of that we can do to honour him we must;" which is in effect the same that we read, "Thou shalt love the Lord thy God with all thy heart, with all thy soul, and with all thy mind:" [Deut. vi. 5] which Law our Saviour doth term "The first and the great commandment" [Matt. xxii. 38].

Touching the next, which as our Saviour addeth is "like unto this," (he meaneth in amplitude and largeness, inasmuch as it is the root out of which all Laws of duty to men-ward have grown, as out of the former all offices of religion towards God,) the like natural inducement hath brought men to know that it is their duty no less to love others than themselves. For seeing those things which are equal must needs all have one measure; if I cannot but wish to receive all good, even as much at every man's hand as any man can wish unto his own soul, how should I look to have any part of my desire herein satisfied, unless myself be careful to satisfy the like desire which is undoubtedly in other men, we all being of one and the same nature? To have any thing offered them repugnant to this desire must needs in all respects grieve them as much as me: so that if I do harm I must look to suffer; there being no reason that others should shew greater measure of love to me than they have by me shewed unto them. My desire therefore to be loved of my equals in nature as much as possible may be, imposeth upon me a natural duty of bearing to themward fully the like affection. From which relation of equality between ourselves and them that are as ourselves, what several rules and canons natural Reason hath drawn for direction of life no man is ignorant; as namely, "That because we would take no harm, we must therefore do none;" "That sith we would not be in any thing extremely dealt with, we must ourselves avoid all extremity in our dealings;" "That from all violence and wrong we are utterly to abstain;" with such like; which further to wade in would be tedious, and to our present purpose not altogether so necessary, seeing that on these two general heads already mentioned all other specialities are dependent.*

[8.] Wherefore the natural measure whereby to judge our doings, is the sentence of Reason, determining and setting down what is good to be done. Which sentence is either mandatory, shewing what must be done; or else permissive, declaring only what may be done; or thirdly admonitory, opening what is the most convenient for us to do. The first taketh place, where the comparison doth stand altogether between doing and not doing of one thing which in itself is absolutely good or evil; as it had been for Joseph to yield or not to yield to the impotent desire of his lewd mistress, the one evil the other good simply [Gen. xxxix. 9]. The second is, when of divers things evil, all being not evitable, we are permitted to take one;

* "On these two commandments hangeth the whole Law." Matt. xxii. 40.

which one saving only in case of so great urgency were not otherwise to be taken; as in the matter of divorce amongst the Jews [Mark x. 4]. The last, when of divers things good, one is principal and most eminent; as in their act who sold their possessions and laid the price at the Apostles' feet [Acts iv. 37; v. 4]; which possessions they might have retained unto themselves without sin: again, in the Apostle St. Paul's own choice [2 Thess. iii. 8] to maintain himself by his own labour; whereas in living by the Church's maintenance, as others did, there had been no offence committed. In Goodness therefore there is a latitude or extent, whereby it cometh to pass that even of good actions some are better than other some; whereas otherwise one man could not excel another, but all should be either absolutely good, as hitting jump that indivisible point or centre wherein goodness consisteth; or else missing it they should be excluded out of the number of well-doers. Degrees of well-doing there could be none, except perhaps in the seldomness and oftenness of doing well. But the nature of Goodness being thus ample, a Law is properly that which Reason in such sort defineth to be good that it must be done. And the Law of Reason or human Nature is that which men by discourse of natural Reason have rightly found out themselves to be all for ever bound unto in their actions.

[9.] Laws of Reason have these marks to be known by. Such as keep them resemble most lively in their voluntary actions that very manner of working which Nature herself doth necessarily observe in the course of the whole world. The works of Nature are all behoveful, beautiful, without superfluity or defect; even so theirs, if they be framed according to that which the Law of Reason teacheth. Secondly, those Laws are investigable by Reason, without the help of Revelation supernatural and divine. Finally, in such sort they are investigable, that the knowledge of them is general, the world hath always been acquainted with them; according to that which one in Sophocles observeth concerning a branch of this Law, "It is no child of to-day's or yesterday's birth, but hath been no man knoweth how long sithence" [*Antigone,* 456]. It is not agreed upon by one, or two, or few, but by all: which we may not so understand, as if every particular man in the whole world did know and confess whatsoever the Law of Reason doth contain; but this Law is such that being proposed no man can reject it as unreasonable and unjust. Again, there is nothing in it but any man (having natural perfection of wit and ripeness of judgment) may by labour and travail find out. And to conclude, the general principles thereof are such, as it is not easy to find men ignorant of them. Law rational therefore, which men commonly use to call the Law of Nature, meaning thereby the Law which human Nature knoweth itself in reason universally bound unto, which also for that cause may be termed most fitly the Law of Reason; this Law, I say, comprehendeth all those things which men by the light of their natural understanding evidently know, or at leastwise may know, to be beseeming or unbeseeming, virtuous or vicious, good or evil for them to do.

[10.] Now although it be true, which some have said, that "whatsoever is done amiss, the Law of Nature and Reason thereby is transgressed," because even those offences which are by their special qualities breaches of supernatural laws, do also, for that they are generally evil, violate in general that principle of Reason, which willeth universally to fly from evil: yet do we not therefore so far extend the Law of Reason, as to contain in it all manner laws whereunto reasonable creatures are bound, but (as hath been shewed) we restrain it to those only duties, which all men by force of natural wit either do or might understand to be such duties as concern all men. "Certain half-waking men there are" (as Saint Augustine noteth), "who neither altogether asleep in folly, nor yet thoroughly awake in the light of true understanding, have thought that there is not at all any thing just and righteous in itself; but look, wherewith nations are inured, the same they take to be right and just. Whereupon their conclusion is, that seeing each sort of people hath a different kind of right from other, and that which is right of its own nature must be everywhere one and the same, therefore in itself there is nothing right. These good folk," saith he, ("that I may not trouble their wits with rehearsal of too many things,) have not looked so far into the world as to perceive that, 'Do as thou wouldest be done unto', is a sentence which all nations under heaven are agreed upon. Refer this sentence to the love of God, and it extinguisheth all heinous crimes; refer it to the love of thy neighbour, and all grievous wrongs it banisheth out of the world." Wherefore as touching the Law of Reason, this was (it seemeth) Saint Augustine's judgment: namely, that there are in it some things which stand as principles universally agreed upon; and that out of those principles, which are in themselves evident, the greatest moral duties we owe towards God or man may without any great difficulty be concluded.

[11.] If then it be here demanded, by what means it should come to pass (the greatest part of the Law moral being so easy for all men to know) that so many thousands of men notwithstanding have been ignorant even of principal moral duties, not imagining the breach of them to be sin: I deny not but lewd and wicked custom, beginning perhaps at the first amongst few, afterwards spreading into greater multitudes, and so continuing from time to time, may be of force even in plain things to smother the light of natural understanding; because men will not bend their wits to examine whether things wherewith they have been accustomed be good or evil. For example's sake, that grosser kind of heathenish idolatry, whereby they worshipped the very works of their own hands, was an absurdity to reason so palpable, that the Prophet David comparing idols and idolaters together maketh almost no odds between them, but the one in a manner as much without wit and sense as the other, "They that make them are like unto them, and so are all that trust in them" [Ps. cxxxv. 18]. That wherein an idolater doth seem so absurd and foolish is by the Wise Man thus exprest, "He is not ashamed to speak unto that which hath no life, he calleth on him that is weak for health, he prayeth for life unto him which is dead, of him which hath no experience he requireth help, for his journey he sueth to him which is not able to go, for gain and work and success in his affairs he seeketh furtherance of him that hath no manner of power" [Wisd. xiii. 17]. The cause of which senseless stupidity is afterwards imputed to custom [Wisd. xiv. 15, 16]. "When a father mourned grievously for his son that was taken away suddenly, he made an image for him that was once dead, whom now he worshippeth as a god, ordaining to his servants ceremonies and sacrifices. Thus by process of time this wicked custom prevailed, and was kept as a law," the authority of rulers, the ambition of craftsmen, and such like means thrusting forward the ignorant, and increasing their superstition.

Unto this which the Wise Man hath spoken somewhat besides may be added. For whatsoever we have hitherto taught, or shall hereafter, concerning the force of man's natural understanding, this we always desire withal to be understood; that there is no kind of faculty or power in man or any other creature, which can rightly perform the functions allotted to it, without perpetual aid and concurrence of that Supreme Cause of all things. The benefit whereof as oft as we cause God in his justice to withdraw, there can no other thing follow than that which the Apostle noteth, even men endued with the light of reason to walk notwithstanding "in the vanity of their mind, having their cogitations darkened, and being strangers from the life of God through the ignorance which is in them, because of the hardness of their hearts" [Ephes. iv. 17, 18]. And this cause is mentioned by the prophet Esay, speaking of the ignorance of idolaters, who see not how the manifest Law of Reason condemneth their gross iniquity and sin. "They have not in them," saith he, "so much wit as to think, 'Shall I bow to the stock of a tree?' All knowledge and understanding is taken from them; for God hath shut their eyes that they cannot see" [Isa. xliv. 18, 19].

That which we say in this case of idolatry serveth for all other things, wherein the like kind of general blindness hath prevailed against the manifest Laws of Reason. Within the compass of which laws we do not only comprehend whatsoever may be easily known to belong to the duty of all men, but even whatsoever may possibly be known to be of that quality, so that the same be by *necessary* consequence deduced out of clear and manifest principles. For if once we descend unto probable collections what is convenient for men, we are then in the territory where free and arbitrary determinations, the territory where Human Laws take place; which laws are after to be considered.

Chapter 9

THE BENEFIT OF KEEPING THAT LAW WHICH REASON TEACHETH

Now the due observation of this Law which Reason teacheth us cannot but be effectual unto their great good that observe the same. For we see the whole world and each part thereof so compacted, that as long as each thing performeth only that work which is natural unto it, it thereby preserveth both other things and also itself. Contrariwise, let any principal thing, as the sun, the moon, any one of the heavens or elements, but once cease or fail, or swerve, and who doth not easily conceive that the sequel thereof would be ruin both to itself and whatsoever dependeth on it? And is it possible, that Man being not only the noblest creature in the world, but even a very world in himself, his transgressing the Law of his Nature should draw no manner of harm after it? Yes, "tribulation and anguish unto every soul that doeth evil". [Rom. ii. 9] Good doth follow unto all things by observing the course of their nature, and on the contrary side evil by not observing it; but not unto natural agents that good which we call *Reward*, not that evil which we properly term *Punishment*. The reason whereof is, because amongst creatures in this world, only Man's observation of the Law of his Nature is *Righteousness*, only Man's transgression *Sin*. And the reason of this is the difference in his manner of observing or transgressing the Law of his Nature. He doth not otherwise than voluntarily the one or the other. What we do against our wills, or constrainedly, we are not properly said to do it, because the motive cause of doing it is not in ourselves, but carrieth us, as if the wind should drive a feather in the air, we no whit furthering that whereby we are driven. In such cases therefore the evil which is done moveth compassion; men are pitied for it, as being rather miserable in such respect than culpable. Some things are likewise done by man, though not through outward force and impulsion, though not against, yet without their wills; as in alienation of mind, or any the like inevitable utter absence of wit and judgment. For which cause, no man did ever think the hurtful actions of furious men and innocents to be punishable. Again, some things we do neither against nor without, and yet not simply and merely with our wills, but with our wills in such sort moved, that albeit there be no impossibility but that we might, nevertheless we are not so easily able to do otherwise. In this consideration one evil deed is made more pardonable than another. Finally, that which we do being evil, is notwithstanding by so much more pardonable, by how much the exigence of so doing or the difficulty of doing otherwise is greater; unless this necessity or difficulty have originally risen from ourselves. It is no excuse therefore unto him, who being drunk committeth incest, and allegeth that his wits were not his own; inasmuch as himself might have chosen whether his wits should by that mean have been taken from him. Now rewards and punishments do always presuppose something willingly done well or ill; without which respect though we may sometimes receive good or harm, yet then the one is only a benefit and not a reward, the other simply an hurt not a punishment. From the sundry dispositions of man's Will, which is the root of all his actions, there groweth variety in the sequel of rewards and punishments, which are by these and the like rules measured: "Take away the will, and all acts are equal: That which we do not, and would do, is commonly accepted as done." By these and the like rules men's actions are determined of and judged, whether they be in their own nature rewardable or punishable.

[2.] Rewards and punishments are not received, but at the hands of such as being above us have power to examine and judge our deeds. How men come to have this authority one over another in external actions, we shall more diligently examine in that which followeth. But for this present, so much all do acknowledge, that sith every man's heart and conscience doth in good or evil, even secretly committed and known to none but itself, either like or disallow itself, and accordingly either rejoice, very nature exulting (as it were) in certain hope of reward, or else grieve (as it were) in a sense of future punishment; neither of which can in this case be looked for from any other, saving only from Him who discerneth and judgeth the very secrets of all hearts: therefore He is the only rewarder and revenger of all such actions; although not of such actions only, but of all whereby the Law of Nature is broken whereof Himself is author. For which cause, the Roman laws, called The Laws of the Twelve Tables, requiring offices of inward affection which the eye of man cannot reach unto, threaten the neglecters of them with none but divine punishment.

Chapter 10

HOW REASON DOTH LEAD MEN UNTO THE MAKING OF HUMAN LAWS WHEREBY POLITIC SOCIETIES ARE GOVERNED; AND TO AGREEMENT ABOUT LAWS WHEREBY THE FELLOWSHIP OR COMMUNION OF INDEPENDENT SOCIETIES STANDETH

That which hitherto we have set down is (I hope) sufficient to shew their brutishness, which imagine that religion and virtue are only as men will account of them; that we might make as much account, if we would, of the contrary, without any harm unto ourselves, and that in nature they are as indifferent one as the other. We see then how nature itself teacheth laws and statutes to live by. The laws which have been hitherto mentioned do bind men absolutely even as they are men, although they have never any settled fellowship, never any solemn agreement amongst themselves what to do or not to do. But forasmuch as we are not by ourselves sufficient to furnish ourselves with competent store of things needful for such a life as our nature doth desire, a life fit for the dignity of man; therefore to supply those defects and imperfections which are in us living single and solely by ourselves, we are naturally induced to seek communion and fellowship with others. This was the cause of men's uniting themselves at the first in politic Societies, which societies could not be without Government, nor Government without a distinct kind of Law from that which hath been already declared. Two foundations there are which bear up public societies; the one, a natural inclination, whereby all men desire sociable life and fellowship; the other, an order expressly or secretly agreed upon touching the manner of their union in living together. The latter is that which we call the Law of a Commonweal, the very soul of a politic body, the parts whereof are by law animated, held together, and set on work in such actions, as the common good requireth. Laws politic, ordained for external order and regiment amongst men, are never framed as they should be, unless presuming the will of man to be inwardly obstinate, rebellious, and averse from all obedience unto the sacred laws of his nature; in a word, unless presuming man to be in regard of his depraved mind little better than a wild beast, they do accordingly provide notwithstanding so to frame his outward actions, that they be no hindrance unto the common good for which societies are instituted: unless they do this, they are not perfect. It resteth therefore that we consider how nature findeth out such laws of government as serve to direct even nature depraved to a right end.

[2.] All men desire to lead in this world a happy life. That life is led most happily, wherein all virtue is exercised without impediment or let. The Apostle [1 Tim. vi. 8], in exhorting men to contentment, although they have in this world no more than very bare food and raiment, giveth us thereby to understand that those are even the lowest of things necessary; that if we should be stripped of all those things without which we might possibly be, yet these must be left; that destitution in these is such an impediment, as till it be removed suffereth not the mind of man to admit any other care. For this cause, first God assigned Adam maintenance of life, and then appointed him a law to observe [Gen. i. 29; ii. 17]. For this cause, after men began to grow to a number, the first thing we read they gave themselves unto was the tilling of the earth and the feeding of cattle. Having by this means whereon to live, the principal actions of their life afterward are noted by the exercise of their religion [Gen. iv. 2, 26]. True it is, that the kingdom of God must be the first thing in our purposes and desires [Matt. vi. 33]. But inasmuch as righteous life presupposeth life; inasmuch as to live virtuously it is impossible except we live; therefore the first impediment, which naturally we endeavour to remove, is penury and want of things without which we cannot live. Unto life many implements are necessary; more, if we seek (as all men naturally do) such a life as hath in it joy, comfort, delight, and pleasure. To this end we see how quickly sundry arts mechanical were found out, in the very prime of the world [Gen. iv. 20, 21, 22]. As things of greatest necessity are always first provided for, so things of greatest dignity are most accounted of by all such as judge rightly. Although therefore riches be a thing which every man wisheth, yet no man of judgment can esteem it better to be rich, than wise, virtuous, and religious. If we be both or either of these, it is not because we are so born. For into the world we come as empty of the one as of the other, as naked in mind as we are in body. Both which necessities of man had at the first no other helps and supplies than only domestical; such as that which the Prophet implieth, saying, "Can a mother forget her child?" [Isa. xlix. 15] such as that which the Apostle mentioneth, saying, "He that careth not for his own is worse than an infidel" [1 Tim. v. 8]; such as that concerning Abraham, "Abraham will command his sons and his household after him, that they keep the way of the Lord." [Gen. xviii. 19]

[3.] But neither that which we learn of ourselves nor that which others teach us can prevail, where wickedness and malice have taken deep root. If therefore when there was but as yet one only family in the world, no means of instruction human or divine could prevent effusion of blood [Gen. iv. 8]; how could it be chosen but that when families were multiplied and increased upon earth, after separation each providing for itself, envy, strife, contention and violence must grow amongst them? For hath not Nature furnished man with wit and valour, as it were with armour, which may be used as well unto extreme evil as good? Yea, were they not used by the rest of the world unto evil; unto the contrary only by Seth, Enoch, and those few the rest in that line? [Gen. vi. 5; Gen. v.]. We all make complaint of the iniquity of our times: not unjustly; for the days are evil. But compare them with those times wherein there were no civil societies, with those times wherein there was as yet no manner of public regiment established, with those times wherein there were not above eight persons righteous living upon the face of the earth [2 Pet. ii. 5]; and we have surely good cause to think that God hath blessed us exceedingly, and hath made us behold most happy days.

[4.] To take away all such mutual grievances, injuries, and wrongs, there was no way but only by growing unto composition and agreement amongst themselves, by ordaining some kind of government public, and by yielding themselves subject thereunto; that unto whom they granted authority to rule and govern, by them the peace, tranquillity, and happy estate of the rest might be procured. Men always knew that when force and injury was offered they might be defenders of themselves; they knew that howsoever men may seek their own commodity, yet if this were done with injury unto others it was not to be suffered, but by all men and by all good means to be withstood; finally they knew that no man might in reason take upon him to determine his own right, and according to his own determination proceed in maintenance thereof, inasmuch as every man is towards himself and them whom he greatly affecteth partial; and therefore that strifes and troubles would be endless, except they gave their common consent all to be ordered by some whom they should agree upon: without which consent there were no reason that one man should take upon him to be lord or judge over another; because, although there be according to the opinion of some very great and judicious men a kind of natural right in the noble, wise, and virtuous, to govern them which are of servile disposition; nevertheless for manifestation of this their right, and men's more peaceable contentment on both sides, the assent of them who are to be governed seemeth necessary.

To fathers within their private families Nature hath given a supreme power; for which cause we see throughout the world even from the foundation thereof, all men have ever been taken as lords and lawful kings in their own houses. Howbeit over a whole grand multitude having no such dependency upon any one, and consisting of so many families as every politic society in the world doth, impossible it is that any should have complete lawful power, but by consent of men, or immediate appointment of God; because not having the natural superiority of fathers, their power must needs be either usurped, and then unlawful; or, if lawful, then either granted or consented unto by them over whom they exercise the same, or else given extraordinarily from God, unto whom all the world is subject. It is no improbable opinion therefore which the arch-philosopher was of, that as the chiefest person in every household was always as it were a king, so when numbers of households joined themselves in civil society together, kings were the first kind of governors amongst them. Which is also (as it seemeth) the reason why the name of *Father* continued still in them, who of fathers were made rulers; as also the ancient custom of governors to do as Melchisedec, and being kings to exercise the office of priests, which fathers did at the first, grew perhaps by the same occasion.

Howbeit not this the only kind of regiment that hath been received in the world. The inconveniences of one kind have caused sundry other to be devised. So that in a word all public regiment of what kind soever seemeth evidently to have risen from deliberate advice, consultation, and composition between men, judging it convenient and behoveful; there being no impossibility in nature considered by itself, but that men might have lived without any public regiment. Howbeit, the corruption of our nature being presupposed, we may not deny but that the Law of Nature doth now require of necessity some kind of regiment, so that to bring things unto the first course they were in, and utterly to take away all kind of public government in the world, were apparently to overturn the whole world.

[5.] The case of man's nature standing therefore as it doth, some kind of regiment the Law of Nature doth require; yet the kinds thereof being many, Nature tieth not to any one, but leaveth the choice as a thing arbitrary. At the first when some certain kind of regiment was once approved, it may be that nothing was then further thought upon for the manner of governing, but all permitted unto their wisdom and discretion which were to rule; till by experience they found this for all parts very inconvenient, so as the thing which they had devised for a remedy did indeed but increase the sore which it should have cured. They saw that to live by one man's will became the cause of all men's misery. This constrained them to come unto laws, wherein all men might see their duties beforehand, and know the penalties of transgressing them. If things be simply good or evil, and withal universally so acknowledged, there needs no new law to be made for such things. The first kind therefore of things appointed by laws human containeth whatsoever being in itself naturally good or evil, is notwithstanding more secret than that it can be discerned by every man's present conceit, without some deeper discourse and judgment. In which discourse because there is difficulty and possibility many ways to err, unless such things were set down by laws, many would be ignorant of their duties which now are not, and many that know what they should do would nevertheless dissemble it, and to excuse themselves pretend ignorance and simplicity, which now they cannot.

[6.] And because the greatest part of men are such as prefer their own private good before all things, even that good which is sensual before whatsoever is most divine; and for that the labour of doing good, together with the pleasure arising from the contrary, doth make men for the most part slower to the one and proner to the other, than that duty prescribed them by law can prevail sufficiently with them: therefore unto laws that men do make for the benefit of men it hath seemed always needful to add rewards, which may more allure unto good than any hardness deterreth from it, and punishments, which may more deter from evil than any sweetness thereto allureth. Wherein as the generality is natural, *virtue rewardable and vice punishable*; so the particular determination of the reward or punishment belongeth unto them by whom laws are made. Theft is naturally punishable, but the kind of punishment is positive, and such lawful as men shall think with discretion convenient by law to appoint.

[7.] In laws, that which is natural bindeth universally, that which is positive not so. To let go those kind of positive laws which men impose upon themselves, as by vow unto God, contract with men, or such like; somewhat it will make unto our purpose, a little more fully to consider what things are incident into the making of the positive laws for the government of them that live united in public society. Laws do not only teach what is good, but they enjoin it, they have in them a certain constraining force. And to constrain men unto any thing inconvenient doth seem unreasonable. Most requisite therefore it is that to devise laws which all men shall be forced to obey none but wise men be admitted. Laws are matters of principal consequence; men of common capacity and but ordinary judgment are not able (for how should they?) to discern what things are fittest for each kind and state of regiment. We cannot be ignorant how much our obedience unto laws dependeth upon this point. Let a man though never so justly oppose himself unto them that are disordered in their ways, and what one amongst them commonly doth not stomach at such contradiction, storm at reproof, and hate such as would reform them? Notwithstanding even they which brook it worst that men should tell them of their duties, when they are told the same by a law, think very well and reasonably of it. For why? They presume that the law doth speak with all indifferency; that the law hath no side-respect to their persons; that the law is as it were an oracle proceeded from wisdom and understanding.

[8.] Howbeit, laws do not take their constraining force from the quality of such as devise them, but from that power which doth give them the strength of laws. That which we spake before concerning the power of government must here be applied unto the power of making laws whereby to govern; which power God hath over all: and by the natural law, whereunto he hath made all subject, the lawful power of making laws to command whole politic societies of men belongeth so properly unto the same entire societies, that for any prince or potentate of what kind soever upon earth to exercise the same of himself, and not either by express commission immediately and personally received from God, or else by authority derived at the first from their consent upon whose persons they impose laws, it is no better than mere tyranny.

Laws they are not therefore which public approbation hath not made so. But approbation not only they give who personally declare their assent by voice, sign, or act, but also when others do it in their names by right originally at the least derived from them. As in parliaments, councils, and the like assemblies, although we be not personally ourselves present, notwithstanding our assent is by reason of others agents there in our behalf. And what we do by others, no reason but that it should stand as our deed, no less effectually to bind us than if ourselves had done it in person. In many things assent is given, they that give it not imagining they do so, because the manner of their assenting is not apparent. As for example, when an absolute monarch commandeth his subjects that which seemeth good in his own discretion, hath not his edict the force of a law whether they approve or dislike it? Again, that which hath been received long sithence and is by custom now established, we keep as a law which we may not transgress; yet what consent was ever thereunto sought or required at our hands?

Of this point therefore we are to note, that sith men naturally have no full and perfect power to command whole politic multitudes of men, therefore utterly without our consent we could in such sort be at no man's commandment living. And to be commanded we do consent, when that society whereof we are part hath at any time before consented, without revoking the same after by the like universal agreement. Wherefore as any man's deed past is good as long as himself continueth; so the act of a public society of men done five hundred years sithence standeth as theirs who presently are of the same societies, because corporations are immortal; we were then alive in our predecessors, and they in their successors do live still. Laws therefore human, of what kind soever, are available by consent.

[9.] If here it be demanded how it cometh to pass that this being common unto all laws which are made, there should be found even in good laws so great variety as there is; we must note the reason hereof to be the sundry particular ends, whereunto the different dispositions of that subject or matter, for which laws are provided, causeth them to have especial respect in making laws. A law there is mentioned amongst the Grecians whereof Pittacus is reported to have been author; and by that law it was agreed, that he which being overcome with drink did then strike any man, should suffer punishment double as much as if he had done the same being sober. No man could ever have thought this reasonable, that had intended thereby only to punish the injury committed according to the gravity of the fact: for who knoweth not that harm advisedly done is naturally less pardonable, and therefore worthy of the sharper punishment? But forasmuch as none did so usually this way offend as men in that case, which they wittingly fell into, even because they would be so much the more freely outrageous; it was for their public good where such disorder was grown to frame a positive law for remedy thereof accordingly. To this appertain those known laws of making laws; as that law-makers must have an eye to the place where, and to the men amongst whom; that one kind of laws cannot serve for all kinds of regiment; that where the multitude beareth sway, laws that shall tend unto preservation of that state must make common smaller offices to go by lot, for fear of strife and division likely to arise; by reason that ordinary qualities sufficing for discharge of such offices they could not but by many be desired, and so with danger contended for, and not missed without grudge and discontentment, whereas at an uncertain lot none can find themselves grieved, on whomsoever it lighteth; contrariwise the greatest, whereof but few are capable, to pass by popular election, that neither the people may envy such as have those honours, inasmuch as themselves bestow them, and that the chiefest may be kindled with desire to exercise all parts of rare and beneficial virtue, knowing they shall not lose their labour by growing in fame and estimation amongst the people: if the helm of chief government be in the hands of a few of the wealthiest, that then laws providing for continuance thereof must make the punishment of contumely and wrong offered unto any of the common sort sharp and grievous, that so the evil may be prevented whereby the rich are most likely to bring themselves into hatred with the people, who are not wont to take so great offence when they are excluded from honours and offices, as when their persons are contumeliously trodden upon. In other kinds of regiment the like is observed concerning the difference of positive laws, which to be every where the same is impossible and against their nature.

[10.] Now as the learned in the laws of this land observe, that our statutes sometimes are only the affirmation or ratification of that which by common law was held before; so here it is not to be omitted that generally all laws human, which are made for the ordering of politic societies, be either such as establish some duty whereunto all men by the law of reason did before stand bound; or else such as make that a duty now which before was none. The one sort we may for distinction's sake call *mixedly*, and the other *merely* human. That which plain or necessary reason bindeth men unto may be in sundry considerations expedient to be ratified by human law. For example, if confusion of blood in marriage, the liberty of having many wives at once, or any other the like corrupt and unreasonable custom doth happen to have prevailed far, and to have gotten the upper hand of right reason with the greatest part; so that no way is left to rectify such foul disorder without prescribing by law the same things which reason necessarily *doth* enforce but is not *perceived* that so it doth; or if many be grown unto that which the Apostle did lament in some, concerning whom he writeth, saying, that "even what things they naturally know, in those very things as beasts void of reason they corrupted themselves;" [Jude 10] or if there be no such special accident, yet forasmuch as the common sort are led by the sway of their sensual desires, and therefore do more shun sin for the sensible evils which follow it amongst men, than for any kind of sentence which reason doth pronounce against it: this very thing is cause sufficient why duties belonging unto each kind of virtue, albeit the Law of Reason teach them, should notwithstanding be prescribed even by human law. Which law in this case we term *mixed*, because the matter whereunto it bindeth is the same which reason necessarily doth require at our hands, and from the Law of Reason it differeth in the manner of binding only. For whereas men before stood bound in conscience to do as the Law of Reason teacheth, they are now by virtue of human law become constrainable, and if they outwardly transgress, punishable. As for laws which are *merely* human, the matter of them is any thing which reason doth but probably teach to be fit and convenient; so that till such time as law hath passed amongst men about it, of itself it bindeth no man. One example whereof may be this. Lands are by human law in some places after the owner's decease divided unto all his children, in some all descendeth to the eldest son. If the Law of Reason did necessarily require but the one of these two to be done, they which by law have received the other should be subject to that heavy sentence, which denounceth against all that decree wicked, unjust, and unreasonable things, *woe* [Isa. x. 1]. Whereas now whichsoever be received there is no Law of Reason transgressed; because there is probable reason why either of them may be expedient, and for either of them more than probable reason there is not to be found.

[11.] Laws whether mixedly or merely human are made by politic societies: some, only as those societies are civilly united; some, as they are spiritually joined and make such a body as we call the Church. Of laws human in this latter kind we are to speak in the third book following. Let it therefore suffice thus far to have touched the force wherewith Almighty God hath graciously endued our nature, and thereby enabled the same to find out both those laws which all men generally are for ever bound to observe, and also such as are most fit for their behoof, who lead their lives in any ordered state of government.

[12.] Now besides that law which simply concerneth men as men, and that which belongeth unto them as they are men linked with others in some form of politic society, there is a third kind of law which toucheth all such several bodies politic, so far forth as one of them hath public commerce with another. And this third is the Law of Nations. Between men and beasts there is no possibility of sociable communion, because the well-spring of that communion is a natural delight which man hath to transfuse from himself into others, and to receive from others into himself especially those things wherein the excellency of his kind doth most consist. The chiefest instrument of human communion therefore is speech, because thereby we impart mutually one to another the conceits of our reasonable understanding. And for that cause seeing beasts are not hereof capable, forasmuch as with them we can use no such conference, they being in degree, although above other creatures on earth to whom nature hath denied sense, yet lower than to be sociable companions of man to whom nature hath given reason; it is of Adam said that amongst the beasts "he found not for himself any meet companion." [Gen. ii. 20] Civil society doth more content the nature of man than any private kind of solitary living, because in society this good of mutual participation is so much larger than otherwise. Herewith notwithstanding we are not satisfied, but we covet (if it might be) to have a kind of society and fellowship even with all mankind. Which thing Socrates intending to signify professed himself a citizen, not of this or that commonwealth, but of the world. And an effect of that very natural desire in us (a manifest token that we wish after a sort an universal fellowship with all men) appeareth by the wonderful delight men have, some to visit foreign countries, some to discover nations not heard of in former ages, we all to know the affairs and dealings of other people, yea to be in league of amity with them: and this not only for traffick's sake, or to the end that when many are confederated each may make other the more strong, but for such cause also as moved the Queen of Sheba to visit Solomon [1 Kings x. 1; 2 Chron. ix. 1; Matt. xii. 42; Luke xi. 31]; and in a word, because nature doth presume that how many men there are in the world, so many gods as it were there are, or at leastwise such they should be towards men.

[13.] Touching laws which are to serve men in this behalf; even as those Laws of Reason, which (man retaining his original integrity) had been sufficient to direct each particular person in all his affairs and duties, are not sufficient but require the access of other laws, now that man and his offspring are grown thus corrupt and sinful; again, as those laws of polity and regiment, which would have served men living in public society together with that harmless disposition which then they should have had, are not able now to serve, when men's iniquity is so hardly restrained within any tolerable bounds: in like manner, the national laws of mutual commerce between societies of that former and better quality might have been other than now, when nations are so prone to offer violence, injury, and wrong. Hereupon hath grown in every of these three kinds that distinction between *Primary* and *Secondary* laws; the one grounded upon sincere, the other built upon depraved nature. Primary laws of nations are such as concern embassage, such as belong to the courteous entertainment of foreigners and strangers, such as serve for commodious traffick, and the like. Secondary laws in the same kind are such as this present unquiet world is most familiarly acquainted with; I mean laws of arms, which yet are much better known than kept. But what matter the Law of Nations doth contain I omit to search.

The strength and virtue of that law is such that no particular nation can lawfully prejudice the same by any their several laws and ordinances, more than a man by his private resolutions the law of the whole commonwealth or state wherein he liveth. For as civil law, being the act of a whole body politic, doth therefore overrule each several part of the same body; so there is no reason that any one commonwealth of itself should to the prejudice of another annihilate that whereupon the whole world hath agreed. For which cause, the Lacedæmonians forbidding all access of strangers into their coasts, are in that respect both by Josephus and Theodoret deservedly blamed, as being enemies to that hospitality which for common humanity's sake all the nations on earth should embrace.

[14.] Now as there is great cause of communion, and consequently of laws for the maintenance of communion, amongst nations; so amongst nations Christian the like in regard even of Christianity hath been always judged needful.

And in this kind of correspondence amongst nations the force of general councils doth stand. For as one and the same law divine, whereof in the next place we are to speak, is unto all Christian churches a rule for the chiefest things; by means whereof they all in that respect make one church, as having all but "one Lord, one faith, and one baptism;" [Ephes. iv. 5] so the urgent necessity of mutual communion for preservation of our unity in these things, as also for order in some other things convenient to be every where uniformly kept, maketh it requisite that the Church of God here on earth have her laws of spiritual commerce between Christian nations; laws by virtue whereof all churches may enjoy freely the use of those reverend, religious, and sacred consultations, which are termed Councils General. A thing whereof God's own blessed Spirit was the author [Acts xv. 28]; a thing practised by the holy Apostles themselves; a thing always afterwards kept and observed throughout the world; a thing never otherwise than most highly esteemed of, till pride, ambition, and tyranny began by factious and vile endeavours to abuse that divine invention unto the furtherance of wicked purposes. But as the just authority of civil courts and parliaments is not therefore to be abolished, because sometime there is cunning used to frame them according to the private intents of men over-potent in the commonwealth; so the grievous abuse which hath been of councils should rather cause men to study how so gracious a thing may again be reduced to that first perfection, than in regard of stains and blemishes sithence growing be held for ever in extreme disgrace.

To speak of this matter as the cause requireth would require very long discourse. All I will presently say is this: whether it be for the finding out of any thing whereunto divine law bindeth us, but yet in such sort that men are not thereof on all sides resolved; or for the setting down of some uniform judgment to stand touching such things, as being neither way matters of necessity, are notwithstanding offensive and scandalous when there is open opposition about them; be it for the ending of strifes touching matters of Christian belief, wherein the one part may seem to have probable cause of dissenting from the other; or be it concerning matters of polity, order, and regiment in the church; I nothing doubt but that Christian men should much better frame themselves to those heavenly precepts, which our Lord and Saviour with so great instancy gave [John xiv. 27] as concerning peace and unity, if we did all concur in desire to have the use of ancient councils again renewed, rather than these proceedings continued, which either make all contentions endless, or bring them to one only determination, and that of all other the worst, which is by sword.

[15.] It followeth therefore that a new foundation being laid, we now adjoin hereunto that which cometh in the next place to be spoken of;

namely, wherefore God hath himself by Scripture made known such laws as serve for direction of men.

Chapter 11

WHEREFORE GOD HATH BY SCRIPTURE FURTHER MADE KNOWN SUCH SUPERNATURAL LAWS AS DO SERVE FOR MEN'S DIRECTION

All things (God only excepted) besides the nature which they have in themselves, receive externally some perfection from other things, as hath been shewed. Insomuch as there is in the whole world no one thing great or small, but either in respect of knowledge or of use it may unto our perfection add somewhat. And whatsoever such perfection there is which our nature may acquire, the same we properly term our good; our sovereign *good* or *blessedness*, that wherein the highest degree of all our perfection consisteth, that which being once attained unto there can rest nothing further to be desired; and therefore with it our souls are fully content and satisfied, in that they have they rejoice, and thirst for no more. Wherefore of good things desired some are such that for themselves we covet them not, but only because they serve as instruments unto that for which we are to seek: of this sort are riches. Another kind there is, which although we desire for itself, as health, and virtue, and knowledge, nevertheless they are not the last mark whereat we aim, but have their further end whereunto they are referred, so as in them we are not satisfied as having attained the utmost we may, but our desires do still proceed. These things are linked and as it were chained one to another; we labour to eat, and we eat to live, and we live to do good, and the good which we do is as seed sown with reference to a future harvest.* But we must come at length to some pause. For, if every thing were to be desired for some other without any stint, there could be no certain end proposed unto our actions, we should go on we know not whither; yea, whatsoever we do were in vain, or rather nothing at all were possible to be done. For as to take away the first efficient of our being were to annihilate utterly our persons, so we cannot remove the last final cause of our working, but we shall cause whatsoever we work to cease. Therefore something there must be desired for itself simply and for no other. That is simply for itself desirable, unto the nature whereof it is opposite and repugnant to be desired with relation unto any other. The ox and the ass desire their food, neither propose they unto themselves any end wherefore; so that of them this is desired for itself; but why? By reason of their imperfection which cannot otherwise desire it;

* "He that soweth to the Spirit shall of the Spirit reap life everlasting." Gal. vi. 8.

whereas that which is desired simply for itself, the excellency thereof is such as permitteth it not in any sort to be referred to a further end.

[2.] Now that which man doth desire with reference to a further end, the same he desireth in such measure as is unto that end convenient; but what he coveteth as good in itself, towards that his desire is ever infinite. So that unless the last good of all, which is desired altogether for itself, be also infinite, we do evil in making it our end; even as they who placed their felicity in wealth or honour or pleasure or any thing here attained; because in desiring any thing as our final perfection which is not so, we do amiss. Nothing may be infinitely desired but that good which indeed is infinite; for the better the more desirable; that therefore most desirable wherein there is infinity of goodness: so that if any thing desirable may be infinite, that must needs be the highest of all things that are desired. No good is infinite but only God; therefore he our felicity and bliss. Moreover, desire tendeth unto union with that it desireth. If then in Him we be blessed, it is by force of participation and conjunction with Him. Again, it is not the possession of any good thing can make them happy which have it, unless they enjoy the thing wherewith they are possessed. Then are we happy therefore when fully we enjoy God, as an object wherein the powers of our souls are satisfied even with everlasting delight; so that although we be men, yet by being unto God united we live as it were the life of God.

[3.] Happiness therefore is that estate whereby we attain, so far as possibly may be attained, the full possession of that which simply for itself is to be desired, and containeth in it after an eminent sort the contentation of our desires, the highest degree of all our perfection. Of such perfection capable we are not in this life. For while we are in the world, subject we are unto sundry imperfections, griefs of body, defects of mind; yea the best things we do are painful, and the exercise of them grievous, being continued without intermission; so as in those very actions whereby we are especially perfected in this life we are not able to persist; forced we are with very weariness, and that often, to interrupt them: which tediousness cannot fall into those operations that are in the state of bliss, when our union with God is complete. Complete union with him must be according unto every power and faculty of our minds apt to receive so glorious an object. Capable we are of God both by understanding and will: by understanding, as He is that sovereign Truth which comprehendeth the rich treasures of all wisdom; by will, as He is that sea of Goodness whereof whoso tasteth shall thirst no more. As the will doth now work upon that object by desire, which is as it were a motion towards the end as yet unobtained; so likewise upon the same hereafter received it shall work also by love. "Appetitus inhiantis fit amor fruentis," saith St. Augustine: "The longing disposition of them that thirst is changed into the sweet affection of them that taste and are replenished." Whereas we now love the thing that is good, but good especially in respect of benefit unto us; we shall then love the thing that is good, only or principally for the goodness of beauty in itself. The soul being in this sort, as it is active, perfected by love of that infinite good, shall, as it is receptive, be also perfected with those supernatural passions of joy, peace, and delight. All this endless and everlasting*. Which perpetuity, in regard whereof our blessedness is termed "a crown which withereth not" [2 Tim. iv. 8; 1 Pet. v. 4], doth neither depend upon the nature of the thing itself, nor proceed from any natural necessity that our souls should so exercise themselves for ever in beholding and loving God, but from the will of God, which doth both freely perfect our nature in so high a degree, and continue it so perfected. Under Man, no creature in the world is capable of felicity and bliss. First, because their chiefest perfection consisteth in that which is best for them, but not in that which is simply best, as ours doth. Secondly, because whatsoever external perfection they tend unto, it is not better than themselves, as ours is. How just occasion have we therefore even in this respect with the Prophet to admire the goodness of God! "Lord, what is man, that thou shouldst exalt him above the works of thy hands," [Ps. viii.] so far as to make thyself the inheritance of his rest and the substance of his felicity?

[4.] Now if men had not naturally this desire to be happy, how were it possible that all men should have it? All men have. Therefore this desire in man is natural. It is not in our power not to do the same; how should it then be in our power to do it coldly or remissly? So that our desire being natural is also in that degree of earnestness whereunto nothing can be added. And is it probable that God should frame the hearts of all men so desirous of that which no man may obtain? It is an axiom of nature that natural desire cannot utterly be frustrate. This desire of ours being natural should be frustrate, if that which may satisfy the same were a thing impossible for man to aspire unto. Man doth seek a triple perfection: first a sensual, consisting in those things which very life itself requireth either as necessary supplements, or as beauties and ornaments thereof; then an intellectual, consisting in those things which none underneath man is either capable of or acquainted with; lastly a spiritual and divine, consisting in those things whereunto we tend by supernatural means here, but cannot here attain unto them. They that make the first of these three the scope of their whole life, are said by the Apostle to have no god but only their belly, to be earthly-minded men [Phil. iii. 19]. Unto the second they bend themselves, who seek especially to excel in all such knowledge and virtue as doth most commend men. To this branch belongeth the law of moral and civil perfection. That there is somewhat higher than either of these two, no other proof doth need than the very process of man's desire, which being natural

* "The just shall go into life everlasting." Matt. xxv [.46]. "They shall be as the angels of God." Matt. xxii [.30].

should be frustrate, if there were not some farther thing wherein it might rest at the length contented, which in the former it cannot do. For man doth not seem to rest satisfied, either with fruition of that wherewith his life is preserved, or with performance of such actions as advance him most deservedly in estimation; but doth further covet, yea oftentimes manifestly pursue with great sedulity and earnestness, that which cannot stand him in any stead for vital use; that which exceedeth the reach of sense; yea somewhat above capacity of reason, somewhat divine and heavenly, which with hidden exultation it rather surmiseth than conceiveth; somewhat it seeketh, and what that is directly it knoweth not, yet very intentive desire thereof doth so incite it, that all other known delights and pleasures are laid aside, they give place to the search of this but only suspected desire. If the soul of man did serve only to give him being in this life, then things appertaining unto this life would content him, as we see they do other creatures; which creatures enjoying what they live by seek no further, but in this contentation do shew a kind of acknowledgment that there is no higher good which doth any way belong unto them. With us it is otherwise. For although the beauties, riches, honours, sciences, virtues, and perfections of all men living, were in the present possession of one; yet somewhat beyond and above all this there would still be sought and earnestly thirsted for. So that Nature even in this life doth plainly claim and call for a more divine perfection than either of these two that have been mentioned.

[5.] This last and highest estate of perfection whereof we speak is received of men in the nature of a Reward [Matt. v. 12]. Rewards do always presuppose such duties performed as are rewardable. Our natural means therefore unto blessedness are our works; nor is it possible that Nature should ever find any other way to salvation than only this. But examine the works which we do, and since the first foundation of the world what one can say, My ways are pure? Seeing then all flesh is guilty of that for which God hath threatened eternally to punish, what possibility is there this way to be saved? There resteth therefore either no way unto salvation, or if any, then surely a way which is supernatural, a way which could never have entered into the heart of man as much as once to conceive or imagine, if God himself had not revealed it extraordinarily. For which cause we term it the Mystery or secret way of salvation. And therefore St. Ambrose in this matter appealeth justly from man to God, "Let God himself that made me, let not man that knows not himself, be my instructor concerning the mystical way to heaven." "When men of excellent wit," saith Lactantius, "had wholly betaken themselves unto study, after farewell bidden unto all kind as well of private as public action, they spared no labour that might be spent in the search of truth; holding it a thing of much more price to seek and to find out the reason of all affairs as well divine as human, than to stick fast in the toil of piling up riches and gathering together heaps of honours. Howbeit, they both did fail of their purpose, and got not as much as to quit their charges; because truth which is the secret of the Most High God, whose proper handy-work all things are, cannot be compassed with that wit and those senses which are our own. For God and man should be very near neighbours, if man's cogitations were able to take a survey of the counsels and appointments of that Majesty everlasting. Which being utterly impossible, that the eye of man by itself should look into the bosom of divine Reason; God did not suffer him being desirous of the light of wisdom to stray any longer up and down, and with bootless expense of travail to wander in darkness that had no passage to get out by. His eyes at the length God did open, and bestow upon him the knowledge of the truth by way of Donative, to the end that man might both be clearly convicted of folly, and being through error out of the way, have the path that leadeth unto immortality laid plain before him." Thus far Lactantius Firmianus, to shew that God himself is the teacher of the truth, whereby is made known the supernatural way of salvation and law for them to live in that shall be saved. In the natural path of everlasting life the first beginning is that ability of doing good, which God in the day of man's creation endued him with; from hence obedience unto the will of his Creator, absolute righteousness and integrity in all his actions; and last of all the justice of God rewarding the worthiness of his deserts with the crown of eternal glory. Had Adam continued in his first estate, this had been the way of life unto him and all his posterity. Wherein I confess notwithstanding with the wittiest of the school-divines [Scotus], "That if we speak of strict justice, God could no way have been bound to requite man's labours in so large and ample manner as human felicity doth import; inasmuch as the dignity of this exceedeth so far the other's value. But be it that God of his great liberality had determined in lieu of man's endeavours to bestow the same by the rule of that justice which best beseemeth him, namely, the justice of one that requiteth nothing mincingly, but all with pressed and heaped and even over-enlarged measure; yet could it never hereupon necessarily be gathered, that such justice should add to the nature of that reward the property of everlasting continuance; sith possession of bliss, though it should be but for a moment, were an abundant retribution." But we are not now to enter into this consideration, how gracious and bountiful our good God might still appear in so rewarding the sons of men, albeit they should exactly perform whatsoever duty their nature bindeth them unto. Howsoever God did propose this reward, we that were to be rewarded must have done that which is required at our hands; we failing in the one, it were in nature an impossibility that the other should be looked for. The light of nature is never able to find out any way of obtaining the reward of bliss, but by performing exactly the duties and works of righteousness.

[6.] From salvation therefore and life all flesh being excluded this way, behold how the wisdom of God hath revealed a way mystical and supernatural, a way directing unto the same end of life by a course which groundeth itself upon the guiltiness of sin, and through sin desert of condemnation and death. For in this way the first thing is the tender compassion of God respecting us drowned and swallowed up in misery; the next is redemption out of the same by the precious death and merit of a mighty Saviour, which hath witnessed of himself, saying [John xiv. 6], "I am the way," the way that leadeth us from misery into bliss. This supernatural way had God in himself prepared before all worlds. The way of supernatural duty which to us he hath prescribed, our Saviour in the Gospel of St. John doth note, terming it by an excellency, The Work of God, "This is the work of God, that ye believe in him whom he hath sent." [John vi. 29] Not that God doth require nothing unto happiness at the hands of men saving only a naked belief (for hope and charity we may not exclude); but that without belief all other things are as nothing, and it the ground of those other divine virtues.

Concerning Faith, the principal object whereof is that eternal Verity which hath discovered the treasures of hidden wisdom in Christ; concerning Hope, the highest object whereof is that everlasting Goodness which in Christ doth quicken the dead; concerning Charity, the final object whereof is that incomprehensible Beauty which shineth in the countenance of Christ the Son of the living God: concerning these virtues, the first of which beginning here with a weak apprehension of things not seen, endeth with the intuitive vision of God in the world to come; the second beginning here with a trembling expectation of things far removed and as yet but only heard of, endeth with real and actual fruition of that which no tongue can express; the third beginning here with a weak inclination of heart towards him unto whom we are not able to approach, endeth with endless union, the mystery whereof is higher than the reach of the thoughts of men; concerning that Faith, Hope, and Charity, without which there can be no salvation, was there ever any mention made saving only in that law which God himself hath from heaven revealed? There is not in the world a syllable muttered with certain truth concerning any of these three, more than hath been supernaturally received from the mouth of the eternal God.

Laws therefore concerning these things are supernatural, both in respect of the manner of delivering them, which is divine; and also in regard of the things delivered, which are such as have not in nature any cause from which they flow, but were by the voluntary appointment of God ordained besides the course of nature, to rectify nature's obliquity withal.

Chapter 12

THE CAUSE WHY SO MANY NATURAL OR RATIONAL LAWS ARE SET DOWN IN HOLY SCRIPTURE

When supernatural duties are necessarily exacted, natural are not rejected as needless. The law of God therefore is, though principally delivered for instruction in the one, yet fraught with precepts of the other also. The Scripture is fraught even with laws of Nature; insomuch that Gratian defining Natural Right, (whereby is meant the right which exacteth those general duties that concern men naturally even as they are men,) termeth "Natural Right, that which the Books of the Law and the Gospel do contain." Neither is it vain that the Scripture aboundeth with so great store of laws in this kind: for they are either such as we of ourselves could not easily have found out, and then the benefit is not small to have them readily set down to our hands; or if they be so clear and manifest that no man endued with reason can lightly be ignorant of them, yet the Spirit as it were borrowing them from the school of Nature, as serving to prove things less manifest, and to induce a persuasion of somewhat which were in itself more hard and dark, unless it should in such sort be cleared, the very applying of them unto cases particular is not without most singular use and profit many ways for men's instruction. Besides, be they plain of themselves or obscure, the evidence of God's own testimony added to the natural assent of reason concerning the certainty of them, doth not a little comfort and confirm the same.

[2.] Wherefore inasmuch as our actions are conversant about things beset with many circumstances, which cause men of sundry wits to be also of sundry judgments concerning that which ought to be done; requisite it cannot but seem the rule of divine law should herein help our imbecility, that we might the more infallibly understand what is good and what evil. The first principles of the Law of Nature are easy; hard it were to find men ignorant of them. But concerning the duty which Nature's law doth require at the hands of men in a number of things particular, so far hath the natural understanding even of sundry whole nations been darkened, that they have not discerned no not gross iniquity to be sin. Again, being so prone as we are to fawn upon ourselves, and to be ignorant as much as may be of our own deformities, without the feeling sense whereof we are most wretched, even so much the more, because not knowing them we cannot so much as desire to have them taken away: how should our festered sores be cured, but that God hath delivered a law as sharp as the two-edged sword, piercing the very closest and most unsearchable corners of the heart [Heb. iv. 12], which the Law of Nature can hardly, human laws by no means possible, reach unto? Hereby we know even secret concupiscence to be sin, and are made fearful to offend though it be but in a wandering cogitation. Finally, of those things which are for direction of all the parts of our life needful, and not impossible to be discerned by the light of Nature itself; are there not many which few men's natural capacity, and some which no man's, hath been able to find out? They are, saith St. Augustine, but a few, and they endued with great ripeness of wit and judgment, free from all such affairs as might trouble their meditations, instructed in the sharpest and the subtlest points of learning, who have, and that very hardly, been able to find out but only the immortality of the soul. The resurrection of the flesh what man did ever at any time dream of, having not heard it otherwise than from the school of Nature? Whereby it appeareth how much we are bound to yield unto our Creator, the Father of all mercy, eternal thanks, for that he hath delivered his law unto the world, a law wherein so many things are laid open, clear, and manifest, as a light which otherwise would have been buried in darkness, not without the hazard, or rather not with the hazard but with the certain loss, of infinite thousands of souls most undoubtedly now saved.

[3.] We see, therefore, that our sovereign good is desired naturally; that God the author of that natural desire had appointed natural means whereby to fulfil it; that man having utterly disabled his nature unto those means hath had other revealed from God, and hath received from heaven a law to teach him how that which is desired naturally must now supernaturally be attained. Finally, we see that because those latter exclude not the former quite and clean as unnecessary, therefore together with such supernatural duties as could not possibly have been otherwise known to the world, the same law that teacheth them, teacheth also with them such natural duties as could not by light of Nature easily have been known.

Chapter 13

THE BENEFIT OF HAVING DIVINE LAWS WRITTEN

In the first age of the world God gave laws unto our fathers, and by reason of the number of their days their memories served instead of books; whereof the manifold imperfections and defects being known to God, he mercifully relieved the same by often putting them in mind of that whereof it behoved them to be specially mindful. In which respect we see how many times one thing hath been iterated unto sundry even of the best and wisest amongst them. After that the lives of men were shortened, means more durable to preserve the laws of God from oblivion and corruption grew in use, not without precise direction from God himslef. First therefore of Moses it is said, that he "wrote all the words of God;" [Exod. xxiv. 4] not by his own private motion and device: for God taketh this act to himself [Hos.

viii. 12], "I have written." Furthermore, were not the Prophets following commanded also to do the like? Unto the holy evangelist St. John, how often express charge is given, "*Scribe*," "Write these things." [Apoc. i. 11; xiv. 13] Concerning the rest of our Lord's disciples, the words of St. Augustine are, "Quicquid ille de suis factis et dictis nos legere voluit, hoc scribendum illis tanquam suis manibus imperavit."*

[2.] Now, although we do not deny it to be a matter merely accidental unto the law of God to be written; although writing be not that which addeth authority and strength thereunto; finally, though his laws do require at our hands the same obedience howsoever they be delivered; his providence, notwithstanding, which hath made principal choice of this way to deliver them, who seeth not what cause we have to admire and magnify? The singular benefit that hath grown unto the world, by receiving the laws of God even by his own appointment committed unto writing, we are not able to esteem as the value thereof deserveth. When the question therefore is, whether we be now to seek for any revealed law of God otherwhere than only in the sacred Scripture; whether we do now stand bound in the sight of God to yield to traditions urged by the Church of Rome the same obedience and reverence we do to his written law, honouring equally and adoring both as divine: our answer is, No. They that so earnestly plead for the authority of tradition, as if nothing were more safely conveyed than that which spreadeth itself by report, and descendeth by relation of former generations unto the ages that succeed, are not all of them (surely a miracle it were if they should be) so simple as thus to persuade themselves; howsoever, if the simple were so persuaded, they could be content perhaps very well to enjoy the benefit, as they account it, of that common error. What hazard the truth is in when it passeth through the hands of report, how maimed and deformed it becometh, they are not, they cannot possibly be ignorant. Let them that are indeed of this mind consider but only that little of things divine which the heathen have in such sort received.† How miserable had the state of the Church of God been long ere this, if wanting the sacred Scripture we had no record of his laws, but only the memory of man receiving the same by report and relation from his predecessors?

[3.] By Scripture it hath in the wisdom of God seemed meet to deliver unto the world much but personally expedient to be practised of certain

*["Whatever He wished us to read about His acts and sayings, He ordered it to be written by them as with His own hands."]

† I mean those historical matters concerning the ancient state of the first world, the deluge, the sons of Noah, the children of Israel's deliverance out of Egypt, the life and doings of Moses their captain, with such like: the certain truth whereof delivered in Holy Scripture is of the heathen, which had them only by report, so intermingled with fabulous vanities, that the most which remaineth in them to be seen is the show of dark and obscure steps, where some part of the truth hath gone.

men; many deep and profound points of doctrine, as being the main original ground whereupon the precepts of duty depend; many prophecies, the clear performance whereof might confirm the world in belief of things unseen; many histories to serve as looking-glasses to behold the mercy, the truth, the righteousness of God towards all that faithfully serve, obey, and honour him; yea many entire meditations of piety, to be as patterns and precedents in cases of like nature; many things needful for explication, many for application unto particular occasions, such as the providence of God from time to time hath taken to have the several books of his holy ordinance written. Be it then that together with the principal necessary laws of God there are sundry other things written, whereof we might haply be ignorant and yet be saved? What? shall we hereupon think them needless? shall we esteem them as riotous branches wherewith we sometimes behold most pleasant vines overgrown? Surely no more than we judge our hands or our eyes superfluous, or what part soever, which if our bodies did want, we might notwithstanding any such defect retain still the complete being of men. As therefore a complete man is neither destitute of any part necessary, and hath some parts whereof though the want could not deprive him of his essence, yet to have them standeth him in singular stead in respect of the special uses for which they serve; in like sort all those writings which contain in them the Law of God, all those venerable books of Scripture, all those sacred tomes and volumes of Holy Writ, they are with such absolute perfection framed, that in them there neither wanteth any thing the lack whereof might deprive us of life, nor any thing in such wise aboundeth, that as being superfluous, unfruitful, and altogether needless, we should think it no loss or danger at all if we did want it.

Chapter 14

THE SUFFICIENCY OF SCRIPTURE UNTO THE END FOR WHICH IT WAS INSTITUTED

Although the Scripture of God therefore be stored with infinite variety of matter in all kinds, although it abound with all sorts of laws, yet the principal intent of Scripture is to deliver the laws of duties supernatural. Oftentimes it hath been in very solemn manner disputed, whether all things necessary unto salvation be necessarily set down in the Holy Scriptures or no.* If we define that necessary unto salvation, whereby the way to salvation is in any sort made more plain, apparent, and easy to be known; then is there no part of true philosophy, no art of account, no kind of science rightly so called, but the Scripture must contain it. If only those things be necessary, as surely none else are, without the knowledge and

* This question proposed by Scotus is affirmatively concluded.

practice whereof it is not the will and pleasure of God to make any ordinary grant of salvation; it may be notwithstanding and oftentimes hath been demanded, how the books of Holy Scripture contain in them all necessary things, when of things necessary the very chiefest is to know what books we are bound to esteem holy; which point is confessed impossible for the Scripture itself to teach. Whereunto we may answer with truth, that there is not in the world any art or science, which proposing unto itself an end (as every one doth some end or other) hath been therefore thought defective, if it have not delivered simply whatsoever is needful to the same end; but all kinds of knowledge have their certain bounds and limits; each of them presupposeth many necessary things learned in other sciences and known beforehand. He that should take upon him to teach men how to be eloquent in pleading causes, must needs deliver unto them whatsoever precepts are requisite unto that end; otherwise he doth not the thing which he taketh upon him. Seeing then no man can plead eloquently unless he be able first to speak; it followeth that ability of speech is in this case a thing most necessary. Notwithstanding every man would think it ridiculous, that he which undertaketh by writing to instruct an orator should therefore deliver all the precepts of grammar; because his profession is to deliver precepts necessary unto eloquent speech, yet so that they which are to receive them be taught beforehand so much of that which is thereunto necessary, as comprehendeth the skill of speaking. In like sort, albeit Scripture do profess to contain in it all things which are necessary unto salvation; yet the meaning cannot be simply of all things that are necessary, but all things that are necessary in some certain kind or form; as all things which are necessary, and either could not at all or could not easily be known by the light of natural discourse; all things which are necessary to be known that we may be saved, but known with presupposal of knowledge concerning certain principles whereof it receiveth us already persuaded, and then instructeth us in all the residue that are necessary. In the number of these principles one is the sacred authority of Scripture. Being therefore persuaded by other means that these Scriptures are the oracles of God, themselves do then teach us the rest, and lay before us all the duties which God requireth at our hands as necessary unto salvation.

[2.] Further, there hath been some doubt likewise, whether *containing in Scripture* do import express setting down in plain terms, or else *comprehending* in such sort that by reason we may from thence conclude all things which are necessary. Against the former of these two constructions instance hath sundry ways been given. For our belief in the Trinity, the co-eternity of the Son of God with his Father, the proceeding of the Spirit from the Father and the Son, the duty of baptizing infants: these with such other principal points, the necessity whereof is by none denied, are notwithstanding in Scripture nowhere to be found by express literal mention, only deduced they are out of Scripture by collection. This kind of comprehension in Scripture being therefore received, still there is doubt how far we are to proceed by collection, before the full and complete measure of things necessary be made up. For let us not think that as long as the world doth endure the wit of man shall be able to sound the bottom of that which may be concluded out of the Scripture; especially if "things contained by collection" do so far extend, as to draw in whatsoever may be at any time out of Scripture but probably and conjecturally surmised. But let *necessary* collection be made requisite, and we may boldly deny, that of all those things which at this day are with so great necessity urged upon this church under the name of reformed church-discipline, there is any one which their books hitherto have made manifest to be contained in the Scripture. Let them, if they can, allege but one properly belonging to their cause, and not common to them and us, and shew the deduction thereof out of Scripture to be necessary.

[3.] It hath been already shewed, how all things necessary unto salvation in such sort as before we have maintained must needs be possible for men to know; and that many things are in such sort necessary, the knowledge whereof is by the light of Nature impossible to be attained. Whereupon it followeth that either all flesh is excluded from possibility of salvation, which to think were most barbarous; or else that God hath by supernatural means revealed the way of life so far forth as doth suffice. For this cause God hath so many times and ways spoken to the sons of men. Neither hath he by speech only, but by writing also, instructed and taught his Church. The cause of writing hath been to the end that things by him revealed unto the world might have the longer continuance, and the greater certainty of assurance, by how much that which standeth on record hath in both those respects preeminence above that which passeth from hand to hand, and hath no pens but the tongues, no books but the ears of men to record it. The several books of Scripture having had each some several occasion and particular purpose which caused them to be written, the contents thereof are according to the exigence of that special end whereunto they are intended. Hereupon it groweth that every book of Holy Scripture doth take out of all kinds of truth, natural [Eph. v. 29], historical [2 Tim. iii. 8], foreign [Tit. i. 12], supernatural [2 Pet. ii. 4], so much as the matter handled requireth.

Now forasmuch as there hath been reason alleged sufficient to conclude, that all things necessary unto salvation must be made known, and that God himself hath therefore revealed his will, because otherwise men could not have known so much as is necessary; his surceasing to speak to the world, since the publishing of the Gospel of Jesus Christ and the delivery of the same in writing, is unto us a manifest token that the way of salvation is now sufficiently opened, and that we need no other means for our full instruction than God hath already furnished us withal.

[4.] The main drift of the whole New Testament is that which St. John setteth down as the purpose of his own history; "These things are written, that ye might believe that Jesus is Christ the Son of God, and that in believing ye might have life through his name." [John xx. 31] The drift of the Old that which the Apostle mentioneth to Timothy, "The Holy Scriptures are able to make thee wise unto salvation." [2 Tim. iii. 15] So that the general end both of Old and New is one; the difference between them consisting in this, that the Old did make wise by teaching salvation through Christ that should come, the New by teaching that Christ the Saviour is come, and that Jesus whom the Jews did crucify, and whom God did raise again from the dead, is he. When the Apostle therefore affirmeth unto Timothy, that the Old was able to make him wise to salvation, it was not his meaning that the Old alone can do this unto us which live sithence the publication of the New. For he speaketh with presupposal of the doctrine of Christ known also unto Timothy; and therefore first it is said, "Continue thou in those things which thou hast learned and art persuaded, knowing of whom thou hast been taught them." [2 Tim. iii. 14] Again, those Scriptures he granteth were able to make him wise to salvation; but he addeth, "through the faith which is in Christ." [2 Tim. iii. 15] Wherefore without the doctrine of the New Testament teaching that Christ hath wrought the redemption of the world, which redemption the Old did foreshew he should work, it is not the former alone which can on our behalf perform so much as the Apostle doth avouch, who presupposeth this when he magnifieth that so highly. And as his words concerning the books of ancient Scripture do not take place but with presupposal of the Gospel of Christ embraced; so our own words also, when we extol the complete sufficiency of the whole entire body of the Scripture, must in like sort be understood with this caution, that the benefit of nature's light be not thought excluded as unnecessary, because the necessity of a diviner light is magnified.

[5.] There is in Scripture therefore no defect, but that any man, what place or calling soever he hold in the Church of God, may have thereby the light of his natural understanding so perfected, that the one being relieved by the other, there can want no part of needful instruction unto any good work which God himself requireth, be it natural or supernatural, belonging simply unto men as men, or unto men as they are united in whatsoever kind of society. It sufficeth therefore that Nature and Scripture do serve in such full sort, that they both jointly, and not severally either of them, be so complete, that unto everlasting felicity we need not the knowledge of any thing more than these two may easily furnish our minds with on all sides; and therefore they which add traditions, as a part of supernatural necessary truth, have not the truth, but are in error. For they only plead, that whatsoever God revealeth as necessary for all Christian men to do or believe, the same we ought to embrace, whether we have received it by writing or otherwise; which no man denieth: when that which they should confirm, who claim so great reverence unto traditions, is, that the same traditions are necessarily to be acknowledged divine and holy. For we do not reject them only because they are not in the Scripture, but because they are neither in Scripture, nor can otherwise sufficiently by any reason be proved to be of God. That which is of God, and may be evidently proved to be so, we deny not but it hath in his kind, although unwritten, yet the selfsame force and authority with the written laws of God. It is by ours acknowledged, "that the Apostles did in every church institute and ordain some rites and customs serving for the seemliness of church-regiment, which rites and customs they have not committed unto writing." Those rites and customs being known to be apostolical, and having the nature of things changeable, were no less to be accounted of in the Church than other things of the like degree; that is to say, capable in like sort of alteration, although set down in the Apostles' writings. For both being known to be apostolical, it is not the manner of delivering them unto the Church, but the author from whom they proceed, which doth give them their force and credit.

Chapter 15

OF LAWS POSITIVE CONTAINED IN SCRIPTURE; THE MUTABILITY OF CERTAIN OF THEM, AND THE GENERAL USE OF SCRIPTURE

Laws being imposed either by each man upon himself, or by a public society upon the particulars thereof, or by all the nations of men upon every several society, or by the Lord himself upon any or every of these; there is not amongst these four kinds any one but containeth sundry both natural and positive laws. Impossible it is but that they should fall into a number of gross errors, who only take such laws for positive as have been made or invented of men, and holding this position hold also, that all positive and none but positive laws are mutable. Laws natural do always bind; laws positive not so, but only after they have been expressly and wittingly imposed. Laws positive there are in every of those kinds before mentioned. As in the first kind the promises which we have passed unto men, and the vows we have made unto God; for these are laws which we tie ourselves unto, and till we have so tied ourselves they bind us not. Laws positive in the second kind are such as the civil constitutions peculiar unto each particular commonweal. In the third kind the law of Heraldry in war is positive: and in the last all the judicials which God gave unto the people of Israel to observe. And although no laws but positive be mutable, yet all are not mutable which be positive. Positive laws are either permanent or else changeable, according as the matter itself is concerning which they were first made. Whether God or man be the maker of them, alteration they so far forth admit, as the matter doth exact.

[2.] Laws that concern supernatural duties are all positive, and either concern men supernaturally as men, or else as parts of a supernatural society, which society we call the Church. To concern men as men supernaturally is to concern them as duties which belong of necessity to all, and yet could not have been known by any to belong unto them, unless God had opened them himself, inasmuch as they do not depend upon any natural ground at all out of which they may be deduced, but are appointed of God to supply the defect of those natural ways of salvation, by which we are not now able to attain thereunto. The Church being a supernatural society doth differ from natural societies in this, that the persons unto whom we associate ourselves, in the one are men simply considered as men, but they to whom we be joined in the other, are God, Angels, and holy men. Again the Church being both a society and a society supernatural, although as it is a society it have the selfsame original grounds which other politic societies have, namely, the natural inclination which all men have unto sociable life, and consent to some certain bond of association, which bond is the law that appointeth what kind of order they shall be associated in: yet unto the Church as it is a society supernatural this is peculiar, that part of the bond of their association which belong to the Church of God must be a law supernatural, which God himself hath revealed concerning that kind of worship which his people shall do unto him. The substance of the service of God therefore, so far forth as it hath in it any thing more than the Law of Reason doth teach, may not be invented of men, as it is amongst the heathens,* but must be received from God himself, as always it hath been in the Church, saving only when the Church hath been forgetful of her duty.

[3.] Wherefore, to end with a general rule concerning all the laws which God hath tied men unto: those laws divine that belong, whether naturally or supernaturally, either to men as men, or to men as they live in politic society, or to men as they are of that politic society which is the Church, without any further respect had unto any such variable accident as the state of men and of societies of men and of the Church itself in this world is subject unto; all laws that so belong unto men, they belong for ever, yea, although they be Positive Laws, unless being positive God himself which made them alter them. The reason is, because the subject or matter of laws in general is thus far forth constant: which matter is that for the ordering whereof laws were instituted, and being instituted are not changeable without cause, neither can they have cause of change, when that which gave them their first institution remaineth for ever one and the same. On the other side, laws that were made for men or societies or churches, in regard

* "Their fear towards me was taught by the precept of men." Isa. xxix. 13.

of their being such as they do not always continue, but may perhaps be clean otherwise a while after, and so may require to be otherwise ordered than before; the laws of God himself which are of this nature, no man endued with common sense will ever deny to be of a different constitution from the former, in respect of the one's constancy and the mutability of the other. And this doth seem to have been the very cause why St. John doth so peculiarly term the doctrine that teacheth salvation by Jesus Christ, *Evangelium æternum*, "an eternal Gospel;" [Apoc. xiv. 6] because there can be no reason wherefore the publishing thereof should be taken away, and any other instead of it proclaimed, as long as the world doth continue: whereas the whole law of rites and ceremonies, although delivered with so great solemnity, is notwithstanding clean abrogated, inasmuch as it had but temporary cause of God's ordaining it.

[4.] But that we may at the length conclude this first general introduction unto the nature and original birth, as of all other laws, so likewise of those which the sacred Scripture containeth, concerning the Author whereof even infidels have confessed that He can neither err nor deceive: albeit about things easy and manifest unto all men by common sense there needeth no higher consultation; because as a man whose wisdom is in weighty affairs admired would take it in some disdain to have his counsel solemnly asked about a toy, so the meanness of some things is such, that to search the Scripture of God for the ordering of them were to derogate from the reverend authority and dignity of the Scripture, no less than they do by whom Scriptures are in ordinary talk very idly applied unto vain and childish trifles: yet better it were to be superstitious than profane; to take from thence our direction even in all things great or small, than to wade through matters of principal weight and moment, without ever caring what the law of God hath either for or against our designs. Concerning the custom of the very Painims, thus much Strabo witnesseth: "Men that are civil do lead their lives after one common law appointing them what to do. For that otherwise a multitude should with harmony amongst themselves concur in the doing of one thing, (for this is civilly to live,) or that they should in any sort manage community of life, it is not possible. Now laws or statutes are of two sorts. For they are either received from gods, or else from men. And our ancient predecessors did surely most honour and reverence that which was from the gods; for which cause consultation with oracles was a thing very usual and frequent in their times." Did they make so much account of the voice of their gods, which in truth were no gods; and shall we neglect the precious benefit of conference with those oracles of the true and living God, whereof so great store is left to the Church, and whereunto there is so free, so plain, and so easy access for all men? "By thy commandments" (this was David's confession unto God) "thou hast made me wiser than mine enemies." [Ps. cxix. 98] Again, "I have had more understanding than all my teachers, because thy testimonies are my meditations." What pains would not they have bestowed in the study of these books, who travelled sea and land to gain the treasure of some few days' talk with men whose wisdom the world did make any reckoning of? That little which some of the heathens did chance to hear, concerning such matter as the sacred Scripture plentifully containeth, they did in wonderful sort affect; their speeches as oft as they make mention thereof are strange, and such as themselves could not utter as they did other things, but still acknowledged that their wits, which did every where else conquer hardness, were with profoundness here over-matched. Wherefore seeing that God hath endued us with sense, to the end that we might perceive such things as this present life doth need; and with reason, lest that which sense cannot reach unto, being both now and also in regard of a future estate hereafter necessary to be known, should lie obscure; finally, with the heavenly support of prophetical revelation, which doth open those hidden mysteries that reason could never have been able to find out, or to have known the necessity of them unto our everlasting good: use we the precious gifts of God unto his glory and honour that gave them, seeking by all means to know what the will of our God is; what righteous before him; in his sight what holy, perfect, and good, that we may truly and faithfully do it.

Chapter 16

A CONCLUSION SHEWING HOW ALL THIS BELONGETH TO THE CAUSE IN QUESTION

Thus far therefore we have endeavoured in part to open, of what nature and force laws are, according unto their several kinds; the law which God with himself hath eternally set down to follow in his own works; the law which he hath made for his creatures to keep; the law of natural and necessary agents; the law which angels in heaven obey; the law whereunto by the light of reason men find themselves bound in that they are men; the law which they make by composition for multitudes and politic societies of men to be guided by; the law which belongeth unto each nation; the law that concerneth the fellowship of all; and lastly the law which God himself hath supernaturally revealed. It might peradventure have been more popular and more plausible to vulgar ears, if this first discourse had been spent in extolling the force of laws, in shewing the great necessity of them when they are good, and in aggravating their offence by whom public laws are injuriously traduced. But forasmuch as with such kind of matter the passions of men are rather stirred one way or other, than their knowledge any way set forward unto the trial of that whereof there is doubt made; I have therefore turned aside from that beaten path, and chosen though a less easy yet a more profitable way in regard of the end we propose. Lest therefore any man should marvel whereunto all these things tend, the drift and purpose of all is this, even to shew in what manner, as every good and perfect gift, so this very gift of good and perfect laws is derived from the Father of lights [James i. 17]; to teach men a reason why just and reasonable laws are of so great force, of so great use in the world; and to inform their minds with some method of reducing the laws whereof there is present controversy unto their first original causes, that so it may be in every particular ordinance thereby the better discerned, whether the same be reasonable, just, and righteous, or no. Is there any thing which can either be thoroughly understood or soundly judged of, till the very first causes and principles from which originally it springeth be made manifest? If all parts of knowledge have been thought by wise men to be then most orderly delivered and proceeded in, when they are drawn to their first original; seeing that our whole question concerneth the quality of ecclesiastical laws, let it not seem a labour superfluous that in the entrance thereunto all these several kinds of laws have been considered, inasmuch as they all concur as principles, they all have their forcible operations therein, although not all in like apparent and manifest manner. By means whereof it cometh to pass that the force which they have is not observed of many.

[2.] Easier a great deal it is for men by law to be taught what they ought to do, than instructed how to judge as they should do of law: the one being a thing which belongeth generally unto all, the other such as none but the wiser and more judicious sort can perform. Yea, the wisest are always touching this point the readiest to acknowledge, that soundly to judge of a law is the weightiest thing which any man can take upon him. But if we will give judgment of the laws under which we live; first let that law eternal be always before our eyes, as being of principal force and moment to breed in religious minds a dutiful estimation of all laws, the use and benefit whereof we see; because there can be no doubt but that laws apparently good are (as it were) things copied out of the very tables of that high everlasting law; even as the book of that law hath said concerning itself, "By me kings reign, and" by me "princes decree justice" [Prov. viii. 15]. Not as if men did behold that book and accordingly frame their laws; but because it worketh in them, because it discovereth and (as it were) readeth itself to the world by them, when the laws which they make are righteous. Furthermore, although we perceive not the goodness of laws made, nevertheless sith things in themselves may have that which we peradventure discern not, should not this breed a fear in our hearts, how we speak or judge in the worse part concerning that, the unadvised disgrace whereof may be no mean dishonour to Him, towards whom we profess all submission and awe? Surely there must be very manifest iniquity in laws, against which we shall be able to justify our contumelious invectives. The chiefest root whereof, when we use them without cause, is ignorance how laws inferior are derived from that supreme or highest law.

[3.] The first that receive impression from thence are natural agents. The law of whose operations might be haply thought less pertinent, when the question is about laws for human actions, but that in those very actions which most spiritually and supernaturally concern men, the rules and axioms of natural operations have their force. What can be more immediate to our salvation than our persuasion concerning the love of Christ towards his Church? What greater assurance of love towards his Church, than the knowledge of that mystical union, whereby the Church is become as near unto Christ as any one part of his flesh is unto other? That the Church being in such sort his he must needs protect it, what proof more strong than if a manifest law so require, which law it is not possible for Christ to violate? And what other law doth the Apostle for this allege, but such as is both common unto Christ with us, and unto us with other things natural; "No man hateth his own flesh, but doth love and cherish it"? [Ephes. v. 29] The axioms of that law therefore, whereby natural agents are guided, have their use in the moral, yea, even in the spiritual actions of men, and consequently in all laws belonging unto men howsoever.

[4.] Neither are the Angels themselves so far severed from us in their kind and manner of working, but that between the law of their heavenly operations and the actions of men in this our state of mortality such correspondence there is, as maketh it expedient to know in some sort the one, for the other's more perfect direction. Would Angels acknowledge themselves "fellow-servants" [Apoc. xix. 10] with the sons of men, but that both having one Lord, there must be some kind of law which is one and the same to both, whereunto their obedience being perfecter is to our weaker both a pattern and a spur? Or would the Apostles, speaking of that which belongeth unto saints as they are linked together in the bond of spiritual society [1 Pet. i. 12; Ephes. iii. 10; 1 Tim. v. 21], so often make mention how Angels therewith are delighted, if in things publicly done by the Church we are not somewhat to respect what the Angels of heaven do? Yea, so far hath the Apostle Saint Paul proceeded, as to signify [1 Cor. xi. 10], that even about the outward orders of the Church which serve but for comeliness, some regard is to be had of Angels, who best like us when we are most like unto them in all parts of decent demeanour. So that the law of Angels we cannot judge altogether impertinent unto the affairs of the Church of God.

[5.] Our largeness of speech how men do find out what things reason bindeth them of necessity to observe, and what it guideth them to choose in things which are left as arbitrary; the care we have had to declare the different nature of laws which severally concern all men, from such as belong unto men either civilly or spiritually associated, such as pertain to the fellowship which nations, or which Christian nations, have amongst themselves, and in the last place such as concerning every or any of these God himself hath revealed by his Holy Word: all serveth but to make manifest, that as the actions of men are of sundry distinct kinds, so the laws thereof must accordingly be distinguished. There are in men operations, some natural, some rational, some supernatural, some politic, some finally ecclesiastical: which if we measure not each by his own proper law, whereas the things themselves are so different, there will be in our understanding and judgment of them confusion.

As that first error sheweth, whereon our opposites in this cause have grounded themselves. For as they rightly maintain that God must be glorified in all things, and that the actions of men cannot tend unto his glory unless they be framed after his law; so it is their error to think that the only law which God hath appointed unto men in that behalf is the sacred Scripture. By that which we work naturally, as when we breathe, sleep, move, we set forth the glory of God as natural agents do [Ps. cxlviii, 7–9], albeit we have no express purpose to make that our end, nor any advised determination therein to follow a law, but do that we do (for the most part) not as much as thinking thereon. In reasonable and moral actions another law taketh place; a law by the observation whereof [Rom. i. 21] we glorify God in such sort, as no creature else under man is able to do; because other creatures have not judgment to examine the quality of that which is done by them, and therefore in that they do they neither can accuse nor approve themselves. Men do both, as the Apostle teacheth; yea, those men which have no written law of God to shew what is good or evil, carry written in their hearts the universal law of mankind, the Law of Reason, whereby they judge as by a rule which God hath given unto all men for that purpose [Rom. ii. 15]. The law of reason doth somewhat direct men how to honour God as their Creator; but how to glorify God in such sort as is required, to the end he may be an everlasting Saviour, this we are taught by divine law, which law both ascertaineth the truth and supplieth unto us the want of that other law. So that in moral actions, divine law helpeth exceedingly the law of reason to guide man's life; but in supernatural it alone guideth.

Proceed we further; let us place man in some public society with others, whether civil or spiritual; and in this case there is no remedy but we must add yet a further law. For although even here likewise the laws of nature and reason be of necessary use, yet somewhat over and besides them is necessary, namely human and positive law, together with that law which is of commerce between grand societies, the law of nations, and of nations Christian. For which cause the law of God hath likewise said, "Let every soul be subject to the higher powers" [Rom. xiii. 1]. The public power of all societies is above every soul contained in the same societies. And the principal use of that power is to give laws unto all that are under it; which laws in such case we must obey, unless there be reason shewed which may necessarily enforce that the law of Reason or of God doth enjoin the contrary. Because except our own private and but probable resolutions be by the law of public determinations overruled, we take away all possibility of sociable life in the world. A plainer example whereof than ourselves we cannot have. How cometh it to pass that we are at this present day so rent with mutual contentions, and that the Church is so much troubled about the polity of the Church? No doubt if men had been willing to learn how many laws their actions in this life are subject unto, and what the true force of each law is, all these controversies might have died the very day they were first brought forth.

[6.] It is both commonly said, and truly, that the best men otherwise are not always the best in regard of society. The reason whereof is, for that the law of men's actions is one, if they be respected only as men; and another, when they are considered as parts of a politic body. Many men there are, than whom nothing is more commendable when they are singled; and yet in society with others none less fit to answer the duties which are looked for at their hands. Yea, I am persuaded, that of them with whom in this cause we strive, there are whose betters amongst men would be hardly found, if they did not live amongst men, but in some wilderness by themselves. The cause of which their disposition so unframable unto societies wherein they live, is, for that they discern not aright what place and force these several kinds of laws ought to have in all their actions. Is there question either concerning the regiment of the Church in general, or about conformity between one church and another, or of ceremonies, offices, powers, jurisdictions in our own church? Of all these things they judge by that rule which they frame to themselves with some show of probability, and what seemeth in that sort convenient, the same they think themselves bound to practise; the same by all means they labour mightily to uphold; whatsoever any law of man to the contrary hath determined they weigh it not. Thus by following the law of private reason, where the law of public should take place, they breed disturbance.

[7.] For the better inuring therefore of men's minds with the true distinction of laws, and of their several force according to the different kind and quality of our actions, it shall not peradventure be amiss to shew in some one example how they all take place. To seek no further, let but that be considered, than which there is not any thing more familiar unto us, our food.

What things are food and what are not we judge naturally by sense [Job xxxiv. 3]; neither need we any other law to be our director in that behalf than the selfsame which is common unto us with beasts.

But when we come to consider of food, as of a benefit which God of his bounteous goodness hath provided for all things living [Ps. cxlv. 15–16]; the law of Reason doth here require the duty of thankfulness at our hands, towards him at whose hands we have it. And lest appetite in the use of food should lead us beyond that which is meet, we owe in this case obedience to that law of Reason, which teacheth mediocrity in meats and drinks. The same things divine law teacheth also, as at large we have shewed it doth all parts of moral duty, whereunto we all of necessity stand bound, in regard of the life to come.

But of certain kinds of food the Jews sometime had, and we ourselves likewise have, a mystical, religious, and supernatural use, they of their paschal lamb and oblations, we of our bread and wine in the Eucharist; which use none but divine law could institute.

Now as we live in civil society, the state of the commonwealth wherein we live both may and doth require certain laws concerning food; which laws, saving only that we are members of the commonwealth where they are of force, we should not need to respect as rules of action, whereas now in their place and kind they must be respected and obeyed.

Yea, the selfsame matter is also a subject wherein sometime ecclesiastical laws have place; so that unless we will be authors of confusion in the Church, our private discretion, which otherwise might guide us a contrary way, must here submit itself to be that way guided, which the public judgment of the Church hath thought better. In which case that of Zonaras concerning fasts may be remembered. "Fastings are good, but let good things be done in good and convenient manner. He that transgresseth in his fasting the orders of the holy fathers," the positive laws of the Church of Christ, must be plainly told, "that good things do lose the grace of their goodness, when in good sort they are not performed."

And as here men's private fancies must give place to the higher judgment of that Church which is in authority a mother over them; so the very actions of whole churches have, in regard of commerce and fellowship with other churches, been subject to laws concerning food, the contrary unto which laws had else been thought more convenient for them to observe; as by that order of abstinence from strangled and blood [Acts xv. 20] may appear; an order grounded upon that fellowship which the churches of the Gentiles had with the Jews.

Thus we see how even one and the selfsame thing is under diverse considerations conveyed through many laws; and that to measure by any one kind of law all the actions of men were to confound the admirable order, wherein God hath disposed all laws, each as in nature, so in degree, distinct from other.

[8.] Wherefore that here we may briefly end: of Law there can be no less acknowledged, than that her seat is the bosom of God, her voice the harmony of the world: all things in heaven and earth do her homage, the very least as feeling her care, and the greatest as not exempted from her power, but Angels and men and creatures of what condition soever, though each in different sort and manner, yet all with uniform consent, admiring her as the mother of their peace and joy.

the second book

CONCERNING THEIR FIRST POSITION WHO URGE REFORMATION IN THE CHURCH OF ENGLAND: NAMELY, THAT SCRIPTURE IS THE ONLY RULE OF ALL THINGS WHICH IN THIS LIFE MAY BE DONE BY MEN

The matter contained in this second book

AS THAT which in the title hath been proposed for the matter whereof we treat, is only the ecclesiastical law whereby we are governed; so neither is it my purpose to maintain any other thing than that which therein truth and reason shall approve. For concerning the dealings of men who administer government, and unto whom the execution of that law belongeth; they have their Judge who sitteth in heaven, and before whose tribunal-seat they are accountable for whatsoever abuse or corruption, which (being worthily misliked in this church) the want either of care or of conscience in them hath bred. We are no patrons of those things therefore, the best defence whereof is speedy redress and amendment. That which is of God we defend, to the uttermost of that ability which he hath given; that which is otherwise, let it wither even in the root from whence it hath sprung. Wherefore all these abuses being severed and set apart, which rise from the corruption of men and not from the laws themselves; come we to those things which in the very whole entire form of our church polity have been (as we persuade ourselves) injuriously blamed by them, who endeavour to overthrow the same, and instead thereof to establish a much worse; only through a strong misconceit they have, that the same is grounded on divine authority.

* Chapters marked with an asterisk are included in this selection. *Ed.*

Now whether it be that through an earnest longing desire to see things brought to a peaceable end, I do but imagine the matters whereof we contend to be fewer than indeed they are; or else for that in truth they are fewer when they come to be discussed by reason, than otherwise they seem when by heat of contention they are divided into many slips, and of every branch an heap is made: surely, as now we have drawn them together, choosing out those things which are requisite to be severally all discussed, and omitting such mean specialties as are likely (without any great labour) to fall afterwards of themselves; I know no cause why either the number or the length of these controversies should diminish our hope of seeing them end with concord and love on all sides; which of his infinite love and goodness the Father of all peace and unity grant.

[2.] Unto which scope that our endeavour may the more directly tend, it seemeth fittest that first those things be examined, which are as seeds from whence the rest that ensue have grown. And of such the most general is that wherewith we are here to make our entrance: a question not moved (I think) any where in other churches, and therefore in ours the more likely to be soon (I trust) determined. The rather, for that it hath grown from no other root, than only a desire to enlarge the necessary use of the Word of God; which desire hath begotten an error enlarging it further than (as we are persuaded) soundness of truth will bear. For whereas God hath left sundry kinds of laws unto men, and by all those laws the actions of men are in some sort directed; they hold that one only law, the Scripture, must be the rule to direct in all things, even so far as to the "taking up of a rush or straw." About which point there should not need any question to grow, and that which is grown might presently end, if they did yield but to these two restraints: the first is, not to extend the actions whereof they speak so low as that instance doth import of taking up a straw, but rather keep themselves at the least within the compass of moral actions, actions which have in them vice or virtue; the second, not to exact at our hands for every action the knowledge of some place of Scripture out of which we stand bound to deduce it, as by divers testimonies they seek to enforce; but rather as the truth is, so to acknowledge, that it sufficeth if such actions be framed according to the law of Reason; the general axioms, rules, and principles of which law being so frequent in Holy Scripture, there is no let but in that regard even out of Scripture such duties may be deduced by some kind of consequence, (as by long circuit of deduction it may be that even all truth out of any truth may be concluded,) howbeit no man bound in such sort to deduce all his actions out of Scripture, as if either the place be to him unknown whereon they may be concluded, or the reference unto that place not presently considered of, the action shall in that respect be condemned as unlawful. In this we dissent, and this we are presently to examine.

Chapter 1
THE FIRST PRETENDED PROOF OF THE FIRST POSITION OUT OF SCRIPTURE, PROV. ii. 9

[3.] In all parts of knowledge rightly so termed things most general are most strong. Thus it must be, inasmuch as the certainty of our persuasion touching particulars dependeth altogether upon the credit of those generalities out of which they grow. Albeit therefore every cause admit not such infallible evidence of proof, as leaveth no possibility of doubt or scruple behind it; yet they who claim the general assent of the whole world unto that which they teach, and do not fear to give very hard and heavy sentence upon as many as refuse to embrace the same, must have special regard that their first foundations and grounds be more than slender probabilities. This whole question which hath been moved about the kind of church regiment, we could not but for our own resolution's sake endeavour to unrip and sift; following therein as near as we might the conduct of that judicial method which serveth best for invention of truth. By means whereof, having found this the head theorem of all their discourses, who plead for the change of ecclesiastical government in England, namely, "That the Scripture of God is in such sort the rule of human actions, that simply whatsoever we do and are not by it directed thereunto, the same is sin;" we hold it necessary that the proofs hereof be weighed. Be they of weight sufficient or otherwise, it is not ours to judge and determine; only what difficulties there are which as yet withhold our assent, till we be further and better satisfied, I hope no indifferent amongst them will scorn or refuse to hear.

[4.] First therefore whereas they allege, "That Wisdom" doth teach men "every good way;" and have thereupon inferred that no way is good in any kind of action unless wisdom do by Scripture lead unto it; see they not plainly how they restrain the manifold ways which wisdom hath to teach men by, unto one only way of teaching, which is by Scripture? The bounds of wisdom are large, and within them much is contained. Wisdom was Adam's instructor in Paradise; wisdom endued the fathers who lived before the law with the knowledge of holy things; by the wisdom of the law of God David attained to excel others in understanding [Ps. cxix. 99]; and Solomon likewise to excel David by the selfsame wisdom of God teaching him many things besides the law. The ways of well-doing are in number even as many as are the kinds of voluntary actions; so that whatsoever we do in this world and may do it ill, we shew ourselves therein by well-doing to be wise. Now if wisdom did teach men by Scripture not only all the ways that are right and good in some certain kind, according to that of St. Paul* concerning the use of Scripture, but did simply without any manner of exception, restraint, or distinction, teach every way of doing well; there is no art, but Scripture should teach it, because every art doth teach the way how to do something or other well. To teach men therefore wisdom professeth, and to teach them every good way; but not every good way by one way of teaching. Whatsoever either men on earth or the Angels of heaven do know, it is as a drop of that unemptiable fountain of wisdom; which wisdom hath diversely imparted her treasures unto the world. As her ways are of sundry kinds, so her manner of teaching is not merely one and the same. Some things she openeth by the sacred books of Scripture; some things by the glorious works of Nature: with some things she inspireth them from above by spiritual influence; in some things she leadeth and traineth them only by worldly experience and practice. We may not so in any one special kind admire her, that we disgrace her in any other; but let all her ways be according unto their place and degree adored.

* * *

Chapter 7

THEIR OPINION CONCERNING THE FORCE OF ARGUMENTS TAKEN FROM HUMAN AUTHORITY FOR THE ORDERING OF MEN'S ACTIONS OR PERSUASIONS

An earnest desire to draw all things unto the determination of bare and naked Scripture hath caused here much pains to be taken in abating the estimation and credit of man. Which if we labour to maintain as far as truth and reason will bear, let not any think that we travail about a matter not greatly needful. For the scope of all their pleading against man's authority is, to overthrow such orders, laws, and constitutions in the Church, as depending thereupon if they should therefore be taken away, would peradventure leave neither face nor memory of Church to continue long in the world, the world especially being such as now it is. That which they have in this case spoken I would for brevity's sake let pass, but that the drift of their speech being so dangerous, their words are not to be neglected.

[2.] Wherefore to say that simply an argument taken from man's authority doth hold no way, "neither affirmatively nor negatively," is hard.

* 2 Tim. iii. 16. "The whole Scripture is given by inspiration of God, and is profitable to teach, to improve, to correct, and to instruct in righteousness, that the man of God may be absolute, being made perfect unto all good works." He meaneth all and only those good works, which belong unto us as we are men of God, and which unto salvation are necessary. Or if we understand by *men of God*, God's ministers, there is not required in them an universal skill of every good work or way, but an ability to teach whatsoever men are bound to do that they may be saved. And with this kind of knowledge the Scripture sufficeth to furnish them as touching matter.

By a man's authority we here understand the force which his word hath for the assurance of another's mind that buildeth upon it; as the Apostle somewhat did upon their report of the house of Chloe [1 Cor. i. 11]; and the Samaritans in a matter of far greater moment upon the report of a simple woman. For so it is said in St. John's Gospel, "Many of the Samaritans of that city believed in him for the saying of the woman, which testified, He hath told me all things that ever I did" [John iv. 39].

The strength of man's authority is affirmatively such that the weightiest affairs in the world depend thereon. In judgment and justice are not hereupon proceedings grounded? Saith not the Law that "in the mouth of two or three witnesses every word shall be confirmed?" [Deut. xix. 15; Matt. xviii. 16]. This the law of God would not say, if there were in a man's testimony no force at all to prove any thing.

And if it be admitted that in matter of fact there is some credit to be given to the testimony of man, but not in matter of opinion and judgment; we see the contrary both acknowledged and universally practised also throughout the world. The sentences of wise and expert men were never but highly esteemed. Let the title of a man's right be called in question; are we not bold to rely and build upon the judgment of such as are famous for their skill in the laws of this land? In matter of state the weight many times of some one man's authority is thought reason sufficient, even to sway over whole nations.

And this not only "with the simpler sort;" but the learneder and wiser we are, the more such arguments in some cases prevail with us. The reason why the simpler sort are moved with authority is the conscience of their own ignorance; whereby it cometh to pass that having learned men in admiration, they rather fear to dislike them than know wherefore they should allow and follow their judgments. Contrariwise with them that are skilful authority is much more strong and forcible; because they only are able to discern how just cause there is why to some men's authority so much should be attributed. For which cause the name of Hippocrates (no doubt) were more effectual to persuade even such men as Galen himself, than to move a silly empiric. So that the very selfsame argument in this kind which doth but induce the vulgar sort to like, may constrain the wiser to yield. And therefore not orators only with the people, but even the very profoundest disputers in all faculties have hereby often with the best learned prevailed most.

As for arguments taken from human authority and that negatively; for example sake, if we should think the assembling of the people of God together by the sound of a bell, the presenting of infants at the holy font by such as commonly we call their godfathers, or any other the like received custom, to be impious, because some men of whom we think very reverently have in their books and writings nowhere mentioned or taught that such things should be in the Church; this reasoning were subject unto just reproof, it were but feeble, weak, and unsound. Notwithstanding even negatively an argument from human authority may be strong, as namely thus: The Chronicles of England mention no more than only six kings bearing the name of Edward since the time of the last conquest; therefore it cannot be there should be more. So that if the question be of the authority of a man's testimony, we cannot simply avouch either that affirmatively it doth not any way hold; or that it hath only force to induce the simpler sort, and not to constrain men of understanding and ripe judgment to yield assent; or that negatively it hath in it no strength at all. For unto every of these the contrary is most plain.

[3.] Neither doth that which is alleged concerning the infirmity of men overthrow or disprove this. Men are blinded with ignorance and error; many things may escape them, and in many things they may be deceived; yea, those things which they do know they may either forget, or upon sundry indirect considerations let pass; and although themselves do not err, yet may they through malice or vanity even of purpose deceive others. Howbeit infinite cases there are wherein all these impediments and lets are so manifestly excluded, that there is no show or colour whereby any such exception may be taken, but that the testimony of man will stand as a ground of infallible assurance. That there is a city of Rome, that Pius Quintus and Gregory the Thirteenth and others have been Popes of Rome, I suppose we are certainly enough persuaded. The ground of our persuasion, who never saw the place nor persons beforenamed, can be nothing but man's testimony. Will any man here notwithstanding allege those mentioned human infirmities, as reasons why these things should be mistrusted or doubted of?

Yea, that which is more, utterly to infringe the force and strength of man's testimony were to shake the very fortress of God's truth. For whatsoever we believe concerning salvation by Christ, although the Scripture be therein the ground of our belief; yet the authority of man is, if we mark it, the key which openeth the door of entrance into the knowledge of the Scripture. The Scripture could not teach us the things that are of God, unless we did credit men who have taught us that the words of Scripture do signify those things. Some way therefore, notwithstanding man's infirmity, yet his authority may enforce assent.

[4.] Upon better advice and deliberation so much is perceived, and at the length confessed; that arguments taken from the authority of men may not only so far forth as hath been declared, but further also be of some force in "human sciences;" which force be it never so small, doth shew that they are not utterly naught. But in "matters divine" it is still maintained stiffly, that they have no manner force at all. Howbeit, the very selfsame reason, which causeth to yield that they are of some force in the one, will at the length constrain also to acknowledge that they are not in the other altogether unforcible. For if the natural strength of man's wit may by experience and study attain unto such ripeness in the knowledge of things human, that men in this respect may presume to build somewhat upon their judgment; what reason have we to think but that even in matters divine, the like wits furnished with necessary helps, exercised in Scripture with like diligence, and assisted with the grace of Almighty God, may grow unto so much perfection of knowledge, that men shall have just cause, when any thing pertinent unto faith and religion is doubted of, the more willingly to incline their minds towards that which the sentence of so grave, wise, and learned in that faculty shall judge most sound? For the controversy is of the weight of such men's judgments. Let it therefore be suspected; let it be taken as gross, corrupt, repugnant unto the truth, whatsoever concerning things divine above nature shall at any time be spoken as out of the mouths of mere natural men, which have not the eyes wherewith heavenly things are discerned. For this we contend not. But whom God hath endued with principal gifts to aspire unto knowledge by; whose exercises, labours, and divine studies he hath so blessed that the world for their great and rare skill that way hath them in singular admiration; may we reject even their judgment likewise, as being utterly of no moment? For mine own part, I dare not so lightly esteem of the Church, and of the principal pillars therein.

[5.] The truth is, that the mind of man desireth evermore to know the truth according to the most infallible certainty which the nature of things can yield. The greatest assurance generally with all men is that which we have by plain aspect and intuitive beholding. Where we cannot attain unto this, there what appeareth to be true by strong and invincible demonstration, such as wherein it is not by any way possible to be deceived, thereunto the mind doth necessarily assent, neither is it in the choice thereof to do otherwise. And in case these both do fail, then which way greatest probability leadeth, thither the mind doth evermore incline. Scripture with Christian men being received as the Word of God; that for which we have probable, yea, that which we have necessary reason for, yea, that which we see with our eyes, is not thought so sure as that which the Scripture of God teacheth; because we hold that his speech revealeth there what himself seeth, and therefore the strongest proof of all, and the most necessarily assented unto by us (which do thus receive the Scripture) is the Scripture. Now it is not required or can be exacted at our hands, that we should yield unto any thing other assent, than such as doth answer the evidence which is to be had of that we assent unto. For which cause even in matters divine, concerning some things we may lawfully doubt and suspend our judgment, inclining neither to one side nor other; as namely touching the time of the fall both of man and angels: of some things we may very well retain an opinion that they are probable and not unlikely to be true, as when we hold that men have their souls rather by creation than propagation, or that the Mother of our Lord lived always in the state of virginity as well after his birth as before (for of these two the one, her virginity before, is a thing which of necessity we must believe; the other, her continuance in the same state always, hath more likelihood of truth than the contrary); finally in all things then are our consciences best resolved, and in most agreeable sort unto God and nature settled, when they are so far persuaded as those grounds of persuasion which are to be had will bear.

Which thing I do so much the rather set down, for that I see how a number of souls are for want of right information in this point oftentimes grievously vexed. When bare and unbuilded conclusions are put into their minds, they finding not themselves to have thereof any great certainty, imagine that this proceedeth only from lack of faith, and that the Spirit of God doth not work in them as it doth in true believers; by this means their hearts are much troubled, they fall into anguish and perplexity: whereas the truth is, that how bold and confident soever we may be in words, when it cometh to the point of trial, such as the evidence is which the truth hath either in itself or through proof, such is the heart's assent thereunto; neither can it be stronger, being grounded as it should be.

I grant that proof derived from the authority of man's judgment is not able to work that assurance which doth grow by a stronger proof; and therefore although ten thousand general councils would set down one and the same definitive sentence concerning any point of religion whatsoever, yet one demonstrative reason alleged, or one manifest testimony cited from the mouth of God himself to the contrary, could not choose but overweigh them all; inasmuch as for them to have been deceived it is not impossible; it is, that demonstrative reason or testimony divine should deceive. Howbeit in defect of proof infallible, because the mind doth rather follow probable persuasions than approve the things that have in them no likelihood of truth at all; surely if a question concerning matter of doctrine were proposed, and on the one side no kind of proof appearing, there should on the other be alleged and shewed that so a number of the learnedest divines in the world have ever thought; although it did not appear what reason or what Scripture led them to be of that judgment, yet to their very bare judgment somewhat a reasonable man would attribute, notwithstanding the common imbecilities which are incident into our nature.

[6.] And whereas it is thought, that especially with "the Church, and those that are called and persuaded of the authority of the Word of God, man's authority" with them especially "should not prevail;" it must and doth prevail even with them, yea with them especially, as far as equity requireth; and farther we maintain it not. For men to be tied and led by authority, as it were with a kind of captivity of judgment, and though there be reason to the contrary not to listen unto it, but to follow like beasts the first in the herd, they know not nor care not whither, this were brutish. Again, that authority of men should prevail with men either against or above Reason, is no part of our belief. "Companies of learned men" be they never so great and reverend, are to yield unto Reason; the weight whereof is no whit prejudiced by the simplicity of his person which doth allege it, but being found to be sound and good, the bare opinion of men to the contrary must of necessity stoop and give place.

Irenæus, writing against Marcion, which held one God author of the Old Testament and another of the New, to prove that the Apostles preached the same God which was known before to the Jews, he copiously allegeth sundry their sermons and speeches uttered concerning that matter and recorded in Scripture. And lest any should be wearied with such store of allegations, in the end he concludeth, "While we labour for these demonstrations out of Scripture, and do summarily declare the things which many ways have been spoken, be contented quietly to hear, and do not think my speech tedious; *Quoniam ostensiones quæ sunt in Scripturis non possunt ostendi nisi ex ipsis Scripturis*; Because demonstrations that are in Scripture may not otherwise be shewed than by citing them out of the Scriptures themselves where they are." Which words make so little unto the purpose, that they seem as it were offended at him which hath called them thus solemnly forth to say nothing.

And concerning the verdict of Jerome; if no man, be he never so well learned, have after the Apostles any authority to publish new doctrine as from heaven, and to require the world's assent as unto truth received by prophetical revelation; doth this prejudice the credit of learned men's judgments in opening that truth, which by being conversant in the Apostles' writings they have themselves from thence learned?

St. Augustine exhorteth not to hear men, but to hearken what God speaketh. His purpose is not (I think) that we should stop our ears against his own exhortation, and therefore he cannot mean simply that audience should altogether be denied unto men, but either that if men speak one thing and God himself teach another, then he not they to be obeyed; or if they both speak the same thing, yet then also man's speech unworthy of hearing, not simply, but in comparison of that which proceedeth from the mouth of God.

"Yea, but we doubt what the will of God is." Are we in this case forbidden to hear what men of judgment think it to be? If not, then this allegation also might very well have been spared.

In that ancient strife which was between the catholic Fathers and Arians, Donatists, and others of like perverse and froward disposition, as long as to Fathers or councils alleged on the one side the like by the contrary side were opposed, impossible it was that ever the question should by this means grow unto any issue or end. The Scripture they both believed: the Scripture they knew could not give sentence on both sides; by Scripture the controversy between them was such as might be determined. In this case what madness was it with such kinds of proofs to nourish their contention, when there were such effectual means to end all controversy that was between them! Hereby therefore it doth not as yet appear, that an argument of authority of man affirmatively is in matters divine nothing worth.

Which opinion being once inserted into the minds of the vulgar sort, what it may grow unto God knoweth. Thus much we see, it hath already made thousands so headstrong even in gross and palpable errors, that a man whose capacity will scarce serve him to utter five words in sensible manner blusheth not in any doubt concerning matter of Scripture to think his own bare *Yea* as good as the *Nay* of all the wise, grave, and learned judgments that are in the whole world: which insolency must be repressed, or it will be the very bane of Christian religion.

[7.] Our Lord's disciples marking what speech he uttered unto them, and at the same time calling to mind a common opinion held by the Scribes, between which opinion and the words of their Master it seemed unto them that there was some contradiction, which they could not themselves answer with full satisfaction of their own minds; the doubt they propose to our Saviour, saying, "Why then say the Scribes that Elias must first come?" [Matt. xvii. 10] They knew that the Scribes did err greatly, and that many ways even in matters of their own profession. They notwithstanding thought the judgment of the very Scribes in matters divine to be of some value; some probability they thought there was that Elias should come, inasmuch as the Scribes said it. Now no truth can contradict any truth; desirous therefore they were to be taught how both might stand together; that which they knew could not be false, because Christ spake it; and this which to them did seem true, only because the Scribes had said it. For the Scripture, from whence the Scribes did gather it, was not then in their heads. We do not find that our Saviour reproved them of error, for thinking the judgment of the Scribes to be worth the objecting, for esteeming it to be of any moment or value in matters concerning God.

[8.] We cannot therefore be persuaded that the will of God is, we should so far reject the authority of men as to reckon it nothing. No, it may be a question, whether they that urge us unto this be themselves so persuaded indeed. Men do sometimes bewray that by deeds, which to confess they are hardly drawn. Mark then if this be not general with all men for the most part. When the judgments of learned men are alleged against them, what do they but either elevate their credit, or oppose unto them the judgments of others as learned? Which thing doth argue that all men acknowledge in them some force and weight, for which they are loath the cause they maintain should be so much weakened as their testimony is available. Again, what reason is there why alleging testimonies as proofs, men give them some title of credit, honour, and estimation, whom they allege, unless beforehand it be sufficiently known who they are; what reason hereof but only a common ingrafted persuasion, that in some men there may be found such qualities as are able to countervail those exceptions which might be taken against them, and that such men's authority is not lightly to be shaken off?

[9.] Shall I add further, that the force of arguments drawn from the authority of Scripture itself, as Scriptures commonly are alleged, shall (being sifted) be found to depend upon the strength of this so much despised and debased authority of man? Surely it doth, and that oftener than we are aware of. For although Scripture be of God, and therefore the proof which is taken from thence must needs be of all other most invincible; yet this strength it hath not, unless it avouch the selfsame thing for which it is brought. If there be either undeniable appearance that so it doth, or reason such as cannot deceive, then Scripture-proof (no doubt) in strength and value exceedeth all. But for the most part, even such as are readiest to cite for one thing five hundred sentences of holy Scripture; what warrant have they, that any one of them doth mean the thing for which it is alleged? Is not their surest ground most commonly, either some probable conjecture of their own, or the judgment of others taking those Scriptures as they do? Which notwithstanding to mean otherwise than they take them, it is not still altogether impossible. So that now and then they ground themselves on human authority, even when they most pretend divine. Thus it fareth even clean throughout the whole controversy about that discipline which is so earnestly urged and laboured for. Scriptures are plentifully alleged to prove that the whole Christian world for ever ought to embrace it. Hereupon men term it *The discipline of God*. Howbeit examine, sift and resolve their alleged proofs, till you come to the very root from whence they spring, the heart wherein their strength lieth; and it shall clearly appear unto any man of judgment, that the most which can be inferred upon such plenty of divine testimonies is only this, That *some things* which they maintain, as far as *some men* can *probably conjecture*, do *seem* to have been out of Scripture *not absurdly* gathered. Is this a warrant sufficient for any man's conscience to build such proceedings upon, as have been and are put in ure for the stablishment of that cause?

[10.] But to conclude, I would gladly understand how it cometh to pass, that they which so peremptorily do maintain that human authority is nothing worth are in the cause which they favour so careful to have the common sort of men persuaded, that the wisest, the godliest and the best learned in all Christendom are that way given, seeing they judge this to make nothing in the world for them. Again how cometh it to pass they cannot abide that authority should be alleged on the other side, if there be no force at all in authorities on one side or other? Wherefore labour they to strip their adversaries of such furniture as doth not help? Why take they such needless pains to furnish also their own cause with the like? If it be void and to no purpose that the names of men are so frequent in their books, what did move them to bring them in, or doth to suffer them there remaining? Ignorant I am not how this is salved, "They do it not but after the truth made manifest first by reason or by Scripture: they do it not but to control the enemies of the truth, who bear themselves bold upon human authority making not for them but against them rather." Which answers are nothing: for in what place or upon what consideration soever it be they do it, were it in their own opinion of no force being done, they would undoubtedly refrain to do it.

Chapter 8

A DECLARATION WHAT THE TRUTH IS IN THIS MATTER

But to the end it may more plainly appear what we are to judge of their sentences, and of the cause itself wherein they are alleged: first it may not well be denied, that all actions of men endued with the use of reason are generally either good or evil. For although it be granted that no action is properly termed good or evil unless it be voluntary; yet this can be no let to our former assertion, That all actions of men endued with the use of reason are generally either good or evil; because even those things are done voluntarily by us which other creatures do naturally, inasmuch as we might stay our doing of them if we would. Beasts naturally do take their food and rest when it offereth itself unto them. If men did so too, and could not do otherwise of themselves, there were no place for any such reproof as that of our Saviour Christ unto his disciples, "Could ye not watch with me one hour?" [Matt. xxvi. 40] That which is voluntarily performed in things tending to the end, if it be well done, must needs be done with deliberate consideration of some reasonable cause wherefore we rather should do it than not. Whereupon it seemeth, that in such actions only those are said to be good or evil which are capable of deliberation: so that many things being hourly done by men, wherein they need not use with themselves any manner of consultation at all, it may perhaps hereby seem that well or ill-doing belongeth only to our weightier affairs, and to those deeds which are of so great importance that they require advice. But thus to determine were perilous, and peradventure unsound also. I do rather incline to think, that seeing all the unforced actions of men are voluntary, and all voluntary actions tending to the end have choice, and all choice presupposeth the knowledge of some cause wherefore we make it: where the reasonable cause of such actions so readily offereth itself that it needeth not to be sought for; in those things, though we do not deliberate, yet they are of their nature apt to be deliberated on, in regard of the will, which may incline either way, and would not any one way bend itself, if there were not some apparent motive to lead it. Deliberation actual we use, when there is doubt what we should incline our wills unto. Where no doubt is, deliberation is not excluded as impertinent unto the thing, but as needless in regard of the agent, which seeth already what to resolve upon. It hath no apparent absurdity therefore in it to think, that all actions of men endued with the use of reason are generally either good or evil.

[2.] Whatsoever is good, the same is also approved of God: and according unto the sundry degrees of goodness, the kinds of divine approbation are in like sort multiplied. Some things are good, yet in so mean a degree of goodness, that men are only not disproved nor disallowed of God for them. "No man hateth his own flesh." [Ephes. v. 29] "If ye do good unto them that do so to you, the very publicans themselves do as much." [Matt. v. 46] "They are worse than infidels that have no care to provide for their own." [1 Tim. v. 8] In actions of this sort, the very light of Nature alone may discover that which is so far forth in the sight of God allowable.

[3.] Some things in such sort are allowed, that they be also required as necessary unto salvation, by way of direct immediate and proper necessity final; so that without performance of them we cannot by ordinary course be saved, nor by any means be excluded from life observing them. In actions of this kind our chiefest direction is from Scripture, for Nature is no sufficient teacher what we should do that we may attain unto life everlasting. The unsufficiency of the light of Nature is by the light of Scripture so fully and so perfectly herein supplied, that further light than this hath added there doth not need unto that end.

[4.] Finally some things, although not so required of necessity that to leave them undone excludeth from salvation, are notwithstanding of so great dignity and acceptation with God, that most ample reward in heaven is laid up for them. Hereof we have no commandment either in Nature or Scripture which doth exact them at our hands; yet those motives there are in both which draw most effectually our minds unto them. In this kind there is not the least action but it doth somewhat make to the accessory augmentation of our bliss. For which cause our Saviour doth plainly witness, that there shall not be as much as a cup of cold water bestowed for his sake without reward [Matt. x. 42]. Hereupon dependeth whatsoever difference there is between the states of saints in glory; hither we refer whatsoever belongeth unto the highest perfection of man by way of service towards God; hereunto that fervour and first love of Christians did bend itself, causing them to sell their possessions, and lay down the price at the blessed Apostles' feet [Acts iv. 34–5]. Hereat St. Paul undoubtedly did aim in so far abridging his own liberty, and exceeding that which the bond of necessary and enjoined duty tied him unto [1 Thess. ii. 7, 9].

[5.] Wherefore seeing that in all these several kinds of actions there can be nothing possibly evil which God approveth; and that he approveth much more than he doth command; and that his very commandments in some kind, as namely his precepts comprehended in the law of nature, may be otherwise known than only by Scripture; and that to do them, howsoever we know them, must needs be acceptable in his sight: let them with whom we have hitherto disputed consider well, how it can stand with reason to make the bare mandate of sacred Scripture the only rule of all good and evil in the actions of mortal men. The testimonies of God are true, the testimonies of God are perfect, the testimonies of God are all sufficient unto that end for which they were given. Therefore accordingly we do receive them, we do not think that in them God hath omitted any thing needful unto his purpose, and left his intent to be accomplished by our devisings. What the Scripture purposeth, the same in all points it doth perform.

Howbeit that here we swerve not in judgment, one thing especially we must observe, namely that the absolute perfection of Scripture is seen by relation unto that end whereto it tendeth. And even hereby it cometh to pass, that first such as imagine the general and main drift of the body of sacred Scripture not to be so large as it is, nor that God did thereby intend to deliver, as in truth he doth, a full instruction in all things unto salvation necessary, the knowledge whereof man by nature could not otherwise in this life attain unto: they are by this very mean induced either still to look for new revelations from heaven, or else dangerously to add to the word of God uncertain tradition, that so the doctrine of man's salvation may be complete; which doctrine, we constantly hold in all respects without any such thing added to be so complete, that we utterly refuse as much as once to acquaint ourselves with any thing further. Whatsoever to make up the doctrine of man's salvation is added, as in supply of the Scripture's unsufficiency, we reject it. Scripture purposing this, hath perfectly and fully done it.

Again, the scope and purpose of God in delivering the Holy Scripture such as do take more largely than behoveth, they on the contrary side, racking and stretching it further than by him was meant, are drawn into sundry as great inconveniences. These pretending the Scripture's perfection infer thereupon, that in Scripture all things lawful to be done must needs be contained. We count those things perfect which want nothing requisite for the end whereto they were instituted. As therefore God created every part and particle of man exactly perfect, that is to say in all points sufficient unto that use for which he appointed it; so the Scripture, yea, every sentence thereof, is perfect, and wanteth nothing requisite unto that purpose for which God delivered the same. So that if hereupon we conclude, that because the Scripture is perfect, therefore all things lawful to be done are comprehended in the Scripture; we may even as well conclude so of every sentence, as of the whole sum and body thereof, unless we first of all prove that it was the drift, scope, and purpose of Almighty God in Holy Scripture to comprise all things which man may practise.

[6.] But admit this, and mark, I beseech you, what would follow. God in delivering Scripture to his Church should clean have abrogated amongst them the law of nature; which is an infallible knowledge imprinted in the minds of all the children of men, whereby both general principles for directing of human actions are comprehended, and conclusions derived from them; upon which conclusions groweth in particularity the choice of good and evil in the daily affairs of this life. Admit this, and what shall the Scripture be but a snare and a torment to weak consciences, filling them with infinite perplexities, scrupulosities, doubts insoluble, and extreme despairs? Not that the Scripture itself doth cause any such thing, (for it tendeth to the clean contrary, and the fruit thereof is resolute assurance and certainty in that it teacheth,) but the necessities of this life urging men to do that which the light of nature, common discretion and judgment of itself directeth them unto; on the other side, this doctrine teaching them that so to do were to sin against their own souls, and that they put forth their hands to iniquity whatsoever they go about and have not first the sacred Scripture of God for direction; how can it choose but bring the simple a thousand times to their wits' end? how can it choose but vex and amaze them? For in every action of common life to find out some sentence clearly and infallibly setting before our eyes what we ought to do, (seem we in Scripture never so expert,) would trouble us more than we are aware. In weak and tender minds we little know what misery this strict opinion would breed, besides the stops it would make in the whole course of all men's lives and actions. Make all things sin which we do by direction of nature's light, and by the rule of common discretion, without thinking at all upon Scripture; admit this position, and parents shall cause their children to sin, as oft as they cause them to do any thing, before they come to years of capacity and be ripe for knowledge in the Scripture: admit this, and it shall not be with masters as it was with him in the Gospel, but servants being commanded to go [Luke vii. 8] shall stand still, till they have their errand warranted unto them by Scripture. Which as it standeth with Christian duty in some cases, so in common affairs to require it were most unfit.

[7.] Two opinions therefore there are concerning sufficiency of Holy Scripture, each extremely opposite unto the other, and both repugnant unto truth. The schools of Rome teach Scripture to be so unsufficient, as if, except traditions were added, it did not contain all revealed and supernatural truth, which absolutely is necessary for the children of men in this life to know that they may in the next be saved. Others justly condemning this opinion grow likewise unto a dangerous extremity, as if Scripture did not only contain all things in that kind necessary, but all things simply, and in such sort that to do any thing according to any other law were not only unnecessary but even opposite unto salvation, unlawful and sinful. Whatsoever is spoken of God or things appertaining to God otherwise than as the truth is, though it seem an honour, it is an injury. And as incredible praises given unto men do often abate and impair the credit of their deserved commendation; so we must likewise take great heed, lest in attributing unto Scripture more than it can have, the incredibility of that do cause even those things which indeed it hath most abundantly to be less reverently esteemed. I therefore leave it to themselves to consider, whether they have in this first point or not overshot themselves; which God doth know is quickly done, even when our meaning is most sincere, as I am verily persuaded theirs in this case was.

the third book

CONCERNING THEIR SECOND ASSERTION, THAT IN SCRIPTURE THERE MUST BE OF NECESSITY CONTAINED A FORM OF CHURCH POLITY, THE LAWS WHEREOF MAY IN NOWISE BE ALTERED

The matter contained in this third book

* Chapters marked with an asterisk are included in this selection. *Ed.*

Chapter 1

WHAT THE CHURCH IS, AND IN WHAT RESPECT LAWS OF POLITY ARE THEREUNTO NECESSARILY REQUIRED

ALBEIT the substance of those controversies whereinto we have begun to wade be rather of outward things appertaining to the Church of Christ, than of any thing wherein the nature and being of the Church consisteth, yet because the subject or matter which this position concerneth is, *A Form of Church Government or Church Polity*, it therefore behoveth us so far forth to consider the nature of the Church, as is requisite for men's more clear and plain understanding in what respect Laws of Polity or Government are necessary thereunto.

[2.] That Church of Christ, which we properly term his body mystical, can be but one; neither can that one be sensibly discerned by any man, inasmuch as the parts thereof are some in heaven already with Christ, and the rest that are on earth (albeit their natural persons be visible) we do not discern under this property, whereby they are truly and infallibly of that body. Only our minds by intellectual conceit are able to apprehend, that such a real body there is, a body collective, because it containeth an huge multitude; a body mystical, because the mystery of their conjunction is removed altogether from sense. Whatsoever we read in Scripture concerning the endless love and the saving mercy which God sheweth towards his Church, the only proper subject thereof is this Church. Concerning this flock it is that our Lord and Saviour hath promised, "I give unto them eternal life, and they shall never perish, neither shall any pluck them out of my hands." [John x. 28] They who are of this society have such marks and notes of distinction from all others, as are not object unto our sense; only unto God, who seeth their hearts and understandeth all their secret cogitations, unto him they are clear and manifest. All men knew Nathanael to be an Israelite. But our Saviour piercing deeper giveth further testimony of him than men could have done with such certainty as he did, "Behold indeed an Israelite in whom is no guile." [John i. 47] If we profess, as Peter did [John xxi. 15], that we love the Lord, and profess it in the hearing of men, charity is prone to believe all things, and therefore charitable men are likely to think we do so, as long as they see no proof to the contrary. But that our love is sound and sincere, that it cometh from "a pure heart and a good conscience and a faith unfeigned," [1 Tim. i. 5] who can pronounce, saving only the Searcher of all men's hearts, who alone intuitively doth know in this kind who are His?

[3.] And as those everlasting promises of love, mercy, and blessedness belong to the mystical Church; even so on the other side when we read of any duty which the Church of God is bound unto, the Church whom this doth concern is a sensibly known company. And this visible Church in like sort is but one, continued from the first beginning of the world to the last end. Which company being divided into two moieties, the one before, the other since the coming of Christ; that part, which since the coming of Christ partly hath embraced and partly shall hereafter embrace the Christian Religion, we term as by a more proper name the Church of Christ. And therefore the Apostle affirmeth plainly of all men Christian [1 Cor. xii. 13], that be they Jews or Gentiles, bond or free, they are all incorporated into one company, they all make but *one body*.* The unity of which visible body and Church of Christ consisteth in that uniformity which all several persons thereunto belonging have, by reason of that *one Lord* whose servants they all profess themselves, that *one Faith* which they all acknowledge, that *one Baptism* wherewith they are all initiated. [Ephes. iv. 5]

[4.] The visible Church of Jesus Christ is therefore one, in outward profession of those things, which supernaturally appertain to the very essence of Christianity, and are necessarily required in every particular Christian man. "Let all the house of Israel know for certainty," saith Peter, "that God hath made him both Lord and Christ, even this Jesus whom you have crucified." [Acts ii. 36] Christians therefore they are not, which call not him their Master and Lord [John xiii. 13; Col. iii. 24, iv. 1]. And from hence it came that first at Antioch, and afterwards throughout the whole world, all that are of the Church visible were called Christians even amongst the heathen. Which name unto them was precious and glorious, but in the estimation of the rest of the world even Christ Jesus himself was execrable [1 Cor. i. 23]; for whose sake all men were so likewise which did acknowledge him to be their Lord. This himself did foresee, and therefore armed his Church, to the end they might sustain it without discomfort. "All these things they will do unto you for my name's sake; yea, the time shall come, that whosoever killeth you will think that he doth God good service." [John xv. 21] "These things I tell you, that when the hour shall come, ye may then call to mind how I told you beforehand of them." [John xvi. 2, 4]

[5.] But our naming of Jesus Christ the Lord is not enough to prove us Christians, unless we also embrace that faith, which Christ hath published unto the world. To shew that the angel of Pergamus continued in Christianity, behold how the Spirit of Christ speaketh, "Thou keepest my name, and thou hast not denied my faith." [Apoc. ii. 13] Concerning which faith, "the rule thereof," saith Tertullian, "is one alone, immovable, and no way possible to be better framed anew." What rule that is he sheweth by rehearsing those few articles of Christian belief. And before Tertullian, Irenaeus; "The Church though scattered through the whole world unto the utmost borders of the earth, hath from the Apostles and their disciples

* "That he might reconcile both unto God in one body." Ephes. ii. 16. "That the Gentiles should be inheritors also, and of the same body." Ephes. iii. 6.

received belief." The parts of which belief he also reciteth, in substance the very same with Tertullian, and thereupon inferreth, "This faith the Church being spread far and wide preserveth as if one house did contain them: these things it equally embraceth, as though it had even one soul, one heart, and no more: it publisheth, teacheth and delivereth these things with uniform consent, as if God had given it but one only tongue wherewith to speak. He which amongst the guides of the Church is best able to speak uttereth no more than this, and less than this the most simple doth not utter," when they make profession of their faith.

[6.] Now although we know the Christian faith and allow of it, yet in this respect we are but entering; entered we are not into the visible Church before our admittance by the door of Baptism. Wherefore immediately upon the acknowledgment of Christian faith, the Eunuch (we see) was baptized by Philip [Acts viii. 38], Paul by Ananias [Acts xxii, 16], by Peter an huge multitude containing three thousand souls [Acts ii. 41], which being once baptized were reckoned in the number of souls added to the visible Church.

[7.] As for those virtues that belong unto moral righteousness and honesty of life, we do not mention them, because they are not proper unto Christian men, as they are Christian, but do concern them as they are men. True it is, the want of these virtues excludeth from salvation. So doth much more the absence of inward belief of heart; so doth despair and lack of hope; so emptiness of Christian love and charity. But we speak now of the visible Church, whose children are signed with this mark, "One Lord, one Faith, one Baptism." In whomsoever these things are, the Church doth acknowledge them for her children; them only she holdeth for aliens and strangers, in whom these things are not found. For want of these it is that Saracens, Jews, and Infidels are excluded out of the bounds of the Church. Others we may not deny to be of the visible Church, as long as these things are not wanting in them. For apparent it is, that all men are of necessity either Christians, or not Christians. If by external profession they be Christians, then are they of the visible Church of Christ: and Christians by external profession they are all, whose mark of recognizance hath in it those things which we have mentioned, yea, although they be impious idolaters, wicked heretics, persons excommunicable, yea, and cast out for notorious improbity. Such withal we deny not to be the imps and limbs of Satan, even as long as they continue such.

[8.] Is it then possible, that the selfsame men should belong both to the synagogue of Satan and to the Church of Jesus Christ? Unto that Church which is his mystical body, not possible; because that body consisteth of none but only true Israelites, true sons of Abraham, true servants and saints of God. Howbeit of the visible body and Church of Jesus Christ those may be and oftentimes are, in respect of the main parts of their outward profession, who in regard of their inward disposition of mind, yea, of external conversation, yea, even of some parts of their very profession, are most worthily both hateful in the sight of God himself, and in the eyes of the sounder parts of the visible Church most execrable. Our Saviour therefore compareth the kingdom of heaven to a net, whereunto all which cometh neither is nor seemeth fish [Matt. xiii. 47]: his Church he compareth unto a field, where tares manifestly known and seen by all men do grow intermingled with good corn [Matt. xiii. 24], and even so shall continue till the final consummation of the world. God hath had ever and ever shall have some Church visible upon earth. When the people of God worshipped the calf in the wilderness [Exod. xxxii; Ps. cvi. 19, 20]; when they adored the brazen serpent [2 Kings xviii. 4]; when they served the gods of nations; when they bowed their knees to Baal [Jer. xi. 13]; when they burnt incense and offered sacrifice unto idols [2 Kings xxii. 17]: true it is, the wrath of God was most fiercely inflamed against them, their prophets justly condemned them, as an adulterous seed [Isa. lvii. 3], and a wicked generation of miscreants, which had forsaken the living God [Isa. i. 4], and of him were likewise forsaken [Isa. lx. 15], in respect of that singular mercy wherewith he kindly and lovingly embraceth his faithful children. Howbeit retaining the law of God and the holy seal of his covenant, the sheep of his visible flock they continued even in the depth of their disobedience and rebellion [Jer. xiii. 11]. Wherefore not only *amongst* them God always had his Church, because he had thousands which never bowed their knees to Baal [1 Kings xix. 18]; but whose knees were bowed unto Baal, even they were also of the visible Church of God. Nor did the Prophet so complain, as if that Church had been quite and clean extinguished; but he took it as though there had not been remaining in the world any besides himself, that carried a true and an upright heart towards God with care to serve him according unto his holy will.

[9.] For lack of diligent observing the difference, first between the Church of God mystical and visible, then between the visible sound and corrupted, sometimes more, sometimes less, the oversights are neither few nor light that have been committed. This deceiveth them, and nothing else, who think that in the time of the first world the family of Noah did contain all that were of the visible Church of God. From hence it grew, and from no other cause in the world, that the African bishops in the council of Carthage, knowing how the administration of baptism belongeth only to the Church of Christ, and supposing that heretics which were apparently severed from the sound believing Church could not possibly be of the Church of Jesus Christ, thought it utterly against reason, that baptism administered by men of corrupt belief should be accounted as a sacrament. And therefore in maintenance of rebaptization their arguments are built upon the fore-alleged ground, "That heretics are not at all any part of the

Church of Christ. Our Saviour founded his Church on a rock, and not upon heresy [Matt. vii. 24, xvi. 18]. Power of baptizing he gave to his Apostles, unto heretics he gave it not [Matt. xxviii. 19]. Wherefore they that are without the Church, and oppose themselves against Christ, do but scatter His sheep and flock, without the Church baptize they cannot." Again, "Are heretics Christians or are they not? If they be Christians, wherefore remain they not in God's Church? If they be no Christians, how make they Christians? Or to what purpose shall those words of the Lord serve: 'He which is not with me is against me;' and, 'He which gathereth not with me scattereth' [Matt. xii. 30]? Wherefore evident it is, that upon misbegotten children and the brood of Antichrist without rebaptization the Holy Ghost cannot descend." But none in this case so earnest as Cyprian: "I know no baptism but one, and that in the Church only; none without the Church, where he that doth cast out the devil hath the devil: he doth examine about belief whose lips and words do breathe forth a canker; the faithless doth offer the articles of faith; a wicked creature forgiveth wickedness; in the name of Christ Antichrist signeth; he which is cursed of God blesseth; a dead carrion promiseth life; a man unpeaceable giveth peace; a blasphemer calleth upon the name of God; a profane person doth exercise priesthood; a sacrilegious wretch doth prepare the altar; and in the neck of all these that evil also cometh, the Eucharist a very bishop of the devil doth presume to consecrate." All this was true, but not sufficient to prove that heretics were in no sort any part of the visible church of Christ, and consequently their baptism no baptism. This opinion therefore was afterwards both condemned by a better advised council, and also revoked by the chiefest of the authors thereof themselves.

[10.] What is it but only the selfsame error and misconceit, wherewith others being at this day likewise possessed, they ask us where our Church did lurk, in what cave of the earth it slept for so many hundreds of years together before the birth of Martin Luther? As if we were of opinion that Luther did erect a New Church of Christ. No, the Church of Christ which was from the beginning is and continueth unto the end: of which Church all parts have not been always equally sincere and sound. In the days of Abia it plainly appeareth that Judah was by many degrees more free from pollution than Israel, as that solemn oration sheweth wherein he pleadeth for the one against the other in this wise [2 Chron. xiii. 4, 9, 10, 11]: "O Jeroboam and all Israel hear you me: have ye not driven away the priests of the Lord, the sons of Aaron and the Levites, and have made you priests like the people of nations? Whosoever cometh to consecrate with a young bullock and seven rams, the same may be a priest of them that are no gods. But we belong unto the Lord our God, and have not forsaken him; and the priests the sons of Aaron minister unto the Lord every morning and every evening burnt-offerings and sweet incense, and the bread is set in order upon the pure table, and the candlestick of gold with the lamps thereof to burn every evening; for we keep the watch of the Lord our God, but ye have forsaken him." In St. Paul's time the integrity of Rome was famous; Corinth many ways reproved; they of Galatia much more out of square. In St. John's time Ephesus and Smyrna in far better state than Thyatira and Pergamus were [Apoc. ii.]. We hope therefore that to reform ourselves, if at any time we have done amiss, is not to sever ourselves from the Church we were of before. In the Church we were, and we are so still. Other difference between our estate before and now we know none but only such as we see in Judah; which having sometime been idolatrous became afterwards more soundly religious by renouncing idolatry and superstition. If Ephraim "be joined unto idols," the counsel of the Prophet is, "Let him alone." "If Israel play the harlot, let not Judah sin." [Hos. iv. 17, 15] "If it seem evil to you," said Joshua [Josh. xxiv. 15], "to serve the Lord, choose you this day whom ye will serve; whether the gods whom your fathers served beyond the flood, or the gods of the Amorites in whose land ye dwell: but I and mine house will serve the Lord." The indisposition therefore of the Church of Rome to reform herself must be no stay unto us from performing our duty to God; even as desire of retaining conformity with them could be no excuse if we did not perform that duty.

Notwithstanding so far as lawfully we may, we have held and do hold fellowship with them. For even as the Apostle doth say of Israel that they are in one respect enemies but in another beloved of God [Rom. xi. 28]; in like sort with Rome we dare not communicate concerning sundry her gross and grievous abominations, yet touching those main parts of Christian truth wherein they constantly still persist, we gladly acknowledge them to be of the family of Jesus Christ; and our hearty prayer unto God Almighty is, that being conjoined so far forth with them, they may at the length (if it be his will) so yield to frame and reform themselves, that no distraction remain in any thing, but that we "all may with one heart and one mouth glorify God the Father of our Lord and Saviour," [Rom. xv. 6] whose Church we are.

As there are which make the Church of Rome utterly no Church at all, by reason of so many, so grievous errors in their doctrines; so we have them amongst us, who under pretence of imagined corruptions in our discipline do give even as hard a judgment of the Church of England itself.

[11.] But whatsoever either the one sort or the other teach, we must acknowledge even heretics themselves to be, though a maimed part, yet a part of the visible Church. If an infidel should pursue to death an heretic professing Christianity, only for Christian profession's sake, could we deny unto him the honour of martyrdom? Yet this honour all men know to be proper unto the Church. Heretics therefore are not utterly cut off from the visible Church of Christ.

If the Fathers do any where, as oftentimes they do, make the true visible Church of Christ and heretical companies opposite; they are to be construed as separating heretics, not altogether from the company of believers, but from the fellowship of sound believers. For where professed unbelief is, there can be no visible Church of Christ; there may be, where sound belief wanteth. Infidels being clean without the Church deny directly and utterly reject the very principles of Christianity; which heretics embrace, and err only by misconstruction: whereupon their opinions, although repugnant indeed to the principles of Christian faith, are notwithstanding by them held otherwise, and maintained as most consonant thereunto. Wherefore being Christians in regard of the general truth of Christ which they openly profess, yet they are by the Fathers every where spoken of as men clean excluded out of the right believing Church, by reason of their particular errors, for which all that are of a sound belief must needs condemn them.

[12.] In this consideration, the answer of Calvin unto Farel concerning the children of Popish parents doth seem crazed. "Whereas," saith he, "you ask our judgment about a matter, whereof there is doubt amongst you, whether ministers of our order professing the pure doctrine of the Gospel may lawfully admit unto baptism an infant whose father is a stranger unto our Churches, and whose mother hath fallen from us unto the Papacy, so that both the parents are popish: thus we have thought good to answer; namely, that it is an absurd thing for us to baptize them which cannot be reckoned members of our body. And sith Papists' children are such, we see not how it should be lawful to minister baptism unto them." Sounder a great deal is the answer of the ecclesiastical college of Geneva unto Knox, who having signified unto them, that himself did not think it lawful to baptize bastards or the children of idolaters (he meaneth Papists) or of persons excommunicate, till either the parents had by repentance submitted themselves unto the Church, or else their children being grown unto the years of understanding should come and sue for their own baptism: "For thus thinking," saith he, "I am thought to be over-severe, and that not only by them which are popish, but even in their judgments also who think themselves maintainers of the truth." Master Knox's oversight herein they controlled. Their sentence was, "Wheresoever the profession of Christianity hath not utterly perished and been extinct, infants are beguiled of their right, if the common seal be denied them." Which conclusion in itself is sound, although it seemeth the ground is but weak whereupon they built it. For the reason which they yield of their sentence, is this; "The promise which God doth make to the faithful concerning their seed reacheth unto a thousand generations; it resteth not only in the first degree of descent. Infants therefore whose great-grandfathers have been holy and godly, do in that respect belong to the body of the church, although the fathers and grandfathers of whom they descend have been apostates: because the tenure of the grace of God which did adopt them three hundred years ago or more in their ancient predecessors, cannot with justice be defeated and broken off by their parents' impiety coming between." By which reason of theirs although it seem that all the world may be baptized, inasmuch as no man living is a thousand descents removed from Adam himself, yet we mean not at this time either to uphold or to overthrow it: only their alleged conclusion we embrace, so it be construed in this sort; "That forasmuch as men remain in the visible Church, till they utterly renounce the profession of Christianity, we may not deny unto infants their right by withholding from them the public sign of holy baptism, if they be born where the outward acknowledgment of Christianity is not clean gone and extinguished." For being in such sort born, their parents are within the Church, and therefore their birth doth give them interest and right in baptism.

[13.] Albeit not every error and fault, yet heresies and crimes which are not actually repented of and forsaken, exclude quite and clean from that salvation which belongeth unto the mystical body of Christ; yea, they also make a separation from the visible sound Church of Christ; altogether from the visible Church neither the one nor the other doth sever. As for the act of excommunication, it neither shutteth out from the mystical, nor clean from the visible, but only from fellowship with the visible in holy duties. With what congruity then doth the Church of Rome deny, that her enemies, whom she holdeth always for heretics, do at all appertain to the Church of Christ; when her own do freely grant, that albeit the Pope (as they say) cannot teach heresy nor propound error, he may notwithstanding himself worship idols, think amiss concerning matters of faith, yea, give himself unto arts diabolical, even being Pope? How exclude they us from being any part of the Church of Christ under the colour and pretence of heresy, when they cannot but grant it possible even for him to be as touching his own personal persuasion heretical, who in their opinion not only is of the Church, but holdeth the chiefest place of authority over the same? But of these things we are not now to dispute. That which already we have set down, is for our present purpose sufficient.

[14.] By the Church therefore in this question we understand no other than only the visible Church. For preservation of Christianity there is not any thing more needful, than that such as are of the visible Church have mutual fellowship and society one with another. In which consideration, as the main body of the sea being one, yet within divers precincts hath divers names; so the Catholic Church is in like sort divided into a number of distinct Societies, every of which is termed a Church within itself. In this sense the Church is always a visible society of men; not an assembly, but a society. For although the name of the Church be given unto Christian assemblies, although any multitude of Christian men congregated may be termed by the name of a Church, yet assemblies properly are rather things that belong to a Church. Men are assembled for performance of public actions; which actions being ended, the assembly dissolveth itself and is no longer in being, whereas the Church which was assembled doth no less continue afterwards than before. "Where but three are, and they of the laity also (saith Tertullian), yet there is a Church:" that is to say, a Christian assembly. But a Church, as now we are to understand it, is a Society; that is, a number of men belonging unto some Christian fellowship, the place and limits whereof are certain. That wherein they have communion is the public exercise of such duties as those mentioned in the Apostles' Acts, *Instruction*, *Breaking of bread,* and *Prayers* [Acts ii. 42]. As therefore they that are of the mystical body of Christ have those inward graces and virtues, whereby they differ from all others, which are not of the same body; again, whosoever appertain to the visible body of the Church, they have also the notes of external profession, whereby the world knoweth what they are: after the same manner even the several societies of Christian men, unto every of which the name of a Church is given with addition betokening severalty, as the Church of Rome, Corinth, Ephesus, England, and so the rest, must be endued with correspondent general properties belonging unto them as they are public Christian societies. And of such properties common unto all societies Christian, it may not be denied that one of the very chiefest is Ecclesiastical Polity.

Which word I therefore the rather use, because the name of Government, as commonly men understand it in ordinary speech, doth not comprise the largeness of that whereunto in this question it is applied. For when we speak of Government, what doth the greatest part conceive thereby, but only the exercise of superiority peculiar unto rulers and guides of others? To our purpose therefore the name of Church-Polity will better serve, because it containeth both government and also whatsoever besides belongeth to the ordering of the Church in public. Neither is any thing in this degree more necessary than Church-Polity, which is a form of ordering the public spiritual affairs of the Church of God.

* * *

Chapter 3

THAT MATTERS OF DISCIPLINE ARE DIFFERENT FROM MATTERS OF FAITH AND SALVATION; AND THAT THEY THEMSELVES SO TEACH WHICH ARE OUR REPROVERS

The mixture of those things by speech which by nature are divided, is the mother of all error. To take away therefore that error which confusion breedeth, distinction is requisite. Rightly to distinguish is by conceit of mind to sever things different in nature, and to discern wherein they differ. So that if we imagine a difference where there is none, because we distinguish where we should not, it may not be denied that we misdistinguish. The only trial whether we do so, yea or no, dependeth upon comparison between our conceit and the nature of things conceived.

[2.] Touching matters belonging unto the Church of Christ this we conceive, that they are not of one suit. Some things are *merely* of faith, which things it doth suffice that we know and believe; some things not only to be known but done, because they concern the actions of men. Articles about the Trinity are matters of *mere* faith, and must be believed. Precepts concerning the works of charity are matters of action; which to know, unless they be practised, is not enough. This being so clear to all men's understanding, I somewhat marvel that they especially should think it absurd to oppose *Church-government*, a plain matter of action, unto matters of faith, who know that themselves divide the Gospel into *Doctrine* and *Discipline*. For if matters of discipline be rightly by them distinguished from matters of doctrine, why not matters of government by us as reasonably set against matters of faith? Do not they under doctrine comprehend the same which we intend by matter of faith? Do not they under discipline comprise the regiment of the Church? When they blame that in us which themselves follow, they give men great cause to doubt that some other thing than judgment doth guide their speech.

[3.] What the Church of God standeth bound to know or do, the same in part nature teacheth. And because nature can teach them but only in part, neither so fully as is requisite for man's salvation, nor so easily as to make the way plain and expedite enough that many may come to the knowledge of it, and so be saved; therefore in Scripture hath God both collected the most necessary things that the school of nature teacheth unto that end, and revealeth also whatsoever we neither could with safety be ignorant of, nor at all be instructed in but by supernatural revelation from him. So that Scripture containing all things that are in this kind any way needful for the Church, and the principal of the other sort, this is the next thing wherewith we are charged as with an error: we teach that whatsoever is unto salvation termed *necessary* by way of excellency, whatsoever it standeth all men upon to know or do that they may be saved, whatsoever there is whereof it may truly be said, "This not to believe is eternal death and damnation," or, "This every soul that will live must duly observe;" of which sort the articles of Christian faith and the sacraments of the Church of Christ are: all such things if Scripture did not comprehend, the Church of God should not be able to measure out the length and the breadth of that way wherein for ever she is to walk, heretics and schismatics never ceasing some to abridge, some to enlarge, all to pervert and obscure the same. But as for those things that are accessory hereunto, those things that so belong to the way of salvation, as to alter them is no otherwise to change that way, than a path is changed by altering only the uppermost face thereof; which be it laid with gravel, or set with grass, or paved with stone, remaineth still the same path; in such things because discretion may teach the Church what is convenient, we hold not the Church further tied herein unto Scripture, than that against Scripture nothing be admitted in the Church, lest that path which ought always to be kept even, do thereby come to be overgrown with brambles and thorns.

[4.] If this be unsound, wherein doth the point of unsoundness lie? It is not that we make some things *necessary,* some things *accessory* and appendent only: for our Lord and Saviour himself doth make that difference, by terming judgment and mercy and fidelity with other things of like nature, "the greater and weightier matters of the law." [Matt. xxiii. 23] Is it then in that we account ceremonies, (wherein we do not comprise sacraments, or any other the like substantial duties in the exercise of religion, but only such external rites as are usually annexed unto Church actions,) is it an oversight that we reckon these things and matters of government in the number of things accessory, not things necessary in such sort as hath been declared? Let them which therefore think us blameable consider well their own words. Do they not plainly compare the one unto garments which cover the body of the Church; the other unto rings, bracelets, and jewels, that only adorn it; the one to that food which the Church doth live by, the other to that which maketh her diet liberal, dainty, and more delicious? Is dainty fare a thing necessary to the sustenance, or to the clothing of the body rich attire? If not, how can they urge the necessity of that which themselves resemble by things not necessary? or by what construction shall any man living be able to make those comparisons true, holding that distinction untrue, which putteth a difference between things of external regiment in the Church and things necessary unto salvation?

* * *

Chapter 8

ANOTHER ANSWER IN DEFENCE OF THE FORMER ASSERTION, WHEREBY THE MEANING THEREOF IS OPENED IN THIS SORT: ALL CHURCH ORDERS MUST BE COMMANDED IN THE WORD, THAT IS TO SAY, GROUNDED UPON THE WORD, AND MADE ACCORDING AT THE LEASTWISE UNTO THE GENERAL RULES OF HOLY SCRIPTURE. AS FOR SUCH THINGS AS ARE FOUND OUT BY ANY STAR OR LIGHT OF REASON, AND ARE IN THAT RESPECT RECEIVED SO THEY BE NOT AGAINST THE WORD OF GOD, ALL SUCH THINGS IT HOLDETH UNLAWFULLY RECEIVED

The last refuge in maintaining this position is thus to construe it, "Nothing ought to be established in the Church, but that which is commanded in the word of God;" that is to say, all Church orders must be "grounded upon the word of God;" in such sort grounded upon the word, not that being found out by some "star, or light of reason, or learning, or other help," they may be received, so they be not against the word of God; but according at leastwise unto the general rules of Scripture they must be made. Which is in effect as much as to say, "We know not what to say well in defence of this position; and therefore lest we should say it is false, there is no remedy but to say that in some sense or other it may be true, if we could tell how."

[2.] First, that scholy had need of a very favourable reader and a tractable, that should think it plain construction, when to be *commanded in the word* and *grounded upon the word* are made all one. If when a man may live in the state of matrimony, seeking that good thereby which nature principally desireth, he make rather choice of a contrary life in regard of St. Paul's judgment [1 Cor. vii. 8, 26]; that which he doth is manifestly *grounded* upon the word of God, yet not *commanded* in his word, because without breach of any commandment he might do otherwise.

[3.] Secondly, whereas no man in justice and reason can be reproved for those actions which are framed according unto that known will of God, whereby they are to be judged; and the will of God which we are to judge our actions by, no sound divine in the world ever denied to be in part made manifest even by light of nature, and not by Scripture alone: if the Church being directed by the former of these two (which God hath given who gave the other, that man might in different sort be guided by them both), if the Church I say do approve and establish that which thereby it judgeth meet, and findeth not repugnant to any word or syllable of holy Scripture; who shall warrant our presumptuous boldness controlling herein the Church of Christ?

[4.] But so it is, the name of the light of nature is made hateful with men; the "star of reason and learning," and all other such like helps, beginneth no otherwise to be thought of than if it were an unlucky comet; or as if God had so accursed it, that it should never shine or give light in things concerning our duty any way towards him, but be esteemed as that *star* in the Revelation [Apoc. viii. 10] called *Wormwood*, which being fallen from heaven, maketh rivers and waters in which it falleth so bitter, that men tasting them die thereof. A number there are, who think they cannot admire as they ought the power and authority of the word of God, if in things divine they should attribute any force to man's reason. For which cause they never use reason so willingly as to disgrace reason. Their usual and common discourses are unto this effect. First, "the natural man perceiveth not the things of the Spirit of God: for they are foolishness unto him: neither can he know them, because they are spiritually discerned." [1 Cor. ii. 14] Secondly, it is not for nothing that St. Paul giveth charge to "beware of philosophy" [Col. ii. 8], that is to say, such knowledge as men by natural reason attain unto. Thirdly, consider them that have from time to time opposed themselves against the Gospel of Christ, and most troubled the Church with heresy. Have they not always been great admirers of human reason? Hath their deep and profound skill in secular learning made them the more obedient to the truth, and not armed them rather against it? Fourthly, they that fear God will remember how heavy his sentences are in this case: "I will destroy the wisdom of the wise, and will cast away the understanding of the prudent. Where is the wise? where is the scribe? where is the disputer of this world? hath not God made the wisdom of this world foolishness? Seeing the world by wisdom knew not God in the wisdom of God, it pleased God by the foolishness of preaching to save believers." [1 Cor. i. 19] Fifthly, the word of God in itself is absolute, exact and perfect. The word of God is a two-edged sword; as for the weapons of natural reason, they are as the armour of Saul, rather cumbersome about the soldier of Christ than needful. They are not of force to do that which the Apostles of Christ did by the power of the Holy Ghost: "My preaching," therefore saith Paul, "hath not been in the enticing speech of man's wisdom, but in plain evidence of the Spirit and of power, that your faith might not be in the wisdom of men, but in the power of God." [1 Cor. ii. 4] Sixthly, if I believe the Gospel, there needeth no reasoning about it to persuade me; if I do not believe, it must be the Spirit of God and not the reason of man that shall convert my heart unto him. By these and the like disputes an opinion hath spread itself very far in the world, as if the way to be ripe in faith were to be raw in wit and judgment; as if reason were an enemy unto religion, childish simplicity the mother of ghostly and divine wisdom.

[5.] The cause why such declamations prevail so greatly, is, for that men suffer themselves in two respects to be deluded; one is, that the wisdom of man being debased either in comparison with that of God, or in regard of some special thing exceeding the reach and compass thereof, it seemeth to them (not marking so much) as if simply it were condemned: another, that learning, knowledge or wisdom, falsely so termed, usurping a name whereof they are not worthy, and being under that name controlled; their reproof is by so much the more easily misapplied, and through equivocation wrested against those things whereunto so precious names do properly and of right belong. This, duly observed, doth to the former allegations itself make sufficient answer. Howbeit, for all men's plainer and fuller satisfaction:

[6.] First, Concerning the inability of reason to search out and to judge of things divine, if they be such as those properties of God and those duties of men towards him, which may be conceived by attentive consideration of heaven and earth; we know that of mere natural men the Apostle testifieth [Rom. i. 21, 32], how they "knew both God, and the Law of God". Other things of God there be which are neither so found, nor though they be shewed can never be approved without the *special* operation of God's good grace and Spirit. Of such things sometime spake the Apostle St. Paul, declaring how Christ had called him to be a witness of his death and resurrection from the dead, according to that which the Prophets and Moses had foreshewed. Festus, a mere natural man, an infidel, a Roman, one whose ears were unacquainted with such matter, heard him, but could not reach unto that whereof he spake; the suffering and the rising of Christ from the dead he rejecteth as idle superstitious fancies not worth the hearing [Acts xxv. 19]. The Apostle that knew them by the Spirit, and spake of them with power of the Holy Ghost, seemed in his eyes but learnedly mad [Acts xxvi. 24]. Which example maketh manifest what elsewhere the same Apostle teacheth, namely, that nature hath need of grace [1 Cor. ii. 14], whereunto I hope we are not opposite, by holding that grace hath use of nature.

[7.] Secondly, Philosophy we are warned to take heed of: not that philosophy which is true and sound knowledge attained by natural discourse of reason; but that philosophy, which to bolster heresy or error casteth a fraudulent show of reason upon things which are indeed unreasonable, and by that mean as by a stratagem spoileth the simple which are not able to withstand such cunning. "Take heed lest any spoil you through philosophy and vain deceit." [Col. ii. 8] He that exhorteth to beware of an enemy's policy doth not give counsel to be impolitic, but rather to use all provident foresight and circumspection, lest our simplicity be overreached by cunning sleights. The way not to be inveigled by them that are so guileful through skill, is thoroughly to be instructed in that which maketh skilful against guile, and to be armed with that true and sincere philosophy, which doth teach, against that deceitful and vain, which spoileth.

[8.] Thirdly, But many great philosophers have been very unsound in belief. And many sound in belief, have been also great philosophers. Could secular knowledge bring the one sort unto the love of Christian faith? Nor Christian faith the other sort out of love with secular knowledge. The harm that heretics did, they did it unto such as were unable to discern between sound and deceitful reasoning; and the remedy against it was ever the skill which the ancient Fathers had to descry and discover such deceit. Insomuch that Cresconius the heretic complained greatly of St. Augustine, as being too full of logical subtilties. Heresy prevaileth only by a counterfeit show of reason; whereby notwithstanding it becometh invincible, unless it be convicted of fraud by manifest remonstrance clearly true and unable to be withstood. When therefore the Apostle requireth ability to convict heretics [Tit. i. 9, 11], can we think he judgeth it a thing unlawful, and not rather needful, to use the principal instrument of their conviction, the light of reason? It may not be denied but that in the Fathers' writings there are sundry sharp invectives against heretics, even for their very philosophical reasonings. The cause whereof Tertullian confesseth not to have been any dislike conceived against the kind of such reasonings, but the end. "We may," saith he, "even in matters of God be made wiser by reasons drawn from the public persuasions, which are grafted in men's minds: so they be used to further the truth, not to bolster error; so they make with, not against, that which God hath determined. For there are some things even known by nature, as the immortality of the soul unto many, our God unto all. I will therefore myself also use the sentence of some such as Plato, pronouncing every soul immortal. I myself too will use the secret acknowledgment of the commonalty, bearing record of the God of gods. But when I hear men allege, 'That which is dead is dead;' and, 'While thou art alive be alive;' and, 'After death an end of all, even of death itself;' then will I call to mind both that the heart of the people with God is accounted dust, and that the very wisdom of the world is pronounced folly. If then an heretic fly also unto such vicious popular and secular conceits, my answer unto him shall be, 'Thou heretic, avoid the heathen; although in this ye be one, that ye both belie God, yet thou that doest this under the name of Christ, differest from the heathen, in that thou seemest to thyself a Christian. Leave him therefore his conceits, seeing that neither will he learn thine. Why dost thou having sight trust to a blind guide; thou which hast put on Christ take raiment of him that is naked? If the Apostle have armed thee, why dost thou borrow a stranger's shield? Let him rather learn of thee to acknowledge, than thou of him to renounce the resurrection of the flesh.' " In a word, the Catholic Fathers did good unto all by that knowledge, whereby heretics hindering the truth in many, might have furthered therewith themselves, but that obstinately following their own ambitious or otherwise corrupted affections, instead of framing their wills to maintain that which reason taught, they bent their wits to find how reason might seem to teach that which their wills were set to maintain. For which cause the Apostle saith of them justly, that they are for the most part *αὐτοκατάκριτοι*, men condemned even in and of themselves [Tit. iii. 11]. For though they be not all persuaded that it is truth which they withstand, yet that to be error which they uphold they might undoubtedly the sooner a great deal attain to know, but that their study is more to defend what once they have stood in, than to find out sincerely and simply what truth they ought to persist in for ever.

[9.] Fourthly, There is in the world no kind of knowledge, whereby any part of truth is seen, but we justly account it precious; yea, that principal truth, in comparison whereof all other knowledge is vile, may receive from it some kind of light; whether it be that Egyptian and Chaldean wisdom mathematical, wherewith Moses and Daniel were furnished [Acts vii. 22; Dan. i. 17]; or that natural, moral, and civil wisdom, wherein Salomon excelled all men [1 Kings iv. 29, 30]; or that rational and oratorial wisdom of the Grecians, which the Apostle St. Paul brought from Tarsus; or that Judaical, which he learned in Jerusalem sitting at the feet of Gamaliel [Acts xxii. 3]: to detract from the dignity thereof were to injury even God himself, who being that light which none can approach unto, hath sent out these lights whereof we are capable, even as so many sparkles resembling the bright fountain from which they rise.

But there are that bear the title of wise men and scribes and great disputers of the world, and are nothing in deed less than what in show they most appear. These being wholly addicted unto their own wills, use their wit, their learning, and all the wisdom they have, to maintain that which their obstinate hearts are delighted with, esteeming in the frantic error of their minds the greatest madness in the world to be wisdom, and the highest wisdom foolishness. Such were both Jews and Grecians, which professed the one sort legal, and the other secular skill, neither enduring to be taught the mystery of Christ: unto the glory of whose most blessed name, whoso study to use both their reason and all other gifts, as well which nature as which grace hath endued them with, let them never doubt but that the same God who is to destroy and confound utterly that wisdom falsely so named in others, doth make reckoning of them as of true Scribes, Scribes by wisdom instructed to the kingdom of heaven [Matt. xiii. 52], not Scribes against that kingdom hardened in a vain opinion of wisdom; which in the end being proved folly, must needs perish, true understanding, knowledge, judgment and reason continuing for evermore.

[10.] Fifthly, Unto the word of God, being in respect of that end for which God ordained it perfect, exact, and absolute in itself, we do not add reason as a supplement of any maim or defect therein, but as a necessary instrument, without which we could not reap by the Scripture's perfection that fruit and benefit which it yieldeth. "The word of God is a twoedged sword" [Heb. iv. 12], but in the hands of reasonable men; and reason as the weapon that slew Goliath, if they be as David was that use it. Touching the Apostles, He which gave them from above such power for miraculous confirmation of that which they taught, endued them also with wisdom from above to teach that which they so did confirm. Our Saviour made choice of twelve simple and unlearned men, that the greater their lack of natural wisdom was, the more admirable that might appear which God supernaturally endued them with from heaven. Such therefore as knew the poor and silly estate wherein they had lived, could not but wonder to hear the wisdom of their speech, and be so much the more attentive unto their teaching. They studied for no tongue, they spake with all, of themselves they were rude, and knew not so much as how to premeditate; the Spirit gave them speech and eloquent utterance.

But because with St. Paul it was otherwise than with the rest, inasmuch as he never conversed with Christ upon earth as they did; and his education had been scholastical altogether, which theirs was not; hereby occasion was taken by certain malignants, secretly to undermine his great authority in the Church of Christ, as though the gospel had been taught him by others than by Christ himself, and as if the cause of the Gentiles' conversion and belief through his means had been the learning and skill which he had by being conversant in their books; which thing made them so willing to hear him, and him so able to persuade them; whereas the rest of the Apostles prevailed, because God was with them, and by miracle from heaven confirmed his word in their mouths. They were mighty in *deeds*: as for him, being absent, his writings had some force; in presence, his power not like unto theirs. In sum, concerning his preaching, their very byword was, λόγος ἐξουθενημένος, *addle speech, empty talk* [2 Cor. x. 10]: his writings full of great words, but in the power of miraculous operations his presence not like the rest of the Apostles.

Hereupon it riseth that St. Paul was so often driven to make his apologies. Hereupon it riseth that whatsoever time he had spent in the study of human learning, he maketh earnest protestation to them of Corinth, that the gospel which he had preached amongst them did not by other means prevail with them, than with others the same gospel taught by the rest of the Apostles of Christ. "My preaching," saith he, "hath not been in the persuasive speeches of human wisdom, but in demonstration of the Spirit and of power: that your faith may not be in the wisdom of men, but in the power of God". [1 Cor. ii. 4, 5] What is it which the Apostle doth here deny? Is it denied that his speech amongst them had been *persuasive*? No: for of him the sacred history plainly testifieth, that for the space of a year and a half he spake in their synagogue every Sabbath; and *persuaded* both Jews and Grecians [Acts xviii. 4, 11]. How then is the speech of men made persuasive? Surely there can be but two ways to bring this to pass, the one human, the other divine. Either St. Paul did *only* by art and natural industry cause his own speech to be credited; or else God by miracle did authorize it, and so bring credit thereunto, as to the speech of the rest of the Apostles. Of which two, the former he utterly denieth. For why? if the preaching of the rest had been effectual by miracle, his *only* by force of his own learning; so great inequality between him and the other Apostles in this thing had been enough to subvert their faith. For might they not with reason have thought, that if he were sent of God as well as they, God would not have furnished them and not him with the power of the Holy Ghost? Might not a great part of them being simple haply have feared, lest their assent had been cunningly gotten unto his doctrine, rather through the weakness of their own wits than the certainty of that truth which he had taught them? How unequal had it been that all believers through the preaching of other Apostles should have their faith strongly built upon the evidence of God's own miraculous approbation, and they whom he had converted should have their persuasion built only upon his skill and wisdom who persuaded them?

As therefore calling from men may authorize us to teach, although it could not authorize him to teach as other Apostles did: so although the wisdom of man had not been sufficient to enable him such a teacher as the rest of the apostles were, unless God's miracles had strengthened both the one and the other's doctrine; yet unto our ability both of teaching and learning the truth of Christ, as we are but mere Christian men, it is not a little which the wisdom of man may add.

[11.] Sixthly, Yea, whatsoever our hearts be to God and to his truth, believe we or be we as yet faithless, for our conversion or confirmation the force of natural reason is great. The force whereof unto those effects is nothing without grace. What then? To our purpose it is sufficient, that whosoever doth serve, honour, and obey God, whosoever believeth in Him, that man would no more do this than innocents and infants do, but for the light of natural reason that shineth in him, and maketh him apt to apprehend those things of God, which being by grace discovered, are effectual to persuade reasonable minds and none other, that honour, obedience, and credit, belong of right unto God. No man cometh unto God to offer him sacrifice, to pour out supplications and prayers before him, or to do him any service, which doth not first believe him both to be, and to be a rewarder of them who in such sort seek unto him [Heb. xi. 6]. Let men be taught this either by revelation from heaven, or by instruction upon earth; by labour, study, and meditation, or by the only secret inspiration of the Holy Ghost; whatsoever the mean be they know it by, if the knowledge thereof were possible without discourse of natural reason, why should none be found capable thereof but only men; nor men till such time as they come unto ripe and full ability to work by reasonable understanding? The whole drift of the Scripture of God, what is it but only to teach Theology? Theology, what is it but the science of things divine? What science can be attained unto without the help of natural discourse and reason? "Judge you of that which I speak" [1 Cor. x. 15], saith the Apostle. In vain it were to speak any thing of God, but that by reason men are able somewhat to judge of that they hear, and by discourse to discern how consonant it is to truth.

[12.] Scripture indeed teacheth things above nature, things which our reason by itself could not reach unto. Yet those things also we believe, knowing by reason that the Scripture is the word of God. In the presence of Festus, a Roman, and of King Agrippa, a Jew, St. Paul omitting the one, who neither knew the Jews' religion nor the books whereby they were taught it, speaketh unto the other of things foreshewed by Moses and the Prophets and performed in Jesus Christ; intending thereby to prove himself so unjustly accused, that unless his judges did condemn both Moses and the Prophets, him they could not choose but acquit, who taught only that fulfilled, which they so long since had foretold. His cause was easy to be discerned; what was done their eyes were witnesses; what Moses and the Prophets did speak their books could quickly shew; it was no hard thing for him to compare them, which knew the one, and believed the other. "King Agrippa, believest thou the Prophets? I know thou dost". [Acts xxvi. 27] The question is how the books of the Prophets came to be credited of King Agrippa. For what with him did authorize the Prophets, the like with us doth cause the rest of the Scripture of God to be of credit.

[13.] Because we maintain that in Scripture we are taught all things necessary unto salvation; hereupon very childishly it is by some demanded, what Scripture can teach us the sacred authority of the Scripture, upon the knowledge whereof our whole faith and salvation dependeth? As though there were any kind of science in the world which leadeth men into knowledge without presupposing a number of things already known. No science doth make known the first principles whereon it buildeth, but they are always either taken as plain and manifest in themselves, or as proved and granted already, some former knowledge having made them evident. Scripture teacheth all supernaturally revealed truth, without the knowledge whereof salvation cannot be attained. The main principle whereupon our belief of all things therein contained dependeth, is, that the Scriptures are the oracles of God himself. This in itself we cannot say is evident. For then all men that hear it would acknowledge it in heart, as they do when they hear that "every whole is more than any part of that whole," because this in itself is evident. The other we know that all do not acknowledge when they hear it. There must be therefore some former knowledge presupposed which doth herein assure the hearts of all believers. Scripture teacheth us that saving truth which God hath discovered unto the world by revelation, and it presumeth us taught otherwise that itself is divine and sacred.

[14.] The question then being by what means we are taught this; some answer that to learn it we have no other way than only tradition; as namely that so we believe because both we from our predecessors and they from theirs have so received. But is this enough? That which all men's experience teacheth them may not in any wise be denied. And by experience we all know, that the first outward motive leading men so to esteem of the Scripture is the authority of God's Church. For when we know the whole Church of God hath that opinion of the Scripture, we judge it even at the first an impudent thing for any man bred and brought up in the Church to be of a contrary mind without cause. Afterwards the more we bestow our labour in reading or hearing the mysteries thereof, the more we find that the thing itself doth answer our received opinion concerning it. So that the former inducement prevailing somewhat with us before, doth now much more prevail, when the very thing hath ministered farther reason. If infidels or atheists chance at any time to call it in question, this giveth us occasion to sift what reason there is, whereby the testimony of the Church concerning Scripture, and our own persuasion which Scripture itself hath confirmed, may be proved a truth infallible. In which case the ancient Fathers being often constrained to shew, what warrant they had so much to rely upon the Scriptures, endeavoured still to maintain the authority of the books of God by arguments such as unbelievers themselves must needs think reasonable, if they judged thereof as they should. Neither is it a thing impossible or greatly hard, even by such kind of proofs so to manifest and clear that point, that no man living shall be able to deny it, without denying some apparent principle such as all men acknowledge to be true.

Wherefore if I believe the Gospel, yet is reason of singular use, for that it confirmeth me in this my belief the more: if I do not as yet believe, nevertheless to bring me to the number of believers except reason did somewhat help, and were an instrument which God doth use unto such purposes, what should it boot to dispute with infidels or godless persons for their conversion and persuasion in that point?

[15.] Neither can I think that when grave and learned men do sometime hold, that of this principle there is no proof but by the testimony of the Spirit, which assureth our hearts therein, it is their meaning to exclude utterly all force which any kind of reason may have in that behalf; but I rather incline to interpret such their speeches, as if they had more expressly set down, that other motives and inducements, be they never so strong and consonant unto reason, are notwithstanding uneffectual of themselves to work faith concerning this principle, if the special grace of the Holy Ghost concur not to the enlightening of our minds. For otherwise I doubt not but men of wisdom and judgment will grant, that the Church, in this point especially, is furnished with reason, to stop the mouths of her impious adversaries; and that as it were altogether bootless to allege against them what the Spirit hath taught us, so likewise that even to our ownselves it needeth caution and explication how the testimony of the Spirit may be discerned, by what means it may be known; lest men think that the Spirit of God doth testify those things which the Spirit of error suggesteth. The operations of the Spirit, especially these ordinary which be common unto all true Christian men, are as we know things secret and undiscernible even to the very soul where they are, because their nature is of another and an higher kind than that they can be by us perceived in this life. Wherefore albeit the Spirit lead us into all truth and direct us in all goodness, yet because these workings of the Spirit in us are so privy and secret, we therefore stand on a plainer ground, when we gather by reason from the quality of things believed or done, that the Spirit of God hath directed us in both, than if we settle ourselves to believe or to do any certain particular thing, as being moved thereto by the Spirit.

[16.] But of this enough. To go from the books of Scripture to the sense and meaning thereof: because the sentences which are by the Apostles recited out of the Psalms [Acts xiii. 36; ii. 34], to prove the resurrection of Jesus Christ, did not prove it, if so be the Prophet David meant them of himself; this exposition therefore they plainly disprove, and shew by manifest reason, that of David the words of David could not possibly be meant. Exclude the use of natural reasoning about the sense of Holy Scripture concerning the articles of our faith, and then that the Scripture doth concern the articles of our faith who can assure us? That which by right exposition buildeth up Christian faith, being misconstrued breedeth error: between true and false construction, the difference reason must shew. Can Christian men perform that which Peter requireth at their hands; is it possible they should both believe and be able, without the use of reason, to render "a reason of their belief," [1 Pet. iii. 15] a reason sound and sufficient to answer them that demand it, be they of the same faith with us or enemies thereunto? may we cause our faith without reason to appear reasonable in the eyes of men? This being required even of learners in the school of Christ, the duty of their teachers in bringing them unto such ripeness must needs be somewhat more, than only to read the sentences of Scripture, and then paraphrastically to scholy them, to vary them with sundry forms of speech, without arguing or disputing about any thing which they contain. This method of teaching may commend itself unto the world by that easiness and facility which is in it: but a law or a pattern it is not, as some do imagine, for all men to follow that will do good in the Church of Christ.

[17.] Our Lord and Saviour himself did hope by disputation to do some good, yea by disputation not only of but against, the truth, albeit with purpose for the truth. That Christ should be the son of David was truth; yet against this truth our Lord in the gospel objecteth, "If Christ be the son of David, how doth David call him Lord?" [Matt. xxii. 43] There is as yet no way known how to dispute, or to determine of things disputed, without the use of natural reason.

If we please to add unto Christ their example, who followed him as near in all things as they could; the sermon of Paul and Barnabas set down in the Acts [Acts xiv. 15], where the people would have offered unto them sacrifice; in that sermon what is there but only natural reason to disprove their act? "O men, why do you these things? We are men even subject to the selfsame passions with you: we preach unto you to leave these vanities and to turn to the living God, the God that hath not left himself without witness, in that he hath done good to the world, giving rain and fruitful seasons, filling our heart with joy and gladness."

Neither did they only use reason in winning such unto Christian belief as were yet thereto unconverted, but with believers themselves they followed the selfsame course. In that great and solemn assembly of believing Jews how doth Peter prove that the Gentiles were partakers of the grace of God as well as they, but by reason drawn from those effects, which were apparently known amongst them? "God which knoweth hearts hath borne them witness in giving unto them the Holy Ghost as unto us." [Acts xv. 8]

The light therefore, which the star of natural reason and wisdom casteth, is too bright to be obscured by the mist of a word or two uttered to diminish that opinion which justly hath been received concerning the force and virtue thereof, even in matters that touch most nearly the principal duties of men and the glory of the eternal God.

[18.] In all which hitherto hath been spoken touching the force and use of man's reason in things divine, I must crave that I be not so understood or construed, as if any such thing by virtue thereof could be done without the aid and assistance of God's most blessed Spirit. The thing we have handled according to the question moved about it; which question is, whether the light of reason be so pernicious, that in devising laws for the Church men ought not by it to search what may be fit and convenient. For this cause therefore we have endeavoured to make it appear, how in the nature of reason itself there is no impediment, but that the selfsame Spirit, which revealeth the things that God hath set down in his law, may also be thought to aid and direct men in finding out by the light of reason what laws are expedient to be made for the guiding of his Church, over and besides them that are in Scripture. Herein therefore we agree with those men, by whom human laws are defined to be ordinances which such as have lawful authority given them for that purpose do probably draw from the laws of nature and God, by discourse of reason aided with the influence of divine grace. And for that cause, it is not said amiss touching ecclesiastical canons, that "by instinct of the Holy Ghost they have been made, and consecrated by the reverend acceptation of all the world."

* * *

the fourth book

CONCERNING THEIR THIRD ASSERTION, THAT OUR FORM OF CHURCH POLITY IS CORRUPTED WITH POPISH ORDERS, RITES, AND CEREMONIES, BANISHED OUT OF CERTAIN REFORMED CHURCHES, WHOSE EXAMPLE THEREIN WE OUGHT TO HAVE FOLLOWED

The matter contained in this fourth book

Chapter 12

THEIR EXCEPTION AGAINST SUCH CEREMONIES AS HAVE BEEN ABUSED BY THE CHURCH OF ROME, AND ARE SAID IN THAT RESPECT TO BE SCANDALOUS

BUT the weightiest exception, and of all the most worthy to be respected, is against such kind of ceremonies, as have been so grossly and shamefully abused in the church of Rome, that where they remain they are scandalous, yea, they cannot choose but be stumbling blocks and grievous causes of offence. Concerning this point therefore we are first to note, what properly it is to be scandalous or offensive; secondly, what kind of ceremonies are such; and thirdly, when they are necessarily for remedy thereof to be taken away, and when not.

[2.] The common conceit of the vulgar sort is, whensoever they see any thing which they mislike and are angry at, to think that every such thing is scandalous, and that themselves in this case are the men concerning whom our Saviour spake in so fearful manner, saying, "whosoever shall scandalize or offend any one of these little ones which believe in me" [Matt. xviii. 6] (that is, as they construe it, whosoever shall anger the meanest and simplest artisan which carrieth a good mind, by not removing out of the Church such rites and ceremonies as displease him), "better he were drowned in the bottom of the sea." But hard were the case of the Church of Christ, if this were to scandalize. Men are scandalized when they are moved, led, and provoked unto sin. At good things evil men may take occasion to do evil; and so Christ himself was a rock of offence in Israel [1 Pet. ii. 8], they taking occasion at his poor estate and at the ignominy of his cross, to think him unworthy the name of that great and glorious Messias, whom the Prophets describe in such ample and stately terms. But that which we therefore term offensive because it inviteth men to offend, and by a dumb kind of provocation encourageth, moveth, or any way leadeth unto sin, must of necessity be acknowledged actively scandalous.

Now some things are so even by their very essence and nature, so that wheresoever they are found they are not, neither can be without this force

* Chapter marked with an asterisk is included in this selection. *Ed.*

of provocation unto evil; of which kind all examples of sin and wickedness are. Thus David was scandalous in that bloody act whereby he caused the enemies of God to be blasphemous [2 Sam. xii. 14]: thus the whole state of Israel scandalous, when their public disorders caused the name of God to be ill-spoken of amongst the nations [Rom. ii. 24; Ezek. xxxvi. 20]. It is of this kind that Tertullian meaneth: "Offence or scandal, if I be not deceived (saith he), is, when the example not of a good but of an evil thing doth set men forward unto sin. Good things can scandalize none save only evil minds:" good things have no scandalizing nature in them.

[3.] Yet that which is of its own nature either good or at least not evil, may by some accident become scandalous at certain times and in certain places and to certain men; the open use thereof nevertheless being otherwise without danger. The very nature of some rites and ceremonies therefore is scandalous, as it was in a number of those which the Manichees did use, and is in all such as the law of God doth forbid. Some are offensive only through the agreement of men to use them unto evil, and not else; as the most of those things indifferent which the heathens did to the service of their false gods, which another, in heart condemning their idolatry, could not do with them in show and token of approbation without being guilty of scandal given. Ceremonies of this kind are either devised at the first unto evil, as the Eunomian heretics in dishonour of the blessed Trinity brought in the laying on of water but once, to cross the custom of the church which in baptism did it thrice; or else having had a profitable use they are afterwards interpreted and wrested to the contrary, as those heretics which held the Trinity to be three distinct not persons but natures, abused the ceremony of three times laying on water in baptism unto the strengthening of their heresy. The element of water is in baptism necessary; once to lay it on or thrice is indifferent. For which cause Gregory making mention thereof saith, "To dive an infant either thrice or but once in baptism, can be no way a thing reprovable; seeing that both in three times washing the Trinity of persons, and in one the Unity of Godhead may be signified." So that of these two ceremonies neither being hurtful in itself, both may serve unto good purpose; yet one was devised, and the other converted, unto evil.

[4.] Now whereas in the church of Rome certain ceremonies are said to have been shamefully abused unto evil, as the ceremony of crossing at baptism, of kneeling at the eucharist, of using wafer-cakes, and such like; the question is, whether for remedy of that evil wherein such ceremonies have been scandalous, and perhaps may be still unto some even amongst ourselves, whom the presence and sight of them may confirm in that former error whereto they served in times past, they are of necessity to be removed. Are these, or any other ceremonies we have common with the church of Rome, scandalous and wicked in their very nature? This no man objecteth. Are any such as have been polluted from their very birth, and instituted even at the first unto that thing which is evil? That which hath been ordained impiously at the first, may wear out that impiety in tract of time; and then what doth let but that the use thereof may stand without offence? The names of our months and of our days we are not ignorant from whence they came, and with what dishonour unto God they are said to have been devised at the first. What could be spoken against any thing more effectual to stir hatred, than that which sometime the ancient Fathers in this case speak? Yet those very names are at this day in use throughout Christendom without hurt or scandal to any. Clear and manifest it is, that things devised by heretics, yea, devised of a very heretical purpose even against religion, and at their first devising worthy to have been withstood, may in time grow meet to be kept; as that custom, the inventors whereof were the Eunomian heretics. So that customs once established and confirmed by long use, being presently without harm, are not in regard of their corrupt original to be held scandalous.

[5.] But concerning those our ceremonies which they reckon for most popish, they are not able to avouch, that any of them was otherwise instituted than unto good, yea, so used at the first. It followeth then that they all are such, as having served to good purpose, were afterwards converted unto the contrary. And sith it is not so much as objected against us, that we retain together with them the evil wherewith they have been infected in the church of Rome, I would demand who they are whom we scandalize, by using harmless things unto that good end for which they were first instituted. Amongst ourselves that agree in the approbation of this kind of good use, no man will say that one of us is offensive and scandalous unto another. As for the favourers of the church of Rome, they know how far we herein differ and dissent from them; which thing neither we conceal, and they by their public writings also profess daily how much it grieveth them; so that of them there will not many rise up against us, as witnesses unto the indictment of scandal, whereby we might be condemned and cast, as having strengthened them in that evil wherewith they pollute themselves in the use of the same ceremonies. And concerning such as withstand the church of England herein, and hate it because it doth not sufficiently seem to hate Rome; they (I hope) are far enough from being by this mean drawn to any kind of popish error. The multitude therefore of them, unto whom we are scandalous through the use of abused ceremonies, is not so apparent, that it can justly be said in general of any one sort of men or other, we cause them to offend. If it be so, that now or then some few are espied, who, having been accustomed heretofore to the rites and ceremonies of the church of Rome, are not so scoured of their former rust as to forsake their ancient persuasion which they have had, howsoever they frame themselves to outward obedience of laws and orders: because such may misconstrue the meaning of our ceremonies, and so take them as though they were in every sort the same they have been, shall this be thought a reason sufficient whereon to conclude that some law must necessarily be made to abolish all such ceremonies?

[6.] They answer, that there is no law of God which doth bind us to retain them. And St. Paul's rule is, that in those things from which without hurt we may lawfully abstain, we should frame the usage of our liberty with regard to the weakness and imbecility of our brethren. Wherefore unto them which stood upon their own defence saying, "All things are lawful unto me"; he replieth, "but all things are not expedient" [1 Cor. vi. 12] in regard of others. "All things are clean, all meats are lawful; but evil unto that man that eateth offensively. If for thy meat's sake thy brother be grieved, thou walkest no longer according to charity. Destroy not him with thy meat for whom Christ died. Dissolve not for food's sake the work of God. We that are strong must bear the imbecilities of the impotent, and not please ourselves." It was a weakness in the Christian Jews, and a maim of judgment in them, that they thought the Gentiles polluted by the eating of those meats which themselves were afraid to touch for fear of transgressing the law of Moses; yea, hereat their hearts did so much rise, that the Apostle had just cause to fear, lest they would rather forsake Christianity than endure any fellowship with such as made no conscience of that which was unto them abominable. And for this cause mention is made of destroying the weak by meats, and of dissolving the work of God [Rom. xiv; xv, 1], which was his Church, a part of the living stones whereof were believing Jews. Now those weak brethren before-mentioned are said to be as the Jews were, and our ceremonies which have been abused in the church of Rome to be as the scandalous meats, from which the Gentiles are exhorted to abstain in the presence of Jews, for fear of averting them from Christian faith. Therefore, as charity did bind them to refrain from that for their brethren's sake, which otherwise was lawful enough for them; so it bindeth us for our brethren's sake likewise to abolish such ceremonies, although we might lawfully else retain them.

[7.] But between these two cases there are great odds. For neither are our weak brethren as the Jews, nor the ceremonies which we use as the meats which the Gentiles used. The Jews were known to be generally weak in that respect; whereas contrariwise the imbecility of ours is not common unto so many, that we can take any such certain notice of them. It is a chance if here and there some one be found; and therefore seeing we may presume men commonly otherwise, there is no necessity that our practice should frame itself by that which the Apostle doth prescribe to the Gentiles.

Again, their use of meats was not like unto of our ceremonies, that being a matter of private action in common life, where every man was free to order that which himself did; but this a public constitution for the ordering of the Church: and we are not to look that the Church should change her public laws and ordinances, made according to that which is judged ordinarily and commonly fittest for the whole, although it chance that for some particular men the same be found inconvenient; especially when there may be other remedy also against the sores of particular inconveniences. In this case therefore where any private harm doth grow, we are not to reject instruction, as being an unmeet plaster to apply unto it; neither can we say, that he which appointeth teachers for physicians in this kind of evil, is "As if a man would set one to watch a child all day long lest he should hurt himself with a knife; whereas by taking away the knife from him, the danger is avoided, and the service of the man better employed." For a knife may be taken away from a child, without depriving them of the benefit thereof which have years and discretion to use it. But the ceremonies which children do abuse if we remove quite and clean, as it is by some required that we should, then are they not taken from children only, but from others also; which is as though because children may perhaps hurt themselves with knives, we should conclude, that therefore the use of knives is to be taken quite and clean even from men also.

[8.] Those particular ceremonies, which they pretend to be so scandalous, we shall in the next Book have occasion more thoroughly to sift, where other things also traduced in the public duties of the Church whereunto each of these appertaineth, are together with these to be touched, and such reasons to be examined as have at any time been brought either against the one or the other. In the meanwhile against the conveniency of curing such evils by instruction, strange it is that they should object the multitude of other necessary matters, wherein preachers may better bestow their time, than in giving men warning not to abuse ceremonies: a wonder it is, that they should object this, which have so many years together troubled the Church with quarrels concerning these things, and are even to this very hour so earnest in them, that if they write or speak publicly but five words, one of them is lightly about the dangerous estate of the church of England in respect of abused ceremonies. How much happier had it been for this whole Church, if they which have raised contention therein about the abuse of rites and ceremonies, had considered in due time that there is indeed store of matters fitter and better a great deal for teachers to spend time and labour in! It is through their importunate and vehement asseverations, more than through any such experience which we have had of our own, that we are forced to think it possible for one or other now and then, at leastwise in the prime of the reformation of our church, to have stumbled at some kind of ceremony; wherein forasmuch as we are contented to take this upon their credit, and to think it may be; sith also they further pretend the same to be so dangerous a snare to their souls that are at any time taken therein; they must give our teachers leave for the saving of those souls (be they never so few) to intermingle sometime with other more necessary things admonition concerning these not unnecessary. Wherein they should in reason more easily yield this leave, considering that hereunto we shall not need to use the hundredth part of that time, which themselves think very needful to bestow in making most bitter invectives against the ceremonies of the Church.

the fifth book

OF THEIR FOURTH ASSERTION, THAT TOUCHING THE SEVERAL PUBLIC DUTIES OF CHRISTIAN RELIGION, THERE IS AMONGST US MUCH SUPERSTITION RETAINED IN THEM; AND CONCERNING PERSONS WHICH FOR PERFORMANCE OF THOSE DUTIES ARE ENDUED WITH THE POWER OF ECCLESIASTICAL ORDER, OUR LAWS AND PROCEEDINGS ACCORDING THEREUNTO ARE MANY WAYS HEREIN ALSO CORRUPT

The matter contained in this fifth book

* Chapters marked with an asterisk are included in this selection. *Ed.*

Chapter 19. Of preaching by reading publicly the books of Holy Scripture; and concerning supposed untruths in those Translations of Scripture which we allow to be read; as also of the choice which we make in reading.

Chapter 20. Of preaching by the public reading of other profitable instructions; and concerning books Apocryphal.

**Chapter 21.* Of preaching by Sermons, and whether Sermons be the only ordinary way of teaching whereby men are brought to the saving knowledge of God's truth.

**Chapter 22.* What they attribute to Sermons only, and what we to reading also.

**Chapter 23.* Of Prayer.

Chapter 24. Of public Prayer.

Chapter 25. Of the form of Common Prayer.

Chapter 26. Of them which like not to have any set form of Common Prayer.

Chapter 27. Of them who allowing a set form of prayer yet allow not ours.

Chapter 28. The form of our Liturgy too near the papists', too far different from that of other reformed Churches, as they pretend.

Chapter 29. Attire belonging to the service of God.

Chapter 30. Of gesture in praying, and of different places chosen to that purpose.

Chapter 31. Easiness of praying after our form.

Chapter 32. The length of our service.

Chapter 33. Instead of such prayers as the primitive Churches have used, and those that be reformed now use, we have (they say) divers short cuts or shreddings, rather wishes than prayers.

**Chapter 34.* Lessons intermingled with our prayers.

**Chapter 35.* The number of our prayers for earthly things, and our oft rehearsing of the Lord's Prayer.

Chapter 36. The people's saying after the minister.

**Chapter 37.* Our manner of reading the Psalms otherwise than the rest of the Scripture.

**Chapter 38.* Of Music with Psalms.

**Chapter 39.* Of singing or saying Psalms, and other parts of Common Prayer wherein the people and the minister answer one another by course.

Chapter 40. Of *Magnificat*, *Benedictus*, and *Nunc Dimittis*.

Chapter 41. Of the Litany.

Chapter 42. Of Athanasius's Creed, and *Gloria Patri*.

Chapter 43. Our want of particular thanksgiving.

Chapter 44. In some things the matter of our prayer, as they affirm, is unsound.

Chapter 45. "When thou hadst overcome the sharpness of death, thou didst open the Kingdom of Heaven unto all believers."

Chapter 46. Touching prayer for deliverance from sudden death.

Chapter 47. Prayer that those things which we for our unworthiness dare not ask, God for the worthiness of his Son would vouchsafe to grant.

Chapter 48. Prayer to be evermore delivered from all adversity.

Chapter 49. Prayer that all men may find mercy.

**Chapter 50*. Of the name, the author, and the force of Sacraments, which force consisteth in this, that God hath ordained them as means to make us partakers of him in Christ, and of life through Christ.

**Chapter 51*. That God is in Christ by the personal incarnation of the Son, who is very God.

**Chapter 52*. The misinterpretations which heresy hath made of the manner how God and man are united in one Christ.

**Chapter 53*. That by the union of the one with the other nature in Christ, there groweth neither gain nor loss of essential properties to either.

**Chapter 54*. What Christ hath obtained according to the flesh, by the union of his flesh with Deity.

**Chapter 55*. Of the personal presence of Christ every where, and in what sense it may be granted he is every where present according to the flesh.

**Chapter 56*. The union or mutual participation which is between Christ and the Church of Christ in this present world.

**Chapter 57*. The necessity of Sacraments unto the participation of Christ.

Chapter 58. The substance of Baptism, the rites or solemnities thereunto belonging, and that the substance thereof being kept, other things in Baptism may give place to necessity.

Chapter 59. The ground in Scripture whereupon a necessity of outward Baptism hath been built.

Chapter 60. What kind of necessity in outward Baptism hath been gathered by the words of our Saviour Christ; and what the true necessity thereof indeed is.

Chapter 61. What things in Baptism have been dispensed with by the Fathers respecting necessity.

Chapter 62. Whether baptism by women be true Baptism, good and effectual to them that receive it.

Chapter 63. Of Interrogatories in Baptism touching faith and the purpose of a Christian life.

Chapter 64. Interrogatories proposed unto infants in Baptism, and answered as in their names by godfathers.

Chapter 65. Of the Cross in Baptism.

Chapter 66. Of Confirmation after Baptism.

**Chapter 67*. Of the Sacrament of the body and blood of Christ.

Chapter 1

TRUE RELIGION IS THE ROOT OF ALL TRUE VIRTUES, AND THE STAY OF ALL WELL-ORDERED COMMONWEALTHS

FEW there are of so weak capacity, but public evils they easily espy; fewer so patient, as not to complain, when the grievous inconveniences thereof work sensible smart. Howbeit to see wherein the harm which they feel consisteth, the seeds from which it sprang, and the method of curing it, belongeth to a skill, the study whereof is so full of toil, and the practice so beset with difficulties, that wary and respective men had rather seek quietly their own, and wish that the world may go well, so it be not long of them than with pain and hazard make themselves advisers for the common good. We which thought it at the very first a sign of cold affection towards the Church of God, to prefer private ease before the labour of appeasing public disturbance, must now of necessity refer events to the gracious providence of Almighty God, and, in discharge of our duty towards him, proceed with the plain and unpartial defence of a common cause. Wherein our endeavour is not so much to overthrow them with whom we contend, as to yield them just and reasonable causes of those things, which, for want of due consideration heretofore, they misconceived, accusing laws for men's oversights, imputing evils, grown through personal defects unto that which is not evil, framing to some sores unwholesome plasters, and applying other some where no sore is.

[2.] To make therefore our beginning that which to both parts is most acceptable, *We agree* that pure and unstained religion ought to be the highest of all cares appertaining to public regiment: as well in regard of that aid and protection [Ps. cxliv. 2] which they who faithfully serve God confess they receive at his merciful hands; as also for the force which religion hath to qualify all sorts of men, and to make them in public affairs the more serviceable, governors the apter to rule with conscience, inferiors for conscience' sake the willinger to obey. It is no peculiar conceit, but a matter of sound consequence, that all duties are by so much the better performed, by how much the men are more religious from whose abilities the same proceed. For if the course of politic affairs cannot in any good sort go forward without fit instruments, and that which fitteth them be their virtues, let Polity acknowledge itself indebted to Religion; godliness being the chiefest top and wellspring of all true virtues, even as God is of all good things.

So natural is the union of Religion with Justice, that we may boldly deem there is neither, where both are not. For how should they be unfeignedly just, whom religion doth not cause to be such; or they religious, which are not found such by the proof of their just actions? If they, which employ their labour and travail about the public administration of justice, follow it only as a trade, with unquenchable and unconscionable thirst of gain, being not in heart persuaded that justice is God's own work [2 Chron. xix. 6], and themselves his agents in this business, the sentence of right God's own verdict, and themselves his priests to deliver it; formalities of justice do but serve to smother right, and that, which was necessarily ordained for the common good, is through shameful abuse made the cause of common misery.

The same piety, which maketh them that are in authority desirous to please and resemble God by justice, inflameth every way men of action with zeal to do good (as far as their place will permit) unto all. For that, they know, is most noble and divine. Whereby if no natural nor casual inability cross their desires, they always delighting to inure themselves with actions most beneficial to others, cannot but gather from thence great experience, and through experience the more wisdom; because conscience, and the fear of swerving from that which is right, maketh them diligent observers of circumstances, the loose regard whereof is the nurse of vulgar folly, no less than Solomon's attention thereunto was of natural furtherances the most effectual to make him eminent above others. For he gave good heed, and pierced every thing to the very ground, and by that mean became the author of many parables. [Eccles. xii. 9]

Concerning fortitude; sith evils great and unexpected (the true touchstone of constant minds) do cause oftentimes even them to think upon divine power with fearfullest suspicions, which have been otherwise the most secure despisers thereof [Wisd. xvii. 13]; how should we look for any constant resolution of mind in such cases, saving only where unfeigned affection to God-ward hath bred the most assured confidence to be assisted by his hand? For proof whereof, let but the acts of the ancient Jews be indifferently weighed; from whose magnanimity, in cases of most extreme hazard, those strange and unwonted resolutions have grown, which for all circumstances no people under the roof of heaven did ever hitherto match. And that which did always so animate them was their mere religion.

Without which, if so be it were possible that all other ornaments of mind might be had in their full perfection, nevertheless the mind that should possess them divorced from piety could be but a spectacle of commiseration; even as that body is, which adorned with sundry other admirable beauties, wanteth eyesight, the chiefest grace that nature hath in that kind to bestow. They which commend so much the felicity of that innocent world, wherein it is said that men of their own accord did embrace fidelity and honesty, not for fear of the magistrate, or because revenge was before their eyes if at any time they should do otherwise, but that which held the people in awe was the shame of ill-doing, the love of equity and right itself a bar against all oppressions which greatness of power causeth; they which describe unto us any such estate of happiness amongst men, though they speak not of religion, do notwithstanding declare that which is in truth her only working. For, if religion did possess sincerely and sufficiently the hearts of all men, there would need no other restraint from evil. This doth not only give life and perfection to all endeavours wherewith it concurreth; but what event soever ensue, it breedeth, if not joy and gladness always, yet always patience, satisfaction, and reasonable contentment of mind. Whereupon it hath been set down as an axiom of good experience, that all things religiously taken in hand are prosperously ended [Ps. i. 3]; because whether men in the end have that which religion did allow them to desire, or that which it teacheth them contentedly to suffer, they are in neither event unfortunate.

[3.] But lest any man should here conceive, that it greatly skilleth not of what sort our religion be, inasmuch as heathens, Turks, and infidels impute to religion a great part of the same effects which ourselves ascribe thereunto, they having ours in the same detestation that we theirs; it shall be requisite to observe well, how far forth there may be agreement in the effects of different religions. First, by the bitter strife which riseth oftentimes from small differences in this behalf, and is by so much always greater as the matter is of more importance; we see a general agreement in the secret opinion of men, that every man ought to embrace the religion which is true, and to shun, as hurtful, whatsoever dissenteth from it, but that most, which doth farthest dissent. The generality of which persuasion argueth, that God hath imprinted it by nature, to the end it might be a spur to our industry in searching and maintaining that religion, from which as to swerve in the least points is error, so the capital enemies thereof God hateth as his deadly foes, aliens, and, without repentance, children of endless perdition. Such therefore touching man's immortal state after this life are not likely to reap benefit by their religion, but to look for the clean contrary, in regard of so important contrariety between it and the true religion.

Nevertheless, inasmuch as the errors of the most seduced this way have been mixed with some truths, we are not to marvel, that although the one did turn to their endless woe and confusion, yet the other had many notable effects as touching the affairs of this present life. There were in these quarters of the world, sixteen hundred years ago, certain speculative men, whose authority disposed the whole religion of those times. By their means it became a received opinion, that the souls of men departing this life do flit out of one body into some other. Which opinion, though false, yet entwined with a true, that the souls of men do never perish, abated the fear of death in them which were so resolved, and gave them courage unto all adventures.

The Romans had a vain superstitious custom, in most of their enterprises to conjecture beforehand of the event by certain tokens which they noted in birds, or in the entrails of beasts, or by other the like frivolous divinations. From whence notwithstanding as oft as they could receive any sign which they took to be favourable, it gave them such hope, as if their gods had made them more than half a promise of prosperous success. Which many times was the greatest cause that they did prevail, especially being men of their own natural inclination hopeful and strongly conceited, whatsoever they took in hand. But could their fond superstition have furthered so great attempts without the mixture of a true persuasion concerning the unresistible force of divine power?

Upon the wilful violation of oaths, execrable blasphemies, and like contempts, offered by deriders of religion even unto false gods, fearful tokens of divine revenge have been known to follow. Which occurrents the devouter sort did take for manifest arguments, that the gods whom they worshipped were of power to reward such as sought unto them, and would plague those that feared them not. In this they erred. For (as the wise man rightly noteth concerning such) it was not the power of them by whom they sware, but the vengeance of them that sinned, which punished the offences of the ungodly [Wisd. xiv. 31]. It was their hurt untruly to attribute so great power unto false gods. Yet the right conceit which they had, that to perjury vengeance is due, was not without good effect as touching the course of their lives, who feared the wilful violation of oaths in that respect.

And whereas we read so many of them so much commended, some for their mild and merciful disposition, some for their virtuous severity, some for integrity of life, all these were the fruits of true and infallible principles delivered unto us in the word of God as the axioms of our religion, which being imprinted by the God of nature in their hearts also, and taking better root in some than in most others, grew, though not from, yet with and amidst the heaps of manifold repugnant errors; which errors of corrupt religion had also their suitable effects in the lives of the selfsame parties.

[4.] Without all controversy, the purer and perfecter our religion is, the worthier effects it hath in them who steadfastly and sincerely embrace it, in others not. They that love the religion which they profess, may have failed in choice, but yet they are sure to reap what benefit the same is able to afford; whereas the best and soundest professed by them that bear it not the like affection, yieldeth them, retaining it in that sort, no benefit. David was a "man after God's own heart," so termed because his affection was hearty towards God. Beholding the like disposition in them which lived under him, it was his prayer to Almighty God, "O keep this for ever in the purpose and thoughts of the heart of this people." [1 Chron. xxix. 18] But when, after that David had ended his days in peace, they who succeeded him in place for the most part followed him not in quality; when those kings (some few excepted) to better their worldly estate, (as they thought,) left their own and their people's ghostly condition uncared for; by woful experience they both did learn, that to forsake the true God of heaven, is to fall into all such evils upon the face of the earth, as men either destitute of grace divine may commit, or unprotected from above endure.

[5.] Seeing therefore it doth thus appear that the safety of all estates dependeth upon religion; that religion unfeignedly loved perfecteth men's abilities unto all kinds of virtuous services in the commonwealth; that men's desire is in general to hold no religion but the true; and that whatsoever good effects do grow out of their religion, who embrace instead of the true a false, the roots thereof are certain sparks of the light of truth intermingled with the darkness of error, because no religion can wholly and only consist of untruths: we have reason to think that all true virtues are to honour true religion as their parent, and all well-ordered commonweals to love her as their chiefest stay.

Chapter 2

THE MOST EXTREME OPPOSITE TO TRUE RELIGION, IS AFFECTED ATHEISM

They of whom God is altogether unapprehended are but few in number, and for grossness of wit such, that they hardly and scarcely seem to hold the place of human being. These we should judge to be of all others most miserable, but that a wretcheder sort there are, on whom whereas nature hath bestowed riper capacity, their evil disposition seriously goeth about therewith to apprehend God as being not God. Whereby it cometh to pass that of these two sorts of men, both godless, the one having utterly no knowledge of God, the other study how to persuade themselves that there is no such thing to be known. The fountain and wellspring of which impiety [Wisd. ii. 21] is a resolved purpose of mind to reap in this world what sensual profit or pleasure soever the world yieldeth, and not to be barred from any whatsoever means available thereunto. And that this is the very radical cause of their atheism, no man I think will doubt which considereth what pains they take to destroy those principal spurs and motives unto all virtue, the creation of the world, the providence of God, the resurrection of the dead, the joys of the kingdom of heaven, and the endless pains of the wicked, yea above all things the authority of Scripture, because on these points it evermore beateth, and the soul's immortality, which granted, draweth easily after it the rest as a voluntary train. Is it not wonderful that base desires should so extinguish in men the sense of their own excellency, as to make them willing that their souls should be like the souls of beasts, mortal and corruptible with their bodies? Till some admirable or unusual accident happen (as it hath in some) to work the beginning of a better alteration in their minds, disputation about the knowledge of God with such kind of persons commonly prevaileth little. For how should the brightness of wisdom shine, where the windows of the soul are of very set purpose closed?* True religion hath many things in it, the only mention whereof galleth and troubleth their minds. Being therefore loth that inquiry into such matters should breed a persuasion in the end contrary unto that they embrace, it is their endeavour to banish as much as in them lieth quite and clean from their cogitation whatsoever may sound that way.

* Susan. ver. 9. "They turned away their mind, and cast down their eyes, that they might not see heaven, nor remember just judgments."

[2.] But it cometh many times to pass (which is their torment) that the thing they shun doth follow them, truth as it were even obtruding itself into their knowledge, and not permitting them to be so ignorant as they would be. Whereupon inasmuch as the nature of man is unwilling to continue doing that wherein it shall always condemn itself, they continuing still obstinate to follow the course which they have begun, are driven to devise all the shifts that wit can invent for the smothering of this light, all that may but with any the least show of possibility stay their minds from thinking that true, which they heartily wish were false, but cannot think it so without some scruple and fear of the contrary.

Now because that judicious learning, for which we commend most worthily the ancient sages of the world, doth not in this case serve the turn, these trencher-mates (for such the most of them be) frame to themselves a way more pleasant; a new method they have of turning things that are serious into mockery, an art of contradiction by way of scorn, a learning wherewith we were long sithence forewarned that the miserable times whereinto we are fallen should abound [2 Peter iii. 3; Jude 18]. This they study, this they practise, this they grace with a wanton superfluity of wit, too much insulting over the patience of more virtuously disposed minds.

For towards these so forlorn creatures we are (it must be confest) too patient. In zeal to the glory of God, Babylon hath excelled Sion. We want that decree [Dan. iii. 29] of Nebuchadnezzar; the fury of this wicked brood hath the reins too much at liberty; their tongues walk at large; the spit-venom of their poisoned hearts breaketh out to the annoyance of others; what their untamed lust suggesteth, the same their licentious mouths do every where set abroach.

With our contentions their irreligious humour also is much strengthened. Nothing pleaseth them better than these manifold oppositions about the matter of religion, as well for that they have hereby the more opportunity to learn on one side how another may be oppugned, and so to weaken the credit of all unto themselves; as also because by this hot pursuit of lower controversies amongst men professing religion, and agreeing in the principal foundations thereof, they conceive hope that about the higher principles themselves time will cause altercations to grow.

For which purpose, when they see occasion, they stick not sometime in other men's persons, yea sometime without any vizard at all, directly to try, what the most religious are able to say in defence of the highest points whereupon all religion dependeth. Now for the most part it so falleth out touching things which generally are received, that although in themselves they be most certain, yet because men presume them granted of all, we are hardliest able to bring such proof of their certainty as may satisfy gainsayers, when suddenly and besides expectation they require the same at our hands. Which impreparation and unreadiness when they find in us, they turn it to the soothing up of themselves in that cursed fancy, whereby they would fain believe that the hearty devotion of such as indeed fear God is nothing else but a kind of harmless error, bred and confirmed in them by the sleights of wiser men.

[3.] For a politic use of religion they see there is, and by it they would also gather that religion itself is a mere politic device, forged purposely to serve for that use. Men fearing God are thereby a great deal more effectually than by positive laws restrained from doing evil; inasmuch as those laws have no farther power than over our outward actions only, whereas unto men's inward cogitations, unto the privy intents and motions of their hearts, religion serveth for a bridle. What more savage, wild, and cruel, than man, if he see himself able either by fraud to overreach, or by power to overbear, the laws whereunto he should be subject? Wherefore in so great boldness to offend, it behoveth that the world should be held in awe, not by a vain surmise, but a true apprehension of somewhat, which no man may think himself able to withstand. This is the politic use of religion.

[4.] In which respect there are of these wise malignants some, who have vouchsafed it their marvellous favourable countenance and speech, very gravely affirming, that religion honoured, addeth greatness, and contemned, bringeth ruin unto commonweals; that princes and states, which will continue, are above all things to uphold the reverend regard of religion, and to provide for the same by all means in the making of their laws.

But when they should define what means are best for that purpose, behold, they extol the wisdom of Paganism; they give it out as a mystical precept of great importance, that princes, and such as are under them in most authority or credit with the people, should take all occasions of rare events, and from what cause soever the same do proceed, yet wrest them to the strengthening of their religion, and not make it nice for so good a purpose to use, if need be, plain forgeries. Thus while they study how to bring to pass that religion may seem but a matter made, they lose themselves in the very maze of their own discourses, as if reason did even purposely forsake them, who of purpose forsake God the author thereof. For surely a strange kind of madness it is, that those men who though they be void of piety, yet because they have wit cannot choose but know that treachery, guile, and deceit are things, which may for a while but do not use long to go unespied, should teach that the greatest honour to a state is perpetuity; and grant that alterations in the service of God, for that they impair the credit of religion, are therefore perilous in commonweals, which have no continuance longer than religion hath all reverence done unto it; and withal acknowledge (for so they do) that when people began to espy the falsehood of oracles, whereupon all Gentility was built, their hearts were utterly averted from it; and notwithstanding counsel princes in sober earnest, for the strengthening of their states to maintain religion, and for the maintenance of religion not to make choice of that which is true, but to authorize that they make choice of by those false and fraudulent means which in the end must needs overthrow it. Such are the counsels of men godless, when they would shew themselves politic devisers, able to create God in man by art.

Chapter 3

OF SUPERSTITION, AND THE ROOT THEREOF, EITHER MISGUIDED ZEAL, OR IGNORANT FEAR OF DIVINE GLORY

Wherefore to let go this execrable crew, and to come to extremities on the contrary hand; two affections there are, the forces whereof, as they bear the greater or lesser sway in man's heart, frame accordingly the stamp and character of his religion; the one zeal, the other fear.

Zeal, unless it be rightly guided, when it endeavoureth most busily to please God, forceth upon him those unseasonable offices which please him not. For which cause, if they who this way swerve be compared with such sincere, sound, and discreet, as Abraham was in matter of religion; the service of the one is like unto flattery, the other like the faithful sedulity of friendship [2 Chron. xx. 7]. Zeal, except it be ordered aright, when it bendeth itself unto conflict with things either in deed, or but imagined to be opposite unto religion, useth the razor many times with such eagerness, that the very life of religion itself is thereby hazarded; through hatred of tares the corn in the field of God is plucked up. So that zeal needeth both ways a sober guide.

Fear, on the other side, if it have not the light of true understanding concerning God, wherewith to be moderated, breedeth likewise superstition. It is therefore dangerous, that in things divine we should work too much upon the spur either of zeal or fear. Fear is a good solicitor to devotion. Howbeit, sith fear in this kind doth grow from an apprehension of Deity endued with irresistible power to hurt, and is of all affections (anger excepted) the unaptest to admit any conference with reason; for which cause the wise man doth say of fear that it is a betrayer of the forces of reasonable understanding [Wisd. xvii. 12]; therefore except men know beforehand what manner of service pleaseth God, while they are fearful they try all things which fancy offereth. Many there are who never think on God but when they are in extremity of fear; and then, because what to think or what to do they are uncertain, perplexity not suffering them to be idle, they think and do as it were in a phrensy they know not what.

[2.] Superstition neither knoweth the right kind, nor observeth the due measure, of actions belonging to the service of God, but is always joined with a wrong opinion touching things divine. Superstition is, when things are either abhorred or observed with a zealous or fearful, but erroneous, relation to God. By means whereof, the superstitious do sometimes serve, though the true God, yet with needless offices, and defraud him of duties necessary; sometime load others than him with such honours as properly are his. The one their oversight, who miss in the choice of that wherewith; the other theirs, who fail in the election of him towards whom they shew devotion: this, the crime of idolatry, that, the fault of voluntary either niceness or superfluity in religion.

[3.] The Christian world itself being divided into two grand parts, it appeareth by the general view of both, that with matter of heresy the West hath been often and much troubled; but the East part never quiet, till the deluge of misery, wherein now they are, overwhelmed them. The chiefest cause whereof doth seem to have lain in the restless wits of the Grecians, evermore proud of their own curious and subtile inventions; which when at any time they had contrived, the great facility of their language served them readily to make all things fair and plausible to men's understanding. Those grand heretical impieties therefore, which most highly and immediately touched God and the glorious Trinity, were all in a manner the monsters of the East. The West bred fewer a great deal, and those commonly of a lower nature, such as more nearly and directly concerned rather men than God; the Latins being always to capital heresies less inclined, yet unto gross superstition more.

[4.] Superstition such as that of the Pharisees was [Mark vii. 9], by whom divine things indeed were less, because other things were more divinely esteemed of than reason would; the superstition that riseth voluntarily, and by degrees which are hardly discerned mingleth itself with the rites even of very divine service done to the only true God, must be considered of as a creeping and encroaching evil, an evil the first beginnings whereof are commonly harmless, so that it proveth only then to be an evil when some farther accident doth grow unto it, or itself come unto farther growth. For in the Church of God sometimes it cometh to pass as in over battle grounds, the fertile disposition whereof is good; yet because it exceedeth due proportion, it bringeth forth abundantly, through too much rankness, things less profitable; whereby that which principally it should yield, being either prevented in place, or defrauded of nourishment, faileth. This (if so large a discourse were necessary) might be exemplified even by heaps of rites and customs now superstitious in the greatest part of the Christian world, which, in their first original beginnings, when the strength of virtuous, devout, or charitable affection bloomed them, no man could justly have condemned as evil.

Chapter 4

OF THE REDRESS OF SUPERSTITION IN GOD'S CHURCH, AND CONCERNING THE QUESTION OF THIS BOOK

But howsoever superstition do grow, that wherein unsounder times have done amiss, the better ages ensuing must rectify, as they may. I now come therefore to those accusations brought against us by pretenders of reformation; the first in the rank whereof is such, that if so be the Church of England did at this day therewith as justly deserve to be touched, as they in this cause have imagined it doth, rather would I exhort all sorts to seek pardon even with tears at the hands of God, than meditate words of defence for our doings, to the end that men might think favourably of them. For as the case of this world, especially now, doth stand, what other stay or succour have we to lean unto, saving the testimony of our conscience, and the comfort we take in this, that we serve the living God (as near as our wits can reach unto the knowledge thereof) even according to his own will, and do therefore trust that his mercy shall be our safeguard against those enraged powers abroad, which principally in that respect are become our enemies? But sith no man can do ill with a good conscience, the consolation which we herein seem to find, is but a mere deceitful pleasing of ourselves in error, which at the length must needs turn to our greater grief, if that which we do to please God most be for the manifold defects thereof offensive unto him. For so it is judged, our prayers, our sacraments, our fasts, our times and places of public meeting together for the worship and service of God, our marriages, our burials, our functions, elections and ordinations ecclesiastical, almost whatsoever we do in the exercise of our religion according to laws for that purpose established, all things are some way or other thought faulty, all things stained with superstition.

[2.] Now although it may be the wiser sort of men are not greatly moved hereat, considering how subject the very best things have been always unto cavil, when wits possessed either with disdain or dislike thereof have set them up as their mark to shoot at: safe notwithstanding it were not therefore to neglect the danger which from hence may grow, and that especially in regard of them, who desiring to serve God as they ought, but being not so skilful as in every point to unwind themselves where the snares of glosing speech do lie to entangle them, are in mind not a little troubled, when they hear so bitter invectives against that which this church hath taught them to reverence as holy, to approve as lawful, and to observe as behoveful for the exercise of Christian duty. It seemeth therefore at the least for their sakes very meet, that such as blame us in this behalf be directly answered, and they which follow us informed plainly in the reasons of that we do.

[3.] On both sides the end intended between us, is to have laws and ordinances such as may rightly serve to abolish superstition, and to establish the service of God with all things thereunto appertaining in some perfect form.

There is an inward reasonable [Rom. xii. 1], and there is a solemn [Luke i. 23] outward serviceable worship belonging unto God. Of the former kind are all manner virtuous duties that each man in reason and conscience to Godward oweth. Solemn and serviceable worship we name for distinction sake, whatsoever belongeth to the Church or public society of God by way of external adoration. It is the later of these two whereupon our present question groweth.

Again, this later being ordered, partly, and as touching principal matters, by none but precepts divine only; partly, and as concerning things of inferior regard, by ordinances as well human as divine: about the substance of religion wherein God's only law must be kept there is here no controversy; the crime now intended against us is, that our laws have not ordered those inferior things as behoveth, and that our customs are either superstitious, or otherwise amiss, whether we respect the exercise of public duties in religion, or the functions of persons authorized thereunto.

* * *

Chapter 18

OF PUBLIC TEACHING, OR PREACHING, AND THE FIRST KIND THEREOF, CATECHISING

Places of public resort being thus provided for, our repair thither is especially for mutual conference, and as it were commerce to be had between God and us.

Because therefore want of the knowledge of God is the cause of all iniquity amongst men, as contrariwise the very ground of all our happiness, and the seed of whatsoever perfect virtue groweth from us, is a right opinion touching things divine; this kind of knowledge we may justly set down for the first and chiefest thing which God imparteth unto his people, and our duty of receiving this at his merciful hands for the first of those religious offices wherewith we publicly honour him on earth. For the instruction therefore of all sorts of men to eternal life it is necessary, that the sacred and saving truth of God be openly published unto them. Which open publication of *heavenly mysteries* is by an excellency termed Preaching. For otherwise there is not any thing *publicly notified*, but we may in that respect, rightly and properly say it is "preached." [Luke viii. 39, xii. 3] So that when the school of God doth use it as *a word of art*, we are accordingly to understand it with restraint to such special matter as that school is accustomed to publish.

[2.] We find not in the world any people that have lived altogether without religion. And yet this duty of religion, which provideth that publicly all sorts of men may be instructed in the fear of God, is to the Church of God and hath been always so peculiar, that none of the heathens, how curious soever in searching out all kinds of outward ceremonies like to ours, could ever once so much as endeavour to resemble *herein* the Church's care for the endless good of her children.

[3.] Ways of teaching there have been sundry always usual in God's Church. For the first introduction of youth to the knowledge of God, the Jews even till this day have their Catechisms. With religion it fareth as with other sciences. The first delivery of the elements thereof must, for like consideration, be framed according to the weak and slender capacity of young beginners: unto which manner of teaching principles in Christianity, the Apostle in the sixth to the Hebrews is himself understood to allude. For this cause therefore, as the Decalogue of Moses declareth summarily those things which we ought to do; the prayer of our Lord whatsoever we should request or desire: so either by the Apostles, or at the leastwise out of their writings, we have the substance of Christian belief compendiously drawn into few and short articles, to the end that the weakness of no man's wit might either hinder *altogether* the knowledge, or excuse the utter ignorance of needful things.

Such as were trained up in these rudiments, and were so made fit to be afterwards by Baptism received into the Church, the Fathers usually in their writings do term Hearers, as having no farther communion or fellowship with the Church than only this, that they were admitted to hear the principles of Christian faith made plain unto them.

Catechising may be in schools, it may be in private families. But when we make it a kind of preaching, we mean always the public performance thereof in the open hearing of men, because things are preached not in that they are taught, but in that they are published.

* * *

Chapter 21

OF PREACHING BY SERMONS; AND WHETHER SERMONS BE THE ONLY ORDINARY WAY OF TEACHING, WHEREBY MEN ARE BROUGHT TO THE SAVING KNOWLEDGE OF GOD'S TRUTH

We marvel the less that our reading of books not canonical is so much impugned, when so little is attributed unto the reading of canonical Scripture itself, that now it hath grown to be a question, whether *the word of God* be any *ordinary* mean to save the souls of men, in that it is either privately studied or publicly read and so made known, or else only as the same is *preached*, that is to say, *explained by lively voice*, and *applied* to the people's use *as the speaker in his wisdom* thinketh meet. For this alone is it which they use to call Preaching. The public reading of the Apocrypha they condemn altogether as a thing effectual unto evil; the *bare* reading *in like sort* of whatsoever, yea even of Scriptures themselves, they mislike, as a thing *uneffectual* to do *that good*, which we are persuaded may grow by it.

[2.] Our desire is in this present controversy, as in the rest, not to be carried up and down with the waves of uncertain arguments, but rather positively to lead on the minds of the simpler sort by plain and easy degrees, till the very nature of the thing itself do make manifest what is truth. First therefore because whatsoever is spoken concerning the efficacy or necessity of God's Word, the same they tie and restrain only unto Sermons, howbeit not Sermons read neither (for such they also abhor in the church) but sermons without book, sermons which spend their life in their birth and may have public audience but once; for this cause to avoid ambiguities wherewith they often entangle themselves, not marking what doth agree to the word of God in itself, and what in regard of outward accidents which may befall it, we are to know that the word of God is his heavenly truth touching matters of eternal life revealed and uttered unto men; unto Prophets and Apostles by immediate divine inspiration, from them to us by their books and writings. We therefore have no *word of God* but the Scripture. Apostolic sermons were unto such as heard them his word, even as properly as to us their writings are. Howbeit not so our own sermons, the expositions which our discourse of wit doth gather and minister out of the word of God. For which cause in this present question, we are when we name the *word of God* always to mean the *Scripture only*.

[3.] The end of the word of God is *to save*, and therefore we term it *the word of life*. The way for all men to be saved is by the knowledge of that truth which the word hath taught. And sith eternal life is a thing of itself communicable unto all, it behoveth that the word of God, the necessary mean thereunto, be so likewise. Wherefore the word of life hath been always a treasure, though precious, yet easy, as well to attain, as to find; lest any man desirous of life should perish through the difficulty of the way. To this end the word of God no otherwise serveth than only in the nature of a doctrinal instrument. It saveth because it maketh "wise to salvation." Wherefore the ignorant it saveth not; they which live by the word must know it. And being itself the instrument which God hath purposely framed, thereby to work the knowledge of salvation in the hearts of men, what cause is there wherefore it should not of itself be acknowledged a most apt and a likely mean to leave an Apprehension of things divine in our understanding, and in the mind an Assent thereunto? For touching the one, sith God, who knoweth and discloseth best the rich treasures of his own wisdom, hath by delivering his word made choice of the Scriptures as the most effectual means whereby those treasures might be imparted unto the world, it followeth that to man's understanding the Scripture must needs be even of itself intended as a full and perfect discovery, sufficient to imprint in us the lively character of all things necessarily required for the attainment of eternal life. And concerning our assent to the mysteries of heavenly truth, seeing that the word of God for the author's sake hath credit with all that confess it (as we all do) to be his word, every proposition of holy Scripture, every sentence being to us a principle; if the principles of all kinds of knowledge else have that virtue in themselves, whereby they are able to procure our assent unto such conclusions as the industry of right discourse doth gather from them; we have no reason to think the principles of that truth which tendeth unto man's everlasting happiness less forcible than any other, when we know that of all other they are for their certainty the most infallible.

But as every thing of price, so this doth require travail. We bring not the knowledge of God with us into the world. And the less our own opportunity or ability is that way, the more we need the help of other men's judgments to be our direction herein. Nor doth any man ever believe, into whom the doctrine of belief is not instilled by instruction some way received at the first from others. Wherein whatsoever fit means there are to notify the mysteries of the word of God, whether publicly (which we call Preaching) or in private howsoever, the word by *every such mean* even "ordinarily" doth save, and not only by being delivered unto men in Sermons.

[4.] *Sermons* are not *the only preaching* which doth save souls. For concerning the use and sense of this word Preaching, which they shut up in so close a prison, although more than enough have already been spoken to redeem the liberty thereof, yet because they insist so much and so proudly insult thereon, we must a little inure their ears with hearing how others whom they more regard are in this case accustomed to use the selfsame language with us whose manner of speech they deride. Justin Martyr doubteth not to tell the Grecians, that even in certain of their *writings* the very judgment to come is preached; nor the council of Vaus to insinuate that presbyters absent through infirmity from their churches might be said to preach by those deputies who in their stead did but read *Homilies*; nor the council of Toledo to call the usual public reading of the *Gospels* in the church Preaching; nor others long before these our days to write, that by him who but readeth *a lesson* in the solemn assembly as part of divine service, the very office of Preaching is so far forth executed. Such kind of speeches were then familiar, those phrases seemed not to them absurd, they would have marvelled to hear the outcries which we do, because we think that the Apostles in writing, and others in reading to the church those books which the Apostles wrote, are neither untruly nor unfitly said "to preach." For although men's *tongues* and their *pens* differ, yet to one and the self-

same general if not particular *effect*, they may both serve. It is no good argument, St. Paul could not "write with his tongue," therefore neither could he "preach with his pen." For Preaching is a general end whereunto writing and speaking do both serve. Men speak not with the instruments of writing, neither write with the instruments of speech, and yet things *recorded* with the one and *uttered* with the other may be *preached* well enough with both. By their patience therefore be it spoken, the Apostles preached as well when they wrote as when they spake the Gospel of Christ, and our usual public Reading of the word of God for the people's instruction is Preaching.

[5.] Nor about words would we ever contend, were not their purpose in so restraining the same injurious to God's most sacred Word and Spirit. It is on both sides confessed that the word of God outwardly administered (his Spirit [John vi. 46; Matt. xvi. 17; 2 Cor. iv. 6; 1 Cor. xii. 3; Acts xvi. 14] inwardly concurring therewith) converteth, edifieth, and saveth souls. Now whereas the external administration of his word is as well by reading barely the Scripture, as by explaining the same when sermons thereon be made; in the one they deny that the finger of God hath *ordinarily* certain *principal operations*, which we most steadfastly hold and believe that it hath in both.

Chapter 22

WHAT THEY ATTRIBUTE TO SERMONS ONLY, AND WHAT WE TO READING ALSO

So worthy a part of divine service we should greatly wrong, if we did not esteem Preaching as the blessed ordinance of God, sermons as keys to the kingdom of heaven, as wings to the soul, as spurs to the good affections of man, unto the sound and healthy as food, as physic unto diseased minds. Wherefore how highly soever it may please them with words of truth to extol sermons, they shall not herein offend us. We seek not to derogate from any thing which they can justly esteem, but our desire is to uphold the just estimation of that from which it seemeth unto us they derogate more than becometh them. That which offendeth us is, first, the great disgrace which they offer unto our custom of bare reading the word of God, and to his gracious Spirit, the *principal* virtue whereof thereby manifesting itself for the endless good of men's souls, even the virtue which it hath to *convert*, to *edify*, to *save* souls, this they mightily strive to obscure; and secondly the shifts wherewith they maintain their opinion of Sermons, whereunto while they labour to appropriate the *saving* power of the Holy Ghost, they separate from all *apparent* hope of life and salvation thousands whom the goodness of Almighty God doth not exclude.

[2.] Touching therefore the use of Scripture, even in that it is openly read, and the inestimable good which the Church of God by that very mean hath reaped; there was, we may very well think, some cause, which moved the Apostle St. Paul to require, that those things which any one church's affairs gave particular occasion to write, might for the instruction of all be published, and that by *reading* [1 Thess. v. 27; Coloss. iv. 16].

1. When the very having of the books of God was a matter of no small charge and difficulty, inasmuch as they could not be had otherwise than only in written copies, it was the necessity not of preaching things agreeable with the word, but of reading the word itself at large to the people, which caused churches throughout the world to have public care, that the sacred oracles of God being procured by common charge, might with great sedulity be kept both entire and sincere. If then we admire the providence of God in the same continuance of Scripture, notwithstanding the violent endeavours of infidels to abolish, and the fraudulent of heretics always to deprave the same, shall we set light by that custom of reading, from whence so precious a benefit hath grown?

2. The voice and testimony of the Church acknowledging Scripture to be the law of the living God, is for the truth and certainty thereof no mean evidence. For if with reason we may presume upon things which a few men's depositions do testify, suppose we that the minds of men are not both at their first access to the school of Christ exceedingly moved, yea and for ever afterwards also confirmed much, when they consider the main consent of all the churches in the whole world witnessing the sacred authority of scriptures, ever sithence the first publication thereof, even till this present day and hour? And that they all have always so testified, I see not how we should possibly wish a proof more palpable, than this manifest received and every where continued custom of reading them publicly as the Scriptures. The reading therefore of the word of God, as the use hath ever been, in open audience, is the plainest evidence we have of the Church's Assent and Acknowledgment that it is his word.

3. A further commodity this custom hath, which is to furnish the very *simplest* and *rudest* sort with such infallible Axioms and Precepts of sacred truth, delivered even in the very letter of the law of God, as may serve them for Rules [John v. 39; Isa. viii. 20] whereby to judge the better all *other doctrines* and instructions which they hear. For which end and purpose I see not how the Scripture could be possibly made familiar unto all, unless far more should be daily read in the people's hearing, than by a Sermon can be opened. For whereas in a manner the whole book of God is by reading every year published, a small part thereof in comparison of the whole may hold very well the readiest interpreter of Scripture occupied many years.

4. Besides, wherefore should any man think, but that reading itself is one of the "ordinary" means, whereby it pleaseth God of his gracious

goodness to instil that celestial verity, which being *but so* received, is nevertheless effectual to *save* souls? Thus much therefore we ascribe to the reading of the word of God as the manner is in our churches.

[3.] And because it were odious if they on their part should altogether despise the same, they yield that reading may "set forward," but not begin the work of salvation; that faith may be "nourished" therewith, but not bred; that herein men's attention to the Scriptures, and their speculation of the creatures of God have like efficacy, both being of power to "augment," but neither to effect belief without sermons; that if any *believe* by reading alone, we are to account it a miracle, an "extraordinary" work of God. Wherein that which they grant we gladly accept at *their* hands, and wish that patiently they would examine how little cause they have to deny that which as yet they grant not.

[4.] The Scripture witnesseth that when the book of the Law of God had been sometime missing, and was after found, the king, which heard it but only read, tare his clothes, and with tears confessed, "Great is the wrath of the Lord upon us, because our fathers have not kept his word to do after all things which are written in this book." [2 Chron. xxxiv. 18, 19, 21] This doth argue, that by bare reading (for of Sermons at that time there is no mention) true repentance may be wrought in the hearts of such as fear God, and yet incur his displeasure, the deserved effect whereof is eternal death. So that their repentance (although it be not their first entrance) is notwithstanding the first step of their reentrance into life, and may be in them wrought by the word only read unto them.

Besides, it seemeth that God would have no man stand in doubt but that the reading of Scripture is effectual, as well *to lay even the first foundation*, as to add degrees of farther perfection in the fear of God. And therefore the Law saith, "Thou shalt *read* this Law before all Israel, that men, women, and *children* may hear, yea even that their children which as yet *have not known* it may hear it, and by hearing it so read, may *learn to fear* the Lord." [Deut. xxxi. 11–13]

Our Lord and Saviour was himself of opinion, that they which would not be drawn to amendment of life by the testimony which Moses and the Prophets have given concerning the miseries that follow sinners after death, were not likely to be persuaded by other means [Luke xvi. 31], although God from the very dead should have raised them up preachers.

Many hear the books of God and believe them not. Howbeit their unbelief in that case we may not impute unto any weakness or unsufficiency in the mean which is used towards them, but to the wilful bent of their obstinate hearts against it. With minds obdurate nothing prevaileth. As well they that preach, as they that read unto such, shall still have cause to complain with the Prophets which were of old, "Who will give credit unto our teaching?" But with whom ordinary means will prevail, surely the power of the word of God, even without the help of interpreters *in God's Church* worketh mightily, not unto their confirmation alone which are converted, but also to their conversion which are not.

It shall not boot them who derogate from reading to excuse it, when they see no other remedy, as if their intent were only to deny that *aliens* and strangers from the family of God are won, or that belief doth use to be wrought at the first in *them*, without sermons. For they know it is our custom of simple reading *not for conversion of infidels* estranged from the house of God, but for *instruction of men baptized*, bred and brought up *in the* bosom of the Church, which they despise as a thing uneffectual to save *such* souls. In *such* they imagine that God hath no ordinary mean to work faith without sermons.

[5.] The reason, why no man can attain belief by the bare contemplation of heaven and earth, is for that they neither are sufficient to give us as much as the least spark of light concerning the very principal mysteries of our faith; and whatsoever we may learn by them, the same we can only attain to know according to the manner of natural sciences, which mere discourse of wit and reason findeth out, whereas the things which we properly believe be only such as are received upon the credit of divine testimony. Seeing therefore that he which considereth the creatures of God findeth therein both these defects, and neither the one nor the other in Scriptures, because he that readeth unto us the Scriptures delivereth all the mysteries of faith, and not any thing amongst them all more than the mouth of the Lord doth warrant: it followeth in those two respects that our consideration of creatures and attention unto Scriptures are not in themselves, and without sermons, things of like disability to *breed* or *beget* faith.

[6.] Small cause also there is, why any man should greatly wonder as at an extraordinary work, if without sermons reading be found to effect thus much. For I would know by some special instance, what one article of Christian faith, or what duty required necessarily unto all men's salvation there is, which the very reading of the word of God is not *apt* to notify. Effects are miraculous and strange when they grow by unlikely means. But did we ever hear it accounted for a wonder, that he which doth read, should believe and live according to the will of Almighty God? Reading doth convey to the mind that truth without addition or diminution, which Scripture hath derived from the Holy Ghost [Exod. xxiv. 7]. And the end of all Scripture is the same which St. John proposeth in the writing of that most divine Gospel, namely Faith, and through faith Salvation [John xx. 31]. Yea all Scripture is to this effect *in itself* available, as they which wrote it were persuaded [Prov. i. 2–4; Rom. i. 16; 2 Tim. iii. 15]; unless we suppose that the Evangelist or others in speaking of their own intent to instruct and to save by writing, had a secret conceit which they never opened unto any, a conceit that no man in the world should ever be that way the better for any sentence by them written, till such time as the same might chance to be preached upon or alleged at the least in a sermon. Otherwise if he which writeth do that which is forcible in itself, how should he which readeth be thought to do that which in itself is of no force to work belief and to save believers?

[7.] Now although we have very just cause to stand in some jealousy and fear, lest by thus overvaluing their sermons, they make the price and estimation of Scripture otherwise notified to fall; nevertheless so impatient they are, that being but requested to let us know what causes they leave for men's encouragement to attend to the reading of the Scripture, if sermons only be the power of God to save every one which believeth; that which we move for our better learning and instruction's sake, turneth unto anger and choler in them, they grow altogether out of quietness with it, they answer fumingly that they are "ashamed to defile their pens with making answer to such idle questions:" yet in this their mood they cast forth somewhat, wherewith under pain of greater displeasure we must rest contented. They tell us the profit of reading is singular, in that it serveth for a preparative unto sermons; it helpeth prettily towards the nourishment of faith which sermons have once engendered; it is some stay to his mind which readeth the Scripture, when he findeth the same things there which are taught in sermons, and thereby perceiveth how God doth concur in opinion with the preacher; besides it keepeth sermons in memory, and doth in that respect, although not feed the soul of man, yet help the retentive force of that stomach of the mind which receiveth ghostly food at the preacher's hand. But the principal cause of *writing* the Gospel was, *that it might be preached* upon or interpreted by public ministers apt and authorized thereunto. Is it credible that a superstitious conceit (for it is no better) concerning sermons should in such sort both darken their eyes and yet sharpen their wits withal, that the only true and weighty cause why Scripture was written, the cause which in Scripture is so often mentioned, the cause which all men have ever till this present day acknowledged, this they should clean exclude as being no cause at all, and load us with so great store of strange concealed causes which did never see light till now? In which number the rest must needs be of moment, when the very chiefest cause of committing the sacred Word of God unto books, is surmised to have been, lest the preacher should want a text whereupon to scholy.

[8.] Men of learning hold it for a slip in judgment, when offer is made to demonstrate that as proper to one thing which reason findeth common unto more. Whereas therefore they take from all kinds of teaching that which they attribute to sermons, it had been their part to yield directly some strong reason why between *sermons alone* and *faith* there should be *ordinarily* that coherence which causes have with their usual effects, why a

Christian man's belief should so naturally grow from sermons, and not possibly from any other kind of teaching.

In belief there being but these two operations, *apprehension* and *assent*, do only sermons cause belief, in that no other way is able to explain the mysteries of God, that the mind may rightly apprehend or conceive them as behoveth? We all know that many things are believed, although they be intricate, obscure, and dark, although they exceed the reach and capacity of our wits, yea although in this world they be no way possible to be understood. Many things believed are likewise so plain, that every common person may therein be unto himself a sufficient expounder. Finally, to explain even those things which need and admit explication, many other usual ways there are besides sermons. Therefore sermons are not the only ordinary means whereby we *first* come to *apprehend* the mysteries of God.

Is it in regard then of sermons only, that apprehending the Gospel of Christ we yield thereunto our unfeigned assent as to a thing infallibly true? They which rightly consider after what sort the heart of man hereunto is framed, must of necessity acknowledge, that whoso assenteth to the words of eternal life, doth it in regard of his *authority* whose words they are. This is in man's conversion unto God τὸ ὅθεν ἡ ἀρχὴ τῆς κινήσεως the first step whereat his race towards heaven beginneth. Unless therefore, clean contrary to our own experience, we shall think it a miracle if any man acknowledge the divine authority of the Scripture, till some sermon have persuaded him thereunto, and that otherwise neither conversation in the bosom of the Church, nor religious education, nor the reading of learned men's books, nor information received by conference, nor whatsoever pain and diligence in hearing, studying, meditating day and night on the Law, is so far blest of God as to work this effect in any man; how would they have us to grant that faith doth not come but only by *hearing sermons*?

[9.] Fain they would have us to believe the Apostle St. Paul himself to be the author of this their paradox, only because he hath said that "it pleaseth God by the foolishness of preaching to save them which believe;" [1 Cor. i. 21] and again, "How shall they call on him in whom they have not believed? how shall they believe in him of whom they have not heard? how shall they hear without a preacher? how shall men preach except they be sent?" [Rom. x. 14, 15]

To answer therefore both allegations at once; the very substance of that they contain is in few but this. Life and salvation God will have *offered unto all*; his will is that *Gentiles* should be saved as well as *Jews*. Salvation belongeth unto none but such "as call upon the name of our Lord Jesus Christ." Which *nations as yet unconverted* neither do *nor possibly can do till they believe*. What they are to believe, impossible it is they should know till they *hear it*. Their hearing requireth *our preaching* unto them.

Tertullian, to draw even Paynims themselves unto Christian belief, willeth *the books* of the Old Testament to be *searched,* which were at that time in *Ptolemy's* library. And if men did not list to travel so far though it were for their endless good, he addeth that *in Rome* and other places the Jews had *synagogues* whereunto every one which would might resort, that this kind of liberty they purchased by payment of a standing tribute, that there they did openly *read* the Scriptures;* and whosoever "will hear", saith Tertullian, "he shall find God; whosoever will study to know, shall be also fain to believe." But sith there is no likelihood that ever voluntarily they will seek instruction at our hands, it remaineth that unless we will suffer them to perish, salvation itself must seek them, it behoveth God to *send* them preachers, as he did his *elect Apostles* throughout the world.

There is *a knowledge* which God hath always revealed unto them in the *works of nature.* This they honour and esteem highly as profound *wisdom*; howbeit this wisdom saveth them not. That which must save believers is *the knowledge of the cross of Christ,* the *only subject* of all our preaching. And in their eyes what doth this seem as yet but *folly*? It pleaseth God by "the
in their eyes what doth this seem as yet but folly? It pleaseth God by "the
foolishness of preaching" to save. These words declare how admirable force those mysteries have which the world doth deride as follies; they shew that the *foolishness of the cross of Christ* is the *wisdom of true believers*; they concern the *object* of our faith, *the matter preached of* and believed in by Christian men†. This we know that the Grecians or Gentiles did account foolishness; but that they ever did think it *a fond* or unlikely *way* to seek men's conversion by *sermons* we have not heard. Manifest therefore it is that the Apostle applying the name of *foolishness* in such sort as they did must needs by "the foolishness of preaching" mean the doctrine of Christ, which we learn that we may be saved; but that sermons are the only manner of teaching whereby it pleaseth our Lord to save he could not mean.

In like sort where the same Apostle proveth that as well the *sending of the Apostles* as their preaching *to the Gentiles* was necessary, dare we affirm it was ever his meaning, that unto their salvation who even from their tender infancy never knew any other faith or religion than only Christian, *no kind of teaching* can be available *saving that* which was so needful for the first universal conversion of Gentiles hating Christianity; neither the *sending* of any sort allowable in the one case, except only of such as had been in the other also most fit and worthy instruments?

Belief in all sorts doth come by hearkening and *attending to the word of life.* Which word sometime proposeth and preacheth itself to the hearer;

* This they did in a tongue which to all learned men amongst the heathens and to a great part of the simplest was familiarly known; as appeareth by a supplication offered unto the emperor Justinian, wherein the Jews make request that it might be lawful for them to read the Greek translation of the LXX interpreters in their synagogues, as their custom before had been.

† The Apostle useth the word *κήρυγμα*, and not *κήρυξις*.

sometime they deliver it whom privately zeal and piety moveth to be instructors of others by conference; sometime of them it is taught whom the Church hath called to the public either reading thereof or interpreting. All these tend unto one effect; neither doth that which St. Paul or other Apostles teach, concerning the necessity of *such teaching* as theirs was, or of *sending such* as they were for *that purpose unto the Gentiles*, prejudice the efficacy of *any other way* of public instruction, or enforce the utter disability of any other men's vocation thought requisite in this Church, for the saving of souls, where means more effectual are wanting.

[10.] Their only proper and direct proof of the thing in question had been to shew, in what sort and how far man's salvation doth necessarily depend upon the knowledge of the word of God; what conditions, properties, and qualities there are, whereby sermons are distinguished from other kinds of administering the word unto that purpose; and what special property or quality that is, which being no where found but in sermons, maketh them effectual to save souls, and leaveth all other doctrinal means besides destitute of vital efficacy. These pertinent instructions, whereby they might satisfy us and obtain the cause itself for which they contend, these things which only would serve they leave, and (which needeth not) sometime they trouble themselves with fretting at the ignorance of such as withstand them in their opinion; sometime they fall upon their poor brethren which can but read, and against *them* they are bitterly eloquent.

If we allege what the Scriptures themselves do usually speak for the saving force of the word of God, not with restraint to any one certain kind of delivery, but howsoever the same shall chance to be made known, yet by one trick or other they always restrain it unto sermons. Our Lord and Saviour hath said, "Search the Scriptures, in them ye think to have eternal life." [John v. 39] But they tell us, he spake to the Jews, which Jews before *had heard his Sermons*; and that peradventure it was his mind they should search, not by reading, nor by hearing them read, but by "attending" whensoever the Scriptures should happen to be "alleged in Sermons."

Furthermore, having *received* apostolic doctrine, the Apostle St. Paul hath taught us to esteem the same as the supreme rule whereby all other doctrines must for ever be examined [Gal. i. 8, 9]. Yea, but inasmuch as the Apostle doth there speak of that he had preached, he "flatly maketh" (as they strangely affirm) "his Preachings or Sermons the rule whereby to examine all." And then I beseech you what rule have we whereby to judge or examine any? For if sermons must be our rule, because the Apostles' sermons were so to their hearers; then, sith we are not as they were, hearers of the Apostles' sermons, it resteth that either the sermons which we hear should be our rule, or (that being absurd) there will (which yet hath greater absurdity) no rule at all be remaining for trial, what doctrines now are corrupt, what consonant with heavenly truth.

Again, let the same Apostle acknowledge "all Scripture" profitable to teach, to improve, to correct, to instruct in righteousness. [2 Tim. iii. 16] Still notwithstanding we err, if hereby we presume to gather, that Scripture read will avail unto any one of all these uses; they teach us the meaning of the words to be, that so much the Scripture can do if the minister that way apply it in his sermons, otherwise not.

Finally, they never hear sentence which mentioneth *the Word* or *Scripture*, but forthwith their glosses upon it are, the Word "preached," the Scripture "explained or delivered unto us *in sermons*." Sermons they evermore understand to be that Word of God, which alone hath vital operation; the dangerous sequel of which construction I wish they did more attentively weigh. For sith speech is the very image whereby the mind and soul of the speaker conveyeth itself into the bosom of him which heareth, we cannot choose but see great reason, wherefore the word that proceedeth from God, who is himself very truth and life, should be (as the Apostle to the Hebrews noteth) lively and mighty in operation, "sharper than any two-edged sword." [Heb. iv. 12] Now if in this and the like places we did conceive that our own sermons are that strong and forcible word, should we not hereby impart even the most peculiar glory of the word of God unto that which is not his word? For touching our sermons, that which giveth them their very being is the wit of man, and therefore they oftentimes accordingly taste too much of that over-corrupt fountain from which they come. In our speech of most holy things, our most frail affections many times are bewrayed.

Wherefore when we read or recite the Scripture, we then deliver to the people *properly* the word of God. As for our sermons, be they never so sound and perfect, his word they are not as the sermons of the prophets were; no, they are but ambiguously termed his word, because his word is commonly the subject whereof they treat, and must be the rule whereby they are framed. Nothwithstanding by these and the like shifts they derive unto sermons alone whatsoever is generally spoken concerning the word.

[11.] Again, what seemeth to have been uttered concerning sermons and their efficacy or necessity, *in regard of divine matter*, and must consequently be verified in sundry other kinds of teaching, if *the matter* be the same in all; their use is to fasten every such speech unto that one only manner of teaching which is by sermons, that still sermons may be all in all. Thus because Solomon declareth that the people decay or "perish" for want of knowledge, where [Prov. xxix. 18] no "prophesying" at all is, they gather that the hope of life and salvation is cut off, where preachers are not which *prophesy by sermons*, how many soever they be in number that read daily the word of God, and deliver, though in other sort, the selfsame matter which sermons do. The people which have no way to come to the knowledge of God, no prophesying, no teaching, perish. But that they should of necessity perish, where any one way of knowledge lacketh, is more than the words of Solomon import.

[12.] Another usual point of their art in this present question, is to make very large and plentiful discourses how Christ is by sermons lifted up *higher* and made *more* apparent to the eye of faith; how the savour of the word [2 Cor. ii. 14–16] is *more* sweet being brayed, and *more* able to nourish being divided by preaching [2 Tim. ii. 15] than by only reading proposed; how sermons are the keys of the kingdom of heaven [Matt. xvi. 19] and do open the Scriptures, which being but read, remain *in comparison* still clasped; how God [1 Cor. iii. 6] giveth *richer* increase of grace to the ground that is planted and watered by preaching, than by bare and simple reading. Out of which premises declaring how attainment unto life is *easier* where sermons are, they conclude an *impossibility* thereof where sermons are not.

Alcidamas the sophister hath many arguments, to prove that voluntary and extemporal far excelleth premeditated speech. The like whereunto and in part the same are brought by them, who commend sermons, as having (which all men I think will acknowledge) sundry peculiar and proper virtues, such as no other way of teaching besides hath. Aptness to follow particular occasions presently growing, to put life into words by countenance, voice, and gesture, to prevail mightily in the sudden affections of men, this sermons may challenge. Wherein notwithstanding so eminent properties whereof lessons are haply destitute, yet lessons being free from some inconveniences whereunto sermons are more subject, they may in this respect no less take, than in other they must give the hand which betokeneth preeminence. For there is nothing which is not someway excelled even by that which it doth excel. Sermons therefore and Lessons may each excel other in some respects, without any prejudice unto either as touching that vital force which they both have in the work of our salvation.

[13.] To which effect when we have endeavoured as much as in us doth lie to find out the strongest causes wherefore they should imagine that reading is itself so unavailable, the most we can learn at their hand is, that sermons are "the ordinance of God," the Scriptures "dark," and the labour of reading "easy."

First therefore as we know that God doth aid with his grace, and by his special providence evermore bless with happy success those things which himself appointeth, so his Church we persuade ourselves he hath not in such sort given over to a reprobate sense, that whatsoever it deviseth for the good of the souls of men, the same he doth still accurse and make frustrate.

Or if he always did defeat the ordinances of his Church, is not reading the ordinance of God [Deut. xxxi. 11–13]? Wherefore then should we think that the force of his secret grace is accustomed to bless the labour of dividing his word according unto each man's private discretion in public sermons, and to withdraw itself from concurring with the public delivery thereof by such selected portions of Scripture, as the whole Church hath solemnly appointed to be read for the people's good, either by ordinary course, or otherwise, according to the exigence of special occasions? Reading (saith Isidore) is to the hearers no small edifying. To them whose delight and meditation is in the law, seeing that happiness and bliss belongeth [Ps. i. 2], it is not in us to deny them the benefit of heavenly grace. And I hope we may presume, that a rare thing it is not in the Church of God, even for that very word which is read to be both presently their joy [Ps. cxix. 16], and afterwards their study that hear it. St. Augustine, speaking of devout men, noteth how they daily frequented the church, how attentive ear they gave unto the lessons and chapters read, how careful they were to remember the same, and to muse thereupon by themselves. St. Cyprian observeth that reading was not without effect in the hearts of men. Their joy and alacrity were to him an argument, that there is in this ordinance a blessing, such as ordinarily doth accompany the administration of the word of life.

It were much if there should be such a difference between the hearing of sermons preached and of lessons read in the church, that he which presenteth himself at the one, and maketh his prayer with the Prophet David, "Teach me O Lord the way of thy statutes, direct me in the path of thy commandments" [Ps. cxix. 33, 35], might have the ground of usual experience, whereupon to build his hope of prevailing with God, and obtaining the grace he seeketh; they contrariwise not so, who crave the like assistance of his Spirit; when they give ear to the reading of the other. In this therefore preaching and reading are equal, that both are approved as his ordinances, both assisted with his grace. And if his grace do assist them both to the nourishment of faith already bred, we cannot, without some very manifest cause yielded, imagine that in breeding or begetting faith, his grace doth cleave to the one and utterly forsake the other.

[14.] Touching *hardness* which is the second pretended impediment, as against Homilies being plain and popular instructions it is no bar, so neither doth it infringe the efficacy no not of Scriptures although but read. The force of reading, how small soever they would have it, must of necessity be granted sufficient to notify that which is plain or easy to be understood. And of things necessary to all men's salvation we have been hitherto accustomed to hold (especially sithence the publishing of the Gospel of Jesus Christ, whereby the simplest having now a key unto knowledge which the Eunuch in the Acts [Acts viii. 31] did want, our children may of themselves by reading understand that, which he without an interpreter could not) they are in Scripture plain and easy to be understood. As for those things which at the first are obscure and dark, when memory hath laid them up for a time, judgment afterwards growing explaineth them. Scripture therefore is not *so hard*, but that the *only reading* thereof may give life unto willing hearers.

[15.] The "easy" performance of which holy labour is in like sort a very cold objection to prejudice the virtue thereof. For what though an *infidel*, yea though *a child* may be able to read? There is no doubt, but the meanest and worst amongst the people under the Law had been as able as the priests themselves were to offer sacrifice. Did this make sacrifice of no effect unto that purpose for which it was instituted? In religion some duties are not commended so much by the hardness of their execution, as by the worthiness and dignity of that acceptation wherein they are held with God.

We admire the goodness of God in nature, when we consider how he hath provided that things most needful to preserve this life should be most prompt and easy for all living creatures to come by. Is it not as evident a sign of his wonderful providence over us, when that food of eternal life, upon the *utter want* whereof our endless death and destruction necessarily ensueth, is prepared and always set in such a readiness, that those very means than which nothing is more easy may suffice to procure the same? Surely if we perish it is not the lack of scribes and learned expounders that can be our just excuse. The word which saveth our souls is near us; we need for knowledge but to read and live [Apoc. i. 3]. The man which readeth the word of God the word itself doth pronounce blessed, if he also observe the same.

[16.] Now all these things being well considered, it shall be no intricate matter for any man to judge with indifferency, on which part the good of the Church is most conveniently sought; whether on ours whose opinion is such as hath been shewed, or else on theirs, who leaving no ordinary way of salvation for them unto whom the word of God is but only read, do seldom name them but with great disdain and contempt who execute that service in the Church of Christ. By means whereof it hath come to pass, that churches, which cannot enjoy the benefit of usual preaching, are judged as it were even forsaken of God, forlorn, and without either hope or comfort: contrariwise those places which every day for the most part are at sermons as the flowing sea, do both by their emptiness at times of reading, and by other apparent tokens, shew to the voice of the living God this way sounding in the ears of men a great deal less reverence than were meet.

[17.] But if no other evil were known to grow thereby, who can choose but think them cruel which doth hear them so boldly teach, that if God (as to Him there is nothing impossible) do haply save any such as continue where they have all other means of instruction, but are not taught by continual preaching, yet this is miraculous, and more than the fitness of so poor instruments can give any man cause to hope for; that sacraments are not effectual to salvation, except men be instructed by *preaching before* they be made partakers of them; yea, that both sacraments and prayers also, where sermons are not, "do not only not feed, but are ordinarily to further condemnation?" What man's heart doth not rise at the mention of these things?

It is true that the weakness of our wits and the dulness of our affections do make us for the most part, even as our Lord's own disciples were for a certain time, hard and slow to believe what is written. For help whereof expositions and exhortations are needful, and that in the most effectual manner. The principal churches throughout the land, and no small part of the rest, being in this respect by the goodness of God so abundantly provided for, they which want the like furtherance unto knowledge, wherewith it were greatly to be desired that they also did abound, are yet we hope not left in so extreme destitution, that justly any man should think the ordinary means of eternal life taken from them, because their teaching is in public for the most part but by reading. For which cause amongst whom there are not those helps that others have to set them forward in the way of life, such to dishearten with fearful sentences, as though their salvation could hardly be hoped for, is not in our understanding so consonant with Christian charity. We hold it safer a great deal and better to give them encouragement [Ecclus. li. 26–7; Matt. xii. 20]; to put them in mind that it is not the deepness of their knowledge, but the singleness of their belief, which God accepteth [1 Tim. i. 5; Rom. xiv. 1; 1 Thes. iii. 10]; that they which "hunger and thirst after righteousness shall be satisfied" [Matt. v. 6]; that no imbecility of means can prejudice the truth of the promise of God herein [Phil. i. 6; 1 Pet. v. 10; Matt. iii. 9]; that the weaker their helps are, the more their need is to sharpen the edge of their own industry [1 Thess. iv. 18; Heb. x. 24; Jude 20, 21; 1 Pet. iv. 10]; and that painfulness by feeble means shall be able to gain that, which in the plenty of more forcible instruments is through sloth and negligence lost [Luke xi. 31].

[18.] As for the men, with whom we have thus far taken pains to confer about the force of the word of God, either read by itself, or opened in sermons; their speeches concerning both the one and the other are in truth such, as might give us very just cause to think, that the reckoning is not great which they make of either. For howsoever they have been driven to devise some odd kinds of blind uses, whereunto they may answer that reading doth serve, yet the reading of the word of God in public more than their preacher's bare text, who will not judge that they deem needless; when if we chance at any time to term it *necessary*, as being a thing which God himself did institute amongst the Jews for purposes that touch as well us as them; a thing which the Apostles commend under the Old, and ordain under the New Testament; a thing whereof the Church of God hath ever sithence the first beginning reaped singular commodity; a thing which without exceeding great detriment no Church can omit: they only are the men that ever we heard of by whom this hath been crossed and gainsaid, they only the men which have given their peremptory sentence to the contrary, "It is untrue that simple reading is necessary in the Church." And why untrue? Because "although it be very convenient which is used in some churches, where before preaching-time the church assembled hath the Scriptures read in such order that the whole canon thereof is oftentimes in one year run through; yet a number of churches which have no such order of simple reading cannot be in this point charged with breach of God's commandment, which they might be if simple reading were necessary." A poor, a cold, and an hungry cavil! Shall we therefore to please them change the word "*necessary*," and say that it hath been a commendable order, a custom very expedient, or an ordinance *most* profitable (whereby they know right well that we mean exceedingly behoveful) to read the word of God at large in the church, whether it be as our manner is, or as theirs is whom they prefer before us? It is not this that will content or satisfy their minds. They have against it a marvellous deep and profound axiom, that "Two things to one and the same end cannot but very improperly be said most profitable." And therefore if preaching be "most profitable" to man's salvation, then is not reading; if reading be, then preaching is not.

[19.] Are they resolved then at the leastwise, if preaching be the only ordinary mean whereby it pleaseth God to save our souls, what kind of preaching it is which doth save? Understand they how or in what respect there is that force and virtue in preaching? We have reason wherefore to make these demands, for that although their pens run all upon *preaching* and *sermons*, yet when themselves do practise that whereof they write, they change their dialect, and those words they shun as if there were in them some secret sting. It is not their phrase to say they "preach," or to give to their own instructions and exhortations the name of sermons; the pain they take themselves in this kind is either "opening," or "lecturing," or "reading," or "exercising," but in no case "preaching." And in this present question they also warily protest, that what they ascribe to the virtue of preaching, they still mean it of "good preaching." Now one of them saith that a good sermon must "expound" and "apply" a "large" portion of the text of Scripture at one time. Another giveth us to understand, that sound preaching "is not to do as one did at London, who spent the most of his time in invectives against good men, and told his audience how the magistrate should have an eye to such as troubled the peace of the Church." The best of them hold it for no good preaching "when a man endeavoureth to make a glorious show of eloquence and learning, rather than to apply himself to the capacity of the simple."

But let them shape us out a good preacher by what pattern soever it pleaseth them best, let them exclude and inclose whom they will with their definitions, we are not desirous to enter into any contention with them about this, or to abate the conceit they have of their own ways, so that when once we are agreed what sermons shall currently pass for good, we may at the length understand from them what that is in a good sermon which doth make it the word of life unto such as hear. If substance of matter, evidence of things, strength and validity of arguments and proofs, or if any other virtue else which words and sentences may contain; of all this what is there in the best sermons being uttered, which they lose by being read? But they utterly deny that the reading either of scriptures or homilies and sermons can ever by the ordinary grace of God save any soul. So that although we had all the sermons word for word which James, Paul, Peter, and the rest of the Apostles made, some one of which sermons was of power to convert thousands of the hearers unto Christian faith; yea although we had all the instructions, exhortations, consolations, which came from the gracious lips of our Lord Jesus Christ himself, and should read them ten thousand times over, to faith and salvation no man could hereby hope to attain.

Whereupon it must of necessity follow, that the vigour and vital efficacy of sermons doth grow from certain accidents which are not in them but in their maker: his virtue, his gesture, his countenance, his zeal, the motion of his body, and the inflection of his voice who first uttereth them as his own, is that which giveth them the form, the nature, the very essence of instruments available to eternal life. If they like neither that nor this, what remaineth but that their final conclusion be, "sermons we know are the only ordinary means to salvation, but why or how we cannot tell?"

[20.] Wherefore to end this tedious controversy, wherein the too great importunity of our over-eager adversaries hath constrained us much longer to dwell, than the barrenness of so poor a cause could have seemed at the first likely either to require or to admit, if they which without partialities and passions are accustomed to weigh all things, and accordingly to give their sentence, shall here sit down to receive our audit, and to cast up the whole reckoning on both sides; the sum which truth amounteth unto will appear to be but this, that as medicines provided of nature and applied by art for the benefit of bodily health, take effect sometimes under and sometimes above the natural proportion of their virtue, according as the mind and fancy of the patient doth more or less concur with them: so whether we barely read unto men the Scriptures of God, or by homilies concerning matter of belief and conversation seek to lay before them the duties which they owe unto God and man; whether we deliver them books to read and consider of in private at their own best leisure, or call them to the hearing of sermons publicly in the house of God; albeit every of these and the like unto these means do truly and daily effect that in the hearts of men for which they are each and all meant, yet the operation which they have in common being most sensible and most generally noted in one kind above the rest, that one hath in some men's opinions drowned altogether the rest, and injuriously brought to pass that they have been thought, not *less effectual* than the other, but without the other *uneffectual* to save souls. Whereas the cause why sermons only are observed to prevail so much while all means else seem to sleep and do nothing, is in truth nothing but that singular affection and attention which the people sheweth every where towards the one, and their cold disposition to the other; the reason hereof being partly the art which our adversaries use for the credit of their sermons to bring men out of conceit with all other teaching besides; partly a custom which men have to let those things carelessly pass by their ears, which they have oftentimes heard before, or know they may hear again whensoever it pleaseth themselves; partly the special advantages which sermons naturally have to procure attention, both in that they come always new, and because by the hearer it is still presumed, that if they be let slip for the present, what good soever they contain is lost, and that without all hope of recovery. This is the true cause of odds between sermons and other kinds of wholesome instruction.

As for the difference which hath been hitherto so much defended on the contrary side, making sermons the only ordinary means unto faith and eternal life, sith this hath neither evidence of truth nor proof sufficient to give it warrant, a cause of such quality may with far better grace and conveniency ask that pardon which common humanity doth easily grant, than claim in challenging manner that assent which is as unwilling when reason guideth it to be yielded where it is not, as withheld where it is apparently due.

All which notwithstanding, as we could greatly wish that the rigour of this their opinion were allayed and mitigated, so because we hold it the part of religious ingenuity to honour virtue in whomsover, therefore it is our most hearty desire, and shall be always our prayer unto almighty God, that in the selfsame fervent zeal wherewith they seem to affect the good of the souls of men, and to thirst after nothing more than that all men might by all means be directed in the way of life, both they and we may constantly persist to the world's end. For in this we are not their adversaries, though they in the other hitherto have been ours.

Chapter 23

OF PRAYER

Between the throne of God in heaven and his Church upon earth here militant if it be so that Angels have their continual intercourse, where should we find the same more verified than in these two ghostly exercises, the one *Doctrine*, and the other *Prayer*? For what is the assembling of the Church to learn, but the receiving of Angels descended from above? What to pray, but the sending of Angels upward? His heavenly inspirations and our holy desires are as so many Angels of intercourse and commerce between God and us. As teaching bringeth us to know that God is our supreme truth; so prayer testifieth that we acknowledge him our sovereign good.

Besides, sith on God as the most high all inferior causes in the world are dependent; and the higher any cause is, the more it coveteth to impart virtue unto things beneath it; how should any kind of service we do or can do find greater acceptance than prayer, which sheweth our concurrence with him in desiring that wherewith his very nature doth most delight?

Is not the name of prayer usual to signify even all the service that ever we do unto God? And that for no other cause, as I suppose, but to shew that there is in religion no acceptable duty which devout invocation of the name of God doth not either presuppose or infer. Prayers are those "calves of men's lips" [Hosea xiv. 2]; those most gracious and sweet odours [Rev. v. 8]; those rich presents and gifts, which being carried up into heaven [Acts x. 4] do best testify our dutiful affection, and are for the purchasing of all favour at the hands of God the most undoubted means we can use.

On others what more easily, and yet what more fruitfully bestowed than our prayers? If we give counsel, they are the simpler only that need it; if alms, the poorer only are relieved; but by prayer we do good to all. And whereas every other duty besides is but to shew itself as time and opportunity require, for this all times are convenient [Rom. i. 9; 1 Thess. v. 17; Luke xviii. 1]; when we are not able to do any other thing for men's behoof, when through maliciousness or unkindness they vouchsafe not to accept any other good at our hands, prayer is that which we always have in our power to bestow, and they never in theirs to refuse. Wherefore "God forbid," said Samuel, speaking unto a most unthankful people, a people weary of the benefit of his most virtuous government over them, "God forbid that I should sin against the Lord, and cease to pray for you." [1 Sam. xii. 23] It is the first thing wherewith a righteous life beginneth, and the last wherewith it doth end.

The knowledge is small which we have on earth concerning things that are done in heaven. Notwithstanding thus much we know even of Saints in heaven, that they pray. And therefore prayer being a work common to the Church as well triumphant as militant, a work common unto men with Angels, what should we think but that so much of our lives is celestial and divine as we spend in the exercise of prayer? For which cause we see that the most comfortable visitations, which God hath sent men from above, have taken especially the times of prayer as their most natural opportunities [Dan. ix. 20; Acts x. 30].

* * *

Chapter 34

LESSONS INTERMINGLED WITH OUR PRAYERS

Again, forasmuch as effectual prayer is joined with a vehement intention of the inferior powers of the soul, which cannot therein long continue without pain, it hath been therefore thought good so by turns to interpose still somewhat for the higher part of the mind, the understanding, to work upon, that both being kept in continual exercise with variety, neither might feel any great weariness, and yet each be a spur to other. For prayer kindleth our desire to behold God by speculation; and the mind delighted with that contemplative sight of God, taketh every where new inflammations to pray, the riches of the mysteries of heavenly wisdom continually stirring up in us correspondent desires towards him. So that he which prayeth in due sort is thereby made the more attentive to hear, and he which heareth the more earnest to pray, for the time which we bestow as well in the one as the other.

[2.] But for what cause soever we do it, this intermingling of lessons with prayers is in their taste a thing as unsavoury, and as unseemly in their sight, as if the like should be done in suits and supplications before some mighty prince of the world. Our speech to worldly superiors we frame in such sort as serveth best to inform and persuade the minds of them, who otherwise neither could nor would greatly regard our necessities: whereas, because we know that God is indeed a King, but *a great* king, who understandeth all things beforehand, which no other king besides doth, a king which needeth not to be informed what we lack, a king readier to grant than we to make our requests; therefore in prayer we do not so much respect what precepts art delivereth touching the method of persuasive utterance in the presence of great men, as what doth most avail to our own edification in piety and godly zeal. If they on the contrary side do think that the same rules of decency which serve for things done unto terrene powers should universally decide what is fit in the service of God; if it be their meaning to hold it for a maxim, that the Church must deliver her public supplications unto God in no other form of speech than such as were decent, if suit should be made to the great Turk, or some other monarch, let them apply their own rule unto their own form of common prayer. Suppose that the people of a whole town with some chosen man before them did continually twice or thrice in a week resort to their king, and every time they come first acknowledge themselves guilty of rebellions and treasons, then sing a song, after that explain some statute of the land to the standers-by, and therein spend at the least an hour; this done, turn themselves again to the king, and for every sort of his subjects crave somewhat of him, at the length sing him another song, and so take their leave. Might not the king well think that either they knew not what they would have, or else that they were distracted in mind, or some other such like cause of the disorder of their supplication? This form of suing unto kings were absurd. This form of praying unto God they allow.

[3.] When God was served with legal sacrifices, such was the miserable and wretched disposition of some men's minds, that the best of every thing they had being culled out for themselves, if there were in their flocks any poor starved or diseased thing not worth the keeping, they thought it good enough for the altar of God, pretending (as wise hypocrites do when they rob God to enrich themselves) that the fatness of calves doth benefit him nothing; to us the best things are most profitable, to him all as one if the mind of the offerer be good, which is the only thing he respecteth. In reproof of which their devout fraud, the Prophet Malachi allegeth that gifts are offered unto God not as supplies of his want indeed, but yet as testimonies of that affection wherewith we acknowledge and honour his greatness. For which cause, sith the greater they are whom we honour, the more regard we have to the quality and choice of those presents which we bring them for honour's sake, it must needs follow that if we dare not disgrace our worldly superiors with offering unto them such refuse as we bring unto God himself, we shew plainly that our acknowledgment of his greatness is but feigned, in heart we fear him not so much as we dread them. "If ye offer the blind for sacrifice it is not evil. Offer it now unto thy prince. Will he be content, or accept thy person? saith the Lord of hosts. Cursed be the deceiver which hath in his flock a male, and having made a vow sacrificeth unto the Lord a corrupt thing. For I am a great king, saith the Lord of hosts" [Mal. i. 8, 14]. Should we hereupon frame a rule that what form of speech or behaviour soever is fit for suitors in a prince's court, the same and no other beseemeth us in our prayers to almighty God?

Chapter 35

THE NUMBER OF OUR PRAYERS FOR EARTHLY THINGS, AND OUR OFT REHEARSING OF THE LORD'S PRAYER

But in vain we labour to persuade them that any thing can take away the tediousness of prayer, except it be brought to the very same both measure and form which themselves assign. Whatsoever therefore our liturgy hath more than theirs, under one devised pretence or other they cut it off. We have of prayers for earthly things in their opinion too great a number; so oft to rehearse the Lord's Prayer in so small a time is as they think a loss of time; the people's praying after the minister they say both wasteth time, and also maketh an unpleasant sound; the Psalms they would not have to be made (as they are) a part of our common prayer, nor to be sung or said by turns, nor such music to be used with them; those evangelical hymns they allow not to stand in our liturgy; the Litany, the Creed of Athanasius, the sentence of Glory wherewith we use to conclude psalms, these things they cancel, as having been instituted in regard of occasions peculiar to the times of old, and as being therefore now superfluous.

[2.] Touching prayers for things earthly, we ought not to think that the Church hath set down so many of them without cause. *They* peradventure, which find this fault, are of the same affection with Solomon, so that if God should offer to grant *them* whatsoever they ask, *they* would neither crave riches, nor length of days, nor yet victory over their enemies, but only an understanding heart: for which cause themselves having eagles' wings, are offended to see others fly so near the ground. But the tender kindness of the Church of God it very well beseemeth to help the weaker sort, which are by so great odds more in number, although some few of the perfecter and stronger may be therewith for a time displeased.

Ignorant we are not, that of such as resorted to our Saviour Christ being present on earth, there came not any unto him with better success for the benefit of their souls' everlasting happiness, than they whose bodily necessities gave them the first occasion to seek relief, where they saw willingness and ability of doing every way good unto all.

The graces of the Spirit are much more precious than worldly benefits; our ghostly evils of greater importance than any harm which the body feeleth. Therefore our desires to heavenward should both in measure and number no less exceed than their glorious object doth every way excel in value. These things are true and plain in the eye of a perfect judgment. But yet it must be withal considered, that the greatest part of the world are they which be farthest from perfection. Such being better able by sense to discern the wants of this present life, than by spiritual capacity to apprehend things above sense, which tend to their happiness in the world to come, are in that respect the more apt to apply their minds even with hearty affection and zeal at the least unto those branches of public prayer, wherein their own particular is moved. And by this mean there stealeth upon them a double benefit: first because that good affection, which things of smaller account have once set on work, is by so much the more easily raised higher; and secondly in that the very custom of seeking so particular aid and relief at the hands of God, doth by a secret contradiction withdraw them from endeavouring to help themselves by those wicked shifts which they know can never have his allowance, whose assistance their prayer seeketh. These multiplied petitions of worldly things in prayer have therefore, besides their direct use, a service, whereby the Church underhand, through a kind of heavenly fraud, taketh therewith the souls of men as with certain baits.

If then their calculation be true (for so they reckon), that a full third of our prayers be allotted unto earthly benefits, for which our Saviour in his platform hath appointed but one petition amongst seven, the difference is without any great disagreement; we respecting what men are, and doing that which is meet in regard of the common imperfection; our Lord contrariwise proposing the most absolute proportion that can be in men's desires, the very highest mark whereat we are able to aim.

[3.] For which cause also our custom is both to place it in the front of our prayers as a guide, and to add it in the end of some principal limbs or parts as a complement which fully perfecteth whatsoever may be defective in the rest. Twice we rehearse it ordinarily, and oftener as occasion requireth more solemnity or length in the form of divine service; not mistrusting, till these new curiosities sprang up, that ever any man would think our labour herein mispent, the time wastefully consumed, and the office itself made worse by so repeating that which otherwise would more hardly be made familiar to the simpler sort; for the good of whose souls there is not in Christian religion any thing of like continual use and force throughout every hour and moment of their whole lives.

I mean not only because prayer, but because this very prayer, is of such efficacy and necessity. For that our Saviour did but set men a bare example how to contrive or devise prayers of their own, and no way bind them to use this, is no doubt an error. John the Baptist's disciples which had been always brought up in the bosom of God's Church from the time of their first infancy till they came to the school of John, were not so brutish that they could be ignorant how to call upon the name of God; but of their master they had received a form of prayer amongst themselves, which form none did use saving his disciples, so that by it as by a mark of special difference they were known from others. And of this the Apostles having taken notice, they request that as John had taught his, so Christ would likewise teach them to pray [Luke xi. 1].

Tertullian and St. Augustine do for that cause term it *Orationem legitimam*, the Prayer which Christ's own law hath tied his Church to use in the same prescript form of words wherewith he himself did deliver it; and therefore what part of the world soever we fall into, if Christian religion have been there received, the ordinary use of this very prayer hath with equal continuance accompanied the same as one of the principal and most material duties of honour done to Jesus Christ. "Seeing that we have (saith St. Cyprian) an Advocate with the Father for our sins, when we that have sinned come to seek for pardon, let us allege unto God the words which our Advocate hath taught. For sith his promise is our plain warrant, that in his name what we ask we shall receive, must we not needs much the rather obtain that for which we sue if not only his name do countenance but also his speech present our requests?"

Though men should speak with the tongues of Angels, yet words so pleasing to the ears of God as those which the Son of God himself hath composed were not possible for men to frame. He therefore which made us to live hath also taught us to pray, to the end that speaking unto the Father in the Son's own prescript form without scholy or gloss of ours, we may be sure that we utter nothing which God will either disallow or deny. Other prayers we use many besides this, and this oftener than any other; although not tied so to do by any commandment of Scripture, yet moved with such considerations as have been before set down: the causeless dislike whereof which others have conceived, is no sufficient reason for us as much as once to forbear in any place a thing which uttered with true devotion and zeal of heart affordeth to God himself that glory, that aid to the weakest sort of men, to the most perfect that solid comfort which is unspeakable.

* * *

Chapter 37

OUR MANNER OF READING THE PSALMS OTHERWISE THAN THE REST OF THE SCRIPTURE

The complaint which they make about Psalms and Hymns, might as well be overpast without any answer, as it is without any cause brought forth. But our desire is to content them if it may be, and to yield them a just reason even of the least things wherein undeservedly they have but as much as dreamed or suspected that we do amiss. They seem sometimes so to speak, as if it greatly offended them, that such Hymns and Psalms as are Scripture should in common prayer be otherwise used than the rest of the Scripture is wont: sometime displeased they are at the artificial music which we add unto psalms of this kind, or of any other nature else; sometime the plainest and the most intelligible rehearsal of them yet they savour not, because it is done by interlocution, and with a mutual return of sentences from side to side.

[2.] They are not ignorant what difference there is between other parts of Scripture and Psalms. The choice and flower of all things profitable in other books the Psalms do both more briefly contain, and more movingly also express, by reason of that poetical form wherewith they are written. The ancient when they speak of the Book of Psalms use to fall into large discourses, shewing how this part above the rest doth of purpose set forth and celebrate all the considerations and operations which belong to God; it magnifieth the holy meditations and actions of divine men; it is of things heavenly an universal declaration, working in them whose hearts God inspireth with the due consideration thereof, an habit or disposition of mind whereby they are made fit vessels both for receipt and for delivery of whatsoever spiritual perfection. What is there necessary for man to know which the Psalms are not able to teach? They are to beginners an easy and familiar introduction, a mighty augmentation of all virtue and knowledge in such as are entered before, a strong confirmation to the most perfect amongst others. Heroical magnanimity, exquisite justice, grave moderation, exact wisdom, repentance unfeigned, unwearied patience, the mysteries of God, the sufferings of Christ, the terrors of wrath, the comforts of grace, the works of Providence over this world, and the promised joys of that world which is to come, all good necessarily to be either known or done or had, this one celestial fountain yieldeth. Let there be any grief or disease incident into the soul of man, any wound or sickness named, for which there is not in this treasure-house a present comfortable remedy at all times ready to be found. Hereof it is that we covet to make the Psalms especially familiar unto all. This is the very cause why we iterate the Psalms oftener than any other part of Scripture besides; the cause wherefore we inure the people together with their minister, and not the minister alone to read them as other parts of Scripture he doth.

Chapter 38

OF MUSIC WITH PSALMS

Touching musical harmony whether by instrument or by voice, it being but of high and low in sounds a due proportionable disposition, such notwithstanding is the force thereof, and so pleasing effects it hath even in that very part of man which is most divine, that some have been thereby induced to think that the soul itself by nature is or hath in it harmony. A thing which delighteth all ages and beseemeth all states; a thing as seasonable in grief as in joy; as decent being added unto actions of greatest weight and solemnity, as being used when men most sequester themselves from action. The reason hereof is an admirable facility which music hath to express and represent to the mind, more inwardly than any other sensible mean, the very standing, rising, and falling, the very steps and inflections every way, the turns and varieties of all passions whereunto the mind is subject; yea so to imitate them, that whether it resemble unto us the same state wherein our minds already are, or a clean contrary, we are not more contentedly by the one confirmed, than changed and led away by the other. In harmony the very image and character even of virtue and vice is perceived, the mind delighted with their resemblances, and brought by having them often iterated into a love of the things themselves. For which cause there is nothing more contagious and pestilent than some kinds of harmony; than some nothing more strong and potent unto good. And that there is such a difference of one kind from another we need no proof but our own experience, inasmuch as we are at the hearing of some more inclined unto sorrow and heaviness; of some, more mollified and softened in mind; one kind apter to stay and settle us, another to move and stir our affections; there is that draweth to a marvellous grave and sober mediocrity, there is also that carrieth as it were into ecstasies, filling the mind with an heavenly joy and for the time in a manner severing it from the body. So that although we lay altogether aside the consideration of ditty or matter, the very harmony of sounds being framed in due sort and carried from the ear to the spiritual faculties of our souls, is by a native puissance and efficacy greatly available to bring to a perfect temper whatsoever is there troubled, apt as well to quicken the spirits as to allay that which is too eager, sovereign against melancholy and despair, forcible to draw forth tears of devotion if the mind be such as can yield them, able both to move and to moderate all affections.

[2.] The Prophet David having therefore singular knowledge not in poetry alone but in music also, judged them both to be things most necessary for the house of God, left behind him to that purpose a number of divinely indited poems, and was farther the author of adding unto poetry melody in public prayer, melody both vocal and instrumental, for the raising up of men's hearts, and the sweetening of their affections towards God. In which considerations the Church of Christ doth likewise at this present day retain it as an ornament to God's service, and an help to our own devotion. They which, under pretence of the Law ceremonial abrogated, require the abrogation of instrumental music, approving nevertheless the use of vocal melody to remain, must shew some reason wherefore the one should be thought a legal ceremony and not the other.

[3.] In church music curiosity and ostentation of art, wanton or light or unsuitable harmony, such as only pleaseth the ear, and doth not naturally serve to the very kind and degree of those impressions, which the matter that goeth with it leaveth or is apt to leave in men's minds, doth rather blemish and disgrace that we do than add either beauty or furtherance unto it. On the other side, these faults prevented, the force and efficacy of the thing itself, when it drowneth not utterly but fitly suiteth with matter altogether sounding to the praise of God, is in truth most admirable, and doth much edify if not the understanding, because it teacheth not, yet surely the affection, because therein it worketh much. They must have hearts very dry and tough, from whom the melody of psalms doth not sometime draw that wherein a mind religiously affected delighteth. Be it as Rabanus Maurus observeth, that at the first the Church in this exercise was more simple and plain than we are, that their singing was little more than only a melodious kind of pronunciation, that the custom which we now use was not instituted so much for their cause which are spiritual, as to the end that into grosser and heavier minds, whom bare words do not easily move, the sweetness of melody might make some entrance for good things. St. Basil himself acknowledging as much, did not think that from such inventions the least jot of estimation and credit thereby should be derogated: "For" (saith he) "whereas the Holy Spirit saw that mankind is unto virtue hardly drawn, and that righteousness is the less accounted of by reason of the proneness of our affections to that which delighteth; it pleased the wisdom of the same Spirit to borrow from melody that pleasure, which mingled with heavenly mysteries, causeth the smoothness and softness of that which toucheth the ear, to convey as it were by stealth the treasure of good things into man's mind. To this purpose were those harmonious tunes of psalms devised for us, that they which are either in years but young, or touching perfection of virtue as yet not grown to ripeness, might when they think they sing, learn. O the wise conceit of that heavenly teacher, which hath by his skill, found out a way, that doing those things wherein we delight, we may also learn that whereby we profit!"

Chapter 39

OF SINGING OR SAYING PSALMS AND OTHER PARTS OF COMMON PRAYER, WHEREIN THE PEOPLE AND THE MINISTER ANSWER ONE ANOTHER BY COURSE

And if the Prophet David did think that the very meeting of men together, and their accompanying one another to the house of God, should make the bond of their love insoluble, and tie them in a league of inviolable amity (Psal. lv. 14); how much more may we judge it reasonable to hope, that the like effects may grow in each of the people towards other, in them all towards their pastor, and in their pastor towards every of them, between whom there daily and interchangeably pass, in the hearing of God himself, and in the presence of his holy Angels, so many heavenly acclamations, exultations, provocations, petitions, songs of comfort, psalms of praise and thanksgiving: in all which particulars, as when the pastor maketh their suits, and they with one voice testify a general assent thereunto; or when he joyfully beginneth, and they with like alacrity follow, dividing between them the sentences wherewith they strive which shall most shew his own and stir up others' zeal, to the glory of that God whose name they magnify; or when he proposeth unto God their necessities, and they their own requests for relief in every of them; or when he lifteth up his voice like a trumpet to proclaim unto them the laws of God, they adjoining though not as Israel did by way of generality a cheerful promise, "All that the Lord hath commanded we will do" [Exod. xix. 8; xxiv, 3; Deut. v. 27; xxvi. 17; Josh. xxiv. 16], yet that which God doth no less approve, that which savoureth more of meekness, that which testifieth rather a feeling knowledge of our common imbecility, unto the several branches thereof, several lowly and humble requests for grace at the merciful hands of God to perform the thing which is commanded; or when they wish reciprocally each other's ghostly happiness; or when he by exhortation raiseth them up, and they by protestation of their readiness declare he speaketh not in vain unto them: these interlocutory forms of speech what are they else, but most effectual partly testifications and partly inflammations of all piety?

[2.] When and how this custom of singing by course came up in the Church it is not certainly known. Socrates maketh Ignatius the Bishop of Antioch in Syria the first beginner thereof, even under the Apostles themselves. But against Socrates they set the authority of Theodoret, who draweth the original of it from Antioch as Socrates doth; howbeit ascribing the invention to others, Flavian and Diodore, men which constantly stood in defence of the apostolic faith against the Bishop of that church, Leontius, a favourer of the Arians. Against both Socrates and Theodoret, Platina is brought as a witness, to testify that Damasus Bishop of Rome began it in his time. Of the Latin church it may be true which Platina saith. And therefore the eldest of that church which maketh any mention thereof is St. Ambrose, Bishop of Milan at the same time when Damasus was of Rome. Amongst the Grecians St. Basil having brought it into his church before they of Neocæsarea used it, Sabellius the heretic and Marcellus took occasion thereat to incense the churches against him, as being an author of new devices in the service of God. Whereupon to avoid the opinion of novelty and singularity, he allegeth for that which himself did the example of the churches of Egypt, Libya, Thebes, Palestina, the Arabians, Phœnicians, Syrians, Mesopotamians, and in a manner all that reverenced the custom of singing psalms together. If the Syrians had it then before Basil, Antioch the mother church of those parts must needs have used it before Basil, and consequently before Damasus. The question is then how long before, and whether so long that Ignatius or as ancient as Ignatius may be probably thought the first inventors. Ignatius in Trajan's days suffered martyrdom. And of the churches in Pontus and Bithynia to Trajan the emperor his own vicegerent there affirmeth, that the only crime he knew of them was, they used to meet together at a certain day, and to praise Christ with hymns as a God, *secum invicem*, "one to another amongst themselves." Which for any thing we know to the contrary might be the selfsame form which Philo Judæus expresseth, declaring how the Essenes were accustomed with hymns and psalms to honour God, sometime all exalting their voices together in one, and sometime one part answering another, wherein as he thought, they swerved not much from the pattern [Exod. xv. 1, 21] of Moses and Miriam.

Whether Ignatius did at any time hear the angels praising God after that sort or no, what matter is it? If Ignatius did not, yet one which must be with us of greater authority did. "I saw the Lord (saith the Prophet Isaiah) on an high throne; the Seraphims stood upon it; *one cried to another* saying, Holy, Holy, Holy, Lord God of Hosts, the whole world is full of his glory". [Isa. vi. 1–3]

But whosoever were the author, whatsoever the time, whencesoever the example of beginning this custom in the Church of Christ; sith we are wont to suspect things only before trial, and afterwards either to approve them as good, or if we find them evil, accordingly to judge of them; their counsel must needs seem very unseasonable, who advise men now to "suspect" that wherewith the world hath had by their own account twelve hundred years' acquaintance and upwards, enough to take away suspicion and jealousy. Men know by this time, if ever they will know, whether it be good or evil which hath been so long retained.

[3.] As for the Devil, which way it should greatly benefit him to have this manner of singing psalms accounted an invention of Ignatius, or an imitation of the angels of heaven, we do not well understand. But we very well see in them who thus plead a wonderful celerity of discourse. For perceiving at the first but only some cause of suspicion and fear lest it should be evil, they are presently in one and the selfsame breath resolved, that "what beginning soever it had, there is no possibility it should be good." The potent arguments which did thus suddenly break in upon them and overcome them are first, that it is not unlawful for the people all jointly to praise God in singing of psalms; secondly, that they are not any where forbidden by the law of God to sing every verse of the whole psalm both with heart and voice quite and clean throughout; thirdly, that it cannot be understood what is sung after our manner. Of which three, forasmuch as lawfulness to sing one way proveth not another way inconvenient, the former two are true allegations, but they lack strength to accomplish their desire; the third so strong that it might persuade, if the truth thereof were not doubtful.

[4.] And shall this enforce us to banish a thing which all Christian churches in the world have received; a thing which so many ages have held; a thing which the most approved councils and laws have so oftentime ratified; a thing which was never found to have any inconvenience in it; a thing which always heretofore the best men and wisest governors of God's people did think they could never commend enough; a thing which, as Basil was persuaded, did both strengthen the meditation of those holy words which were uttered in that sort, and serve also to make attentive, and to raise up the hearts of men; a thing whereunto God's people of old did resort, with hope and thirst that thereby especially their souls might be edified; a thing which filleth the mind with comfort and heavenly delight, stirreth up flagrant desires and affections correspondent unto that which the words contain, allayeth all kind of base and earthly cogitations, banisheth and driveth away those evil secret suggestions which our invisible enemy is always apt to minister, watereth the heart to the end it may fructify, maketh the virtuous in trouble full of magnanimity and courage, serveth as a most approved remedy against all doleful and heavy accidents which befall men in this present life, to conclude, so fitly accordeth with the Apostle's own exhortation [Eph. v. 19], "Speak to yourselves in psalms and hymns and spiritual songs, making melody, and singing to the Lord in your hearts," that surely there is more cause to fear lest the want thereof be a maim, than the use a blemish to the service of God?

[5.] It is not our meaning, that what we attribute unto the Psalms should be thought to depend altogether on that only form of singing or reading them by course as with us the manner is; but the end of our speech is to shew that because the Fathers of the Church, with whom the selfsame custom was so many ages ago in use, have uttered all these things concerning the fruit which the Church of God did then reap, observing that and no other form, it may be justly avouched that we ourselves retaining it and besides it also the other more newly and not unfruitfully devised, do neither want that good which the later invention can afford, nor lose any thing of that for which the ancient so oft and so highly commend the former. Let novelty therefore in this give over endless contradictions, and let ancient custom prevail.

* * *

Chapter 50

OF THE NAME, THE AUTHOR, AND THE FORCE OF SACRAMENTS; WHICH FORCE CONSISTETH IN THIS, THAT GOD HATH ORDAINED THEM AS MEANS TO MAKE US PARTAKERS OF HIM IN CHRIST, AND OF LIFE THROUGH CHRIST

Instruction and Prayer whereof we have hitherto spoken, are duties which serve as elements, parts, or principles, to the rest that follow, in which number the Sacraments of the Church are chief. The Church is to us that very mother of our new birth [Gal. iv. 26; Isai. liv. 3], in whose bowels we are all bred, at whose breasts we receive nourishment. As many therefore as are apparently to our judgment born of God, they have the seed of their regeneration by the ministry of the Church, which useth to that end and purpose not only the Word, but the Sacraments, both having generative force and virtue.

[2.] As oft as we mention a Sacrament properly understood, (for in the writings of the ancient Fathers all articles which are peculiar to the Christian faith, all duties of religion containing that which sense or natural reason cannot of itself discern, are most commonly named Sacraments,) our restraint of the word to some few principal divine ceremonies importeth in every such ceremony two things, the substance of the ceremony itself which is visible, and besides that somewhat else more secret in reference whereunto we conceive that ceremony to be a Sacrament. For we all admire and honour the holy Sacraments, not respecting so much the service which we do unto God in receiving them, as the dignity of that sacred and secret gift which we thereby receive from God. Seeing that Sacraments therefore consist altogether in relation to some such gift or grace supernatural as only God can bestow, how should any but the Church administer those ceremonies as Sacraments which are not thought to be Sacraments by any but by the Church?

[3.] There is in Sacraments to be observed their force and their form of administration. Upon their force their necessity dependeth. So that how they are necessary we cannot discern till we see how effectual they are. When Sacraments are said to be visible signs of invisible grace, we thereby conceive how grace is indeed the very end for which these heavenly mysteries were instituted, and besides sundry other properties observed in them, the matter whereof they consist is such as signifieth, figureth, and representeth their end. But still their efficacy resteth obscure to our understanding, except we search somewhat more distinctly what grace in particular that is whereunto they are referred, and what manner of operation they have towards it.

The use of Sacraments is but only in this life, yet so that here they concern a far better life than this, and are for that cause accompanied with "grace which worketh salvation." Sacraments are the powerful instruments of God to eternal life. For as our natural life consisteth in the union of the body with the soul; so our life supernatural in the union of the soul with God. And forasmuch as there is no union of God with man without that mean beween both which is both, it seemeth requisite that we first consider how God is in Christ, then how Christ is in us, and how the Sacraments do serve to make us partakers of Christ. In other things we may be more brief, but the weight of these requireth largeness.

Chapter 51

THAT GOD IS IN CHRIST BY THE PERSONAL INCARNATION OF THE SON WHO IS VERY GOD*

"The Lord our God is but one God." In which indivisible unity notwithstanding we adore the Father as being altogether of himself, we glorify that consubstantial Word which is the Son, we bless and magnify that co-essential Spirit eternally proceeding from both which is the Holy Ghost. Seeing therefore the Father is of none, the Son is of the Father and the Spirit is of both, they are by these their several properties really distinguishable each from other. For the substance of God with this property *to be of none* doth make the person of the Father; the very selfsame substance in number with this property *to be of the Father* maketh the person of the Son; the same substance having added unto it the property of *proceeding from the other two* maketh the person of the Holy Ghost. So that in every person there is implied both the substance of God which is one, and also that property which causeth the same person really and truly to differ from the other two. Every person hath his own subsistence which no other besides hath, although there be others besides that are of the same substance. As no man but Peter can be the person which Peter is, yet Paul hath the selfsame nature which Peter hath. Again, angels have every of them the nature of pure and invisible spirits, but every Angel is not that Angel which appeared in a dream to Joseph.

[2.] Now when God became man, lest we should err in applying this to the person of the Father, or of the Spirit, St. Peter's confession unto Christ was, "Thou art the *Son* of the living God," [Matt. xvi. 16] and St. John's exposition thereof was plain, that it is the *Word* [John i. 14] which was made Flesh. "The Father and the Holy Ghost (saith Damascene) have no communion with the incarnation of the Word otherwise than only by approbation and assent."

Notwithstanding, forasmuch as the Word and Deity are one subject, we must beware we exclude not the nature of God from incarnation, and so make the Son of God incarnate not to be very God. For undoubtedly even the nature of God itself in the only person of the Son is incarnate, and hath taken to itself flesh. Wherefore incarnation may neither be granted to any person but only one, nor yet denied to that nature which is common unto all three.

[3.] Concerning the cause of which incomprehensible mystery, forasmuch as it seemeth a thing unconsonant that the world should honour any other as the Saviour but him whom it honoureth as the Creator of the world, and in the wisdom of God it hath not been thought convenient to

* Isai. ix. 6; Jer. xxiii. 6; Rom. ix. 5; John xvi. 15, v. 21; Col. ii. 9; 1 John v. 20.

admit any way of saving man but by man himself, though nothing should be spoken of the love and mercy of God towards man, which this way are become such a spectacle as neither men nor angels can behold without a kind of heavenly astonishment, we may hereby perceive there is cause sufficient why divine nature should assume human, that so God might be in Christ reconciling to himself the world [2 Cor. v. 19]. And if some cause be likewise required why rather to this end and purpose the Son than either the Father or the Holy Ghost should be made man, could we which are born the children of wrath be adopted the sons of God through grace, any other than the natural son of God being mediator between God and us? It became therefore him by whom all things are to be the way of salvation to all, that the institution and restitution of the world might be both wrought by one hand [Heb. ii. 10]. The world's salvation was without the incarnation of the Son of God a thing impossible, not simply impossible, but impossible it being presupposed that the will of God was no otherwise to have it saved than by the Death of his own Son. Wherefore taking to himself our flesh, and by his incarnation making it his own flesh, he had now of his own although from us what to offer unto God for us.

And as Christ took manhood that by it he might be capable of death whereunto he humbled himself, so because manhood is the proper subject of compassion and feeling pity, which maketh the sceptre of Christ's regency even in the kingdom of heaven amiable, he which without our nature could not on earth suffer for the sins of the world, doth now also [Heb. iv. 15] by means thereof both make intercession to God for sinners and exercise dominion over all men with a true, a natural, and a sensible touch of mercy.

Chapter 52

THE MISINTERPRETATIONS WHICH HERESY HATH MADE OF THE MANNER HOW GOD AND MAN ARE UNITED IN ONE CHRIST

It is not in man's ability either to express perfectly or conceive the manner how this was brought to pass. But the strength of our faith is tried by those things wherein our wits and capacities are not strong. Howbeit because this divine mystery is more true than plain, divers having framed the same to their own conceits and fancies are found in their expositions thereof more plain than true. Insomuch that by the space of five hundred years after Christ, the Church was almost troubled with nothing else saving only with care and travail to preserve this article from the sinister construction of heretics. Whose first mists when the light of the Nicene council had dispelled, it was not long ere Macedonius transferred unto God's most Holy Spirit the same blasphemy wherewith Arius had already dishonoured his co-eternally begotten Son; not long ere Apollinarius began to pare away from Christ's humanity. In refutation of which impieties when the Fathers of the Church, Athanasius, Basil, and the two Gregories, had by their painful travails sufficiently cleared the truth, no less for the Deity of the Holy Ghost than for the complete humanity of Christ, there followed hereupon a final conclusion, whereby those controversies, as also the rest which Paulus Samosatenus, Sabellius, Photinus, Aëtius, Eunomius, together with the whole swarm of pestilent Demi-Arians had from time to time stirred up sithence the council of Nice, were both privately first at Rome in a smaller synod, and then at Constantinople, in a general famous assembly brought to a peaceable and quiet end, seven-score bishops and ten agreeing in that confession which by them set down remaineth at this present hour a part of our church liturgy, a memorial of their fidelity and zeal, a sovereign preservative of God's people from the venomous infection of heresy.

[2.] Thus in Christ the verity of God and the complete substance of man were with full agreement established throughout the world, till such time as the heresy of Nestorius broached itself, "dividing Christ into two persons, the Son of God and the Son of man, the one a person begotten of God before all worlds, the other also a person born of the Virgin Mary, and in special favour chosen to be made entire to the Son of God above all men, so that whosoever will honour God must together honour Christ, with whose person God hath vouchsafed to join himself in so high a degree of gracious respect and favour." But that the selfsame person which verily is man should properly be God also, and that, by reason not of two persons linked in amity but of two natures human and divine conjoined in one and the same person, the God of glory may be said as well to have suffered death as to have raised the dead from their graves, the Son of man as well to have made as to have redeemed the world, Nestorius in no case would admit.

[3.] That which deceived him was want of heed to the first beginning of that admirable combination of God with man. "The Word (saith St. John) was made flesh and dwelt *in us*." [John i. 14] The Evangelist useth the plural number, men for manhood, *us* for the nature whereof we consist, even as the Apostle denying the assumption of *angelical nature*, saith likewise in the plural number, "He took not *Angels* but the seed of Abraham." [Heb. ii. 16] It pleased not the Word or Wisdom of God to take to itself some one person amongst men, for then should that one have been advanced which was assumed and no more, but Wisdom to the end she might save many built her house of that *nature* which is common unto all, she made not *this or that man* her habitation, but dwelt *in us*. The seeds of herbs and plants at the first are not in act but in possibility that which they afterwards grow to be. If the Son of God had taken to himself a man now made and already perfected, it would of necessity follow that there are in Christ two persons, the one assuming and the other assumed; whereas the Son of God did not assume a man's person unto his own, but a man's nature to his own person, and therefore took *semen*, the seed of Abraham, the very first original element of our nature, before it was come to have any personal human subsistence. The flesh and the conjunction of the flesh with God began both at one instant; his making and taking to himself our flesh, was but one act, so that in Christ there is no personal subsistence but one, and that from everlasting. By taking only the nature of man he still continueth one person, and changeth but the manner of his subsisting, which was before in the mere glory of the Son of God, and is now in the habit also of our flesh.

Forasmuch therefore as Christ hath no personal subsistence but one whereby we acknowledge him to have been eternally the Son of God, we must of necessity apply to the *person* of the Son of God even that which is spoken of Christ according to his human nature. For example, according to the flesh he was born of the Virgin Mary, baptized of John in the river Jordan, by Pilate adjudged to die, and executed by the Jews. We cannot say properly that the Virgin bore, or John did baptize, or Pilate condemn, or the Jews crucify the nature of man, because these all are personal attributes; his person is the subject which receiveth them, his nature that which maketh his Person capable or apt to receive. If we should say that the person of a man in our saviour Christ was the subject of these things, this were plainly to entrap ourselves in the very snare of the Nestorians' heresy, between whom and the Church of God there was no difference, saving only that Nestorius imagined in Christ as well a personal human subsistence as a divine, the Church acknowledging a substance both divine and human, but no other personal subsistence than divine, because the Son of God took not to himself a man's person, but the nature only of a man.

Christ is a person both divine and human, howbeit not therefore two persons in one, neither both these in one sense, but a Person divine, because he is *personally* the Son of God, human, because *he hath* really *the nature* of the children of men. In Christ therefore God and man "there is" (saith Paschasius) "a twofold substance, not a twofold person, because one person extinguisheth another, whereas one nature cannot in another become extinct." For the personal being which the Son of God already had, suffered not the substance to be personal which he took, although together with the nature which he had the nature also which he took continueth. Whereupon it followeth against Nestorius, that no person was born of the Virgin but the Son of God, no person but the Son of God baptized, the Son of God condemned, the Son of God and no other person crucified; which one only point of Christian belief, *the infinite worth of the Son of God*, is the very ground of all things believed concerning life and salvation by that which Christ either did or suffered as man in our behalf.

[4.] But forasmuch as St. Cyril, the chiefest of those two hundred bishops assembled in the Council of Ephesus, where the heresy of Nestorius was condemned, had in his writings against the Arians avouched that the Word or Wisdom of God hath *but one nature* which is eternal, and whereunto he assumed flesh (for the Arians were of opinion that besides God's own eternal wisdom, there is a wisdom which God created before all things, to the end he might thereby create all things else, and that this created wisdom was the Word which took flesh): again, forasmuch as the same Cyril had given instance in the body and the soul of man no farther than only to enforce by example against Nestorius, that a visible and an invisible, a mortal and an immortal substance may united make *one person*: the words of Cyril were in process of time so taken as though it had been his drift to teach, that even as in us the body and the soul, so in Christ God and man make but *one nature*. Of which error, six hundred and thirty fathers in the Council of Chalcedon condemned Eutyches. For as Nestorius teaching rightly that God and man are distinct natures, did thereupon misinfer that in Christ those natures can by no conjunction make one person; so Eutyches, of sound belief as touching their true personal copulation, became unsound by denying the difference which still continueth between the one and the other nature. We must therefore keep warily a middle course, shunning both that distraction of persons wherein Nestorius went awry, and also this later confusion of natures which deceived Eutyches.

These natures from the moment of their first combination have been and are for ever inseparable. For even when his soul forsook the tabernacle of his body, his Deity forsook neither body nor soul. If it had, then could we not truly hold either that the person of Christ was buried, or that the person of Christ did raise up itself from the dead. For the body separated from the Word can in no true sense be termed the person of Christ; nor is it true to say that the Son of God in raising up that body did raise up himself, if the body were not both with him and of him even during the time it lay in the sepulchre. The like is also to be said of the soul, otherwise we are plainly and inevitably Nestorians. The very person of Christ therefore for ever one and the selfsame was only touching bodily substance concluded within the grave, his soul only from thence severed, but by personal union his deity still unseparably joined with both.

Chapter 53

THAT BY THE UNION OF THE ONE WITH THE OTHER NATURE IN CHRIST THERE GROWETH NEITHER GAIN NOR LOSS OF ESSENTIAL PROPERTIES TO EITHER

The sequel of which conjunction of natures in the person of Christ is no abolishment of natural properties appertaining to either substance, no transition or transmigration thereof out of one substance into another, finally no such mutual infusion as really causeth the same natural operations or properties to be made common unto both substances; but whatsoever is natural to deity the same remaineth in Christ uncommunicated unto his manhood, and whatsoever natural to manhood his deity thereof is uncapable. The true properties and operations of his Deity are to know that which is not possible for *created natures* to comprehend; to be simply the highest cause of all things, the wellspring of immortality and life; to have neither end nor beginning of days; to be every where present, and enclosed no where; to be subject to no alteration nor passion; to produce of itself those effects which cannot proceed but from infinite majesty and power. The true properties and operations of his manhood are such as Irenæus reckoneth up: "If Christ," saith he, "had not taken flesh from the very earth, he would not have coveted those earthly nourishments, wherewith bodies which be taken from thence are fed. This was the nature which felt hunger after long fasting, was desirous of rest after travail, testified compassion and love by tears, groaned in heaviness, and with extremity of grief even melted away itself into bloody sweats." To Christ we ascribe both working of wonders and suffering of pains, we use concerning him speeches as well of humility as of divine glory. But the one we apply unto that nature which he took of the Virgin Mary, the other to that which was in the beginning.

[2.] We may not therefore imagine that the properties of the weaker nature have vanished with the presence of the more glorious, and have been therein swallowed up as in a gulf. We dare not in this point give ear to them who over-boldly affirm that "the nature which Christ took weak and feeble from us by being mingled with deity became the same which deity is, that the assumption of our substance unto his was like the blending of a drop of vinegar with the huge Ocean, wherein although it continue still, yet not with those properties which severed it hath, because sithence the instant of their conjunction, all distinction and difference of the one from the other is extinct, and whatsover we can now conceive of the Son of God, is nothing else but mere deity," which words are so plain and direct for Eutyches, that I stand in doubt they are not his whose name they carry. Sure I am they are far from truth, and must of necessity give place to the better-advised sentences of other men. "He which in himself was appointed," saith Hilary, "a mediator to save his Church, and for performance of that mystery of mediation between God and man, is become God and man, doth now being but one consist of both those natures united, neither hath he through the union of both incurred the damage or loss of either, lest by being born a man we should think he hath given over to be God, or that because he continueth God, therefore he cannot be man also, whereas the true belief which maketh a man happy proclaimeth jointly God and man, confesseth the Word and flesh together." Cyril more plainly: "His two natures have knit themselves the one to the other, and are in that nearness as uncapable of confusion as of distraction. Their coherence hath not taken away the difference between them. Flesh is not become God, but doth still continue flesh, although it be now the flesh of God." Yea, "of each substance," saith Leo, "the properties are all preserved and kept safe."

[3.] These two natures are as causes and original grounds of all things which Christ hath done. Wherefore some things he doth as God, because his Deity alone is the wellspring from which they flow; some things as man, because they issue from his mere human nature; some things jointly as both God and man, because both natures concur as principles thereunto. For albeit the properties of each *nature* do cleave only to that nature whereof they are properties, and therefore Christ cannot *naturally be* as God the same which he *naturally is* as man; yet both natures may very well concur unto *one effect*, and Christ in that respect be truly said to *work* both as God and as man one and the selfsame thing. Let us therefore set it down for a rule or principle so necessary as nothing more to the plain deciding of all doubts and questions about the union of natures in Christ, that of both natures there is a *co-operation* often, an *association* always, but never any mutual *participation*, whereby the properties of the one are infused into the other.

[4.] Which rule must serve for the better understanding of that which Damascene hath touching cross and circulatory speeches, wherein there are attributed to God such things as belong to manhood, and to man such as properly concern the deity of Christ Jesus. The cause whereof is the *association* of natures in one subject. A kind of mutual commutation there is whereby those concrete names, *God* and *Man*, when we speak of *Christ*, do take interchangeably one another's room, so that for truth of speech it skilleth not whether we say that the Son of God hath created the world, and the Son of man by his death hath saved it, or else that the Son of man did create, and the Son of God die to save the world. Howbeit, as oft as we attribute to God what the manhood of Christ claimeth, or to man what his Deity hath right unto, we understand by the name of God and the name of Man neither the one nor the other nature, but the whole person of Christ, in whom both natures are. When the Apostle saith of the Jews that they crucified the Lord of glory, and when the Son of man being on earth affirmeth that the Son of man was in heaven at the same instant, there is in these two speeches that mutual circulation before-mentioned. In the one [1 Cor. ii. 8], there is attributed to God or the Lord of glory death, whereof divine nature is not capable; in the other ubiquity unto man [John iii. 13], which human nature admitteth not. Therefore by the Lord of glory we must needs understand the whole person of Christ, who being Lord of Glory, was indeed crucified, but not in that nature for which he is termed the Lord of glory. In like manner by the Son of man the whole person of Christ must necessarily be meant, who being man upon earth, filled heaven with his glorious presence, but not according to that nature for which the title of man is given him.

Without this caution the Fathers whose belief was sincere and their meaning most sound, shall seem in their writings one to deny what another constantly doth affirm. Theodoret disputeth with great earnestness that *God* cannot be said to suffer. But he thereby meaneth Christ's *divine nature* against Apollinarius, which held even deity itself passible. Cyril on the other side against Nestorius as much contendeth, that whosoever will deny *very God* to have suffered death, doth forsake the faith. Which notwithstanding to hold were heresy, if the name of God in this assertion did not import as it doth the person of Christ, who being verily God suffered death, but in the flesh, and not in that substance for which the name of God is given him.

Chapter 54

WHAT CHRIST HATH OBTAINED ACCORDING TO THE FLESH, BY THE UNION OF HIS FLESH WITH DEITY

If then both natures do remain with their properties in Christ thus distinct as hath been shewed, we are for our better understanding what either nature receiveth from other, to note that Christ is by three degrees a receiver: first, in that he is the Son of God; secondly, in that his human nature hath had the honour of union with deity bestowed upon it; thirdly, in that by means thereof sundry eminent graces have flowed as effects from deity into that nature which is coupled with it. On Christ therefore there is bestowed the gift of eternal generation, the gift of union, and the gift of unction.

[2.] By the gift of eternal generation Christ hath received of the Father one and in number the selfsame substance, which the Father hath of himself unreceived from any other. For every *beginning* [Ephes. iii. 15] *is a Father* unto that which cometh of it; and every *offspring is a Son* unto that out of which it groweth. Seeing therefore the Father alone is originally [James i. 17] that deity which Christ originally is not, (for Christ is God by being of God, light by issuing out of light [Heb. i. 3; Sap. vii. 25–6],) it followeth hereupon that whatsoever Christ hath common unto him with his heavenly Father, the same of necessity must be *given* him, but naturally and eternally given, not bestowed by way of benevolence and favour, as the other gifts both are. And therefore where the fathers give it out for a rule, that whatsoever Christ is said in Scripture to have *received*, the same we ought to apply only to the manhood of Christ; their assertion is true of all things which Christ hath received *by grace,* but to that which he hath received of the Father by eternal nativity or birth it reacheth not.

[3.] Touching union of diety with manhood, it is by grace, because there can be no greater grace shewed towards man, than that God should vouchsafe to unite to man's nature the person of his only begotten Son. Because [John iii. 35] "the Father loveth the Son" as man, he hath by uniting Deity with manhood, "*given* all things into his hands." It hath *pleased* the Father, that in him "all fulness should dwell." [Ephes. i. 5] The "name" which he hath "above all names" is *given* him [Phil. ii. 9] "As the Father hath life in himself," the "Son in himself hath life also" by the *gift* of the Father [John v. 26]. The gift whereby God hath made Christ a fountain of life is that "conjunction of the nature of God with the nature of man" [1 John v. 20] in the person of Christ, "*which gift,*" (saith Christ to the woman of Samaria,) "if thou didst know and *in that respect* understand *who it is* which asketh water of thee, thou wouldest ask of him that he might give thee living water." [John iv. 10] The union therefore of the flesh with Deity is to *that flesh* a gift of principal grace and favour. For by virtue of this grace, man is really made God, a creature is exalted above the dignity of all creatures, and hath all creatures else under it.

[4.] This admirable union of God with man can enforce in that higher nature no alteration, because unto God there is nothing more natural than not to be subject to any change. Neither is it a thing impossible that the Word being made flesh should be that which it was not before as touching the manner of subsistence, and yet continue in all qualities or properties of nature the same it was, because the incarnation of the Son of God consisteth *merely in the union* of natures, which union doth add perfection to the weaker, to the nobler no alteration at all. If therefore it be demanded what the person of the Son of God hath attained by assuming manhood, surely, the whole sum of all is this, to be as we are truly, really, and naturally man, by means whereof he is made capable of meaner offices than otherwise his person could have admitted, the only gain he thereby purchased for himself was to be capable of loss and detriment for the good of others.

[5.] But may it rightly be said concerning the incarnation of Jesus Christ, that as our nature hath in no respect changed his, so from his to ours as little alteration hath ensued? The very cause of his taking upon him our nature was to change it, to better the quality, and to advance the condition thereof, although in no sort to abolish the substance which he took, nor to infuse into it the natural forces and properties of his Deity. As therefore we have shewed how the Son of God by his incarnation hath changed the manner of that personal subsistence which before was solitary, and is now in the association of flesh, no alteration thereby accruing to the nature of God; so neither are the *properties of man's nature* in the person of Christ by force and virtue of the same conjunction so much altered, as not to stay within those limits which our substance is bordered withal; nor the *state and quality* of our substance so unaltered, but that there are in it many glorious effects proceeding from so near copulation with deity. God from us can receive nothing, we by him have obtained much. For albeit the natural properties of deity be not communicable to man's nature, the supernatural gifts, graces, and effects thereof are.

The honour which our flesh hath by being the flesh of the Son of God is in many respects great. If we respect but that which is common unto us with him, the glory provided for him and his in the kingdom of heaven, his right and title thereunto even in that he is man differeth from other men's, because he is that man of whom God is himself a part. We have right to the same inheritance with Christ, but not the same right which he hath, his being such as we cannot reach, and ours such as he cannot stoop unto.

Furthermore, to be the way, the truth, and the life; to be the wisdom, righteousness, sanctification, resurrection; to be the peace of the whole world, the hope of the righteous, the heir of all things; to be that supreme head whereunto all power both in heaven and in earth is given: these are not honours common unto Christ with other men, they are titles above the dignity and worth of any which were but a mere man, yet true of Christ even in that he is man, but man with whom deity is personally joined, and unto whom it hath added those excellencies which make him more than worthy thereof.

Finally, sith God hath deified our nature, though not by turning it into himself, yet by making it his own inseparable habitation, we cannot now conceive how God should without man either exercise divine power, or receive the glory of divine praise. For man is in both an associate of Deity.

[6.] But to come to the grace of *unction*: did the parts of our nature, the soul and body of Christ, receive by the influence of Deity wherewith they were matched no ability of operation, no virtue or quality above nature? Surely as the sword which is made fiery doth not only cut by reason of the sharpness which simply it hath, but also burn by means of that heat which it hath from fire, so there is no doubt but the deity of Christ hath enabled that nature which it took of man to do more than man in this world hath power to comprehend; forasmuch as (the bare essential properties of deity excepted) he hath imparted unto it all things, he hath replenished it with all such perfections as the same is any way apt to receive [Luc. ii. 47, 52], at the least according to the exigence of that economy or service for which it pleased him in love and mercy to be made man. For as the parts, degrees, and offices of that mystical administration did require which he voluntarily undertook, the beams of deity did in operation always accordingly either restrain or enlarge themselves.

[7.] From hence we may somewhat conjecture how the powers of that soul are illuminated, which being so inward unto God cannot choose but be privy unto all things which God worketh, and must therefore of necessity be endued with knowledge so far forth universal [Col. ii. 3], though not with infinite knowledge peculiar to deity itself. The soul of Christ that saw in this life the face of God was here through so visible presence of deity filled with all manner graces and virtues in that unmatchable degree of perfection, for which of him we read it written, that "God with the oil of gladness anointed him above his fellows." [Isa. xi. 2; lxi. 1; Luke iv. 18; Acts iv. 27, x. 38; Heb. i. 9; 2 Cor. i. 21; 1 John ii. 20, 27]

[8.] And as God hath in Christ unspeakably glorified the nobler, so likewise the meaner part of our nature, the very bodily substance of man. Where also that must again be remembered which we noted before concerning degrees of the influence of deity proportionable unto his own purposes, intents, and counsels. For in this respect his body which by natural condition was corruptible wanted the gift of everlasting immunity from death, passion, and dissolution, till God which gave it to be slain for sin had for righteousness' sake restored it to life with certainty of endless continuance. Yea in this respect the very glorified body of Christ retained in it the scars and marks of former mortality [John xx. 27].

[9.] But shall we say that in heaven his glorious body by virtue of the same cause hath now power to present itself in all places and to be every where at once present? We nothing doubt but God hath many ways above the reach of our capacities exalted that body which it hath pleased him to make his own, that body wherewith he hath saved the world, that body which hath been and is the root of eternal life, the instrument wherewith deity worketh, the sacrifice which taketh away sin, the price which hath ransomed souls from death, the leader of the whole army of bodies that shall rise again. For though it had a beginning from us, yet God hath given it vital efficacy, heaven hath endowed it with celestial power, that virtue it hath from above, in regard whereof all the angels of heaven adore it. Notwithstanding, a body still it continueth, a body consubstantial with our bodies, a body of the same both nature and measure which it had on earth.

[10.] To gather therefore into one sum all that hitherto hath been spoken touching this point, there are but four things which concur to make complete the whole state of our Lord Jesus Christ: his deity, his manhood, the conjunction of both, and the distinction of the one from the other being joined in one. Four principal heresies there are which have in those things withstood the truth: Arians by bending themselves against the deity of Christ; Apollinarians by maiming and misinterpreting that which belongeth to his human nature; Nestorians by rending Christ asunder, and dividing him into two persons; the followers of Eutyches by confounding in his person those natures which they should distinguish. Against these there have been four most famous ancient general Councils: the Council of Nice to define against Arians, against Apollinarians the Council of Constantinople, the Council of Ephesus against Nestorians, against Eutychians the Chalcedon Council. In four words, *ἀληθῶς, τελέως, ἀδιαιρέτως, ἀσυγχύτως, truly, perfectly, indivisibly, distinctly*, the first applied to his being God, and the second to his being Man, the third to his being of both one, and the fourth to his still continuing in that one both, we may fully by way of abridgment comprise whatsoever antiquity hath at large handled either in declaration of Christian belief, or in refutation of the foresaid heresies. Within the compass of which four heads, I may truly affirm, that all heresies which touch but the person of Jesus Christ, whether they have risen in these later days, or in any age heretofore, may be with great facility brought to confine themselves.

We conclude therefore that to save the world it was of necessity the Son of God should be thus incarnate, and that God should so be in Christ as hath been declared.

Chapter 55

OF THE PERSONAL PRESENCE OF CHRIST EVERY WHERE, AND IN WHAT SENSE IT MAY BE GRANTED HE IS EVERY WHERE PRESENT ACCORDING TO THE FLESH

Having thus far proceeded in speech concerning the person of Jesus Christ, his two natures, their conjunction, that which he either is or doth in respect of both, and that which the one receiveth from the other; sith God in Christ is generally the medicine which doth cure the world, and Christ in us is that receipt of the same medicine, whereby we are every one particularly cured, inasmuch as Christ's incarnation and passion can be available to no man's good which is not made partaker of Christ, neither can we participate him without his presence, we are briefly to consider how Christ is present, to the end it may thereby better appear how we are made partakers of Christ both otherwise and in the sacraments themselves.

[2.] All things are in such sort divided into finite and infinite, that no one substance, nature, or quality, can be possibly capable of both. The world and all things in the world are stinted, all effects that proceed from them, all the powers and abilities whereby they work, whatsoever they do, whatsoever they may, and whatsoever they are, is limited. Which limitation of each creature is both the perfection and also the preservation thereof. Measure is that which perfecteth all things, because every thing is for some end, neither can that thing be available to any end which is not proportionable thereunto, and to proportion as well excesses as defects are opposite. Again, forasmuch as nothing doth perish but only through excess or defect of that, the due proportioned measure whereof doth give perfection, it followeth that measure is likewise the preservation of all things. Out of which premises we may conclude not only that nothing created can possibly be unlimited, or can receive any such accident, quality, or property, as may really make it infinite, (for then should it cease to be a creature,) but also that every creature's limitation is according to his own kind, and, therefore as oft as we note in them any thing above their kind, it argueth that the same is not properly theirs, but groweth in them from a cause more powerful than they are.

[3.] Such as the substance of each thing is, such is also the presence thereof. Impossible it is that God should withdraw his presence from any thing [Ps. cxxxix. 7, 8], because the very substance of God is infinite. He filleth heaven and earth [Jer. xxiii. 24], although he take up no room in either, because his substance is immaterial, pure, and of us in this world so incomprehensible, that albeit no part of us be ever absent from him who is present whole unto every particular thing, yet his presence with us we no way discern farther than only that God is present, which partly by reason and more perfectly by faith we know to be firm and certain.

[4.] Seeing therefore that presence every where is the sequel of an infinite and incomprehensible substance, (for what can be every where but that which can no where be comprehended?) to inquire whether Christ be every where is to inquire of a natural property, a property that cleaveth to the deity of Christ. Which deity being common unto him with none but only the Father and the Holy Ghost, it followeth that nothing of Christ which is limited, that nothing created, that neither the soul nor the body of Christ, and consequently not Christ as man or Christ according to his human nature can possibly be every where present, because those phrases of limitation and restraint do either point out the principal subject whereunto every such attribute adhereth, or else they intimate the radical cause out of which it groweth. For example, when we say that Christ as man or according to his human nature suffered death, we shew what nature was the proper subject of mortality; when we say that as God or according to his deity he conquered death, we declare his deity to have been the cause, by force and virtue whereof he raised himself from the grave. But neither is the manhood of Christ that subject whereunto universal presence agreeth, neither is it the cause original by force whereof his person is enabled to be every where present. Wherefore Christ is essentially present with all things, in that he is very God, but not present with all things as man, because manhood and the parts thereof can neither be the cause nor the true subject of such presence.

[5.] Notwithstanding, somewhat more plainly to shew a true immediate reason wherefore the manhood of Christ can neither be every where present, nor cause the person of Christ so to be; we acknowledge that of

St. Augustine concerning Christ most true, "In that he is personally the Word he created all things, in that he is naturally man he himself is created of God," and it doth not appear that any one creature hath power to be present with all creatures. Whereupon, nevertheless it will not follow that Christ cannot therefore be thus present, because he is himself a creature, forasmuch as only infinite presence is that which cannot possibly stand with the essence or being of any creature: as for presence with all things that are, sith the whole race, mass, and body of them is finite, Christ by being *a creature* is not *in that respect* excluded from possibility of presence with them. That which excludeth him therefore as man from so great largeness of presence, is only his being *man*, a creature *of this particular kind*, whereunto the God of nature hath set those bounds of restraint and limitation, beyond which to attribute unto it any thing more than a creature *of that sort* can admit, were to give it another nature, to make it a creature of some other kind than in truth it is.

[6.] Furthermore if Christ in that he is man be every where present, seeing this cometh not by the nature of manhood itself, there is no other way how it should grow but either by the grace of union with deity, or by the grace of unction received from deity. It hath been already sufficiently proved that by force of union the properties of both natures are imparted *to the person only* in whom they are, and not what belongeth to the one nature really conveyed or translated into the other; it hath been likewise proved that natures united in Christ continue the very same which they are where they are not united. And concerning the grace of unction, wherein are contained the gifts and virtues which Christ as man hath above men, they make him really and habitually a man more excellent than we are, they take not from him the nature and substance that we have, they cause not his soul nor body to be of another kind than ours is. Supernatural endowments are an advancement, they are no extinguishment of that nature whereto they are given.

The substance of the body of Christ hath no presence, neither can have, but only local. It was not therefore every where seen, nor did it every where suffer death, every where it could not be entombed, it is not every where now being exalted into heaven. There is no proof in the world strong to enforce that Christ had a true body but by the true and natural properties of his body. Amongst which properties, definite or local presence is chief. "How is it true of Christ (saith Tertullian) that he died, was buried, and rose again, if Christ had not that very flesh the nature whereof is capable of these things, flesh mingled with blood, supported with bones, woven with sinews, embroidered with veins?" If his majestical body have now any such new property, by force whereof it may every where really even *in substance* present itself, or may at once be in many places, then hath the majesty of his estate extinguished the verity of his nature. "Make thou no doubt or question of it (saith St. Augustine) but that the man Christ Jesus is now in that very place from whence he shall come in the same form and substance of flesh which he carried thither, and from which he hath not taken nature, but given thereunto immortality. According to this form he spreadeth not out himself into all places. For it behoveth us to take great heed, lest while we go about to maintain the glorious deity of him which is man, we leave him not the true bodily substance of a man." According to St. Augustine's opinion therefore that majestical body which we make to be every where present, doth thereby cease to have the substance of a true body.

[7.] To conclude, we hold it in regard of the fore-alleged proofs a most infallible truth that Christ as man is not every where present. There are which think it as infallibly true, that Christ is every where present as man. Which peradventure in some sense may be well enough granted. His human substance in itself is naturally absent from the earth, his soul and body not on earth but in heaven only. Yet because this substance is inseparably joined to that personal Word which by his very divine essence is present with all things, the nature which cannot have in itself universal presence hath it *after a sort* by being *nowhere severed* from that which every where is present. For inasmuch as that infinite Word is not divisible into parts, it could not in part but must needs be wholly incarnate, and consequently, wheresoever the Word is, it hath with it manhood. Else should the Word be in part or somewhere God only and not man, which is impossible. For the *person of Christ is whole*, perfect God and perfect man wheresoever, although the parts of his manhood being finite and his deity infinite, we cannot say that the *whole of Christ* is simply every where, as we may that his deity is, and that his person is by force of deity. For *somewhat of the person* of Christ is not every where in that sort, namely his manhood, the *only conjunction* whereof with deity is extended as far as deity, the actual *position* restrained and tied to a certain place. Yet presence *by way of conjunction* is in some sort presence.

[8.] Again, as the manhood of Christ may after a sort be every where said to be present, because that person is every where present, from whose divine substance manhood nowhere is severed: so the same universality of presence may likewise seem in another respect appliable thereunto, namely by *co-operation* with deity, and that *in all things*. The light created of God in the beginning did first by itself illuminate the world; but after that the Sun and Moon were created, the world sithence hath *by them* always enjoyed the same. And that deity of Christ which before our Lord's incarnation wrought all things without man, doth now work nothing wherein the nature which it hath assumed is either absent from it or idle. Christ as man hath [Matt. xxviii. 18] all power both in heaven and earth given him. He hath as man, not as God only, supreme dominion over quick and dead

[Rom. xiv. 9]. For so much his ascension into heaven and his session at the right hand of God do import. The Son of God which did first humble himself by taking our flesh upon him, descended afterwards much lower and became according to the flesh obedient so far as to suffer death, even the death of the cross, for all men, because such was his Father's will. The former was an humiliation of deity, the latter an humiliation of manhood. For which cause there followed upon the latter an exaltation of that which was humbled [Phil. ii. 8, 9; Heb. ii. 9; Rev. v. 12]. For with power he created the world, but restored it by obedience. In which obedience as according to his manhood he had glorified God on earth, so God hath glorified in heaven that nature which yielded him obedience, and hath given unto Christ even in that he is man such fulness of power over the whole world [Luke xxi. 27], that he which before fulfilled in the state of humility and patience whatsoever God did require, doth now reign in glory till the time that all things be restored [Acts iii. 21]. He which came down from heaven and descended into the lowest parts of the earth is ascended far above all heavens [Ephes. iv. 9], that sitting at the right hand of God he might from thence fill all things with the gracious and happy fruits of his saving presence. Ascension into heaven is a plain local translation of Christ according to his manhood from the lower to the higher parts of the world. Session at the right hand of God is the actual exercise of that regency and dominion wherein the manhood of Christ is joined and matched with the Deity of the Son of God. Not that his manhood was before without the possession of the same power, but because the full use thereof was suspended till that humility, which had been before as a veil to hide and conceal majesty, were laid aside. After his rising again from the dead, then did God set him at his right hand in heavenly places [Ephes. i. 20–23] far above all principality, and power, and might, and domination, and every name that is named not in this world only but also in that which is to come, and hath put all things under his feet [Ps. viii. 6; Heb. ii. 8], and hath appointed him over all the head to the Church which is his body, the fulness of him that filleth all in all. The sceptre of which spiritual regiment over us in this present world is at the length to be yielded up into the hands of the Father which gave it [1 Cor. xv. 24]; that is to say the use and exercise thereof shall cease, there being no longer on earth any militant Church to govern. This government therefore he exerciseth both as God and as man, as God by essential presence with all things, as man by co-operation with that which essentially is present. Touching the manner how he worketh as man in all things, the principal powers of the soul of man are the will and the understanding, the one of which two in Christ assenteth unto all things, and from the other nothing which deity doth work is hid. So that by knowledge and assent the soul of Christ is present with all things which the deity of Christ worketh.

[9.] And even the body of Christ itself, although the definite limitation thereof be most sensible, doth notwithstanding admit in some sort a kind of infinite and unlimited presence likewise. For his body being a part of that nature which whole nature is presently joined unto deity wheresoever deity is, it followeth that his bodily substance hath every where a presence of true conjunction with deity. And forasmuch as it is by virtue of that conjunction made the body of the Son of God, by whom also it was made a sacrifice for the sins of the whole world, this giveth it a *presence of force and efficacy* throughout all generations of men. Albeit therefore nothing be *actually* infinite *in substance* but God only in that he is God, nevertheless as every number is infinite by possibility of addition, and every line by possibility of extension infinite, so there is no stint which can be set to the value or merit of the sacrificed body of Christ, it hath no measured certainty of limits, bounds of efficacy unto life it knoweth none, but is also itself infinite in *possibility of application.*

Which things indifferently every way considered, that gracious promise of our Lord and Saviour Jesus Christ concerning presence with his to the very end of the world, I see no cause but that we may well and safely interpret he doth perform both as God by essential presence of deity, and as Man in that order, sense, and meaning, which hath been shewed.

Chapter 56

THE UNION OR MUTUAL PARTICIPATION WHICH IS BETWEEN CHRIST AND THE CHURCH OF CHRIST IN THIS PRESENT WORLD

We have hitherto spoken of the person and of the presence of Christ. Participation is that mutual inward hold which Christ hath of us and we of him, in such sort that each possesseth other by way of special interest, property, and inherent copulation. For plainer explication whereof we may from that which hath been before sufficiently proved assume to our purpose these two principles, "That every original cause imparteth itself unto those things which come of it;" and "whatsoever taketh being from any other, the same is after a sort in that which giveth it being."

[2.] It followeth hereupon that the Son of God being light of light, must needs be also light in light [John i. 18]. The persons of the Godhead, by reason of the unity of their substance, do as necessarily remain one within another, as they are of necessity to be distinguished one from another, because two are the issue of one, and one the offspring of the other two, only of three one not growing out of any other. And sith they all are but one God in number, one indivisible essence or substance, their distinction cannot possibly admit separation. For how should that subsist *solitarily* by itself which hath no substance but *individually* the very same whereby others subsist with it; seeing that the multiplication of substances *in particular* is necessarily required to make those things subsist apart which have the selfsame general nature, and the persons of that trinity are not three particular substances to whom one *general* nature is common, but three that subsist by one substance *which itself is particular*, yet they all three have it, and their several ways of having it are that which maketh their personal distinction? The Father therefore is in the Son, and the Son in him, they both in the Spirit, and the Spirit in both them. So that the Father's first offspring, which is the Son, remaineth eternally in the Father; the Father eternally also in the Son, no way severed or divided by reason of the sole and single unity of their substance. The Son in the Father as light in that light out of which it floweth without separation; the Father in the Son as light in that light which it causeth and leaveth not. And because in this respect his eternal being is of the Father, which eternal being is his life, therefore he by the Father liveth.

[3.] Again, sith all things do accordingly love their offspring as themselves are more or less contained in it, he which is thus the only-begotten, must needs be in this degree the only-beloved of the Father. He therefore which is in the Father by eternal derivation of being and life from him, must needs be in him through an eternal affection of love.

[4.] His Incarnation causeth him also as man to be now in the Father, and the Father to be in him. For in that he is man, he receiveth life from the Father as from the fountain of that everliving deity, which in the person of the Word hath combined itself with manhood, and doth thereunto impart such life as to no other creature besides him is communicated. In which consideration likewise the love of the Father towards him is more than it can be towards any other [Luke iii. 22; John iii. 34–5; v. 20; x. 17], neither can any attain unto that perfection of love which he beareth towards his heavenly Father [John xiv. 31; xv. 10]. Wherefore God is not so in any, nor any so in God as Christ, whether we consider him as the personal Word of God, or as the natural son of man.

[5.] All other things that are of God have God in them and he them in himself likewise. Yet because their substance and his wholly differeth, their coherence and communion either with him or amongst themselves is in no sort like unto that before-mentioned.

God hath his influence into the very essence of all things, without which influence of deity supporting them their utter annihilation could not choose but follow. Of him all things have both received their first being and their continuance to be that which they are. All things are therefore partakers of God, they are his offspring, his influence is in them, and the personal wisdom of God is for that very cause said to excel in nimbleness or agility, to [Wisd. vii. 23] pierce into all intellectual, pure, and subtile spirits, to go through all, and to reach unto every thing which is. Otherwise, how should the same wisdom be that which supporteth, beareth up [Heb. i. 3], and sustaineth all?

Whatsoever God doth work, the hands of all three persons are jointly and equally in it according to *the order of that connexion* whereby they each depend upon other. And therefore albeit in that respect the Father be first, the Son next, the Spirit last, and consequently nearest unto every effect which groweth from all three, nevertheless, they all being of one essence, are likewise all of one efficacy. Dare any man unless he be ignorant altogether how inseparable the persons of the Trinity are, persuade himself that every of them may have their sole and several possessions, or that [John xiv. 23] we being not partakers of all, can have fellowship with any one? The Father as goodness, the Son as wisdom, the Holy Ghost as power do all concur in every particular outwardly issuing from that one only glorious deity which they all are. For that which moveth God to work is goodness, and that which ordereth his work is wisdom, and that which perfecteth his work is power. All things which God in their times and seasons hath brought forth were eternally and before all times in God, as a work unbegun is in the artificer which afterward bringeth it unto effect. Therefore whatsoever we do behold now in this present world, it was enwrapped within the bowels of divine mercy, written in the book of eternal wisdom, and held in the hands of omnipotent power, the first foundations of the world being as yet unlaid.

So that all things which God hath made are in that respect the offspring of God [Acts. xvii. 28, 29], they are *in him* as effects in their highest cause, he likewise actually is *in them*, the assistance and influence of his deity is *their life* [John i. 4, 10; Isai. xl. 26].

[6.] Let hereunto *saving efficacy* be added, and it bringeth forth a special offspring amongst men, containing them to whom God hath himself given the gracious and amiable name of sons [1 John iii. 1]. We are by nature the sons of Adam. When God created Adam he created us, and as many as are descended from Adam have in themselves the root out of which they spring. The sons of God we neither are all nor any one of us otherwise than only by grace and favour. The sons of God have God's own natural son as a second Adam [1 Cor. xv. 47] from heaven, whose race and progeny they are by spiritual and heavenly birth. God therefore loving eternally his Son, he must needs eternally in him have loved and preferred before all others them which are spiritually sithence descended and sprung out of him [Ephes. i. 3, 4]. These were in God as in their Saviour, and not as in their creator only. It was the purpose of his *saving* goodness, his *saving* wisdom, and his *saving* power which inclined itself towards them.

[7.] They which thus were in God eternally by their intended admission to life, have by vocation or adoption God actually now in them, as the artificer is in the work which his hand doth presently frame. Life as all other gifts and benefits groweth originally from the Father, and cometh not to us but by the Son [1 John v. 11], nor by the Son to any of us in particular but through the Spirit [Rom. viii. 10]. For this cause the Apostle wisheth to the church of Corinth, "The grace of our Lord Jesus Christ, and the love of God, and the fellowship of the Holy Ghost." [2 Cor. xiii. 13] Which three St. Peter comprehendeth in one, "The participation of divine nature." [2 Pet. i. 4] We are therefore in God through Christ eternally according to that intent and purpose whereby we were chosen to be made his in this present world before the world itself was made, we are in God through the knowledge which is had of us, and the love which is borne towards us from everlasting. But in God we actually are no longer than only from the time of our actual adoption into the body of his true Church, into the fellowship of his children. For his Church he knoweth and loveth, so that they which are in the Church are thereby known to be in him. Our being in Christ by eternal foreknowledge saveth us not without our actual and real adoption into the fellowship of his Saints in this present world. For in him we actually are by our actual incorporation into that society which hath him for their head [Col. ii. 10], and doth make together with him one body, (he and they in that respect having one name [1 Cor. xii. 12,],) for which cause, by virtue of this mystical conjunction, we are of him and in him even as though our very flesh and bones should be made continuate with his [Ephes. v. 30]. We are in Christ because he [John xv. 9] knoweth and loveth us even as parts of himself. No man actually is in him but they in whom he actually is. For "he which hath not the Son of God hath not life." [1 John v. 12] "I am the vine and you are the branches: he which abideth in me and I in him the same bringeth forth much fruit;" but the branch severed from the vine withereth [John xv. 5, 6]. We are therefore adopted sons of God to eternal life by participation of the only-begotten Son of God, whose life is the well-spring and cause of ours [John xiv. 19; Ephes. v. 23].

It is too cold an interpretation, whereby some men expound our being in Christ to import nothing else, but only that the selfsame nature which maketh us to be men, is in him, and maketh him man as we are. For what man in the world is there which hath not so far forth communion with Jesus Christ? It is not this that can sustain the weight of such sentences as speak of the mystery of our coherence [John xiv. 20; xv. 4] with Jesus Christ. The Church is in Christ as Eve was in Adam. Yea by grace we are every of us in Christ and in his Church, as by nature we are in those our first parents. God made Eve of the rib of Adam. And his Church he frameth out of the very flesh, the very wounded and bleeding side of the Son of man. His body crucified and his blood shed for the life of the world, are the true elements of that heavenly being, which maketh us such as himself is of whom we come [1 Cor. xv. 48]. For which cause the words of Adam may be fitly the words of Christ concerning his Church, "flesh of my flesh, and bone of my bones," a true native extract out of mine own body. So that in him even according to his manhood we according to our heavenly being are as branches in that root out of which they grow.

To all things he is life, and to men light [John i. 4–9], *as the Son of God*; to the Church both life and light eternal [John vi. 57] by being made the Son of man for us, and by being in us a Saviour, whether we respect him as God, or as man. Adam is in us as an original cause of our nature, and of that corruption of nature which causeth death, Christ as the cause original of restoration to life [Heb. v. 9]; the person of Adam is not in us, but his nature, and the corruption of his nature derived into all men by propagation; Christ having Adam's nature as we have, but incorrupt, deriveth not nature but incorruption and that immediately from his own person into all that belong unto him. As therefore we are really partakers of the body of sin and death received from Adam, so except we be truly partakers of Christ, and as really possessed of his Spirit, all we speak of eternal life is but a dream.

[8.] That which quickeneth us is the Spirit of the second Adam [1 Cor. xv. 22, 45], and his flesh that wherewith he quickeneth. That which in him made our nature uncorrupt, was the union of his deity with our nature. And in that respect the sentence of death and condemnation which only taketh hold upon sinful flesh, could no way possibly extend unto him. This caused his voluntary death for others to prevail with God, and to have the force of an expiatory sacrifice. The blood of Christ, as the Apostle witnesseth, doth therefore take away sin, because "through the eternal Spirit he offered himself unto God without spot." [Heb. ix. 14] That which sanctified our nature in Christ, that which made it a sacrifice available to take away sin, is the same which quickeneth it, raised it out of the grave after death, and exalted it unto glory. Seeing therefore that Christ is in us as a quickening Spirit, the first degree of communion with Christ must needs consist in the participation of his spirit, which Cyprian in that respect well termeth *germanissimam societatem*, the highest and truest society that can be between man and him which is both God and man in one.

[9.] These things St Cyril duly considering, reproveth their speeches which taught that only the deity of Christ is the vine whereupon we by faith do depend as branches, and that neither his flesh nor our bodies are comprised in this resemblance. For doth any man doubt but that even from the flesh of Christ our very bodies do receive that life which shall make them glorious at the later day, and for which they are already accounted parts of his blessed body? Our corruptible bodies could never live the life they shall live, were it not that here they are joined with his body which is incorruptible, and that his is in ours as a cause of immortality, a cause by removing through the death and merit of his own flesh that which hindered the life of ours. Christ is therefore both as God and as man that true vine whereof we both spiritually and corporally are branches. The mixture of his bodily substance with ours is a thing which the ancient Fathers disclaim. Yet the mixture of his flesh with ours they speak of, to signify what our very bodies through mystical conjunction receive from that vital efficacy which we know to be in his: and from bodily mixtures they borrow divers similitudes rather to declare the truth, than the manner of coherence between his sacred and the sanctified bodies of Saints.

[10.] Thus much no Christian man will deny, that when Christ sanctified his own flesh, giving as God and taking as man the Holy Ghost, he did not this for himself only but for our sakes, that the grace of sanctification and life which was first received in him might pass from him to his whole race, as malediction came from Adam unto all mankind. Howbeit, because the work of his Spirit to those effects is in us prevented by sin and death possessing us before, it is of necessity that as well our present sanctification unto newness of life, as the future restoration of our bodies should presuppose a participation of the grace, efficacy, merit or virtue of his body and blood, without which foundation first laid there is no place for those other operations of the Spirit of Christ to ensue. So that Christ imparteth plainly himself by degrees.

It pleaseth him in mercy to account himself incomplete and maimed without us [Ephes. i. 23]. But most assured we are that we all receive of his fulness, because he is in us as a moving and working cause; from which many blessed effects are really found to ensue, and that in sundry both kinds and degrees, all tending to eternal happiness. It must be confessed that of Christ, working as a creator, and a governor of the world by providence, all are partakers; not all partakers of that grace whereby he inhabiteth whom he saveth.

Again, as he dwelleth not by grace in all, so neither doth he equally work in all them in whom he dwelleth. "Whence is it (saith St. Augustine) that some be holier than others are, but because God doth dwell in some more plentifully than in others?"

And because the divine substance of Christ is equally in all, his human substance equally distant from all, it appeareth that the participation of Christ wherein there are many degrees and differences, must needs consist in such effects as being derived from both natures of Christ really into us, are made our own, and we by having them in us are truly said to have him from whom they come, Christ also more or less to inhabit and impart himself as the graces are fewer or more, greater or smaller, which really flow into us from Christ.

Christ is whole with the whole Church, and whole with every part of the Church, as touching his person, which can no way divide itself, or be possessed by degrees and portions. But the participation of Christ importeth, besides the presence of Christ's person, and besides the mystical copulation thereof with the parts and members of his whole Church, a true actual influence of grace whereby the life which we live according to godliness is his [Gal. ii. 20], and from him we receive those perfections wherein our eternal happiness consisteth.

[11]. Thus we participate Christ partly by imputation, as when those things which he did and suffered for us are imputed unto us for righteousness [Isa. liii. 5; Ephes. i. 7]; partly by habitual and real infusion, as when grace is inwardly bestowed while we are on earth, and afterwards more fully both our souls and bodies made like unto his in glory. The first thing of his so infused into our hearts in this life is the Spirit of Christ [Rom. viii. 9; Gal. iv. 6], whereupon because the rest of what kind soever do all both necessarily depend and infallibly also ensue, therefore the apostles term it sometime the seed of God [1 John iii. 9], sometime the pledge of our heavenly inheritance [Ephes. i. 14], sometime the handsel or earnest of that which is to come [Rom. viii. 23]. From hence it is that they which belong to the mystical body of our Savour Christ, and be in number as the stars of heaven, divided successively by reason of their mortal condition into many generations, are notwithstanding coupled every one to Christ their head [1 Cor. xii. 27; Ephes. iv. 15], and all unto every particular person amongst themselves [Rom. xii. 5; Ephes. iv. 25], inasmuch as the same Spirit, which anointed the blessed soul of our Saviour Christ, doth so formalize, unite and actuate his whole race, as if both he and they were so many limbs compacted into one body, by being quickened all with one and the same soul.

[12.] That wherein we are partakers of Jesus Christ by imputation, agreeth equally unto all that have it. For it consisteth in such acts and deeds of his as could not have longer continuance than while they were in doing, nor at that very time belong unto any other but to him from whom they came, and therefore how men either then or before or sithence should be made partakers of them, there can be no way imagined but only by imputation. Again, a deed must either not be imputed to any, but rest altogether in him whose it is, or if at all it be imputed, they which have it by imputation must have it such as it is whole. So that degrees being neither in the personal presence of Christ, nor in the participation of those effects which are ours by imputation only, it resteth that we wholly apply them to the participation of Christ's infused grace, although even in this kind also the first beginning of life, the seed of God, the first-fruits of Christ's Spirit be without latitude. For we have hereby only the being of the Sons of God, in which number how far soever one may seem to excel another, yet touching this that all are sons, they are all equals, some haply better sons than the rest are, but none any more a son than another.

[13.] Thus therefore we see how the Father is in the Son, and the Son in the Father; how they both are in all things, and all things in them; what communion Christ hath with his Church, how his Church and every member thereof is in him by original derivation, and he personally in them by way of mystical association wrought through the gift of the Holy Ghost, which they that are his receive from him, and together with the same what benefit soever the vital force of his body and blood may yield, yea by steps and degrees they receive the complete measure of all such divine grace, as doth sanctify and save throughout, till the day of their final exaltation to a state of fellowship in glory, with him whose partakers they are now in those things that tend to glory. As for any mixture of the substance of his flesh with ours, the participation which we have of Christ includeth no such kind of gross surmise.

Chapter 57

THE NECESSITY OF SACRAMENTS UNTO THE PARTICIPATION OF CHRIST

It greatly offendeth, that some, when they labour to shew the use of the holy Sacraments, assign unto them no end but only *to teach* the mind, by other senses, that which the Word doth teach by hearing. Whereupon, how easily neglect and careless regard of so heavenly mysteries may follow, we see in part by some experience had of those men with whom that opinion is most strong. For where the word of God may be heard, which teacheth with much more expedition and more full explication any thing we have to learn, if all the benefit we reap by Sacraments be instruction, they which at all times have opportunity of using the better mean to that purpose, will surely hold the worse in less estimation. And unto infants which are not capable of instruction, who would not think it a mere superfluity that any sacrament is administered, if to administer the Sacraments be but to teach receivers what God doth for them? There is of Sacraments therefore undoubtedly some other more excellent and heavenly use.

[2.] Sacraments, by reason of their mixed nature, are more diversely interpreted and disputed of than any other part of religion besides, for that in so great store of properties belonging to the selfsame thing, as every man's wit hath taken hold of some especial consideration above the rest, so they have accordingly seemed one to cross another as touching their several opinions about the necessity of sacraments, whereas in truth their disagreement is not great. For let respect be had to the duty which every communicant doth undertake, and we may well determine concerning the use of Sacraments, that they serve as bonds of obedience to God, strict obligations to the mutual exercise of Christian charity, provocations to godliness, preservations from sin, memorials of the principal benefits of Christ; respect the time of their institution, and it thereby appeareth that God hath annexed them for ever unto the New Testament, as other rites were before with the Old; regard the weakness which is in us, and they are warrants for the more security of our belief; compare the receivers of them with such as receive them not, and sacraments are marks of distinction to separate God's own from strangers: so that in all these respects, they are found to be most necessary.

[3.] But their chiefest force and virtue consisteth not herein so much as in that they are heavenly ceremonies, which God hath sanctified and ordained to be administered in his Church, first, as marks whereby to know when God doth impart the vital or saving grace of Christ unto all that are capable thereof, and secondly as means conditional which God requireth in them unto whom he imparteth grace. For sith God in himself is invisible, and cannot by us be discerned working, therefore when it seemeth good in the eyes of his heavenly wisdom, that men for some special intent and purpose should take notice of his glorious presence, he giveth them some plain and sensible token whereby to know what they cannot see. For Moses to see God and live was impossible. Yet Moses by fire knew where the glory of God extraordinarily was present [Exod. iii. 2]. The angel, by whom God endued the waters of the pool called Bethesda with supernatural virtue to heal, was not seen of any, yet the time of the Angel's presence known by the troubled motions of the waters themselves [John v. 4]. The Apostles by fiery tongues which they saw, were admonished when the Spirit, which they could not behold, was upon them [Acts ii. 3]. In like manner, it is with us. Christ and his Holy Spirit with all their blessed effects, though entering into the soul of man we are not able to apprehend or express how, do notwithstanding give notice of the times when they use to make their access, because it pleaseth Almighty God to communicate by sensible means those blessings which are incomprehensible.

[4.] Seeing therefore that grace is a consequent of sacraments, a thing which accompanieth them as their end, a benefit which he that hath receiveth from God himself the author of sacraments, and not from any other natural or supernatural quality in them, it may be hereby both understood that sacraments are necessary, and that the manner of their necessity to life supernatural is not in all respects as food unto natural life, because they contain *in themselves* no vital force or efficacy, they are not physical but *moral instruments* of salvation, duties of service and worship, which unless we perform as the author of grace requireth, they are unprofitable. For all receive not the grace of God which receive the sacraments of his grace. Neither is it *ordinarily* his will to bestow the grace of sacraments on any, but by the sacraments; which grace also they that receive by sacraments or with sacraments, receive it from him and not from them. For of sacraments the very same is true which Solomon's wisdom observeth in the brazen serpent, "He that turned towards it was not healed by the thing he saw, but by thee, O saviour of all." [Wisd. xvi. 7]

[5.] This is therefore the necessity of sacraments. That saving grace which Christ originally is or hath for the general good of his whole Church, by sacraments he severally deriveth into every member thereof; sacraments serve as the instruments of God to that end and purpose, moral instruments, the use whereof is in our hands, the effect in his; for the use we have his express commandment, for the effect his conditional promise: so that without our obedience to the one, there is of the other no apparent assurance, as contrariwise where the signs and sacraments of his grace are not either through contempt unreceived, or received with contempt, we are not to doubt but that they really give what they promise, and are what they signify. For we take not Baptism nor the Eucharist for bare *resemblances* or memorials of things absent, neither for *naked signs* and testimonies assuring us of grace received before, but (as they are indeed and in verity) for means effectual whereby God when we take the sacraments delivereth into our hands that grace available unto eternal life, which grace the sacraments represent or signify.

[6.] There have grown in the doctrine concerning sacraments many difficulties for want of distinct explication what kind or degree of grace doth belong unto each sacrament. For by this it hath come to pass, that the true immediate cause why baptism, and why the supper of our Lord is necessary, few do rightly and distinctly consider. It cannot be denied but sundry the same effects and benefits which grow unto men by the one sacrament may rightly be attributed unto the other. Yet then doth baptism challenge to itself but the inchoation of those graces, the consummation whereof dependeth on mysteries ensuing. We receive Christ Jesus in baptism once as the first beginner, in the Eucharist often as being by continual degrees the finisher of our life. By baptism therefore we receive Christ Jesus, and from him that saving grace which is proper unto baptism. By the other sacrament we receive him also, imparting therein himself and that grace which the eucharist properly bestoweth. So that each sacrament having both that which is general or common, and that also which is peculiar unto itself, we may hereby gather that the participation of Christ which properly belongeth to any one sacrament, is not otherwise to be obtained but by the sacrament whereunto it is proper.

* * *

Chapter 67

OF THE SACRAMENT OF THE BODY AND BLOOD OF CHRIST

The grace which we have by the holy Eucharist doth not begin but continue life. No man therefore receiveth this sacrament before baptism, because no dead thing is capable of nourishment. That which groweth must of necessity first live. If our bodies did not daily waste, food to restore them were a thing superfluous. And it may be that the grace of Baptism would serve to eternal life, were it not that the state of our spiritual being is daily so much hindered and impaired after baptism. In that life therefore where neither body nor soul can decay, our souls shall as little require this sacrament as our bodies corporal nourishment. But as long as the days of our warfare last, during the time that we are both subject to diminution and capable of augmentation in grace, the words of our Lord and Saviour Christ will remain forcible, "Except ye eat the flesh of the son of man, and drink his blood, ye have no life in you." [John vi. 53]

Life being therefore proposed unto all men as their end, they which by baptism have laid the foundation and attained the first beginning of a new life have here their nourishment and food prescribed for *continuance* of life in them. Such as will live the life of God must eat the flesh and drink the blood of the Son of man, because this is a part of that diet which if we want we cannot live. Whereas therefore in our infancy we are incorporated into Christ and by baptism receive the grace of his Spirit without any sense or feeling of the gift which God bestoweth, in the Eucharist we so receive the gift of God, that we know by grace what the grace is which God giveth us, the degrees of our own increase in holiness and virtue we see and can judge of them, we understand that the strength of our life begun in Christ is Christ, that his flesh is meat and his blood drink, not by surmised imagination but truly, even so truly that through faith we perceive in the body and blood sacramentally presented the very taste of eternal life, the grace of the sacrament is here as the food which we eat and drink.

[2.] This was it that some did exceedingly fear, lest Zwinglius and Œcolampadius would bring to pass, that men should account of this sacrament but only as of a shadow, destitute, empty and void of Christ. But seeing that by opening the several opinions which have been held, they are grown for aught I can see on all sides at the length to a general agreement concerning that which alone is material, namely the *real participation* of Christ and of life in his body and blood *by means of this sacrament*; wherefore should the world continue still distracted and rent with so manifold contentions, when there remaineth now no controversy saving only about the subject *where* Christ is? Yea even in this point no side denieth but that *the soul of man* is the receptacle of Christ's presence. Whereby the question is yet driven to a narrower issue, nor doth any thing rest doubtful but this, whether when the sacrament is administered Christ be whole *within man only*, or else his body and blood be also externally seated in the very consecrated elements themselves; which opinion they that defend are driven either to *consubstantiate* and incorporate Christ with elements sacramental, or to *transubstantiate* and change their substance into his; and so the one to hold him really but invisibly moulded up with the substance of those elements, the other to hide him under the only visible show of bread and wine, the substance whereof (as they imagine) is abolished and his succeeded in the same room.

[3.] All things considered and compared with that success which truth hath hitherto had by so bitter conflicts with errors in this point, shall I wish that men would more give themselves to meditate with silence what we have by the sacrament, and less to dispute of the manner how? If any man suppose that this were too great stupidity and dulness, let us see whether the apostles of our Lord themselves have not done the like. It appeareth by many examples that they of their own disposition were very scrupulous and inquisitive, yea in other cases of less importance and less difficulty always apt to move questions. How cometh it to pass that so few words of so high a mystery being uttered, they receive with gladness the gift of Christ and make no show of doubt or scruple? The reason hereof is not dark to them which have any thing at all observed how the powers of the mind are wont to stir when that which we infinitely long for presenteth itself above and besides expectation. Curious and intricate speculations do hinder, they abate, they quench such inflamed motions of delight and joy as divine graces use to raise when extraordinarily they are present. The mind therefore feeling present joy is always marvellous unwilling to admit any other cogitation, and in that case casteth off those disputes whereunto the intellectual part at other times easily draweth.

A manifest effect whereof may be noted if we compare with our Lord's disciples in the twentieth of John the people that are said in the sixth of John to have gone after him to Capernaum. These leaving him on the one side the sea of Tiberias, and finding him again as soon as themselves by ship were arrived on the contrary side, whither they knew that by ship he came not, and by land the journey was longer than according to the time he could have to travel, as they wondered so they asked also, "Rabbi, when camest thou hither?" [John vi. 25] The disciples when Christ appeared to them in far more strange and miraculous manner moved no question, but rejoiced greatly in that they saw. For why? The one sort beheld only that in Christ which they knew was more than natural, but yet their affection was not rapt therewith through any great extraordinary gladness, the other when they looked on Christ were not ignorant that they saw the wellspring of their own everlasting felicity; the one because they enjoyed not disputed, the other disputed not because they enjoyed.

[4.] If then the presence of Christ with them did so much move, judge what their thoughts and affections were at the time of this new presentation of Christ not before their eyes but within their souls. They had learned before that his flesh and blood are the true cause of eternal life; that this they are not by the bare force of their own substance, but through the dignity and worthiness of his person which offered them up by way of sacrifice for the life of the whole world, and doth make them still effectual thereunto; finally that to us they are life in particular by being particularly received. Thus much they knew, although as yet they understood not perfectly to what effect or issue the same would come, till at the length being assembled for no other cause which they could imagine but to have eaten the Passover only that Moses appointeth, when they saw their Lord and Master with hands and eyes lifted up to heaven first bless and consecrate for the endless good of all generations till the world's end the chosen elements of bread and wine, which elements made for ever the instruments of life by virtue of his divine benediction they being the first that were commanded to receive from him, the first which were warranted by his promise that not only unto them at the present time but to whomsoever they and their successors after them did duly administer the same, those mysteries should serve as conducts of life and conveyances of his body and blood unto them: was it possible they should hear that voice, "Take, eat, this is my body; drink ye all of this, this is my blood;" possible that doing what was required and believing what was promised, the same should have present effect in them, and not fill them with a kind of fearful admiration at the heaven which they saw in themselves? They had at that time a sea of comfort and joy to wade in, and we by that which they did are taught that this heavenly food is given for the satisfying of our empty souls, and not for the exercising of our curious and subtle wits.

[5.] If we doubt what those admirable words may import, let him be our teacher for the meaning of Christ to whom Christ was himself a schoolmaster, let our Lord's Apostle be his interpreter, content we ourselves with his explication, *My body,* "*the communion of my body*", *My blood,* "*the communion of my blood*". Is there any thing more expedite, clear, and easy, than that as Christ is termed our life because through him we obtain life, so the parts of this sacrament are his body and blood for that they are so to us who receiving them receive that by them which they are termed? The bread and cup are his body and blood because they are causes instrumental upon the receipt whereof the *participation* of his body and blood ensueth. For that which produceth any certain effect is not vainly nor improperly said to be that very effect whereunto it tendeth.

Every cause is in the effect which groweth from it. Our souls and bodies quickened to eternal life are effects the cause whereof is the person of Christ, his body and his blood are the true wellspring out of which this life floweth. So that his body and blood are in that very subject whereunto they minister life not only by effect or operation, even as the influence of the heavens is in plants, beasts, men, and in every thing which they quicken, but also by a far more divine and mystical kind of union, which maketh us one with him even as he and the Father are one.

[6.] The real presence of Christ's most blessed body and blood is not therefore to be sought for in the sacrament, but in the worthy receiver of the sacrament.

And with this the very order of our Saviour's words agreeth, first "Take and eat;" then "This is my Body which was broken for you:" first "Drink ye all of this;" then followeth "This is my Blood of the new testament which is shed for many for the remission of sins." [Mark xiv. 22] I see not which way it should be gathered by the words of Christ, when and where the bread is His body or the cup His blood, but only in the very heart and soul of him which receiveth them. As for the sacraments, they really exhibit, but for aught we can gather out of that which is written of them, they are not really nor do really contain in themselves that grace which with them or by them it pleaseth God to bestow.

If on all sides it be confessed that the grace of baptism is poured into the soul of man, that by water we receive it although it be neither seated in the water nor the water changed into it, what should induce men to think that the grace of the Eucharist must needs be in the Eucharist before it can be in us that receive it?

The fruit of the Eucharist is the participation of the body and blood of Christ. There is no sentence of Holy Scripture which saith that we cannot by this sacrament be made partakers of his body and blood except they be first contained in the sacrament, or the sacrament converted into them. "This is my body," and "This is my blood," being words of promise, sith we all agree that by the sacrament Christ doth really and truly in us perform his promise, why do we vainly trouble ourselves with so fierce contentions whether by consubstantiation, or else by transubstantiation the sacrament itself be first possessed with Christ, or no? A thing which no way can either further or hinder us howsoever it stand, because our participation of Christ in this sacrament dependeth on the co-operation of his omnipotent power which maketh it his body and blood to us, whether with change or without alteration of the element, such as they imagine, we need not greatly to care nor inquire.

[7.] Take therefore that wherein all agree, and then consider by itself what cause why the rest in question should not rather be left as superfluous than urged as necessary. It is on all sides plainly confessed, first that this sacrament is a true and a real participation of Christ, who thereby imparteth himself even his whole entire person *as a mystical head* unto every soul that receiveth him, and that every such receiver doth thereby incorporate or unite himself unto Christ as a *mystical member of* him, yea of them also whom he acknowledgeth to be his own; secondly that to whom *the person of Christ* is thus communicated, to them he giveth by the same sacrament his Holy Spirit to sanctify them as it sanctifieth him which is their head; thirdly that what *merit, force or virtue soever there is in his sacrificed body and blood*, we freely, fully and wholly have it by this sacrament; fourthly that *the effect thereof in us is a real transmutation of our souls and bodies* from sin to righteousness, from death and corruption to immortality and life; fifthly that because the sacrament being of itself but a corruptible and earthly creature must needs be thought an unlikely instrument to work so admirable effects in man, we are therefore to rest ourselves altogether upon *the strength of his glorious power* who is able and will bring to pass that the bread and cup which he giveth us shall be truly the thing he promiseth.

[8.] It seemeth therefore much amiss that against them whom they term Sacramentaries so many invective discourses are made all running upon two points, that the Eucharist is not a bare sign or figure only, and that the efficacy of his body and blood is not all we receive in this sacrament. For no man having read their books and writings which are thus traduced can be ignorant that both these assertions they plainly confess to be most true. They do not so interpret the words of Christ as if the name of his body did import but the figure of his body, and to be were only to signify his blood. They grant that these holy mysteries received in due manner do instrumentally both make us partakers of the grace of that body and blood which were given for the life of the world, and besides also impart unto us even in true and real though mystical manner the very person of our Lord himself, whole, perfect, and entire, as hath been shewed.

[9.] Now whereas all three opinions do thus far accord in one, that strong conceit which two of the three have embraced as touching a literal, corporal, and oral manducation of the very substance of his flesh and blood is surely an opinion no where delivered in Holy Scripture, whereby they should think themselves bound to believe it, and (to speak with the softest terms we can use) greatly prejudiced in that when some others did so conceive of eating his flesh, our Saviour to abate that error in them gave them directly to understand how his flesh so eaten could profit them nothing, because the words which he spake were spirit, that is to say, they had a reference to a mystical participation, which mystical participation giveth life. Wherein there is small appearance of likelihood that his meaning should be only to make them Marcionites by inversion, and to teach them that as Marcion did think Christ seemed to be a man but was not, so they contrariwise should believe that Christ in truth would so give them as they thought his flesh to eat, but yet lest the horror thereof should offend them, he would not seem to do that he did.

[10.] When they which have this opinion of Christ in that blessed sacrament go about to explain themselves, and to open after what manner things are brought to pass, the one sort lay the union of Christ's deity with his manhood as their first foundation and ground; from thence they infer a power which the body of Christ hath *thereby* to present itself in all places; out of which ubiquity of his body they gather the presence thereof with that sanctified bread and wine of our Lord's table; the conjunction of his body and blood with those elements they use as an argument to shew how the bread may as well in that respect be termed his body because his body is therewith joined, as the Son of God may be named man by reason that God and man in the person of Christ are united; to this they add how the words of Christ commanding us to eat must needs import that as he hath coupled the substance of his flesh and the substance of bread together, so we together should receive both; which labyrinth as the other sort doth justly shun, so the way which they take to the same inn is somewhat more short but no whit more certain. For through God's omnipotent power they imagine that transubstantiation followeth upon the words of consecration, and upon transubstantiation the participation of Christ's both body and blood in the only shape of sacramental elements.

So that they all three do plead God's omnipotency: Sacramentaries to that alteration which the rest confess he accomplisheth; the patrons of transubstantiation over and besides that to the change of one substance into another; the followers of consubstantiation to the kneading up of both substances as it were into one lump.

[11.] Touching the sentence of antiquity in this cause, first forasmuch as they knew that the force of this sacrament doth necessarily presuppose the verity of Christ's both body and blood, they used oftentimes the same as an argument to prove that Christ hath as truly the substance of man as of God, because here we receive Christ and those graces which flow from him in that he is man. So that if he have no such being, neither can the sacrament have any such meaning as we all confess it hath. Thus Tertullian, thus Irenaeus, thus Theodoret disputeth.

Again, as evident it is how they teach that Christ is *personally* there present, yea present whole, albeit a part of Christ be *corporally* absent from thence; that Christ assisting this heavenly banquet with his personal and true presence doth by his own divine power add to the natural substance thereof supernatural efficacy, which addition to the nature of those consecrated elements changeth them and maketh them that unto us which otherwise they could not be; that to us they are thereby made such instruments as mystically yet truly, invisibly yet really work our communion or fellowship with the person of Jesus Christ as well in that he is man as God, our participation also in the fruit, grace and efficacy of his body and blood, whereupon there ensueth a kind of transubstantiation in us, a true change both of soul and body, an alteration from death to life. In a word, it appeareth not that of all the ancient fathers of the Church any one did ever conceive or imagine other than only a mystical participation of Christ's both body and blood in the sacrament, neither are their speeches concerning the change of the elements themselves into the body and blood of Christ such, that a man can thereby in conscience assure himself it was their meaning to persuade the world either of a corporal consubstantiation of Christ with those sanctified and blessed elements before we receive them, or of the like transubstantiation of them into the body and blood of Christ. Which both to our mystical communion with Christ are so unnecessary, that the fathers who plainly hold but this mystical communion cannot easily be thought to have meant any other change of sacramental elements than that which the same spiritual communion did require them to hold.

[12.] These things considered, how should that mind which, loving truth and seeking comfort out of holy mysteries, hath not perhaps the leisure, perhaps not the wit nor capacity to tread out so endless mazes, as the intricate disputes of this cause have led men into, how should a virtuously disposed mind better resolve with itself than thus? "Variety of judgments and opinions argueth obscurity in those things whereabout they differ. But that which all parts receive for truth, that which every one having sifted is by no one denied or doubted of, must needs be matter of infallible certainty. Whereas therefore there are but three expositions made of 'this is my body,' the first, 'this is in itself before participation *really and truly the natural substance of my body by reason of the coexistence which my omnipotent body hath with the sanctified element of bread*', which is the Lutherans' interpretation; the second, 'this is itself and before participation *the very true and natural substance of my body, by force of that deity which with the words of consecration abolisheth the substance of bread and substituteth in the place thereof my body,*' which is the popish construction; the last, '*this hallowed food, through concurrence of divine power, is in verity and truth, unto faithful receivers, instrumentally a cause of that mystical participation, whereby as I make myself wholly theirs, so I give them in hand an actual possession of all such saving grace as my sacrificed body can yield, and as their souls do presently need, this is* to them and in them *my body*:' of these three rehearsed interpretations the last hath in it nothing but what the rest do all approve and acknowledge to be most true, nothing but that which the words of Christ are on all sides confessed to enforce, nothing but that which the Church of God hath always thought necessary, nothing but that which alone is sufficient for every Christian man to believe concerning the use and force of this sacrament, finally nothing but that wherewith the writings of all antiquity are consonant and all Christian confessions agreeable. And as truth in what kind soever is by no kind of truth gainsayed, so the mind which resteth itself on this is never troubled with those perplexities which the other do both find, by means of so great contradiction between their opinions and true principles of reason grounded upon experience, nature and sense. Which albeit with boisterous courage and breath they seem oftentimes to blow away, yet whoso observeth how again they labour and sweat by subtlety of wit to make some show of agreement between their peculiar conceits and the general edicts of nature, must needs perceive they struggle with that which they cannot fully master. Besides sith of that which is proper to themselves their discourses are hungry and unpleasant, full of tedious and irksome labour, heartless and hitherto without fruit; on the other side read we them or hear we others, be they of our own or of ancienter times, to what part soever they be thought to incline touching that whereof there is controversy, yet in this where they all speak but one thing their discourses are heavenly, their words sweet as the honeycomb, their tongues melodiously tuned instruments, their sentences mere consolation and joy: are we not hereby almost even with voice from heaven, admonished which we may safeliest cleave unto?

"He which hath said of the one sacrament, 'wash and be clean,' hath said concerning the other likewise, 'eat and live.' If therefore without any such particular and solemn warrant as this is, that poor distressed woman coming unto Christ for health could so constantly resolve herself, 'May I but touch the skirt of his garment I shall be whole,' what moveth us to argue of the manner how life should come by bread, our duty being here but to take what is offered, and most assuredly to rest persuaded of this, that can we but eat we are safe? When I behold with mine eyes some small and scarce discernible grain or seed whereof nature maketh promise that a tree shall come, and when afterwards of that tree any skilful artificer undertaketh to frame some exquisite and curious work, I look for the event, I move no question about performance either of the one or of the other. Shall I simply credit nature in things natural, shall I in things artificial rely myself on art, never offering to make doubt, and in that which is above both art and nature refuse to believe the author of both, except he acquaint me with his ways, and lay the secret of his skill before me? Where God himself doth speak those things which either for height and sublimity of matter, or else for secresy of performance we are not able to reach unto, as we may be ignorant without danger, so it can be no disgrace to confess we are ignorant. Such as love piety will as much as in them lieth know all things that God commandeth, but especially the duties of service which they owe to God. As for his dark and hidden works, they prefer as becometh them in such cases simplicity of faith before that knowledge, which curiously sifting what it should adore, and disputing too boldly of that which the wit of man cannot search, chilleth for the most part all warmth of zeal, and bringeth soundness of belief many times into great hazard. Let it therefore be sufficient for me presenting myself at the Lord's table to know what there I receive from him, without searching or inquiring of the manner how Christ performeth his promise; let disputes and questions, enemies to piety, abatements of true devotion, and hitherto in this cause but over-patiently heard, let them take their rest; let curious and sharp-witted men beat their heads about what questions themselves will, the very letter of the word of Christ giveth plain security that these mysteries do as nails fasten us to his very cross, that by them we draw out, as touching efficacy, force, and virtue, even the blood of his gored side, in the wounds of our redeemer we there dip our tongues, we are dyed red both within and without, our hunger is satisfied and our thirst for ever quenched; they are things wonderful which he feeleth, great which he seeth, and unheard of which he uttereth, whose soul is possessed of this paschal lamb and made joyful in the strength of this new wine; this bread hath in it more than the substance which our eyes behold, this cup hallowed with solemn benediction availeth to the endless life and welfare both of soul and body, in that it serveth as well for a medicine to heal our infirmities and purge our sins as for a sacrifice of thanksgiving; with touching it sanctifieth, it enlighteneth with belief, it truly conformeth us unto the image of Jesus Christ; what these elements are in themselves it skilleth not, it is enough that to me which take them they are the body and blood of Christ, his promise in witness hereof sufficeth, his word he knoweth which way to accomplish; why should any cogitation possess the mind of a faithful communicant but this, *O my God thou art true, O my Soul thou art happy*"?

[13.] Thus therefore we see that howsoever men's opinions do otherwise vary, nevertheless touching baptism and the supper of the Lord, we may with consent of the whole Christian world conclude they are necessary, the one to initiate or begin, the other to consummate or make perfect our life in Christ.

* * *

Chapter 69

OF FESTIVAL DAYS AND THE NATURAL CAUSES OF THEIR CONVENIENT INSTITUTION

As the substance of God alone is infinite and hath *no kind* of limitation, so likewise his continuance is from everlasting to everlasting and knoweth neither beginning nor end. Which demonstrable conclusion being presupposed, it followeth necessarily that besides him all things are finite both in substance and in continuance. If in substance all things be finite, it cannot be but that there are bounds without the compass whereof their substance doth not extend; if in continuance also limited, they all have, it cannot be denied, their set and their certain terms before which they had no being at all. This is the reason why first we do most admire those things which are greatest, and secondly those things which are ancientest, because the one are least distant from the infinite substance, the other from the infinite continuance of God. Out of this we gather that only God hath true immortality or eternity, that is to say continuance wherein there groweth no difference by addition of hereafter unto now, whereas the noblest and perfectest of all things besides have continually through continuance the time of former continuance lengthened, so that they could not heretofore be said to have continued so long as now, neither now so long as hereafter.

[2.] God's own eternity is the hand which leadeth angels in the course of their perpetuity; their perpetuity the hand that draweth out celestial motion, the line of which motion and the thread of time are spun together. Now as nature bringeth forth time with motion, so we by motion have learned how to divide time, and by the smaller parts of time both to measure the greater and to know how long all things else endure. For time considered in itself is but the flux of that very instant wherein the motion of the heaven began. Being coupled with other things it is the quantity of their continuance measured by the distance of two instants. As the time of a man is a man's continuance from the instant of his first breath till the instant of his last gasp.

Hereupon some have defined time to be the measure of the motion of heaven, because the first thing which time doth measure is that motion wherewith it began and by the help whereof it measureth other things, as when the Prophet David saith, that a man's continuance doth not commonly exceed threescore and ten years, he useth the help both of motion and number to measure time. They which make time an effect of motion, and motion to be in nature before time, ought to have considered with themselves that albeit we should deny as Melissus did all motion, we might notwithstanding acknowledge time, because time doth but signify the quantity of continuance, which continuance may be in things that rest and are never moved. Besides we may also consider in rest both that which is past, and that which is present, and that which is future, yea farther, even length and shortness in every of these, although we never had conceit of motion. But to *define* without motion *how* long or *how* short such continuance is were impossible. So that herein we must of necessity use the benefit of years, days, hours, minutes, which all grow from celestial motion.

Again forasmuch as that motion is circular whereby we make our divisions of time, and the compass of that circuit such, that the heavens which are therein continually moved and keep in their motions uniform celerity must needs touch often the same points, they cannot choose but bring unto us by equal distances frequent returns of the same times.

Furthermore, whereas time is nothing but the mere quantity of that continuance which all things have that are not as God is, without beginning, that which is proper unto all quantities agreeth also to this kind, so that time doth but measure other things, and neither worketh in them any real effect nor is itself ever capable of any. And therefore when commonly we use to say that time doth eat or fret out all things, that time is the wisest thing in the world because it bringeth forth all knowledge, and that nothing is more foolish than time which never holdeth any thing long, but whatsoever one day learneth the same another day forgetteth again, that some men see prosperous and happy days and that some men's days are miserable: in all these and the like speeches that which is uttered of the time is not verified of time itself, but agreeth unto those things which are in time, and do by means of so near conjunction either lay their burden upon the back, or set their crown upon the head of time. Yea, the very opportunities which we ascribe to time do in truth cleave to the things themselves wherewith time is joined; as for time it neither causeth things nor opportunities of things, although it comprise and contain both.

[3.] All things whatsoever having their time, the works of God have always that time which is seasonablest and fittest for them. His works are some ordinary, some more rare, all worthy of observation, but not all of like necessity to be often remembered, they all have their times, but they all do not add the same estimation and glory to the times wherein they are. For as God by being every where yet doth not give unto all places one and the same degree of holiness, so neither one and the same dignity to all times by working in all. For if all either places or times were in respect of God alike, wherefore was it said unto Moses by particular designation, "This very place wherein thou standest is holy ground"? [Exod. iii. 5] Why doth the Prophet David choose out of all the days of the year but one whereof he speaketh by way of principal admiration, "This is the day which the Lord hath made"? [Ps. cxviii. 24] No doubt as God's extraordinary presence hath hallowed and sanctified certain places, so they are his extraordinary works that have truly and worthily advanced certain times, for which cause they ought to be with all men that honour God more holy than other days.

The wise man therefore compareth herein not unfitly the times of God with the persons of men. If any should ask how it cometh to pass that one day doth excel another, seeing the light of all the days in the year proceedeth from one sun, to this he answereth [Ecclus. xxxiii. 7–12], that "the knowledge of the Lord hath parted them asunder, he hath by them disposed the times and solemn feasts; some he hath chosen out and sanctified, some he hath put among the days to number:" even as Adam and all other men are of one substance, all created of the earth, "but the Lord hath divided them by great knowledge and made their ways divers, some he hath blessed and exalted, some he hath sanctified and appropriated unto himself, some he hath cursed, humbled and put them out of their dignity."

So that the cause being natural and necessary for which there should be a difference in days, the solemn observation whereof declareth religious thankfulness towards him whose works of principal reckoning we thereby admire and honour, it cometh next to be considered what kinds of duties and services they are wherewith such times should be kept holy.

*   *   *

the sixth book

CONTAINING THEIR FIFTH ASSERTION, WHICH IS, THAT OUR LAWS ARE CORRUPT AND REPUGNANT TO THE LAWS OF GOD, IN MATTER BELONGING TO THE POWER OF ECCLESIASTICAL JURISDICTION, IN THAT WE HAVE NOT THROUGHOUT ALL CHURCHES CERTAIN LAY-ELDERS ESTABLISHED FOR THE EXERCISE OF THAT POWER

Chapter 1

THE QUESTION BETWEEN US, WHETHER ALL CONGREGATIONS OR PARISHES OUGHT TO HAVE LAY-ELDERS INVESTED WITH POWER OF JURISDICTION IN SPIRITUAL CAUSES

THE same men which in heat of contention do hardly either speak or give ear to reason, being after sharp and bitter conflict retired to a calm remembrance of all their former proceedings; the causes that brought them into quarrel, the course which their stirring affections have followed, and the issue whereunto they are come; may peradventure, as troubled waters, in small time, of their own accord, by certain easy degrees settle themselves again, and so recover that clearness of well-advised judgment, whereby they shall stand at the length indifferent, both to yield and admit any reasonable satisfaction, where before they could not endure with patience to be gainsayed. Neither will I despair of the like success in these unpleasant controversies touching ecclesiastical policy; the time of silence which both parts have willingly taken to breathe, seeming now as it were a pledge of all men's quiet contentment to hear with more indifferency the weightiest and last remains of that cause, Jurisdiction [Book VI], Dignity [Book VII], Dominion Ecclesiastical [Book VIII]. For, let not any man imagine, that the bare and naked difference of a few ceremonies could either have kindled so much fire, or have caused it to flame so long; but that the parties which herein laboured mightily for change, and (as they say) for Reformation, had somewhat more than this mark only whereat to aim.

[2.] Having therefore drawn out a complete form, as they supposed, of public service to be done to God, and set down their plot for the office of the ministry in that behalf; they very well knew how little their labours so far forth bestowed would avail them in the end, without a claim of jurisdiction to uphold the fabric which they had erected; and this neither likely to be obtained but by the strong hand of the people, nor the people unlikely to favour it, the more if overture were made of their own interest, right, and title thereunto. Whereupon there are many which have conjectured this to be the cause, why in all the projects of their discipline (it being manifest that their drift is to wrest the key of spiritual authority out of the hands of former governors, and equally to possess therewith the pastors of all several congregations) the people, first for surer accomplishment, and then for better defence thereof, are pretended necessary actors in those things, whereunto their ability for the most part is as slender, as their title and challenge unjust.

[3.] Notwithstanding whether they saw it necessary for them to persuade the people, without whose help they could do nothing; or else, (which I rather think,) the affection which they bare towards this new form of government made them to imagine it God's own ordinance, their doctrine is "that by the law of God, there must be for ever in all congregations certain lay-elders, ministers of ecclesiastical jurisdiction," inasmuch as our Lord and Saviour by testament (for so they presume) hath left all ministers or pastors in the Church executors equally to the whole power of spiritual jurisdiction, and with them hath joined the people as colleagues. By maintenance of which assertion there is unto that part apparently gained a twofold advantage; both because the people in this respect are much more easily drawn to favour it, as a matter of their own interest; and for that, if they chance to be crossed by such as oppose against them, the colour of divine authority, assumed for the grace and countenance of that power in the vulgar sort, furnisheth their leaders with great abundance of matter, behoveful for their encouragement to proceed always with hope of fortunate success in the end, considering their cause to be as David's was, a just defence of power given them from above, and consequently, their adversaries' quarrel the same with Saul's, by whom the ordinance of God was withstood.

[4.] Now on the contrary side, if this their surmise prove false; if such, as in justification whereof no evidence sufficient either hath been or can be alleged (as I hope it shall clearly appear after due examination and trial), let them then consider whether those words of Corah, Dathan and Abiram against Moses and against Aaron, "It is too much that ye take upon you, seeing all the congregation is holy," [Numb. xvi. 3] be not the very true abstract and abridgment of all their published Admonitions, Demonstrations, Supplications, and Treatises whatsoever, whereby they have laboured to void the rooms of their spiritual superiors before authorized, and to advance the new fancied sceptre by lay presbyterial power.

Chapter 2

THE NATURE OF SPIRITUAL JURISDICTION

But before there can be any settled determination, whether truth do rest on their part, or on ours, touching lay-elders; we are to prepare the way thereunto, by explication of some things requisite and very needful to be considered; as first, how besides that spiritual power which is of Order, and was instituted for performance of those duties whereof there hath been speech already had, there is in the Church no less necessary a second kind, which we call the power of Jurisdiction. When the Apostle doth speak of ruling the Church of God [Acts xx. 28], and of receiving accusations [1 Tim. v. 19], his words have evident reference to the power of jurisdiction. Our Saviour's words to the power of order, when he giveth his disciples charge [Mark xvi. 15; Matt. xxviii. 19; 1 Cor. xi. 24], saying, "Preach; baptize; do this in remembrance of me." "A Bishop" (saith Ignatius) "doth bear the image of God and of Christ; of God in ruling, of Christ in administering, holy things." By this therefore we see a manifest difference acknowledged between the power of Ecclesiastical Order, and the power of Jurisdiction ecclesiastical.

[2.] The spiritual power of the Church being such as neither can be challenged by right of nature, nor could by human authority be instituted, because the forces and effects thereof are supernatural and divine; we are to make no doubt or question, but that from him which is the Head it hath descended unto us that are the body now invested therewith. He gave it for the benefit and good of souls, as a mean to keep them in the path which leadeth unto endless felicity, a bridle to hold them within their due and convenient bounds, and if they do go astray, a forcible help to reclaim them. Now although there be no kind of spiritual power, for which our Lord Jesus Christ did not give both commission to exercise, and direction how to use the same, although his laws in that behalf recorded by the holy evangelists be the only ground and foundation, whereupon the practice of the Church must sustain itself: yet, as all multitudes, once grown to the form of societies, are even thereby naturally warranted to enforce upon their own subjects particularly those things which public wisdom shall judge expedient for the common good: so it were absurd to imagine the Church itself, the most glorious amongst them, abridged of this liberty; or to think that no law, constitution, or canon, can be further made either for limitation or amplification in the practice of our Saviour's ordinances, whatsoever occasion be offered through variety of times and things, during the state of this inconstant world, which bringeth forth daily such new evils as must of necessity by new remedies be redrest, did both of old enforce our venerable predecessors, and will always constrain others, sometime to make, sometime to abrogate, sometime to augment, and again to abridge sometime; in sum, often to vary, alter, and change customs incident into the manner of exercising that power which doth itself continue always one and the same. I therefore conclude, that spiritual authority is a power which Christ hath given to be used over them which are subject unto it for the eternal good of their souls, according to his own most sacred laws and the wholesome positive constitutions of his Church.

In doctrine referred unto action and practice, as this is which concerns spiritual jurisdiction, the first step towards sound and perfect understanding is the knowledge of the end, because thereby both use doth frame, and contemplation judge all things.

Chapter 3

OF PENITENCY, THE CHIEFEST END PROPOUNDED BY SPIRITUAL JURISDICTION. TWO KINDS OF PENITENCY; THE ONE A PRIVATE DUTY TOWARDS GOD, THE OTHER A DUTY OF EXTERNAL DISCIPLINE. OF THE VIRTUE OF REPENTANCE, FROM WHICH THE FORMER DUTY PROCEEDETH; AND OF CONTRITION, THE FIRST PART OF THAT DUTY.

Seeing then that the chiefest cause of spiritual jurisdiction is to provide for the health and safety of men's souls, by bringing them to see and repent their grievous offences committed against God, as also to reform all injuries offered with the breach of Christian love and charity, toward their brethren, in matters of ecclesiastical cognizance; the use of this power shall by so much the plainlier appear, if first the nature of repentance itself be known.

We are by repentance to appease whom we offend by sin. For which cause, whereas all sin deprives us of the favour of Almighty God, our way of reconciliation with him is the inward secret repentance of the heart; which inward repentance alone sufficeth, unless some special thing, in the quality of sin committed, or in the party that hath done amiss, require more. For besides our submission in God's sight, repentance must not only proceed to the private contentation of men, if the sin be a crime injurious; but also farther, where the wholesome discipline of God's Church exacteth a more exemplary and open satisfaction. Now the Church being satisfied with outward repentance, as God is with inward, it shall not be amiss, for more perspicuity, to term this latter always the Virtue, the former the Discipline of Repentance: which discipline hath two sorts of penitents to work upon, inasmuch as it hath been accustomed to lay the offices of repentance on some seeking, others shunning them; on some at their own voluntary request, on others altogether against their wills; as shall hereafter appear by store of ancient examples. Repentance being therefore either in the sight of God alone, or else with the notice also of men: without the one, sometimes thoroughly performed, but always practised more or less, in our daily devotions and prayers, we have no remedy for any fault; whereas the other is only required in sins of a certain degree and quality: the one necessary for ever, the other so far forth as the laws and orders of God's Church shall make it requisite: the nature, parts, and effects of the one always the same; the other limited, extended, varied by infinite occasions.

[2.] The virtue of repentance in the heart of man is God's handy work, a fruit or effect of divine grace. Which grace continually offereth itself, even unto them that have forsaken it, as may appear by the words of Christ in St. John's Revelation, "I stand at the door and knock:" nor doth he only knock without, but also within assist to open, whereby access and entrance is given to the heavenly presence of that saving power, which maketh man a repaired Temple for God's good Spirit again to inhabit. And albeit the whole train of virtues which are implied in the name of grace be infused at one instant; yet because when they meet and concur unto any effect in man, they have their distinct operations rising orderly one from another; it is no unnecessary thing that we note the way or method of the Holy Ghost in framing man's sinful heart to repentance.

A work, the first foundation whereof is laid by opening and illuminating the eye of faith, because by faith are discovered the principles of this action, whereunto unless the understanding do first assent, there can follow in the will towards penitency no inclination at all. Contrariwise, the resurrection of the dead, the judgment of the world to come, and the endless misery of sinners being apprehended, this worketh fear; such as theirs was, who feeling their own distress and perplexity, in that passion besought our Lord's Apostles earnestly to give them counsel what they should do [Acts ii. 37]. For fear is impotent and unable to advise itself; yet this good it hath, that men are thereby made desirous to prevent, if possibly they may, whatsoever evil they dread. The first thing that wrought the Ninevites' repentance, was fear of destruction within forty days [Jonah iii. 5]: signs and miraculous works of God, being extraordinary representations of divine power, are commonly wont to stir any the most wicked with terror, lest the same power should bend itself against them. And because tractable minds, though guilty of much sin, are hereby moved to forsake those evil ways which make his power in such sort their astonishment and fear; therefore our Saviour denounced his curse against Corazin and Bethsaida, saying, that if Tyre and Sidon had seen that which they did, those signs which prevailed little with the one would have wrought the other's repentance [Matt. xi. 21]. As the like thereunto did in the men given to curious arts, of whom the apostolic history saith, that "fear came upon them, and many which had followed vain sciences, burnt openly the very books out of which they had learned the same." As fear of contumely and disgrace amongst men, together with other civil punishments, are a bridle to restrain from any heinous acts whereinto men's outrage would otherwise break; so the fear of divine revenge and punishment, where it taketh place, doth make men desirous to be rid likewise from that inward guiltiness of sin, wherein they would else securely continue.

[3.] Howbeit, when faith hath wrought a fear of the event of sin, yet repentance hereupon ensueth not, unless our belief conceive both the possibility and means to avert evil: the possibility, inasmuch as God is merciful, and most willing to have sin cured; the means, because he hath plainly taught what is requisite and shall suffice unto that purpose. The nature of all wicked men is, for fear of revenge to hate whom they most wrong; the nature of hatred, to wish that destroyed which it cannot brook; and from hence ariseth the furious endeavours of godless and obdurate sinners to extinguish in themselves the opinion of God, because they would not have him to be, whom execution of endless woe doth not suffer them to love. Every sin against God abateth, and continuance in sin extinguisheth our love towards him. It was therefore said to the angel of Ephesus having sinned, "Thou art fallen away from thy first love," so that, as we never decay in love till we sin, in like sort neither can we possibly forsake sin, unless we first begin again to love. What is love towards God, but a desire of union with God? And shall we imagine a sinner converting himself to God, in whom there is no desire of union with God presupposed? I therefore conclude, that fear worketh no man's inclination to repentance, till somewhat else have wrought in us love also. Our love and desire of union with God ariseth from the strong conceit which we have of his admirable goodness. The goodness of God which particularly moveth unto repentance, is his mercy towards mankind, notwithstanding sin: for let it once sink deeply into the mind of man, that howsoever we have injuried God, his very nature is averse from revenge, except unto sin we add obstinacy; otherwise always ready to accept our submission as a full discharge or recompense for all wrongs; and can we choose but begin to love him whom we have offended? or can we but begin to grieve that we have offended him whom we love? Repentance considereth sin as a breach of the law of God, an act obnoxious to that revenge, which notwithstanding may be prevented, if we pacify God in time.

The root and beginning of penitency therefore is the consideration of our own sin, as a cause which hath procured the wrath, and a subject which doth need the mercy of God. For unto man's understanding there being presented, on the one side, tribulation and anguish upon every soul that doth evil; on the other, eternal life unto them which by continuance in well-doing seek glory, and honour, and immortality: on the one hand, a curse to the children of disobedience; on the other, to lovers of righteousness all grace and benediction: yet between these extremes, that eternal God, from whose unspotted justice and undeserved mercy the lot of each inheritance proceedeth, is so inclinable rather to shew compassion than to take revenge, that all his speeches in Holy Scripture are almost nothing else but entreaties of men to prevent destruction by amendment of their wicked lives; all the works of his providence little other than mere allurements of the just to continue steadfast, and of the unrighteous to change their course; all his dealings and proceedings such towards true converts, as have even filled the grave writings of holy men with these and the like most sweet sentences: "Repentance (if I may so speak) stoppeth God in his way, when being provoked by crimes past he cometh to revenge them with most just punishments; yea, it tieth as it were the hands of the avenger, and doth not suffer him to have his will." Again, "The merciful eye of God towards men hath no power to withstand penitency, at what time soever it comes in presence." And again, "God doth not take it so in evil part, though we wound that which he hath required us to keep whole, as that after we have taken hurt there should be in us no desire to receive his help." Finally, lest I be carried too far in so large a sea, "There was never any man condemned of God but for neglect, nor justified except he had care, of repentance."

[4.] From these considerations, setting before our eyes our inexcusable both unthankfulness in disobeying so merciful, and foolishness in provoking so powerful a God, there ariseth necessarily a pensive and corrosive desire that we had done otherwise; a desire which suffereth us to foreslow no time, to feel no quietness within ourselves, to take neither sleep nor food with contentment, never to give over supplications, confessions, and other penitent duties, till the light of God's reconciled favour shine in our darkened soul.

Fulgentius asking the question, why David's confession should be held for effectual penitence, and not Saul's; answereth, that the one hated sin, the other feared only punishment in this world: Saul's acknowledgment of sin was fear, David's both fear and also love. This was the fountain of Peter's tears, this the life and spirit of David's eloquence, in those most admirable hymns entitled Penitential, where the words of sorrow for sin do melt the very bowels of God remitting it, and the comforts of grace in remitting sin carry him which sorrowed rapt as it were into heaven with ecstasies of joy and gladness. The first motive of the Ninevites unto repentance was their belief in a sermon of fear, but the next and most immediate, an axiom of love [Jon. iii. 9]; "Who can tell whether God will turn away his fierce wrath, that we perish not?" No conclusion such as theirs, "Let every man turn from his evil way," but out of premises such as theirs were, fear and love. Wherefore the well-spring of repentance is faith, first breeding fear, and then love; which love causeth hope, hope resolution of attempt; "I will go to my Father, and say, I have sinned against heaven and against thee;" that is to say, I will do what the duty of a convert requireth.

[5.] Now in a penitent's or convert's duty, there are included, first, the aversion of the will from sin; secondly, the submission of ourselves to God by supplication and prayer; thirdly, the purpose of a new life, testified with present works of amendment: which three things do very well seem to be comprised in one definition, by them which handle repentance, as a virtue that hateth, bewaileth, and sheweth a purpose to amend sin. We offend God in thought, word, and deed. To the first of which three, they make contrition; to the second, confession; and to the last, our works of satisfaction, answerable.

Contrition doth not here import those sudden pangs and convulsions of the mind which cause sometimes the most forsaken of God to retract their own doings; it is no natural passion or anguish, which riseth in us against our wills, but a deliberate aversion of the will of man from sin; which being always accompanied with grief, and grief oftentimes partly with tears, partly with other external signs, it hath been thought, that in these things contrition doth chiefly consist: whereas the chiefest thing in contrition is that alteration whereby the will, which was before delighted with sin, doth now abhor and shun nothing more. But forasmuch as we cannot hate sin in ourselves without heaviness and grief, that there should be in us a thing of such hateful quality, the will averted from sin must needs make the affection suitable; yea, great reason why it should so do: for sith the will by conceiving sin hath deprived the soul of life; and of life there is no recovery without repentance, the death of sin; repentance not able to kill sin, but by withdrawing the will from it; the will unpossible to be withdrawn, unless it concur with a contrary affection to that which accompanied it before in evil: is it not clear that as an inordinate delight did first begin sin, so repentance must begin with a just sorrow, a sorrow of heart, and such a sorrow as renteth the heart; neither a feigned nor slight sorrow; not feigned, lest it increase sin; nor slight, lest the pleasures of sin overmatch it.

[6.] Wherefore of Grace, the highest cause from which man's penitency doth proceed; of faith, fear, love, hope, what force and efficiency they have in repentance; of parts and duties thereunto belonging, comprehended in the schoolmen's definitions; finally, of the first among those duties, contrition, which disliketh and bewaileth iniquity, let this suffice.

And because God will have offences by repentance not only abhorred within ourselves, but also with humble supplication displayed before him, and a testimony of amendment to be given, even by present works, worthy repentance, in that they are contrary to those we renounce and disclaim: although the virtue of repentance do require that her other two parts, confession and satisfaction, should here follow; yet seeing they belong as well to the discipline as to the virtue of repentance, and only differ for that in the one they are performed to man, in the other to God alone; I had rather distinguish them in joint handling, than handle them apart, because in quality and manner of practice they are distinct.*

* * *

* Three long, largely historical chapters on confession, satisfaction, and absolution make up the balance of what is traditionally printed as Book VI of the *Polity*, but these were very possibly not intended by Hooker to be part of the work at all. (See above, p. 27)

the seventh book

THEIR SIXTH ASSERTION, THAT THERE OUGHT NOT TO BE IN THE CHURCH, BISHOPS ENDUED WITH SUCH AUTHORITY AND HONOUR AS OURS ARE

The matter contained in this seventh book

**Chapter 1.* The state of Bishops, although some time oppugned, and that by such as therein would most seem to please God, yet by his providence upheld hitherto, whose glory it is to maintain that whereof himself is the author.

**Chapter 2.* What a Bishop is, what his name doth import, and what doth belong unto his office as he is a Bishop.

Chapter 3. In Bishops two things traduced; of which two, the one their authority; and in it the first thing condemned, their superiority over other ministers: what kind of superiority in ministers it is which the one part holdeth, and the other denieth lawful.

**Chapter 4.* From whence it hath grown that the Church is governed by Bishops.

Chapter 5. The time and cause of instituting every where Bishops with restraint.

Chapter 6. What manner of power Bishops from the first beginning have had.

Chapter 7. After what sort Bishops, together with presbyters, have used to govern the churches which were under them.

Chapter 8. How far the power of Bishops hath reached from the beginning in respect of territory, or local compass.

Chapter 9. In what respects episcopal regiment hath been gainsaid of old by Aërius.

Chapter 10. In what respect episcopal regiment is gainsaid by the authors of pretended reformation at this day.

Chapter 11. Their arguments in disgrace of regiment by Bishops, as being a mere invention of man, and not found in Scripture, answered.

Chapter 12. Their arguments to prove there was no necessity of instituting Bishops in the Church.

Chapter 13. The fore-alleged arguments answered.

Chapter 14. An answer unto those things which are objected concerning the difference between that power which Bishops now have, and that which ancient Bishops had more than other presbyters.

Chapter 15. Concerning the civil power and authority which our Bishops have.

* Chapters marked with an asterisk are included in this selection. *Ed.*

Chapter 1

THE STATE OF BISHOPS ALTHOUGH SOMETIME OPPUGNED, AND THAT BY SUCH AS THEREIN WOULD MOST SEEM TO PLEASE GOD, YET BY HIS PROVIDENCE UPHELD HITHERTO, WHOSE GLORY IT IS TO MAINTAIN THAT WHEREOF HIMSELF IS THE AUTHOR

I HAVE heard that a famous kingdom in the world being solicited to reform such disorders as all men saw the Church exceedingly burdened with, when of each degree great multitudes thereunto inclined, and the number of them did every day so increase that this intended work was likely to take no other effect than all good men did wish and labour for; a principal actor herein (for zeal and boldness of spirit) thought it good to shew them betimes what it was which must be effected, or else that there could be no work of perfect reformation accomplished. To this purpose, in a solemn sermon, and in a great assembly, he described unto them the present quality of their public estate by the parable of a tree, huge and goodly to look upon, but without that fruit which it should and might bring forth; affirming that the only way of redress was a full and perfect establishment of Christ's discipline (for so their manner is to entitle a thing hammered out upon the forge of their own invention), and that to make way of entrance for it, there must be three great limbs cut off from the body of that stately tree of the kingdom: those three limbs were three sorts of men; nobles, whose high estate would make them otherwise disdain to put their necks under that yoke; lawyers, whose courts being not pulled down, the new church consistories were not like to flourish; finally, prelates, whose ancient dignity, and the simplicity of their intended church discipline, could not possibly stand together. The proposition of which device being plausible to active spirits, restless through desire of innovation, whom commonly nothing doth more offend than a change which goeth fearfully on by slow and suspicious paces; the heavier and more experienced sort began presently thereat to pull back their feet again, and exceedingly to fear the stratagem of reformation for ever after. Whereupon ensued those extreme conflicts of the one part with the other, which continuing and increasing to this very day, have now made the state of that flourishing kingdom even such, as whereunto we may most fitly apply those words of the Prophet Jeremiah [Lam. i. 3], "Thy breach is great like the sea, who can heal thee?"

[2.] Whether this were done in truth, according to the constant affirmation of some avouching the same, I take not upon me to examine; that which I note therein is, how with us that policy hath been corrected. For to the authors of pretended reformation with us, it hath not seemed expedient to offer the edge of the axe unto all three boughs at once, but rather to single them, and strike at the weakest first, making show that the lop of that one shall draw the more abundance of sap to the other two, that they may thereby the better prosper.

All prosperity, felicity and peace we wish multiplied on each estate, as far as their own hearts' desire is: but let men know that there is a God, whose eye beholdeth them in all their ways; a God, the usual and ordinary course of whose justice is to return upon the head of malice the same devices which it contriveth against others. The foul practices which have been used for the overthrow of bishops, may perhaps wax bold in process of time to give the like assault even there, from whence at this present they are most seconded.

[3.] Nor let it over dismay them who suffer such things at the hands of this most unkind world, to see that heavenly estate and dignity thus conculcated, in regard whereof so many their predecessors were no less esteemed than if they had not been men, but angels amongst men. With former bishops it was as with Job in the days of that prosperity which at large he describeth [Job xxix. 21–5], saying, "Unto me men gave ear, they waited and held their tongue at my counsel; after my words they replied not; I appointed out their way and did sit as chief; I dwelt as it had been a king in an army." At this day the case is otherwise with them; and yet no otherwise than with the selfsame Job at what time the alteration of his estate wrested these contrary speeches from him [Job xxx. 1–9],

"But now they that are younger than I mock at me, the children of fools, and offspring of slaves, creatures more base than the earth they tread on, such as if they did shew their heads, young and old would shout at them and chase them through the streets with a cry, their song I am, I am a theme for them to talk on." An injury less grievous if it were not offered by them whom Satan hath through his fraud and subtilty so far beguiled as to make them imagine herein they do unto God a part of most faithful service. Whereas the lord in truth, whom they serve herein, is as St. Cyprian telleth them, like, not Christ, (for he it is that doth appoint and protect bishops,) but rather Christ's adversary and enemy of his Church.

[4.] A thousand five hundred years and upward the Church of Christ hath now continued under the sacred regiment of bishops. Neither for so long hath Christianity been ever planted in any kingdom throughout the world but with this kind of government alone; which to have been ordained of God, I am for mine own part even as resolutely persuaded, as that any other kind of government in the world whatsoever is of God. In this realm of England, before Normans, yea before Saxons, there being Christians, the chief pastors of their souls were bishops. This order from about the first establishment of Christian religion, which was publicly begun through the virtuous disposition of King Lucius not fully two hundred years after Christ, continued till the coming in of the Saxons; by whom Paganism being every where else replanted, only one part of the island, whereinto the ancient natural inhabitants the Britons were driven, retained constantly the faith of Christ, together with the same form of spiritual regiment, which their fathers had before received. Wherefore in the histories of the Church we find very ancient mention made of our own bishops. At the council of Ariminum, about the year three hundred and fifty-nine, Britain had three of her bishops present. At the arrival of Augustine the monk, whom Gregory sent hither to reclaim the Saxons from Gentility about six hundred years after Christ, the Britons he found observers still of the selfsame government by bishops over the rest of the clergy; under this form Christianity took root again, where it had been exiled. Under the selfsame form it remained till the days of the Norman conqueror. By him and his successors thereunto sworn, it hath from that time till now by the space of five hundred years more been upheld.

O nation utterly without knowledge, without sense! We are not through error of mind deceived, but some wicked thing hath undoubtedly bewitched us, if we forsake that government, the use whereof universal experience hath for so many years approved, and betake ourselves unto a regiment neither appointed of God himself, as they who favour it pretend, nor till yesterday ever heard of among men. By the Jews Festus was much complained of, as being a governor marvellous corrupt, and almost intolerable: such notwithstanding were they who came after him, that men which thought the public condition most afflicted under Festus, began to wish they had him again, and to esteem him a ruler commendable. Great things are hoped for at the hands of these new presidents, whom reformation would bring in: notwithstanding the time may come, when bishops whose regiment doth now seem a yoke so heavy to bear, will be longed for again even by them that are the readiest to have it taken off their necks.

But in the hands of Divine Providence we leave the ordering of all such events, and come now to the question itself which is raised concerning bishops. For the better understanding whereof we must beforehand set down what is meant, when in this question we name a bishop.

Chapter 2

WHAT A BISHOP IS, WHAT HIS NAME DOTH IMPORT, AND WHAT DOTH BELONG TO HIS OFFICE AS HE IS A BISHOP

For whatsoever we bring from antiquity, by way of defence in this cause of bishops, it is cast off as impertinent matter, all is wiped away with an odd kind of shifting answer, "That the bishops which now are, be not like unto them which were." We therefore beseech all indifferent judges to weigh sincerely with themselves how the case doth stand. If it should be at this day a controversy whether kingly regiment were lawful or no, peradventure in defence thereof, the long continuance which it hath had sithence the first beginning might be alleged; mention perhaps might be made what kings there were of old even in Abraham's time, what sovereign princes both before and after. Suppose that herein some man purposely bending his wit against sovereignty, should think to elude all such allegations by making ample discovery through a number of particularities, wherein the kings that are do differ from those that have been, and should therefore in the end conclude, that such ancient examples are no convenient proofs of that royalty which is now in use. Surely for decision of truth in this case there were no remedy, but only to shew the nature of sovereignty, to sever it from accidental properties, make it clear that ancient and present regality are one and the same in substance, how great odds soever otherwise may seem to be between them. In like manner, whereas a question of late hath grown, whether ecclesiastical regiment by bishops be lawful in the Church of Christ or no: in which question, they that hold the negative, being pressed with that general received order, according whereunto the most renowned lights of the Christian world have governed the same in every age as bishops; seeing their manner is to reply, that such bishops as those ancient were, ours are not; there is no remedy but to shew, that to be a bishop is now the selfsame thing which it hath been; that one definition agreeth fully and truly as well to those elder, as to these latter bishops.

Sundry dissimilitudes we grant there are, which notwithstanding are not such that they cause any equivocation in the name, whereby we should think a bishop in those times to have had a clean other definition than doth rightly agree unto bishops as they are now. Many things there are in the state of bishops, which the times have changed; many a parsonage at this day is larger than some ancient bishoprics were; many an ancient bishop poorer than at this day sundry under them in degree. The simple hereupon lacking judgment and knowledge to discern between the nature of things which changeth not, and these outward variable accidents, are made believe that a bishop heretofore and now are things in their very nature so distinct that they cannot be judged the same. Yet to men that have any part of skill, what more evident and plain in bishops, than that augmentation or diminution in their precincts, allowances, privileges, and such like, do make a difference indeed, but no essential difference between one bishop and another? As for those things in regard whereof we use properly to term them bishops, those things whereby they essentially differ from other pastors, those things which the natural definition of a bishop must contain; what one of them is there more or less appliable unto bishops now than of old?

[2.] The name Bishop hath been borrowed from the Grecians, with whom it signifieth one which hath principal charge to guide and oversee others. The same word in ecclesiastical writings being applied unto church governors, at the first unto all and not unto the chiefest only [Acts xx. 28; Phil. i. 1], grew in short time peculiar and proper to signify such episcopal authority alone, as the chiefest governors exercised over the rest. For with all names this is usual, that inasmuch as they are not given till the things whereunto they are given have been sometime first observed, therefore generally things are ancienter than the names whereby they are called [Gen. ii. 19].

Again, sith the first things that grow into general observation, and do thereby give men occasion to find names for them, are those which being in many subjects, are thereby the easier, the oftener, and the more universally noted; it followeth that names imposed to signify common qualities or operations are ancienter, than is the restraint of those names, to note an excellency of such qualities or operations in some one or few amongst others. For example, the name disciple being invented to signify generally a learner, it cannot choose but in that signification be more ancient than when it signifieth as it were by a kind of appropriation, those learners who being taught of Christ* were in that respect termed disciples by an excellency. The like is to be seen in the name Apostle, the use whereof to signify a messenger must needs be more ancient than that use which restraineth it unto messengers sent concerning evangelical affairs; yea this use more

* So also the name *deacon*, a minister appropriated to a certain order of ministers.

ancient than that whereby the same word is yet restrained further to signify only those whom our Saviour himself immediately did send. After the same manner the title or name of a Bishop having been used of old to signify both an ecclesiastical overseer in general, and more particularly also a principal ecclesiastical overseer; it followeth, that this latter restrained signification is not so ancient as the former, being more common.* Yet because the things themselves are always ancienter than their names; therefore that thing which the restrained use of the word doth import, is likewise ancienter than the restraint of the word is, and consequently that power of chief ecclesiastical overseers, which the term of a bishop importeth, was before the restrained use of the name which doth import it. Wherefore a lame and an impotent kind of reasoning it is, when men go about to prove that in the Apostles' times there was no such thing as the restrained name of a bishop doth now signify, because in their writings there is found no restraint of that name, but only a general use whereby it reacheth unto all spiritual governors and overseers.

[3.] But to let go the name, and come to the very nature of that thing which is thereby signified. In all kinds of regiment whether ecclesiastical or civil, as there are sundry operations public, so likewise great inequality there is in the same operations, some being of principal respect, and therefore not fit to be dealt in by every one to whom public actions, and those of good importance, are notwithstanding well and fitly enough committed. From hence have grown those different degrees of magistrates or public persons, even ecclesiastical as well as civil. Amongst ecclesiastical persons therefore bishops being chief ones, a bishop's function must be defined by that wherein his chiefty consisteth.

A Bishop is a minister of God, unto whom with permanent continuance there is given not only power of administering the Word and Sacraments, which power other Presbyters have; but also a further power to ordain ecclesiastical persons, and a power of chiefty in government over Presbyters as well as Laymen, a power to be by way of jurisdiction a Pastor even to Pastors themselves. So that this office, as he is a Presbyter or Pastor, consisteth in those things which are common unto him with other pastors, as in ministering the Word and Sacraments: but those things incident unto his office, which do properly make him a Bishop, cannot be common unto him with other Pastors.

Now even as pastors, so likewise bishops being principal pastors, are either at large or else with restraint. At large, when the subject of their regiment is indefinite, and not tied to any certain place; bishops with restraint are they whose regiment over the Church is contained within some

* The name likewise of a minister was common to divers degrees, which now is peculiarly among ourselves given only to pastors, and not, as anciently, to deacons also.

definite, local compass, beyond which compass their jurisdiction reacheth not. Such therefore we always mean when we speak of that regiment by bishops which we hold a thing most lawful, divine and holy in the Church of Christ.

* * *

Chapter 4

FROM WHENCE IT HATH GROWN THAT THE CHURCH IS GOVERNED BY BISHOPS

The first Bishops in the Church of Christ were his blessed Apostles; for the office whereunto Matthias was chosen the sacred history doth term *ἐπισκοπὴν*, an episcopal office. Which being spoken expressly of one, agreeth no less unto them all than unto him. For which cause St. Cyprian speaking generally of them all doth call them Bishops. They which were termed Apostles, as being sent of Christ to publish his gospel throughout the world, and were named likewise Bishops, in that the care of government was also committed unto them, did no less perform the offices of their episcopal authority by governing, than of their apostolical by teaching. The word *ἐπισκοπὴ*, expressing that part of their office which did consist in regiment, proveth not (I grant) their chiefty in regiment over others, because as then that name was common unto the function of their inferiors, and not peculiar unto theirs. But the history of their actions sheweth plainly enough how the thing itself which that name appropriated importeth, that is to say, even such spiritual chiefty as we have already defined to be properly episcopal, was in the holy Apostles of Christ. Bishops therefore they were at large.

[2.] But was it lawful for any of them to be a bishop with restraint? True it is their charge was indefinite; yet so, that in case they did all whether severally or jointly discharge the office of proclaiming every where the gospel and of guiding the Church of Christ, none of them casting off his part in their burden [Rom. ii. 14. 15; 1 Cor. ix. 16; John xxi. 15, 16] which was laid upon them, there doth appear no impediment but that they having received their common charge indefinitely might in the execution thereof notwithstanding restrain themselves, or at leastwise be restrained by the after commandment of the Spirit, without contradiction or repugnancy unto that charge more indefinite and general before given them: especially if it seemed at any time requisite, and for the greater good of the Church, that they should in such sort tie themselves unto some special part of the flock of Jesus Christ, guiding the same in several as bishops. For first, notwithstanding our Saviour's commandment unto them all to go and preach unto all nations; yet some restraint we see there was made, when by agreement between Paul and Peter [Gal. ii. 8], moved with those effects of their labours which the providence of God brought forth, the one betook himself unto the Gentiles, the other unto the Jews, for the exercise of that office of every where preaching. A further restraint of their apostolic labours as yet there was also made, when they divided themselves into several parts of the world; John for his charge taking Asia, and so the residue other quarters to labour in. If nevertheless it seem very hard that we should admit a restraint so particular, as after that general charge received to make any Apostle notwithstanding the bishop of some one church; what think we of the bishop of Jerusalem, James, whose consecration unto that mother see of the world, because it was not meet that it should at any time be left void of some Apostle, doth seem to have been the very cause of St. Paul's miraculous vocation, to make up the number of the twelve again, for the gathering of nations abroad, even as the martyrdom of the other James, the reason why Barnabas in his stead [Acts xii. 2; xiii. 2] was called.

Finally, Apostles, whether they did settle in any one certain place, as James, or else did otherwise, as the Apostle Paul, episcopal authority either at large or with restraint they had and exercised. Their episcopal power they sometimes gave unto others to exercise as agents only in their stead, and as it were by commission from them. Thus Titus [Titus i. 5], and thus Timothy, at the first, though afterwards endued with apostolic power of their own.

[3.] For in process of time the Apostles gave episcopal authority, and that to continue always with them which had it. "We are able to number up them," saith Irenæus, "who by the Apostles were made bishops." In Rome he affirmeth that the Apostles themselves made Linus the first bishop. Again of Polycarp he saith likewise, that the Apostles made him bishop of the church of Smyrna. Of Antioch they made Evodius bishop, as Ignatius witnesseth, exhorting that church to tread in his holy steps, and to follow his virtuous example.

The Apostles therefore were the first which had such authority, and all others who have it after them in orderly sort are their lawful successors, whether they succeed in any particular church, where before them some Apostle hath been seated, as Simon succeeded James in Jerusalem; or else be otherwise endued with the same kind of bishoply power, although it be not where any Apostle before hath been. For to succeed them, is after them to have that episcopal kind of power which was first given to them. "All bishops are," saith Jerome, "the Apostles' successors." In like sort Cyprian doth term bishops, "Præpositos qui Apostolis vicaria ordinatione succedunt." From hence it may haply seem to have grown, that they whom we now call Bishops were usually termed at the first Apostles, and so did carry their very names in whose rooms of spiritual authority they succeeded.

[4.] Such as deny Apostles to have any successors at all in the office of their apostleship, may hold that opinion without contradiction to this of ours, if they well explain themselves in declaring what truly and properly apostleship is. In some things every presbyter, in some things only bishops, in some things neither the one nor the other are the Apostles' successors. The Apostles were sent [Acts i. 21, 22; 1 John i. 3; Gal. i. 1; Apoc. xxi. 14; Matt. xxviii. 19] as special chosen eyewitnesses of Jesus Christ, from whom immediately they received their whole embassage, and their commission to be the principal first founders of an house of God, consisting as well of Gentiles as of Jews. In this there are not after them any other like unto them; and yet the Apostles have now their successors upon earth, their true successors, if not in the largeness, surely in the kind of that episcopal function, whereby they had power to sit as spiritual ordinary judges, both over laity and over clergy, where churches Christian were established.

* * *

Chapter 24

THAT FOR THEIR UNWORTHINESS TO DEPRIVE BOTH THEM AND THEIR SUCCESSORS OF SUCH GOODS, AND TO CONVEY THE SAME UNTO MEN OF SECULAR CALLING, WERE EXTREME SACRILEGIOUS INJUSTICE

But beware we of following Christ as thieves follow true men, to take their goods by violence from them. Be it that bishops were all unworthy, not only of living, but even of life, yet what hath our Lord Jesus Christ deserved, for which men should judge him worthy to have the things that are his given away from him unto others that have no right unto them? For at this mark it is that the head lay-reformers do all aim. Must these unworthy prelates give place? What then? Shall better succeed in their rooms? Is this desired, to the end that others may enjoy their honours, which shall do Christ more faithful service than they have done? Bishops are the worst men living upon earth; therefore let their sanctified possessions be divided: amongst whom? O blessed reformation! O happy men, that put to their helping hands for the furtherance of so good and glorious a work!

[2.] Wherefore albeit the whole world at this day do already perceive, and posterity be like hereafter a great deal more plainly to discern, not that the clergy of God is thus heaved at because they are wicked, but that means are used to put it into the heads of the simple multitude that they are such indeed, to the end that those who thirst for the spoil of spiritual possessions may till such time as they have their purpose be thought to covet nothing but only the just extinguishment of unreformable persons; so that in regard of such men's intentions, practices, and machinations against them, the part that suffereth these things may most fitly pray with David [Ps. vii. 8], "Judge thou me, O Lord, according to my righteousness, and according unto mine innocency: O let the malice of the wicked come to an end, and be thou the guide of the just:" notwithstanding, forasmuch as it doth not stand with Christian humility otherwise to think, than that this violent outrage of men is a rod in the ireful hands of the Lord our God, the smart whereof we deserve to feel; let it not seem grievous in the eyes of my reverend lords the Bishops, if to their good consideration I offer a view of those sores which are in the kind of their heavenly function most apt to breed, and which being not in time cured, may procure at the length that which God of his infinite mercy avert.

[3.] Of bishops in his time St. Jerome complaineth, that they took it in great disdain to have any fault great or small found with them. Epiphanius likewise before Jerome noteth their impatiency this way to have been the very cause of a schism in the Church of Christ; at what time one Audius, a man of great integrity of life, full of faith and zeal towards God, beholding those things which were corruptly done in the Church, told the bishops and presbyters their faults in such sort as those men are wont, who love the truth from their hearts, and walk in the paths of a most exact life. Whether it were covetousness or sensuality in their lives, absurdity or error in their teaching; any breach of the laws and canons of the Church wherein he espied them faulty, certain and sure they were to be thereof most plainly told. Which thing they whose dealings were justly culpable could not bear; but instead of amending their faults bent their hatred against him who sought their amendment, till at length they drove him by extremity of infestation, through weariness of striving against their injuries, to leave both them and with them the Church.

Amongst the manifold accusations, either generally intended against the bishops of this our Church, or laid particularly to the charge of any of them, I cannot find that hitherto their spitefullest adversaries have been able to say justly, that any man for telling them their personal faults in good and Christian sort hath sustained in that respect much persecution. Wherefore notwithstanding mine own inferior estate and calling in God's Church, the consideration whereof assureth me, that in this kind the sweetest sacrifice which I can offer unto Christ is meek obedience, reverence and awe unto the prelates which he hath placed in seats of higher authority over me, emboldened I am, so far as may conveniently stand with that duty of humble subjection, meekly to crave, my good lords, your favourable pardon, if it shall seem a fault thus far to presume; or if otherwise, your wonted courteous acceptation.

——"Sine me hæc haud mollia fatu
"Sublatis aperire dolis." *Æneid.* lib. xii. [25.]*

[4.] First, In government, be it of what kind soever, but especially if it be such kind of government as prelates have over the Church, there is not one thing publicly more hurtful than that an hard opinion should be conceived of governors at the first: and a good opinion how should the world ever conceive of them for their after-proceedings in regiment, whose first access and entrance thereunto giveth just occasion to think them corrupt men, which fear not that God in whose name they are to rule? Wherefore a scandalous thing it is to the Church of God, and to the actors themselves dangerous, to have aspired unto rooms of prelacy by wicked means. We are not at this day troubled much with that tumultuous kind of ambition wherewith the elections of Damasus in St. Jerome's age, and of Maximus in Gregory's time, and of others, were long sithence stained. Our greatest fear is rather the evil which Leo and Anthemius did by imperial constitution endeavour as much as in them lay to prevent. He which granteth, or he which receiveth the office and dignity of a bishop, otherwise than beseemeth a thing divine and most holy; he which bestoweth, and he which obtaineth it after any other sort than were honest and lawful to use, if our Lord Jesus Christ were present himself on earth to bestow it even with his own hands, sinneth a sin by so much more grievous than the sin of Belshazzar, by how much offices and functions heavenly are more precious than the meanest ornaments or implements which thereunto appertain. If it be as the Apostle saith, that the Holy Ghost doth make bishops and that the whole action of making them is God's own deed, men being therein but his agents; what spark of the fear of God can there possibly remain in their hearts, who representing the person of God in naming worthy men to ecclesiastical charge, do sell that which in his name they are to bestow; or who standing as it were at the throne of the living God do bargain for that which at his hands they are to receive? Woe worth such impious and irreligious profanations. The Church of Christ hath been hereby made, not a den of thieves, but in a manner the very dwelling-place of foul spirits; for undoubtedly such a number of them have been in all ages who thus have climbed into seat of episcopal regiment.

[5.] Secondly, Men may by orderly means be invested with spiritual authority and yet do harm by reason of ignorance how to use it to the good of the Church. "It is," saith Chrysostom, "a thing highly to be accounted of, but an hard thing, to be that which a bishop should be." Yea a hard and a toilsome thing it is for a bishop to know the things that belong unto a bishop. A right good man may be a very unfit magistrate. And for

* ["Suffer me to utter this hard saying, stripped of all disguise"; tr. H. R. Fairclough, Loeb Library.]

discharge of a bishop's office, to be well-minded is not enough, no not to be well learned also. Skill to instruct is a thing necessary, skill to govern much more necessary in a bishop. It is not safe for the Church of Christ, when bishops learn what belongeth unto government, as empirics learn physic by killing of the sick. Bishops were wont to be men of great learning in the laws both civil and of the Church; and while they were so, the wisest men in the land for counsel and government were bishops.

[6.] Thirdly, Know we never so well what belongeth unto a charge of so great moment, yet can we not therein proceed but with hazard of public detriment, if we rely on ourselves alone, and use not the benefit of conference with others. A singular mean to unity and concord amongst themselves, a marvellous help unto uniformity in their dealings, no small addition of weight and credit unto that which they do, a strong bridle unto such as watch for occasions to stir against them, finally, a very great stay unto all that are under their government, it could not choose but be soon found, if bishops did often and seriously use the help of mutual consultation.

[7.] These three rehearsed are things only preparatory unto the course of episcopal proceedings. But the hurt is more manifestly seen which doth grow to the Church of God by faults inherent in their several actions, as when they carelessly ordain, when they institute negligently, when corruptly they bestow church-livings, benefices, prebends, and rooms especially of jurisdiction, when they visit for gain's sake rather than with serious intent to do good, when their courts erected for the maintenance of good order, are disordered, when they regard not the clergy under them, when neither clergy nor laity are kept in that awe for which this authority should serve, when any thing appeareth in them rather than a fatherly affection towards the flock of Christ, when they have no respect to posterity, and finally when they neglect the true and requisite means whereby their authority should be upheld. Surely the hurt which groweth out of these defects must needs be exceeding great. In a minister, ignorance and disability to teach is a maim; nor is it held a thing allowable to ordain such, were it not for the avoiding of a greater evil which the church must needs sustain, if in so great scarcity of able men, and unsufficiency of most parishes throughout the land to maintain them, both public prayer and the administration of sacraments should rather want, than any man thereunto be admitted lacking dexterity and skill to perform that which otherwise was most requisite. Wherefore the necessity of ordaining such is no excuse for the rash and careless ordaining of every one that hath but a friend to bestow some two or three words of ordinary commendation in his behalf. By reason whereof the Church groweth burdened with silly creatures more than need, whose noted baseness and insufficiency bringeth their very order itself into contempt.

It may be that the fear of a *Quare impedit* doth cause institutions to pass more easily than otherwise they would. And to speak plainly the very truth, it may be that writs of *Quare non impedit* were for these times most necessary in the other's place: yet where law will not suffer men to follow their own judgment, to shew their judgment they are not hindered. And I doubt not but that even conscienceless and wicked patrons, of which sort the swarms are too great in the church of England, are the more emboldened to present unto bishops any refuse, by finding so easy acceptation thereof. Somewhat they might redress this sore, notwithstanding so strong impediments, if it did plainly appear that they took it indeed to heart, and were not in a manner contented with it.

[8.] Shall we look for care in admitting whom others present, if that which some of yourselves confer be at any time corruptly bestowed? A foul and an ugly kind of deformity it hath, if a man do but think what it is for a bishop to draw commodity and gain from those things whereof he is left a free bestower, and that in trust, without any other obligation than his sacred order only, and that religious integrity which hath been presumed on in him. Simoniacal corruption I may not for honour's sake suspect to be amongst men of so great place. So often they do not I trust offend by sale, as by unadvised gift of such preferments, wherein that ancient canon should specially be remembered, which forbiddeth a bishop to be led by human affection in bestowing the things of God. A fault no where so hurtful, as in bestowing places of jurisdiction, and in furnishing cathedral churches, the prebendaries and other dignities whereof are the very true successors of those ancient presbyters which were at the first as counsellors unto bishops. A foul abuse it is, that any one man should be loaded as some are with livings in this kind, yea some even of them who condemn utterly the granting of any two benefices unto the same man, whereas the other is in truth a matter of far greater sequel, as experience would soon shew, if churches cathedral being furnished with the residence of a competent number of virtuous, grave, wise and learned divines, the rest of the prebends of every such church were given within the diocess unto men of worthiest desert, for their better encouragement unto industry and travel; unless it seem also convenient to extend the benefit of them unto the learned in universities, and men of special employment otherwise in the affairs of the Church of God. But howsoever, surely with the public good of the Church it will hardly stand, that in any one person such favours be more multiplied than law permitteth in those livings which are with cure.

[9.] Touching bishops' visitations, the first institution of them was profitable, to the end that the state and condition of churches being known, there might be for evils growing convenient remedies provided in due time. The observation of church laws, the correction of faults in the service of

God and manners of men, these are things that visitors should seek. When these things are inquired of formally, and but for custom's sake, fees and pensions being the only thing which is sought, and little else done by visitations; we are not to marvel if the baseness of the end doth make the action itself loathsome. The good which bishops may do not only by these visitations belonging ordinarily to their office, but also in respect of that power which the founders of colleges have given them of special trust, charging even fearfully their consciences therewith: the good, I say, which they might do by this their authority, both within their own diocess, and in the well-springs themselves, the universities, is plainly such as cannot choose but add weight to their heavy accounts in that dreadful day if they do it not.

[10.] In their courts, where nothing but singular integrity and justice should prevail, if palpable and gross corruptions be found, by reason of offices so often granted unto men who seek nothing but their own gain, and make no account what disgrace doth grow by their unjust dealings unto them under whom they deal, the evil hereof shall work more than they which procure it do perhaps imagine.

[11.] At the hands of a bishop the first thing looked for is a care of the clergy under him, a care that in doing good they may have whatsoever comforts and encouragements his countenance, authority and place may yield. Otherwise what heart shall they have to proceed in their painful course, all sorts of men besides being so ready to malign, despise and every way oppress them? Let them find nothing but disdain in bishops; in the enemies of present government, if that way they list to betake themselves, all kind of favourable and friendly helps; unto which part think we it likely that men having wit, courage and stomach, will incline?

As great a fault is the want of severity when need requireth, as of kindness and courtesy in bishops. But touching this, what with ill usage of their power amongst the meaner, and what with disusage amongst the higher sort, they are in the eyes of both sorts as bees that have lost their sting. It is a long time sithence any great one hath felt, or almost any one much feared the edge of that ecclesiastical severity, which sometime held lords and dukes in a more religious awe than now the meanest are able to be kept.

[12.] A bishop, in whom there did plainly appear the marks and tokens of a fatherly affection towards them that are under his charge, what good might he do ten thousand ways more than any man knows how to set down? But the souls of men are not loved, that which Christ shed his blood for is not esteemed precious. This is the very root, the fountain of all negligence in church-government.

[13.] Most wretched are the terms of men's estate when once they are at a point of wretchedness so extreme, that they bend not their wits any further than only to shift out the present time, never regarding what shall become of their successors after them. Had our predecessors so loosely cast off from them all care and respect to posterity, a Church Christian there had not been about the regiment whereof we should need at this day to strive. It was the barbarous affection of Nero, that the ruin of his own imperial seat he could have been well enough contented to see, in case he might also have seen it accompanied with the fall of the whole world: an affection not more intolerable than theirs, who care not to overthrow all posterity, so they may purchase a few days of ignominious safety unto themselves and their present estates; if it may be termed a safety which tendeth so fast unto their very overthrow that are the purchasers of it in so vile and base manner. Men whom it standeth upon to uphold a reverend estimation of themselves in the minds of others, without which the very best things they do are hardly able to escape disgrace, must before it be over late remember how much easier it is to retain credit once gotten, than to recover it being lost. The executors of bishops are sued if their mansion-house be suffered to go to decay: but whom shall their successors sue for the dilapidations which they make of that credit, the unrepaired diminutions whereof will in time bring to pass, that they which would most do good in that calling shall not be able, by reason of prejudice generally settled in the minds of all sorts against them?

[14.] By what means their estimation hath hitherto decayed, it is no hard thing to discern. Herod and Archelaus are noted to have sought out purposely the dullest and most ignoble that could be found amongst the people, preferring such to the high priest's office, thereby to abate the great opinion which the multitude had of that order, and to procure a more expedite course for their own wicked counsels, whereunto they saw the high priests were no small impediment, as long as the common sort did much depend upon them. It may be there hath been partly some show and just suspicion of like practice in some, in procuring the undeserved preferments of some unworthy persons, the very cause of whose advancement hath been principally their unworthiness to be advanced. But neither could this be done altogether without the inexcusable fault of some preferred before, and so oft we cannot imagine it to have been done, that either only or chiefly from thence this decay of their estimation may be thought to grow. Somewhat it is that the malice of their cunning adversaries, but much more which themselves have effected against themselves.

[15.] A bishop's estimation doth grow from the excellency of virtues suitable unto his place. Unto the place of a bishop those high divine virtues are judged suitable, which virtues being not easily found in other sorts of great men, do make him appear so much the greater in whom they are found. Devotion and the feeling sense of religion are not usual in the noblest, wisest, and chiefest personages of state, by reason their wits are so much employed another way, and their minds so seldom conversant in heavenly things. If therefore wherein themselves are defective they see that bishops do blessedly excel, it frameth secretly their hearts to a stooping kind of disposition, clean opposite to contempt. The very countenance of Moses was glorious after that God had conferred with him. And where bishops are, the powers and faculties of whose souls God hath possessed, those very actions, the kind whereof is common unto them with other men, have notwithstanding in them a more high and heavenly form, which draweth correspondent estimation unto it, by virtue of that celestial impression, which deep meditation of holy things, and as it were conversation with God doth leave in their minds. So that bishops which will be esteemed of as they ought, must frame themselves to that very pattern from whence those Asian bishops unto whom St. John writeth were denominated, even so far forth as this our frailty will permit; shine they must as angels of God in the midst of perverse men. They are not to look that the world should always carry the affection of Constantine, to bury that which might derogate from them, and to cover their imbecilities. More than high time it is that they bethink themselves of the Apostle's admonition, *Attende tibi*, "Have a vigilant eye to thyself." They err if they do not persuade themselves that wheresoever they walk or sit, be it in their churches or in their consistories, abroad and at home, at their tables or in their closets, they are in the midst of snares laid for them. Wherefore as they are with the prophet every one of them to make it their hourly prayer unto God, "Lead me O Lord in thy righteousness, because of enemies;" so it is not safe for them, no not for a moment, to slacken their industry in seeking every way that estimation which may further their labours unto the Church's good. Absurdity, though but in words, must needs be this way a maim, where nothing but wisdom, gravity and judgment is looked for. That which the son of Sirach hath concerning the writings of the old sages, "Wise sentences are found in them," should be the proper mark and character of bishops' speeches, whose lips, as doors, are not to be opened, but for egress of instruction and sound knowledge. If base servility and dejection of mind be ever espied in them, how should men esteem them as worthy the rooms of the great ambassadors of God? A wretched desire to gain by bad and unseemly means standeth not with a mean man's credit, much less with that reputation which Fathers of the Church should be in. But if besides all this there be also coldness in works of piety and charity, utter contempt even of learning itself, no care to further it by any such helps as they easily might and ought to afford, no not as much as that due respect unto their very families about them, which all men that are of account do order as near as they can in such sort that no grievous offensive deformity be therein noted; if there still continue in that most reverend order, such as by so many engines, work day and night to pull down the whole frame of their own estimation amongst men, some of the rest secretly also permitting others their industrious opposites every day more and more to seduce the multitude; how should the Church of God hope for great good at their hands?

[16.] What we have spoken concerning these things, let not malicious accusers think themselves therewith justified, no more than Shimei was by his sovereign's most humble and meek acknowledgment even of that very crime which so impudent a caitiff's tongue upbraided him withal; the one in the virulent rancour of a cankered affection, took that delight for the present, which in the end did turn to his own more tormenting woe; the other in the contrite patience even of deserved malediction had yet this comfort, "It may be the Lord will look on mine affliction, and do me good for his cursing this day." [2 Sam. xvi. 12] As for us over whom Christ hath placed them to be the chiefest guides and pastors of our souls, our common fault is, that we look for much more in our governors than a tolerable sufficiency can yield, and bear much less than humanity and reason do require we should. Too much perfection over rigorously exacted in them, cannot but breed in us perpetual discontentment, and on both parts cause all things to be unpleasant. It is exceedingly worth the noting, which Plato hath about the means whereby men fall into an utter dislike of all men with whom they converse: "This sourness of mind which maketh every man's dealings unsavoury in our taste, entereth by an unskilful overweening, which at the first we have of one, and so of another, in whom we afterwards find ourselves to have been deceived, they declaring themselves in the end to be frail men, whom we judged demigods. When we have oftentimes been thus beguiled, and that far besides expectation, we grow at the length to this plain conclusion, that there is nothing at all sound in any man. Which bitter conceit is unseemly, and plain to have risen from lack of mature judgment in human affairs; which if so be we did handle with art, we would not enter into dealings with men, otherwise than being beforehand grounded in this persuasion, that the number of persons notably good or bad is but very small; that the most part of good have some evil, and of evil men some good in them." [*Phaedo*] So true our experience doth find those aphorisms of Mercurius Trismegistus: "to purge goodness quite and clean from all mixture of evil here is a thing impossible." Again, "when in this world we term a thing good, we cannot by exact construction have any other true meaning, than that the said thing so termed is not noted to be a thing exceedingly evil." And again, "Amongst men, O Æsculapius, the name of that which is good we find, but no where the very true thing itself." When we censure the deeds and dealings of our superiors, to bring with us a fore-conceit thus qualified shall be as well on our part as theirs a thing available unto quietness.

[17.] But howsoever the case doth stand with men's either good or bad quality, the verdict which our Lord and Saviour hath given, should continue for ever sure; "Quæ Dei sunt, Deo;" let men bear the burden of their own iniquity; as for those things which are God's, let not God be deprived of them. For if only to withhold that which should be given be no better than [Mal. iii. 8] to rob God, if to withdraw any mite of that which is but in purpose only bequeathed, though as yet undelivered into the sacred treasure of God, be a sin for which Ananias [Acts v. 2] and Sapphira felt so heavily the dreadful hand of divine revenge; quite and clean to take that away which we never gave, and that after God hath for so many ages therewith been possessed, and that without any other shew of cause, saving only that it seemeth in their eyes who seek it to be too much for them which have it in their hands, can we term it or think it less than most impious injustice, most heinous sacrilege? Such was the religious affection of Joseph [Gen. xlvii. 22], that it suffered him not to take that advantage, no not against the very idolatrous priests of Egypt, which he took for the purchasing of other men's lands to the king; but he considered, that albeit their idolatry deserved hatred, yet for the honour's sake due unto priesthood, better it was the king himself should yield them relief in public extremity, than permit that the same necessity should constrain also them to do as the rest of the people did.

[18.] But it may be men have now found out, that God hath proposed the Christian clergy as a prey for all men freely to seize upon; that God hath left them as the fishes of the sea, which every man that listeth to gather into his net may; or that there is no God in heaven to pity them, and to regard the injuries which man doth lay upon them: yet the public good of this church and commonwealth doth, I hope, weigh somewhat in the hearts of all honestly disposed men. Unto the public good no one thing is more directly available, than that such as are in place, whether it be of civil or of ecclesiastical authority, be so much the more largely furnished even with external helps and ornaments of this life, how much the more highly they are in power and calling advanced above others. For nature is not contented with bare sufficiency unto the sustenance of man, but doth evermore covet a decency proportionable unto the place which man hath in the body or society of others. For according unto the greatness of men's calling, the measure of all their actions doth grow in every man's secret expectation, so that great men do always know that great things are at their hands expected. In a bishop great liberality, great hospitality, actions in every kind great are looked for: and for actions which must be great, mean instruments will not serve. Men are but men, what room soever amongst men they hold. If therefore the measure of their worldly abilities be beneath that proportion which their calling doth make to be looked for at their hands, a stronger inducement it is than perhaps men are aware of unto evil and corrupt dealings for supply of that defect. For which cause we must needs think it a thing necessary unto the common good of the Church, that great jurisdiction being granted unto bishops over others, a state of wealth proportionable should likewise be provided for them. Where wealth is had in so great admiration, as generally in this golden age it is, that without it angelical perfections are not able to deliver from extreme contempt, surely to make bishops poorer than they are, were to make them of less account and estimation than they should be. Wherefore if detriment and dishonour do grow to religion, to God, to his Church, when the public account which is made of the chief of the clergy decayeth, how should it be but in this respect for the good of religion, of God, of his Church, that the wealth of bishops be carefully preserved from further diminution?

The travels and crosses wherewith prelacy is never unaccompanied, they which feel them know how heavy and how great they are. Unless such difficulties therefore annexed unto that estate be tempered by co-annexing thereunto things esteemed of in this world, how should we hope that the minds of men, shunning naturally the burdens of each function, will be drawn to undertake the burden of episcopal care and labour in the Church of Christ? Wherefore if long we desire to enjoy the peace, quietness, order and stability of religion, which prelacy (as hath been declared) causeth, then must we necessarily, even in favour of the public good, uphold those things, the hope whereof being taken away, it is not the mere goodness of the charge, and the divine acceptation thereof, that will be able to invite many thereunto.

[19.] What shall become of that commonwealth or church in the end, which hath not the eye of learning to beautify, guide and direct it? At the length what shall become of that learning, which hath not wherewith any more to encourage her industrious followers? And finally, what shall become of that courage to follow learning, which hath already so much failed through the only diminution of her chiefest rewards, bishoprics? Surely wheresoever this wicked intendment of overthrowing cathedral churches, or of taking away those livings, lands and possessions which bishops hitherto have enjoyed, shall once prevail, the handmaids attending thereupon will be paganism and extreme barbarity.

[20.] In the Law of Moses, how careful provision is made that goods of this kind might remain to the Church for ever: "Ye shall not make common the holy things of the children of Israel, lest ye die, saith the Lord." [Numb. xviii. 32] Touching the fields annexed unto Levitical cities, the law was plain, they might not be sold; and the reason of the law, this, "for it was their possession for ever:" [Lev. xxv. 34] He which was Lord and owner of it, his will and pleasure was, that from the Levites it should never pass to be enjoyed by any other. The Lord's own portion, without his own commission and grant, how should any man justly hold? They which hold it by his appointment had it plainly with this condition [Ezek. xlviii. 14], "They shall not sell of it, neither change it, nor alienate the first-fruits of the land; for it is holy unto the Lord." It falleth sometimes out, as the prophet Habakkuk noteth, that the very "prey of savage beasts becometh dreadful unto themselves." [Habak. ii. 17] It did so in Judas, Achan, Nebuchadnezzar; their evil-purchased goods were their snare, and their prey their own terror; a thing no where so likely to follow, as in those goods and possessions, which being laid where they should not rest, have by the Lord's own testimony his most bitter curse their undividable companion [Mal. iii. 9].

[21.] These persuasions we use for other men's cause, not for theirs with whom God and religion are parts of the abrogated law of ceremonies. Wherefore not to continue longer in the cure of a sore desperate, there was a time when the clergy had almost as little as these good people wish. But the kings of this realm and others whom God had blest, considered devoutly with themselves, as David in like case sometimes had done, "Is it meet that we at the hands of God should enjoy all kinds of abundance, and God's clergy suffer want?" They considered that of Solomon, "Honour God with thy substance, and the chiefest of all thy revenue; so shall thy barns be filled with corn, and thy vessels shall run over with new wine." [Prov. iii. 9] They considered how the care which Jehosaphat had [2 Chron. xix], in providing that the Levites might have encouragement to do the work of the Lord cheerfully, was left of God as a fit pattern to be followed in the Church for ever. They considered what promise our Lord and Saviour had made unto them, at whose hands his prophets should receive but the least part of the meanest kind of friendliness, though it were but a draught of water; which promise seemeth now to be taken, as if Christ had made them of any higher courtesy uncapable, and had promised reward not unto such as give them but that, but unto such as leave them but that. They considered how earnest the Apostle is, that if the ministers of the law were so amply provided for, less care then ought not to be had of them, who under the gospel of Jesus Christ possess correspondent rooms in the Church. They considered how needful it is that they who provoke all others unto works of mercy and charity should especially have wherewith to be examples of such things, and by such means to win them, with whom other means without those do commonly take very small effect. In these and the like considerations, the Church revenues were in ancient times augmented; our Lord thereby performing manifestly the promise made to his servants, that they which did "leave either father, or mother, or lands, or goods, for his sake, should receive even in this world an hundred fold." For some hundreds of years together, they which joined themselves to the Church were fain to relinquish all worldly emoluments and to endure the hardness of an afflicted estate. Afterward the Lord gave rest to his Church, kings and princes became as fathers thereunto, the hearts of all men inclined towards it, and by his providence there grew unto it every day earthly possessions in more and more abundance, till the greatness thereof bred envy, which no diminutions are able to satisfy.

[22.] For as those ancient nursing Fathers thought they did never bestow enough; even so in the eye of this present age, as long as any thing remaineth, it seemeth to be too much. Our fathers we imitate *in perversum*, as Tertullian speaketh; like them we are, by being in equal degree the contrary unto that which they were. Unto those earthly blessings which God as then did with so great abundance pour down upon the ecclesiastical state, we may in regard of most near resemblance apply the selfsame words which the prophet hath, "God blessed them exceedingly, and by this very mean turned the hearts of their own brethren to hate them, and to deal politicly with his servants." [Ps. cv. 24–5] Computations are made, and there are huge sums set down, for princes to see how much they may amplify and enlarge their own treasure; how many public burdens they may ease; what present means they may have to reward their servants about them, if they please but to grant their assent, and to accept of the spoil of bishops, by whom church goods are but abused unto pomp and vanity. Thus albeit they deal with one whose princely virtue giveth them small hope to prevail in impious and sacrilegious motions, yet shame they not to move her royal majesty even with a suit not much unlike unto that wherewith the Jewish high priests tried Judas, whom they solicited unto treason against his Master, and proposed unto him a number of silver pence in lieu of so virtuous and honest a service. But her sacred majesty disposed to be always like herself, her heart so far estranged from willingness to gain by pillage of that estate, the only awe whereof under God she hath been unto this present hour, as of all other parts of this noble commonwealth, whereof she hath vowed herself a protector till the end of her days on earth, which if nature could permit, we wish, as good cause we have, endless: this her gracious inclination is more than a seven times sealed warrant, upon the same assurance whereof, touching any action so dishonourable as this, we are on her part most secure, not doubting but that unto all posterity it shall for ever appear, that from the first to the very last of her sovereign proceedings there hath not been one authorized deed other than consonant with that Symmachus saith, "Fiscus bonorum principum, non sacerdotum damnis, sed hostium spoliis augeatur:"* consonant with that imperial law, "Ea quæ ad beatissimæ ecclesiæ jura pertinent, tanquam ipsam sacrosanctam et religiosam ecclesiam, intacta convenit venerabiliter custodiri; ut sicut ipsa religionis et fidei mater perpetua est, ita ejus patrimonium jugiter servetur illæsum."†

* ["The treasury of good princes is increased with the spoils of enemies, not with the losses of priests."]

† ["Things pertaining to the rights of the most blessed Church should be kept reverently untouched like the inviolable and religious Church herself, so that just as the mother of religion and faith is perpetual, so may her patrimony be preserved ever unharmed."]

[23.] As for the case of public burdens, let any politician living make it appear, that by confiscation of bishops' livings, and their utter dissolution at once, the commonwealth shall ever have half that relief and ease which it receiveth by their continuance as now they are, and it shall give us some cause to think, that albeit we see they are impiously and irreligiously minded, yet we may esteem them at least to be tolerable commonwealth's-men. But the case is too clear and manifest, the world doth but too plainly see it that no one order of subjects whatsoever within this land doth bear the seventh part of that proportion which the clergy beareth in the burdens of the commonwealth. No revenue of the crown like unto it, either for certainty or for greatness. Let the good which this way hath grown to the commonwealth by the dissolution of religious houses, teach men what ease unto public burdens there is like to grow by the overthrow of the clergy. My meaning is not hereby to make the state of bishopricks and of those dissolved companies alike, the one no less unlawful to be removed than the other. For those religious persons were men which followed only a special kind of contemplative life in the commonwealth, they were properly no portion of God's clergy (only such amongst them excepted as were also priests), their goods (that excepted which they unjustly held through the pope's usurped power of appropriating ecclesiastical livings unto them) may in part seem to be of the nature of civil possessions, held by other kinds of corporations, such as the city of London hath divers. Wherefore as their institution was human, and their end for the most part superstitious, they had not therein merely that holy and divine interest which belongeth unto bishops, who being employed by Christ in the principal service of his Church, are receivers and disposers of his patrimony, as hath been shewed, which whosoever shall withhold or withdraw at any time from them, he undoubtedly robbeth God himself.

[24.] If they abuse the goods of the Church unto pomp and vanity, such faults we do not excuse in them. Only we wish it to be considered whether such faults be verily in them, or else but objected against them by such as gape after spoil, and therefore are no competent judges what is moderate and what excessive in them, whom under this pretence they would spoil. But the accusation may be just. In plenty and fulness it may be we are of God more forgetful than were requisite. Notwithstanding men should remember how not to the clergy alone it was said by Moses in Deuteronomy, "Ne cum manducaveris et biberis et domos optimas ædificaveris."* If the remedy prescribed for this disease be good, let it unpartially be applied. "Interest reipub. ut re sua *quisque* bene utatur."† Let all states be put to their moderate pensions, let their livings and lands be taken away from

* Deut. viii. 12. ["Lest when thou hast eaten and art full, and hast built goodly houses, and dwelt therein."]

† ["It concerns the commonwealth that *each* should enjoy what is his."]

them whosoever they be, in whom such ample possessions are found to have been matters of grievous abuse: were this just? would noble families think this reasonable? The title which bishops have to their livings is as good as the title of any sort of men unto whatsoever we account to be most justly held by them; yea in this one thing the claim of bishops hath preeminence above all secular titles of right, in that God's own interest is the tenure whereby they hold, even as also it was to the priests of the law an assurance of their spiritual goods and possessions, whereupon, though they many times abused greatly the goods of the Church, yet was not God's patrimony therefore taken away from them, and made saleable unto other tribes. To rob God, to ransack the Church, to overthrow the whole order of Christian bishops, and to turn them out of land and living, out of house and home, what man of common honesty can think it for any manner of abuse to be a remedy lawful or just? We must confess that God is righteous in taking away that which men abuse: but doth that excuse the violence of thieves and robbers?

[25.] Complain we will not with St. Jerome, "That the hands of men are so straitly tied, and their liberal minds so much bridled and held back from doing good by augmentation of the Church patrimony." For we confess that herein mediocrity may be and hath been sometime exceeded. There did want heretofore a Moses to temper men's liberality, to say unto them who enriched the Church, *Sufficit*, Stay your hands, lest fervour of zeal do cause you to empty yourselves too far. It may be the largeness of men's hearts being then more moderate, had been after more durable; and one state by too much overgrowing the rest, had not given occasion unto the rest to undermine it. That evil is now sufficiently cured: the Church treasury, if then it were over-full, hath since been reasonable well emptied. That which Moses spake unto givers, we must now inculcate unto takers away from the Church, Let there be same stay, some stint in spoiling. If "grape-gatherers came unto them," saith the prophet [Obad. 5], "would they not leave some remnant behind?" But it hath fared with the wealth of the Church as with a tower, which being built at the first with the highest, overthroweth itself after by its own greatness; neither doth the ruin thereof cease with the only fall of that which hath exceeded mediocrity, but one part bearth down another, till the whole be laid prostrate. For although the state ecclesiastical, both others and even bishops themselves, be now fallen to so low an ebb, as all the world at this day doth see; yet because there remaineth still somewhat which unsatiable minds can thirst for, therefore we seem not to have been hitherto sufficiently wronged. Touching that which hath been taken from the Church in appropriations known to amount to the value of one hundred twenty-six thousand pounds yearly, we rest contentedly and quietly without it, till it shall please God to touch the hearts of men, of their own voluntary accord, to restore it to him again; judging thereof no otherwise than some others did of those goods which were by Sylla taken away from the citizens of Rome, that albeit they were in truth *male capta*, unconscionably taken away from the right owners at the first, nevertheless, seeing that such as were after possessed of them held them not without some title, which law did after a sort made good, *repetitio eorum proculdubio labefactabat compositam civitatem*.* What hath been taken away as dedicated unto uses superstitious, and consequently not given unto God, or at the leastwise not so rightly given, we repine not thereat. That which hath gone by means secret and indirect, through corrupt compositions or compacts, we cannot help. What the hardness of men's hearts doth make them loth to have exacted, though being due by law, even thereof the want we do also bear. Out of that which after all these deductions cometh clearly unto our hands, I hope it will not be said that towards the public charge we disburse nothing. And doth the residue seem yet excessive? The ways whereby temporal men provide for themselves and their families are fore-closed unto us. All that we have to sustain our miserable life with, is but a remnant of God's own treasure, so far already diminished and clipped, that if there were any sense of common humanity left in this hard-hearted world, the impoverished estate of the clergy of God would at the length even of very commiseration be spared. The mean gentleman that hath but an hundred pound land to live on, would not be hasty to change his worldly estate and condition with many of these so over abounding prelates; a common artisan or tradesman of the city, with ordinary pastors of the Church.

[26.] It is our hard and heavy lot, that no other sort of men being grudged at, how little benefit soever the public weal reap by them, no state complained of for holding that which hath grown unto them by lawful means; only the governors of our souls, they that study day and night so to guide us, that both in this world we may have comfort and in the world to come endless felicity and joy (for even such is the very scope of all their endeavours, this they wish, for this they labour, how hardly soever we use to construe of their intents): hard, that only they should be thus continually lifted at for possessing but that whereunto they have by law both of God and man most just title. If there should be no other remedy but that the violence of men in the end must needs bereave them of all succour, further than the inclination of others shall vouchsafe to cast upon them, as it were by way of alms for their relief but from hour to hour; better they are not than their fathers, which have been contented with as hard a portion at the world's hands: let the light of the sun and moon, the common benefit of heaven and earth be taken from bishops, if the question were whether God should lose his glory, and the safety of his Church be hazarded, or they

* ["Demanding them back again was undoubtedly to shake the city after it was once more at peace."]

relinquish the right and interest which they have in the things of this world. But sith the question in truth is whether Levi shall be deprived of the portion of God or no, to the end that Simeon or Reuben may devour it as their spoil, the comfort of the one in sustaining the injuries which the other would offer, must be that prayer poured out by Moses, the prince of prophets, in most tender affection to Levi, "Bless, O Lord, his substance, accept thou the work of his hands; smite through the loins of them that rise up against him, and of them which hate him, that they rise no more." [Deut. xxxiii. 10–11]

the eighth book

THEIR SEVENTH ASSERTION, THAT UNTO NO CIVIL PRINCE OR GOVERNOR THERE MAY BE GIVEN SUCH POWER OF ECCLESIASTICAL DOMINION AS BY THE LAWS OF THIS LAND BELONGETH UNTO THE SUPREME REGENT THEREOF

The matter contained in this eighth book

Chapter 1

WE COME now to the last thing whereof there is controversy moved, namely the *power* of *Supreme Jurisdiction*, which for distinction's sake we call the power of *Ecclesiastical Dominion*.

It was not thought fit in the Jews' commonwealth, that the exercise of supremacy ecclesiastical should be denied unto him, to whom the exercise of chiefty civil did appertain; and therefore their kings were invested with both. This power they gave unto Simon [1 Maccab. xiv. 42], when they consented that he should be "their prince", not only "to set men over the works, and over the country, and over the weapons, and over the fortresses", but also "to provide for the holy things", and "that he should be obeyed of every man, and that all the writings in the country should be made in his name, and that it should not be lawful for any of the people or priests to withstand his words, or to call any congregation in the country without him."

And if it be haply surmised, that thus much was given unto Simon, as being both prince and high priest; which otherwise, being only their civil governor, he could not lawfully have enjoyed: we must note, that all this is no more than the ancient kings of that people had, being kings and not priests. By this power David, Asa, Jehosaphat, Ezekias, Josias, and the rest, made those laws and orders which the Sacred History speaketh of, concerning matter of mere religion, the affairs of the temple, and service of God. Finally, had it not been by the virtue of this power, how should it possibly have come to pass, that the piety or impiety of the king did always accordingly change the public face of religion, which thing the priests by themselves never did, neither could at any time hinder from being done? Had the priests alone been possessed with all power in spiritual affairs, how should any law concerning matter of religion have been made but only by them? In them it had been, and not in the king, to change the face of religion at any time. The altering of religion, the making of ecclesiastical laws, with other the like actions belonging unto the power of dominion, are still termed *the deeds of the king*; to shew that in him was placed supremacy of power even in this kind over all, and that unto their high priests the same was never committed, saving only at such times as their priests were also kings or princes over them.

[2.] According to the pattern of which example, the like power in causes ecclesiastical is by the laws of this realm annexed unto the crown. And there are which imagine, that kings, being mere lay persons, do by this means exceed the lawful bounds of their calling. Which thing to the end that they may persuade, they first make a necessary separation perpetual and personal between the Church and commonwealth. Secondly, they so tie all kind of power ecclesiastical unto the Church, as if it were in every degree their only right which are by proper spiritual function termed Church-governors, and might not to Christian princes any wise appertain.

To lurk under shifting ambiguities and equivocations of words in matters of principal weight is childish. A church and a commonwealth we grant are things in nature the one distinguished from the other. A commonwealth is one way, and a church another way, defined. In their opinion the church and the commonwealth are corporations, not distinguished only in nature and definition, but in subsistence perpetually severed; so that they that are of the one can neither appoint nor execute, in whole nor in part, the duties which belong unto them which are of the other, without open breach of the law of God, which hath divided them, and doth require that being so divided they should distinctly and severally work, as depending both upon God, and not hanging one upon the other's approbation for that which either hath to do.

We say that the care of religion being common unto all societies politic, such societies as do embrace the true religion have the name of the Church given unto every of them for distinction from the rest; so that every body politic hath some religion, but the Church that religion which is only true. Truth of religion is that proper difference whereby a church is distinguished from other politic societies of men. We here mean true religion in gross, and not according to every particular: for they which in some particular points of religion do swerve from the truth, may nevertheless most truly, if we compare them to men of an heathenish religion, be said to hold and profess that religion which is true. For which cause, there being of old so many politic societies established throughout the world, only the commonwealth of Israel, which had the truth of religion, was in that respect the Church of God: and the Church of Jesus Christ is every such politic society of men, as doth in religion hold that truth which is proper to Christianity. As a politic society it doth maintain religion; as a church, that religion which God hath revealed by Jesus Christ.

With us therefore the name of a church importeth only a society of men, first united into some public form of regiment, and secondly distinguished from other societies by the exercise of Christian religion. With them on the other side the name of the Church in this present question importeth not only a multitude of men so united and so distinguished, but also further the same divided necessarily and perpetually from the body of the commonwealth: so that even in such a politic society as consisteth of none but Christians, yet the Church of Christ and the commonwealth are two corporations, independently each subsisting by itself.

We hold, that seeing there is not any man of the Church of England but the same man is also a member of the commonwealth; nor any man a member of the commonwealth, which is not also of the Church of England; therefore as in a figure triangular the base doth differ from the sides thereof, and yet one and the selfsame line is both a base and also a side; a side simply, a base if it chance to be the bottom and underlie the rest: so, albeit properties and actions of one kind do cause the name of a commonwealth, qualities and functions of another sort the name of a Church to be given unto a multitude, yet one and the selfsame multitude may in such sort be both, and is so with us, that no person appertaining to the one can be denied to be also of the other. Contrariwise, unless they against us should hold, that the Church and the commonwealth are two, both distinct and separate societies, of which two, the one comprehendeth always persons not belonging to the other; that which they do they could not conclude out of the difference between the Church and the commonwealth; namely, that bishops may not meddle with the affairs of the commonwealth, because they are governors of another corporation, which is the Church; nor kings with making laws for the Church, because they have government not of this corporation, but of another divided from it, the commonwealth; and the walls of separation between these two must for ever be upheld. They hold the necessity of personal separation, which clean excludeth the power of one man's dealing in both; we of natural, which doth not hinder but that one and the same person may in both bear a principal sway.

[3.] The causes of common received error in this point seem to have been especially two: one, that they who embrace true religion living in such commonwealths as are opposite thereunto, and in other public affairs retaining civil communion with such, are constrained, for the exercise of their religion, to have a several communion with those who are of the same religion with them. This was the state of the Jewish Church both in Egypt and Babylon, the state of Christian Churches a long time after Christ. And in this case, because the proper affairs and actions of the Church, as it is the Church, have no dependencie upon the laws, or upon the governors of the civil state, an opinion hath thereby grown, that even so it should be always. This was it which deceived Allen in the writing of his Apology: "The Apostles," saith he, "did govern the church in Rome when Nero did bear rule, even as at this day in all the Turk's dominions, the Church hath a spiritual regiment without dependence, and so ought she to have, live she amongst heathens, or with Christians."

[4.] Another occasion of which misconceit is, that things appertaining unto religion are both distinguished from other affairs, and have always had in the Church special persons chosen to be exercised about them. By which distinction of spiritual affairs and persons therein employed from temporal, the error of personal separation always necessary between the Church and the commonwealth hath strengthened itself. For of every politic society that being true which Aristotle hath, namely, "that the scope thereof is not simply to live, nor the duty so much to provide for life, as for means of living well:" and that even as the soul is the worthier part of man, so human societies are much more to care for that which tendeth properly unto the soul's estate, than for such temporal things as this life doth stand in need of: other proof there needs none to shew that as by all men the kingdom of God is first to be sought for [Matt. vi. 33], so in all commonwealths things spiritual ought above temporal to be provided for. And of things spiritual, the chiefest is religion. For this cause, persons and things employed peculiarly about the affairs of religion, are by an excellency termed spiritual. The heathen themselves had their spiritual laws, causes, and offices, always severed from their temporal; neither did this make two independent states amongst them. God by revealing true religion doth make them that receive it his Church. Unto the Jews he so revealed the truth of religion, that he gave them in special consideration laws, not only for the administration of things spiritual, but also temporal. The Lord himself appointing both the one and the other in that commonwealth, did not thereby distract it into several independent communities, but institute several functions of one and the same community. Some reason therefore must be alleged why it should be otherwise in the Church of Christ.

THREE KINDS OF PROOFS FOR CONFIRMATION OF THE FORESAID SEPARATION BETWEEN THE CHURCH AND COMMONWEALTH THE FIRST TAKEN FROM DIFFERENCE OF AFFAIRS AND OFFICES IN EACH

I shall not need to spend any great store of words in answering that which is brought out of holy Scripture to shew that secular and ecclesiastical affairs and offices are distinguished; neither that which hath been borrowed from antiquity, using by phrase of speech to oppose the commonwealth to the Church of Christ; nor yet the reasons which are wont to be brought forth as witnesses, that the Church and commonwealth are always distinct. For whether a church and a commonwealth do differ, is not the question we strive for; but our controversy is concerning the kind of distinction, whereby they are severed the one from the other; whether as under heathen kings the Church did deal with her own affairs within herself, without depending at all upon any in civil authority, and the commonwealth in hers, altogether without the privity of the Church; so it ought to continue still, even in such commonwealths as have now publicly embraced the truth of Christian religion; whether they ought to be evermore two societies, in such sort, several and distinct.

I ask therefore, what society that was, that was in Rome, whereunto the Apostle did give the name of the Church of Rome in his time? If they answer, as needs they must, that the Church of Rome in those days was that whole society of men which in Rome professed the name of Christ, and not that religion which the laws of the commonwealth did then authorize; we say as much, and therefore grant that the commonwealth of Rome was one society, and the Church of Rome another, in such sort as there was between them no mutual dependency. But when whole Rome became Christian, when they all embraced the gospel, and made laws in the defence thereof, if it be held that the church and the commonwealth of Rome did then remain as before; there is no way how this could be possible, save only one, and that is, they must restrain the name of the Church in a Christian commonwealth to the clergy, excluding all the residue of believers, both prince and people. For if all that believe be contained in the name of the Church, how should the Church remain by personal subsistencie divided from the commonwealth, when the whole commonwealth doth believe?

The Church and the commonwealth therefore are in this case personally one society, which society being termed a commonwealth as it liveth under whatsoever form of secular law and regiment, a church as it hath the spiritual law of Jesus Christ; forasmuch as these two laws contain so many and so different offices, there must of necessity be appointed in it some to one charge, and some to another, yet without dividing the whole, and making it two several impaled societies.

The difference therefore either of affairs or offices ecclesiastical from secular [2 Chron. xix. 8, 11; Heb. v. 1; 1 Thess. v. 12], is no argument that the Church and the commonwealth are always separate and independent the one from the other: which thing even Allen himself considering somewhat better, doth in this point a little correct his former judgment before mentioned, and confesseth in his Defence of English Catholics, that "the power political hath her princes, laws, tribunals; the spiritual, her prelates, canons, councils, judgments; and those (when the princes are pagans) wholly separate, but in Christian commonwealths joined though not confounded." Howbeit afterwards his former sting appeareth again; for in a Christian commonwealth he holdeth, that the Church ought not to depend at all upon the authority of any civil person whatsoever, as in England he saith it doth.

PROOFS OF SEPARATION BETWEEN THE CHURCH AND COMMONWEALTH, TAKEN FROM THE SPEECHES OF THE FATHERS OPPOSING THE ONE TO THE OTHER

[5.] It will be objected, that "the Fathers do oftentimes mention the commonwealth and the Church of God by way of opposition. Can the same thing be opposite unto itself? If one and the same society be both, what sense can there be in that speech which saith, that 'they suffer and flourish together'? What sense in that which maketh one thing adjudged to the Church, another to the commonwealth? Finally, in that which putteth a difference between the causes of the province and of the Church? Doth it not hereby appear that the Church and the commonwealth are things evermore personally separate?"

No, it doth not hereby appear that there is perpetually any such separation; we may speak of them as two, we may sever the rights and causes of the one well enough from the other, in regard of that difference which we grant there is between them, albeit we make no personal difference. For the truth is, that the Church and the commonwealth are names which import things really different; but those things are accidents, and such accidents as may and should always lovingly dwell together in one subject. Wherefore the real difference between the accidents signified by those names, doth not prove different subjects for them always to reside in. For albeit the subjects wherein they are resident be sometime different, as when the people of God have their being among infidels; yet the nature of them is not such but that their subject may be one, and therefore it is but a changeable accident, in those accidents, when the subjects they are in be diverse.

There can be no error in our conceit concerning this point, if we remember still what accident that is, for which a society hath the name of a commonwealth, and what accident that which doth cause it to be termed a Church. A commonwealth we name it simply in regard of some regiment or policy under which men live; a church for the truth of that religion which they profess. Now names betokening accidents unabstracted, do betoken not only those accidents, but also together with them the subjects whereunto they cleave. As when we name a schoolmaster and a physician, these names do not only betoken two accidents, teaching and curing, but also some person or persons in whom these accidents are. For there is no impediment but both may be one man, as well as they are for the most part diverse. The commonwealth and the Church therefore being such names, they do not only betoken those accidents of civil government and Christian religion which we have mentioned, but also together with them such multitudes as are the subjects of those accidents. Again, their nature being such that they may well enough dwell together in one subject, it followeth that their names, though always implying that difference of accidents which hath been set down, yet do not always imply different subjects also. When we oppose the Church therefore and the commonwealth in a Christian society, we mean by the commonwealth that society with relation unto all the public affairs thereof, only the matter of true religion excepted; by the Church, the same society with only reference unto the matter of true religion, without any other affairs besides: when that society which is both a church and a commonwealth doth flourish in those things which belong unto it as a commonwealth, we then say, the *commonwealth* doth flourish; when in those things which concern it as a church, the *Church* doth flourish; when in both, then the *Church* and *commonwealth* flourish together.

The Prophet Isaiah, to note corruptions in the commonwealth, complaineth, "That where judgment and justice had lodged now were murderers; princes were become companions of thieves; every one loved gifts and rewards; but the fatherless was not judged, neither did the widow's cause come before them." [Isai. i. 21, 23] To shew abuses in the Church, Malachy doth make his complaint: "Ye offer unclean bread upon mine altar: if ye offer the blind for sacrifice, it is not amiss as ye think; if the lame and the sick, nothing is amiss." [Mal. i. 7, 8] The treasures which David did bestow upon the temple [1 Chron. xxix. 3] do argue the love which he bare to the Church: the pains that Nehemias took for building the walls of the city [Nehem. ii. 17] are tokens of his care for the commonwealth. Causes of the commonwealth, or province, are such as Gallio was content to be judge of: "If it were a matter of wrong, or an evil deed,

O ye Jews, I would according to reason maintain you." [Acts xviii. 14] Causes of the Church are such as Gallio there rejecteth: "If it be a question of your law, look you unto it, I will be no judge of those things." [Acts xviii. 15] In respect of these differences therefore the Church and the commonwealth may in speech be compared or opposed aptly enough the one to the other; yet this is no argument that they are two independent societies.

PROOFS OF PERPETUAL SEPARATION AND INDEPENDENCY BETWEEN THE COMMONWEALTH AND THE CHURCH, TAKEN FROM THE EFFECTS OF PUNISHMENTS INFLICTED AND RELEASED BY THE ONE OR THE OTHER

[6.] Some other reasons there are, which seem a little more nearly to make for the purpose, as long as they are but heard and not sifted. For what though a man being severed by excommunication from the Church, be not thereby deprived of freedom in the city; nor being there discommoned, is thereby forthwith excommunicated and excluded from the Church? what though the Church be bound to receive them upon repentance, whom the commonwealth may refuse again to admit if it chance the same men to be shut out of both? That division of the church and commonwealth, which they contend for, will very hardly hereupon follow.

For we must note that members of a Christian commonwealth have a triple state; a *natural*, a *civil*, and a *spiritual*. No man's natural estate is cut off otherwise than by that capital execution, after which he that is gone from the body of the commonwealth doth not, I think, remain still in the body of the visible Church.

And concerning man's *civil* state, the same is subject partly to inferior abatements of liberty, and partly unto diminution in the very highest degree, such as banishment is; which, sith it casteth out quite and clean from the body of the commonwealth, must needs also consequently cast the banished party even out of the very Church he was of before, because that Church and the commonwealth he was of were both one and the same society: so that whatsoever doth separate utterly a man's person from the one, it separateth also from the other. As for such abatements of civil state as take away only some privilege, dignity, or other benefit which a man enjoyeth in the commonwealth, they reach only unto our dealing with public affairs, from which what should let but that men may be excluded and thereunto restored again, without diminishing or augmenting the number of persons in whom either church or commonwealth consisteth? He that by way of punishment loseth his voice in a public election of magistrates, ceaseth not thereby to be a citizen. A man disfranchised may notwithstanding enjoy as a subject the common benefit of protection under laws and magistrates. So that these inferior diminutions which touch men civilly, but neither do clean extinguish their estate as they belong to the commonwealth, nor impair a whit their condition as they are of the Church of God: these I say clearly do prove a difference of the affairs of the one from the other, but such a difference as maketh nothing for their surmise of distracted societies.

And concerning excommunication, it cutteth off indeed from the Church, and yet not from the commonwealth; howbeit so, that the party excommunicate is not thereby severed from one body which subsisteth in itself, and retained of another in like sort subsisting; but he that before had fellowship with that society whereof he was a member, as well touching things spiritual as civil, is now by force of excommunication, although not severed from the same body in civil affairs, nevertheless for the time cut off from it as touching communion in those things which belong to the said body, as it is the Church.

A man which having been both excommunicated by the Church, and deprived of civil dignity in the commonwealth, is upon his repentance necessarily readunited into the one, but not of necessity into the other. What then? that which he is adunited unto is a communion in things divine, whereof saints are partakers; that from which he is withheld is the benefit of some human privilege or right which other citizens haply enjoy. But are not those Saints and Citizens one and the same people? are they not one and the same society? doth it hereby appear that the Church which receiveth an excommunicate man, can have no dependency of any person which is of chief authority and power, in those things of the commonwealth whereunto the said party is not admitted?

[7.] Wherefore to end this point, I conclude: First, that under dominions of infidels, the Church of Christ, and their commonwealth, were two societies independent. Secondly, that in those commonwealths where the bishop of Rome beareth sway, one society is both the Church and the commonwealth; but the bishop of Rome doth divide the body into two diverse bodies, and doth not suffer the Church to depend upon the power of any civil prince or potentate. Thirdly, that within this realm of England the case is neither as in the one, nor as in the other of the former two: but from the state of pagans we differ, in that with us one society is both the Church and commonwealth, which with them it was not; as also from the state of those nations which subject themselves to the bishop of Rome, in that our Church hath dependency upon the chief in our commonwealth, which it hath not under him. In a word, our estate is according to the pattern of God's own ancient elect people, which people was not part of them the commonwealth, and part of them the Church of God, but the selfsame people whole and entire were both under one chief Governor, on whose supreme authority they did [all] depend.

Chapter 2

[1.] Now the drift of all that hath been alleged to prove perpetual separation and independency between the Church and the commonwealth is, that this being held necessary, it might consequently be thought, that in a Christian kingdom he whose power is greatest over the commonwealth may not lawfully have supremacy of power also over the Church, as it is a church; that is to say, so far as to order and dispose of spiritual affairs, as the highest uncommanded commander in them. Whereupon it is grown a question, whether power ecclesiastical over the Church, power of dominion in such degree as the laws of this land do grant unto the sovereign governor thereof, may by the said supreme Head and Governor lawfully be enjoyed and held?

For resolution wherein, we are, first, to define what the power of dominion is: then to shew by what right: after what sort: in what measure: with what conveniency: according unto whose example Christian kings may have it. And when these generalities are opened, to examine afterwards how lawful that is which we in regard of dominion do attribute unto our own: namely, the title of headship over the Church, so far as the bounds of this kingdom do reach: the prerogative of calling and dissolving greater assemblies, about spiritual affairs public: the right of assenting unto all those orders concerning religion, which must after be in force as laws: the advancement of principal church-governors to their rooms of prelacy: judicial authority higher than others are capable of: and exemption from being punishable with such kind of censures as the platform of reformation doth teach that they ought to be subject unto.

WHAT THEIR POWER OF DOMINION IS

[2.] Without order there is no living in public society, because the want thereof is the mother of confusion, whereupon division of necessity followeth, and out of division, inevitable destruction [Luke xi. 17]. The Apostle therefore giving instruction to public societies, requireth that all things be orderly done [1 Cor. xiv. 40]. Order can have no place in things, unless it be settled amongst the persons that shall by office be conversant about them. And if things or persons be ordered, this doth imply that they are distinguished by degrees. For order is a gradual disposition.

The whole world consisting of parts so many, so different, is by this only thing upheld; he which framed them hath set them in order. Yea, the very Deity itself both keepeth and requireth for ever this to be kept as a law, that wheresoever there is a coagmentation of many, the lowest be knit to the highest by that which being interjacent may cause each to cleave unto other, and so all to continue one.

This order of things and persons in public societies is the work of polity, and the proper instrument thereof in every degree is *power*; power being that ability which we have of ourselves, or receive from others, for performance of any action. If the action which we are to perform be conversant about matter of mere religion, the power of performing it is then spiritual; and if that power be such as hath not any other to overrule it, we term it dominion, or power supreme, so far as the bounds thereof do extend.

[3.] When therefore Christian kings are said to have spiritual dominion or supreme power in ecclesiastical affairs and causes, so the meaning is, that within their own precincts and territories they have authority and power to command even in matters of Christian religion, and that there is no higher nor greater that can in those causes over-command them, where they are placed to reign as kings. But withal we must likewise note that their power is termed *supremacy*, as being the highest, not simply without exception of any thing. For what man is there so brain-sick, as not to except in such speeches God himself, the King of all the kings of the earth? Besides, where the law doth give dominion, who doubteth but that the king who receiveth it must hold it of and under the law? according to that old axiom, "Attribuat rex legi, quod lex attribuit ei, potestatem et dominium"*: and again, "Rex non debet esse sub homine, sed sub Deo et lege."† Thirdly, whereas it is not altogether without reason, "that kings are judged to have by virtue of their dominion, although greater power than any, yet not than all the states of those societies conjoined, wherein such sovereign rule is given them;" there is not hereunto any thing contrary by us affirmed, no, not when we grant supreme authority unto kings, because *supremacy* is no otherwise intended or meant than to exclude partly foreign powers, and partly the power which belongeth in several unto others, contained as parts within that politic body over which those kings have supremacy. "Where the king hath power of dominion, or supreme power, there no foreign state or potentate, no state or potentate domestical, whether it consist of one or of many, can possibly have in the same affairs and causes authority higher than the king."

Power of spiritual dominion therefore is in causes ecclesiastical that ruling authority, which neither any foreign state, nor yet any part of that politic body at home, wherein the same is established, can lawfully overrule.

BY WHAT RIGHT, NAMELY, SUCH AS THOUGH MEN DO GIVE, GOD DOTH RATIFY

[4.] Unto which supreme power in kings two kinds of adversaries there are that have opposed themselves: one sort defending, "that supreme

* ["Let the king grant the law what the law grants him: power and dominion."]
† ["A king ought not to be under any man, but under God and the law."]

power in causes ecclesiastical throughout the world appertaineth of divine right to the bishop of Rome:" another sort, "that the said power belongeth in every national church unto the clergy thereof assembled." We which defend as well against the one as the other, "that kings within their own precincts may have it," must shew by what right it may come unto them.

[5.] First, unto me it seemeth almost out of doubt and controversy, that every independent multitude, before any certain form of regiment established, hath, under God's supreme authority, full dominion over itself, even as a man not tied with the bond of subjection as yet unto any other, hath over himself the like power. God creating mankind did endue it naturally with full power to guide itself, in what kinds of societies soever it should choose to live. A man which is born lord of himself may be made another's servant: and that power which naturally whole societies have, may be derived into many, few, or one, under whom the rest shall then live in subjection.

Some multitudes are brought in subjection by force, as they who being subdued are fain to submit their necks unto what yoke it pleaseth their conquerors to lay upon them; which conquerors by just and lawful wars do hold their power over such multitudes as a thing descending unto them, divine providence itself so disposing. For it is God who giveth victory in the day of war, and unto whom dominion in this sort is derived, the same they enjoy according unto that law of nations, which law authorizeth conquerors to reign as absolute lords over them whom they vanquish.

Sometimes it pleaseth God himself by special appointment to choose out and nominate such as to whom dominion shall be given, which thing he did often in the commonwealth of Israel. They who in this sort receive power have it immediately from God, by mere divine right; they by human, on whom the same is bestowed according unto men's discretion, when they are left free by God to make choice of their own governor. By which of these means soever it happen that kings or governors be advanced unto their seats, we must acknowledge both their lawful choice to be approved of God, and themselves for God's lieutenants [Dan. ii. 21, iv.; Is. xlv; Rom. xiii] and confess their power his.

[6.] Again, on whom the same is bestowed even of men's discretion, they likewise do hold it by divine right, if God in his own revealed word have appointed such power to be, although himself extraordinarily bestow it not, but leave the appointment of the persons unto men.

As for supreme power in ecclesiastical affairs, the word of God doth no where appoint that all kings should have it, neither that any should not have it; for which cause it seemeth to stand altogether by human right, that unto Christian kings there is such dominion given. Yea, albeit God do neither appoint the thing nor assign the person; nevertheless when men have established both, who doth doubt but that sundry duties and offices depending thereupon are prescribed in the word of God, and consequently by that very right to be exacted?

For example's sake, the power which the Roman emperors had over foreign provinces was not a thing which the law of God did ever institute, neither was Tiberius Cæsar by special commission from heaven therewith invested; and yet the payment of tribute unto Cæsar being made emperor is the plain law of Jesus Christ. Unto kings by human right, honour by very divine right, is due; man's ordinances are many times presupposed as grounds in the statutes of God. And therefore of what kind soever the means be whereby governors are lawfully advanced unto their seats, as we by the law of God stand bound meekly to acknowledge them for God's lieutenants, and to confess their power his, so they by the same law are both authorized and required to use that power as far as it may be in any sort available to his honour. The law appointeth no man to be an husband, but if a man have betaken himself unto that condition, it giveth him then authority over his own wife. That the Christian world should be ordered by kingly regiment, the law of God doth not any where command; and yet the law of God doth give them right, which once are exalted to that estate, to exact at the hands of their subjects general obediences in whatsoever affairs their power may serve to command. So God doth ratify the works of that sovereign authority which kings have received by men.

AFTER WHAT SORT

[7.] This is therefore the right whereby kings do hold their power; but yet in what sort the same doth rest and abide in them it somewhat further behoveth to search. Wherein, that we be not enforced to make overlarge discourses about the different conditions of sovereign or supreme power, that which we speak of kings shall be with respect to the state and according to the nature of this kingdom, where the people are in no subjection, but such as willingly themselves have condescended unto, for their own most behoof and security. In kingdoms therefore of this quality the highest governor hath indeed universal dominion, but with dependence upon that whole entire body, over the several parts whereof he hath dominion; so that it standeth for an axiom in this case, The king is "major singulis, universis minor".*

[8.] The king's dependency we do not construe as some have done, who are of opinion that no man's birth can make him a king, but every particular person advanced unto such authority hath at his entrance into his reign the same bestowed upon him, as an estate in condition, by the voluntary deed of the people, in whom it doth lie to put by any one, and

* ["Greater than each, less than all."]

to prefer some other before him, better liked of, or judged fitter for the place, and that the party so rejected hath herein no injury, no not although this be done in a place where the crown doth go *κατὰ γένος*, by succession, and to a person which being capable hath apparently, if blood be respected, the nearest right. They plainly affirm, that "in all well-appointed kingdoms, the custom evermore hath been, and is, that children succeed not their deceased parents till the people after a sort have created them anew, neither that they grow to their fathers as natural and proper heirs, but are then to be reckoned for kings, when at the hands of such as represent the people's majesty they have by a sceptre and diadem received as it were the investiture of kingly power." Their very words are, "That where such power is settled into a family or kindred, the stock itself is thereby chosen, but not the twig that springeth of it. The next of the stock unto him which reigneth are not through nearness of blood made kings, but rather set forth to stand for the kingdom. Where regal dominion is hereditary, it is notwithstanding if ye look to the persons themselves which have it altogether elective." To this purpose are alleged heaps of Scriptures concerning the solemn coronation or inauguration of Saul, of David, of Solomon, of others, by the nobles, ancients, and people of the commonwealth of Israel; as if these solemnities were a kind of deed, whereby the right of dominion is given. Which strange, untrue, and unnatural conceits, set abroad by seedsmen of rebellion, only to animate unquiet spirits, and to feed them with a possibility of aspiring unto thrones and sceptres, if they can win the hearts of the people, what hereditary title soever any other before them may have, I say, these unjust and insolent positions I would not mention, were it not thereby to make the countenance of truth more orient: for unless we will openly proclaim defiance unto all law, equity, and reason, we must (there is no remedy) acknowledge, that in kingdoms hereditary birth giveth right unto sovereign dominion; and the death of the predecessor putteth the successor by blood in seisin. Those public solemnities before mentioned do but either serve for an open testification of the inheritor's right, or belong to the form of inducting him into possession of that thing he hath right unto. And therefore in case it do happen that without right of blood a man in such wise be possessed, all those things are utterly void, they make him no indefeasible estate, the inheritor by blood may dispossess him as an usurper.

[9.] The case thus standing, albeit we judge it a thing most true, that kings, even inheritors, do hold their right to the power of dominion, with dependency upon the whole entire body politic over which they rule as kings; yet so it may not be understood, as if such dependency did grow, for that every supreme governor doth personally take from thence his power by way of gift, bestowed of their own free accord upon him at the time of his entrance into the said place of sovereign government. But the cause of dependency is in that first original conveyance, when power was derived by the whole into one; to pass from him into them, whom out of him nature by lawful birth should produce, and no natural or legal inability make incapable. Neither can any man with reason think, but that the first institution of kings is a sufficient consideration wherefore their power should always depend on that from which it did then flow. Original influence of power from the body into the king, is cause of the king's dependency in power upon the body.

[10.] By dependency we mean subordination and subjection. A manifest token of which dependency may be this: as there is no more certain argument that lands are held under any as lord, than if we see that such lands in defect of heirs do fall by escheat unto him; in like manner it doth rightly follow, that seeing dominion, when there is none to inherit it, returneth unto the body, therefore they which before were inheritors thereof did hold it with dependency upon the body. So that by comparing the body with the head, as touching power, it seemeth always to reside in both, fundamentally or radically in the one, in the other derivatively; in the one the habit, in the other the act of power.

May then a body politic at all times withdraw in whole or in part that influence of dominion which passeth from it, if inconvenience doth grow thereby? It must be presumed, that supreme governors will not in such case oppose themselves, and be stiff in detaining that, the use whereof is with public detriment: but surely without their consent I see not how the body should be able by any just means to help itself, saving when dominion doth escheat. Such things therefore must be thought upon beforehand, that power may be limited ere it be granted; which is the next thing we are to consider.

IN WHAT MEASURE

[11.] In power of dominion, all kings have not an equal latitude. Kings by conquest make their own charter: so that how large their power, either civil or spiritual, is, we cannot with any certainty define, further than only to set them in general the law of God and nature for bounds. Kings by God's own special appointment have also that largeness of power, which he doth assign or permit with approbation. Touching kings which were first instituted by agreement and composition made with them over whom they reign, how far their power may lawfully extend, the articles of compact between them must shew: not the articles only of compact at the first beginning, which for the most part are either clean worn out of knowledge, or else known unto very few, but whatsoever hath been after in free and voluntary manner condescended unto, whether by express consent, whereof positive laws are witnesses, or else by silent allowance famously notified through custom reaching beyond the memory of man. By which means of after-agreement, it cometh many times to pass in kingdoms, that they whose ancient predecessors were by violence and force made subject, do grow even by little and little into that most sweet form of kingly government which philosophers define to be "regency, willingly sustained and endued with chiefty of power in the greatest things."

[12.] Many of the ancients in their writings do speak of kings with such high and ample terms, as if universality of power, even in regard of things and not of persons only, did appertain to the very being of a king. The reason is, because their speech concerning kings they frame according to the state of those monarchs to whom unlimited authority was given: which some not observing, imagine that all kings, even in that they are kings, ought to have whatsoever power they find any sovereign ruler lawfully to have enjoyed. But that most judicious philosopher, whose eye scarce any thing did escape which was to be found in the bosom of nature, he considering how far the power of one sovereign ruler may be different from another regal authority, noteth in Spartan kings, "that of all others they were most tied to law, and so had the most restrained power." A king which hath not supreme power in the greatest things, is rather entitled a king, than invested with real sovereignty. We cannot properly term him a king, of whom it may not be said, at the leastwise as touching certain the very chiefest affairs of state, "his right in them is to have rule, not subject to any other predominant." I am not of opinion that simply always in kings the most, but the best limited power is best: the most limited is, that which may deal in fewest things; the best, that which in dealing is tied unto the soundest, perfectest, and most indifferent rule; which rule is the law; I mean not only the law of nature and of God, but very national or municipal law consonant thereunto. Happier that people whose law is their king in the greatest things, than that whose king is himself their law. Where the king doth guide the state, and the law the king, that commonwealth is like an harp or melodious instrument, the strings whereof are tuned and handled all by one hand, following as laws the rules and canons of musical science. Most divinely therefore Archytas maketh unto public felicity these four steps, every later whereof doth spring from the former, as from a mother cause; *ὁ μὲν βασιλεὺς νόμιμος, ὁ δὲ ἄρχων ἀκόλουθος ὁ δὲ ἀρχόμενος ἐλεύθερος, ἁ δ' ὅλα κοινωνία εὐδαίμων*;* adding on the contrary side, that "where this order is not, it cometh by transgression thereof to pass that the king grows a tyrant; he that ruleth under him abhorreth to be guided and commanded by him; the people subject under both, have freedom under neither; and the whole community is wretched."

[13.] In which respect, I cannot choose but commend highly their

* "The king ruling by law, the magistrate following, the subject free, and the whole society happy."

wisdom, by whom the foundations of this commonwealth have been laid; wherein though no manner person or cause be unsubject to the king's power, yet so is the power of the king over all and in all limited, that unto all his proceedings the law itself is a rule. The axioms of our regal government are these: "Lex facit regem:" the king's grant of any favour made contrary to law is void; "Rex nihil potest nisi quod jure potest." Our kings therefore, when they take possession of the room they are called unto, have it painted out before their eyes, even by the very solemnities and rites of their inauguration, to what affairs by the said law their supreme authority and power reacheth. Crowned we see they are, and enthronized, and anointed: the crown a sign of military; the throne, of sedentary or judicial; the oil, of religious or sacred power.

[14.] It is not on any side denied, that kings may have such authority in secular affairs. The question then is, "What power they lawfully may have and exercise in causes of God." "A prince, or magistrate, or a community," saith D. Stapleton, "may have power to lay corporal punishments on them which are teachers of perverse things; power to make laws for the peace of the Church; power to proclaim, to defend, and even by revenge to preserve from violation *dogmata*, very articles of religion themselves." Others in affection no less devoted unto the papacy, do likewise yield, that "the civil magistrate may by his edicts and laws keep all ecclesiastical persons within the bounds of their duties, and constrain them to observe the canons of the Church, to follow the rules of ancient discipline." That "if Joas were commended for his care and provision concerning so small a part of religion as the church-treasury; it must needs be both unto Christian kings themselves greater honour, and to Christianity a larger benefit, when the custody of religion whole and of the worship of God in general is their charge." If therefore all these things mentioned be most properly the affairs of God, and ecclesiastical causes; if the actions specified be works of power; and if that power be such as kings may use of themselves, without the leave of any other power superior in the same things: it followeth necessarily, that kings may have supreme power, not only in civil, but also in ecclesiastical affairs; and consequently, that they may withstand what bishop or pope soever shall, under the pretended claim of higher spiritual authority, oppose himself against their proceedings. But they which have made us the former grant, will hereunto never condescend. What they yield that princes may do, it is with secret exception always understood, if the bishop of Rome give leave, if he interpose no prohibition: wherefore somewhat it is in show, in truth nothing, which they grant.

Our own reformers do the very like. When they make their discourses in general concerning the authority which magistrates may have, a man would think them far from withdrawing any jot of that which with reason may be thought due. "The prince and civil magistrate," saith one of them, "hath to see that the laws of God touching his worship, and touching all matters and orders of the Church be executed, and duly observed; and to see that every ecclesiastical person do that office whereunto he is appointed, and to punish those which fail in their office accordingly." Another acknowledgeth, that "the magistrate may lawfully uphold all truth by his sword, punish all persons, enforce all to do their duties unto God and men; maintain by his laws every point of God's word, punish all vice in all men; see into all causes, visit the ecclesiastical state, and correct the abuses thereof; finally, so look to his subjects, that under him they may lead their lives in all godliness and honesty." A third more frankly professeth, that in case their church-discipline were established, so little it shorteneth the arms of sovereign dominion in causes ecclesiastical, that her gracious Majesty, for any thing which they teach or hold to the contrary, may no less than now "remain still over all persons, in all things supreme governess, even with that full and royal authority, superiority, preeminence, supremacy, and prerogative, which the laws already established do give her, and her Majesty's injunctions, and the articles of the Convocation-house, and other writings apologetical of her royal authority and supreme dignity, do declare and explain."

[15.] Posidonius was wont to say of the Epicure, "That he thought there were no gods, but that those things which he spake concerning the gods were only given out for fear of growing odious amongst men; and therefore that in words he left gods remaining, but in very deed overthrew them, inasmuch as he gave them no kind of motion, no kind of action." After the very selfsame manner, when we come unto those particular effects and prerogatives of dominion which the laws of this land do grant unto the kings thereof, it will appear how those men, notwithstanding their large and liberal speeches, abate such parcels out of the fore-alleged grand and flourishing sum, that a man comparing the one with the other may half stand in doubt, lest their opinions in very truth be against that authority which by their speeches they seem mightily to uphold, partly for the avoiding of public obloquy, envy, and hatred; partly to the intent they may both in the end, by establishment of their discipline, extinguish the force of supreme power which princes have, and yet in the meanwhile by giving forth these smooth discourses, obtain that their favourers may have somewhat to allege for them by way of apology, and that in such words as sound towards all kind of fulness in power. But for myself, I had rather construe such their contradictions in the better part, and impute their general acknowledgment of the lawfulness of kingly power unto the force of truth, presenting itself before them sometimes alone; their particular contrarieties, oppositions, denials, unto that error which having so fully possessed their minds, casteth things inconvenient upon them; of which things in their due place.

[16.] Touching that which is now in hand, we are on all sides fully agreed: first, that there is not any restraint or limitation of matter for regal authority and power to be conversant in, but of religion whole, and of whatsoever cause thereto appertaineth, kings may lawfully have charge, they lawfully may therein exercise dominion, and use the temporal sword: secondly, that some kinds of actions conversant about such affairs are denied unto kings; as, namely, actions of the power of order, and of that power of jurisdiction, which is with it unseparably joined; power to administer the word and sacraments, power to ordain, to judge as an ordinary, to bind and loose, to excommunicate, and such like: thirdly, that even in these very actions which are proper unto dominion, there must be some certain rule, whereunto kings in all their proceedings ought to be strictly tied; which rule for proceedings in ecclesiastical affairs and causes by regal power, hath not hitherto been agreed upon with so uniform consent and certainty as might be wished. The different sentences of men herein I will not now go about to examine, but it shall be enough to propose what rule doth seem in this case most reasonable.

[BY WHAT RULE]

[17.] It hath been declared already in general, how "the best established dominion is where the law doth most rule the king:" the true effect whereof particularly is found as well in ecclesiastical as in civil affairs. In these the king, through his supreme power, may do great things and sundry himself, both appertaining unto peace and war, both at home, by commandment and by commerce with states abroad, because so much the law doth permit. Some things on the other side, the king alone hath no power to do without consent of the lords and commons assembled in parliament: the king of himself cannot change the nature of pleas, nor courts, no not so much as restore blood; because the law is a bar unto him; not any law divine or natural, for against neither it were though kings of themselves might do both, but the positive laws of the realm have abridged therein and restrained the king's power; which positive laws, whether by custom or otherwise established without repugnancy unto the law of God and nature, ought no less to be of force even in the spiritual affairs of the Church. Wherefore in regard of ecclesiastical laws, we willingly embrace that of Ambrose, "kings have dominion to exercise in ecclesiastical causes, but according to the laws of the Church." Whether it be therefore the nature of courts, or the form of pleas, or the kind of governors, or the order of proceedings in whatsoever spiritual business; for the received laws and liberties of the Church the king hath supreme authority and power, but against them, none.

What such positive laws have appointed to be done by others than the king, or by others with the king, and in what form they have appointed the doing of it, the same of necessity must be kept, neither is the king's sole authority to alter it.

Yea, even as it were a thing unreasonable, if in civil affairs the king (albeit the whole universal body did join with him) should do any thing by their absolute supreme power for the ordering of their state at home, in prejudice of any of those ancient laws of nations which are of force throughout the world, because the necessary commerce of kingdoms dependeth on them; so in principal matters belonging to Christian religion, a thing very scandalous and offensive it must needs be thought, if either kings or laws should dispose of the affairs of God, without any respect had to that which of old hath been reverently thought of throughout the world, and wherein there is no law of God which forceth us to swerve from the way wherein so many and so holy ages have gone.

Wherefore not without good consideration the very law itself hath provided, "That judges ecclesiastical appointed under the king's commission shall not adjudge for heresy any thing but that which heretofore hath been so adjudged by the authority of the canonical scriptures, or by the first four general councils, or by some other general council wherein the same hath been declared heresy by the express words of the said canonical scriptures, or such as hereafter shall be termed heresy by the high court of parliament of this realm, with the assent of the clergy in the convocation." By which words of the law who doth not plainly see, how in that one branch of proceeding by virtue of the king's supreme authority, the credit which those four general councils have throughout all churches evermore had, was judged by the makers of the foresaid act a just cause wherefore it should be mentioned in that case, as a requisite part of the rule wherewith dominion was to be limited. But of this we shall further consider, when we come unto that which sovereign power may do in making ecclesiastical laws.

WITH WHAT CONVENIENCY

[18.] The cause of deriving supreme power from an whole entire multitude unto some special part thereof, is partly the necessity of expedition in public affairs; partly the inconveniency of confusion and trouble, where a multitude of equals dealeth; and partly the dissipation which must needs ensue in companies, where every man wholly seeketh his own particular (as we all would do, even with other men's hurt) and haply the very overthrow of ourselves in the end also, if for procurement of the common good of all men, by keeping every several man in order, some were not armed with authority over all, and encouraged with prerogatives of honour to sustain the weighty burden of that charge. The good which is proper unto each man belongeth to the common good of all, as a part of the whole's perfection; but yet these two are things different; for men by that which is proper are severed, united they are by that which is common. Wherefore, besides that which moveth each man in particular to seek his private, there must of necessity in all public societies be also a general mover, directing unto the common good, and framing every man's particular to it. The end whereunto all government was instituted, was *bonum publicum*, the universal or common good. Our question is of dominion, for that end and purpose derived into one. Such as in one public state have agreed that the supreme charge of all things should be committed unto one, they I say, considering what inconveniences may grow where states are subject unto sundry supreme authorities, were for fear of those inconveniences withdrawn from liking to establish many; *οὐκ ἀγαθὸν πολυκοιρανίη*, the multitude of supreme commanders is troublesome. "No man," saith our Saviour, "can serve two masters:" surely two supreme masters would make any one man's service somewhat uneasy in such cases as might fall out. Suppose that to-morrow the power which hath dominion in justice require thee at the court; that which in war, at the field; that which in religion, at the temple: all have equal authority over thee, and impossible it is, that thou shouldest be in such case obedient to all: by choosing any one whom thou wilt obey, certain thou art for thy disobedience to incur the displeasure of the other two.

Chapter 3

ACCORDING UNTO WHAT EXAMPLE OR PATTERN

But there is nothing for which some colourable reason or other may not be found. Are we able to shew any commendable state of government, which by experience and practice hath felt the benefit of being in all causes subject unto the supreme authority of one? Against the polity of Israel, I hope there will no man except, where Moses deriving so great a part of his burden in government unto others, did notwithstanding retain to himself universal supremacy. Jehosaphat appointing one to be chief in the affairs of God, and another in the king's affairs, did this as having himself dominion over them in both. If therefore, with approbation from heaven, the kings of God's own chosen people had in the affairs of Jewish religion supreme power, why not Christian kings the like power also in Christian religion? Unless men will answer, as some have done, "that touching the Jews, first their religion was of far less perfection and dignity than ours is, ours being that truth whereof theirs was but a shadowish prefigurative resemblance." Secondly, "That all parts of their religion, their laws, their sacrifices, their rites and ceremonies, being fully set down to their hands, and needing no more but only to be put in execution, the kings might well have highest authority to see that done: whereas with us there are a number of mysteries even in belief, which were not so generally for them, as for us, necessary to be with sound express acknowledgment understood; a number of things belonging unto external regiment, and our manner of serving God, not set down by particular ordinances, and delivered unto us in writing; for which cause the state of the Church doth now require that the spiritual authority of ecclesiastical persons be large, absolute, and not subordinate to regal power." Thirdly, "that whereas God armeth religion Jewish, with temporal, Christian, with a sword but of spiritual punishment; the one with power to imprison, to scourge, and to put to death, the other with bare authority to censure and excommunicate; there is no reason that the Church, which now hath no visible sword, should in regiment be subject unto any other power, than only unto theirs which have authority to bind and loose." Fourthly, "that albeit while the Church was restrained unto one people, it seemed not incommodious to grant their kings the general chiefty of power; yet now, the Church having spread itself over all nations, great inconveniency must thereby grow, if every Christian king in his several territory should have the like power." Of all these differences, there is not one which doth prove it a thing repugnant unto the law either of God or nature, that all supremacy of external power be in Christian kingdoms granted unto the kings thereof, for preservation of quietness, unity, order, and peace, in such manner as hath been shewed.

[2.] The service which we do unto the true God who made heaven and earth, is far different from that which heathens have done unto their supposed gods, though nothing else were respected but only the odds between their hope and ours. The offices of piety or true religion sincerely performed have the promises both of this life and of the life to come: the practices of superstition have neither. If notwithstanding the heathens, reckoning upon no other reward for all which they did but only protection and favour in the temporal estate and condition of this present life, and perceiving how great good did hereby publicly grow, as long as fear to displease (they knew not what) divine power was some kind of bridle unto them, did therefore provide that the highest degree of care for their religion should be the principal charge of such as having otherwise also the greatest and chiefest power were by so much the more fit to have custody thereof: shall the like kind of provision be in us thought blameworthy?

[REPLY TO THE FIRST OBJECTION]

A gross error it is, to think that regal power ought to serve for the good of the body, and not of the soul; for men's temporal peace, and not their eternal safety: as if God had ordained kings for no other end and purpose but only to fat up men like hogs, and to see that they have their mash? Indeed, to lead men unto salvation by the hand of secret, invisible, and ghostly regiment, or by the external administration of things belonging unto priestly order (such as the word and sacraments are), this is denied unto Christian kings: no cause in the world to think them uncapable of supreme authority in the outward government which disposeth the affairs of religion so far forth as the same are disposable by human authority, and to think them uncapable thereof, only for that the said religion is everlastingly beneficial to them that faithfully continue in it. And even as little cause there is, that being admitted thereunto amongst the Jews, they should amongst the Christians of necessity be delivered from ever exercising any such power, for the dignity and perfection which is in our religion more than in theirs [2 Cor. iii. 7, 8].

[TO THE SECOND]

[3.] It may be a question, whether the affairs of Christianity require more wit, more study, more knowledge of divine things in him which shall order them, than the Jewish religion did. For although we deny not the form of external government, together with all other rites and ceremonies, to have been in more particular manner set down; yet withal it must be considered also, that even this very thing did in some respects make the burthen of their spiritual regiment the harder to be borne; by reason of infinite doubts and difficulties which the very obscurity and darkness of their law did breed, and which being not first decided, the law could not possibly have due execution.

Besides, inasmuch as their law did also dispose even of all kind of civil affairs; their clergy, being the interpreters of the whole law, sustained not only the same labour which divines do amongst us, but even the burthen of our lawyers too. Nevertheless, be it granted that moe things do now require to be publicly deliberated and resolved upon with exacter judgment in matters divine than kings for the most part have: their personal inability to judge, in such sort as professors do, letteth not but that their regal authority may have the selfsame degree or sway which the kings of Israel had in the affairs of their religion, to rule and command according to the manner of supreme governors.

[TO THE THIRD]

[4.] As for the sword, wherewith God armed his Church of old, if that were a reasonable cause why kings might then have dominion, I see not but that it ministreth still as forcible an argument for the lawfulness and expediency of their continuance therein now. As we degrade and excommunicate, even so did the Church of the Jews both separate offenders from the temple, and depose the clergy also from their rooms, when cause required. The other sword of corporal punishment is not by *Christ's own appointment* in the hands of the Church of Christ, as God did place it himself in the hands of the Jewish Church. For why? He knew that they whom he sent abroad to gather a people unto him only by persuasive means, were to build up his Church even within the bosom of kingdoms, the chiefest governors whereof would be open enemies unto it every where for the space of many years. Wherefore such commission for discipline he gave them, as they might any where exercise in quiet and peaceable manner; the subjects of no commonwealth being touched in goods or person, by virtue of that spiritual regiment whereunto Christian religion embraced did make them subject.

Now when afterwards it came to pass, that whole kingdoms were made Christian, I demand whether that authority, which served before for the furtherance of religion, may not as effectually [serve] to the maintenance of Christian religion. Christian religion hath the sword of spiritual discipline. But doth that suffice? The Jewish which had it also, did nevertheless stand in need to be aided with the power of the civil sword. The help whereof, although when Christian religion cannot have, it must without it sustain itself as far as the other which it hath will serve; notwithstanding, where both may be had, what forbiddeth the Church to enjoy the benefit of both? Will any man deny that the Church doth need the rod of corporal punishment to keep her children in obedience withal, such a law as Macabeus made amongst the Scots, that he which continued an excommunicate two years together, and reconciled not himself to the church, should forfeit all his goods and possessions?

Again, the custom which many Christian churches have to fly to the civil magistrate for coercion of those that will not otherwise be reformed these things are proof sufficient that even in Christian religion, the power wherewith ecclesiastical persons were endued at the first is unable to do of itself so much as when secular power doth strengthen it; and that, not by way of ministry or service, but of predominancy, such as the kings of Israel in their time exercised over the Church of God.

[TO THE FOURTH]

[5.] Yea, but the Church of God was then restrained more narrowly to one people and one king, which now being spread throughout all kingdoms, it would be a cause of great dissimilitude in the exercise of Christian religion if every king should be over the affairs of the church where he reigneth supreme ruler.

Dissimilitude in great things is such a thing which draweth great inconvenience after it, a thing which Christian religion must always carefully prevent. And the way to prevent it is, not as some do imagine, the yielding up of supreme power over all churches into one only pastor's hands; but the framing of their government, especially for matter of substance, every where according to the rule of one only law, to stand in no less force than the law of nations doth, to be received in all kingdoms, all sovereign rulers to be sworn no otherwise unto it than some are to maintain the liberties, laws, and received customs of the country where they reign. This shall cause uniformity even under several dominions, without those woeful inconveniences whereunto the state of Christendom was subject heretofore, through the tyranny and oppression of that one universal Nimrod who alone did all.

And, till the Christian world be driven to enter into the peaceable and true consultation about some such kind of general law concerning those things of weight and moment wherein now we differ, if one church hath not the same order which another hath: let every church keep as near as may be the order it should have, and commend the just defence thereof unto God, even as Juda did, when it differed in the exercise of religion from that form which Israel followed.

[6.] Concerning therefore the matter whereof we have hitherto spoken, let it stand for our final conclusion, that in a free Christian state or kingdom, where one and the selfsame people are the Church and the commonwealth, God through Christ directing that people to see it for good and weighty considerations expedient that their sovereign lord and governor in causes civil have also in ecclesiastical affairs a supreme power; forasmuch as the light of reason doth lead them unto it, and against it God's own revealed law hath nothing: surely they do not in submitting themselves thereunto any other than that which a wise and religious people ought to do.

It was but a little overflowing of wit in Thomas Aquinas, so to play upon the words of Moses in the Old [Exod. xix. 6], and of Peter in the New Testament [1 Pet. ii. 9], as though because the one did term the Jews "a priestly kingdom," the other as "a kingly priesthood," those two substantives "kingdom" and "priesthood" should import, that Judaism did stand through the kings' superiority over priests, Christianity through the priests' supreme authority over kings. Is it probable, that Moses and Peter had herein so nice and curious conceits? Or else more likely that both meant one and the same thing; namely that God doth glorify and sanctify his, even with full perfection in both; which thing St. John doth in plainer sort express, saying that "Christ hath made us both kings and priests." [Rev. i. 6]

Chapter 4

OF THEIR TITLE OF HEADSHIP WHICH WE GIVE TO THE KINGS OF ENGLAND IN RELATION UNTO THE CHURCH

[1.] For the title or style itself, although the laws of this land have annexed it to the crown, yet so far we would not strive, if so be men were nice and scrupulous in this behalf only, because they do wish that for reverence unto Christ Jesus, the civil magistrate did rather use some other form of speech wherewith to express that sovereign authority which he lawfully hath over all, both persons and causes of the Church. But I see that hitherto they which condemn utterly the name so applied, do it because they mislike that any such power should be given unto civil governors. The greatest exception that Sir Thomas More took against that title, who suffered death for denial of it, was "for that it maketh a lay, or secular person, the head of the state spiritual or ecclesiastical;" as though God himself did not name even Saul the head of all the tribes of Israel; and consequently of that tribe also among the rest, whereunto the state spiritual or ecclesiastical belonged. When the authors of the *Centuries* reprove it in kings and civil governors, the reason is, "such kind of power is too high for them, they fit it not." In excuse of Mr. Calvin, by whom this realm is condemned of blasphemy for entitling Henry the Eighth Supreme Head of this Church under Christ, a charitable conjecture is made, that he spake by misinformation, and thought we had meant thereby far otherwise than we do; howbeit, as he professeth utter dislike of that name, so whether the name be used or no, the very power itself which we give unto civil magistrates he much complaineth of, and testifieth, "That their power over all things was it which had ever wounded him deeply; that unadvised persons had made them too spiritual; that through Germany this fault did reign; that in those very parts where Calvin himself was, it prevailed more than were to be wished; that rulers, by imagining themselves so spiritual, have taken away ecclesiastical regiment; that they think they cannot reign unless they abolish all authority of the Church, and be themselves the chief judges, as well in doctrine, as in the whole spiritual regency." So that in truth the question is, whether the magistrate, by being head in such sense as we term him, do use or exercise any part of that authority, not which belongeth unto Christ, but which other men ought to have.

[2.] These things being thus first considered, it will be the easier to judge concerning our own estate, whether by force of ecclesiastical dominion with us kings have any other kind of prerogative than they may lawfully hold and enjoy. It is as some do imagine too much, that kings of England should be termed Heads, in relation to the Church. That which we understand by headship, is their only supreme power in ecclesiastical affairs or causes. That which lawfully princes are, what should make it unlawful for men by special styles or titles to signify? If the having of supreme power be allowed, why is the expressing thereof by the title of head condemned? They seem in words, at the leastwise some of them, now at the length to acknowledge that kings may have supreme government even over all, both persons and causes. We in terming our princes *Heads of the Church*, do but testify that we acknowledge them such governors.

[3.] Against this peradventure it will be replied, that howsoever we interpret ourselves, it is not fit for a mortal man, and therefore not fit for a civil magistrate, to be entitled *Head of the Church*. Why so? First, "this title, Head of the Church, was given unto our Saviour Christ [Ephes. i. 21; Col. i. 18], to lift him above all powers, rules, and dominions, either in heaven or in earth. Where if this title belong also to the civil magistrate, then it is manifest that there is a power in earth whereunto our Saviour Christ is not in this point superior." Again, "if the civil magistrate may have this title, he may be also termed the first-begotten of all creatures, the first-begotten of the dead, yea the Redeemer of his people. For these are alike given him as dignities whereby he is lifted up above all creatures." Besides this, "the whole argument of the Apostle in both places doth lead to shew that this title, Head of the Church, cannot be said of any creature." And further, "the very demonstrative article, among the Hebrews especially, whom St. Paul doth follow, serveth to tie that which is verified of one, unto himself alone: so that when the apostle doth say that Christ is ἡ κεφαλή, the Head; it is as much as if he should say, Christ, and no other, is the Head of the Church."

[4.] Thus have we against the entitling of the highest magistrates, Head, with relation unto the Church, four several arguments, gathered by strong surmise out of words marvellous unlikely to have been written for any such purpose as that whereunto they are now urged. To the Ephesians, the Apostle writeth [Ephes. i. 20–23], that "Christ, God hath seated on his own right hand in the heavenly places, above all regency, and authority, and power, and dominion, and whatsoever name is named, not in this world only, but in that which shall be also: and hath under his feet set all things, and hath given him head above all things unto the Church, which is his body, even the complement of him which accomplisheth all in all." To the Colossians in like manner [Col. i. 18], that "He is the head of the body of the Church, who is a first-born regency out of the dead, to the end he might be made amongst them all such an one as hath the chiefty:" he meaneth, amongst all them whom before he mentioned, saying [Col. i. 16], "In him all things that are, were made; the things in the heavens, and the things on the earth, the things that are visible, and the things that are invisible, whether they be thrones, or dominations, or regencies." &c.

Unto the fore-alleged arguments therefore we answer: first, that it is not simply the title of Head, which lifteth our Saviour above all powers, but the title of Head in such sort understood, as the apostle himself meant it: so that the same being imparted in another sense unto others, doth not any way make those others therein his equals; inasmuch as diversity of things is usual to be understood, even when of words there is no diversity; and it is only the adding of one and the selfsame thing unto diverse persons, which doth argue equality in them. If I term Christ and Cæsar lords, yet this is no equalling of Cæsar with Christ, because it is not thereby intended. "To term the emperor Lord," saith Tertullian, "I for mine own part will not refuse, so that I be not required to term him Lord in the same sense that God is so termed."

Neither doth it follow, which is objected in the second place, that if the civil magistrate may be entitled an Head, he may be also as well termed, "the first-begotten of all creatures," "the first-begotten of the dead," and "the Redeemer of his people." For albeit the former dignity do lift him up no less than these, yet these terms are not appliable and apt to signify any other inferior dignity, as the former term of Head was.

The argument or matter which the Apostle followeth hath small evidence for proof, that his meaning was to appropriate unto Christ the foresaid title, otherwise than only in such sense as doth make it, being so understood, too high to be given to any creature.

As for the force of the article, whereby our Lord and Saviour is named the Head, it serveth to tie that unto him by way of excellency, which in a meaner degree is common to others; it doth not exclude any other utterly from being termed Head, but from being entitled as Christ is, the Head, by way of the very highest degree of excellency. Not in the communication of names, but in the confusion of things, is error.

[5.] Howbeit, if Head were a name which well could not be, or never had been used to signify that which a magistrate may be in relation unto some church, but were by continual use of speech appropriated unto that only thing which it signifieth, being applied unto Jesus Christ; then, although we might carry in ourselves a right understanding, yet ought we otherwise rather to speak, unless we interpret our own meaning by some clause of plainer speech; because we are else in manifest danger to be understood according to that construction and sense wherein such words are usually taken. But here the rarest construction, and most removed from common sense, is that which the word doth import being applied unto Christ; that which we signify by it in giving it unto the magistrate, is a great deal more familiar in the common conceit of men. The word is so fit to signify all kinds of superiority, preeminence, and chiefty, that no one thing is more ordinary than so to use it even in vulgar speech, and in common understanding so to take it. If therefore a Christian king may have any preeminence or chiefty above all other in the Church, (albeit it were less than Theodore Beza giveth, who placeth kings amongst the principal members whereunto public function in the Church belongeth, and denieth not, but that of them which have public function, the civil magistrate's power hath all the rest at commandment, in regard of that part of his office, which is to procure that peace and good order be especially kept in things concerning the first Table;) even hereupon to term him the *Head* of that *Church* which is his *Kingdom*, should not seem so unfit a thing: which title surely we would not communicate to any other, no not although it should at our hands be exacted with torments, but that our meaning herein is made known to the whole world, so that no man which will understand can easily be ignorant, that we do not impart to kings when we term them *Heads* the honour which properly is given to our Lord and Saviour Christ, when the blessed Apostles in Scripture do term him the *Head of the Church*.

DIFFERENCES BETWEEN CHRIST'S HEADSHIP AND THAT WHICH WE GIVE TO KINGS

[6.] The power which we signify by that name, differeth in three things plainly from that which Christ doth challenge.

It differeth in order, measure, and kind. In order, because God hath given him to his Church for the Head above all, "far above all principality, and power, and might, and dominion, and every name that is named, not in this world only, but also in that which is to come:" [Ephes. i. 21, 22] whereas the power which others have is subordinated unto his.

Again, as he differeth in order, so in measure of power also; because God hath given unto him [Ps. ii. 8] the ends of the earth for his possession; unto him, dominion from sea to sea; unto him, all power in heaven and in earth; unto him, such sovereignty, as doth not only reach over all places, persons, and things, but doth rest in his one only person, and is not by any succession continued; he reigneth as Head and King for ever, nor is there any kind of law which tieth him, but his own proper will and wisdom; his power is absolute, the same jointly over all which it is severally over each. Not so the power of any other headship. How kings are restrained, and in what sort their authority is limited, we have shewed before. So that unto him is given by the title of Headship over the Church, that largeness of power, wherein neither man nor angel can be matched or compared with him.

The last and the weightiest difference between him and them, is in the very kind of their power. The head being of all other parts of man's body the most divine, hath dominion over all the rest: it is the fountain of sense, of motion; the throne where the guide of the soul doth reign; the court from whence direction of all things human proceedeth. Why Christ is called *Head of his Church*, these causes they themselves do yield. As the head is the highest part of a man, above which there is none, always joined with the body: so Christ is the highest in his Church, inseparably knit with it. Again, as the head giveth sense and moving to all the body, so he quickeneth, and together with understanding of heavenly things, giveth strength to walk therein. Seeing therefore, that they cannot affirm Christ sensibly present, or always visibly joined unto his body the Church which is on earth, inasmuch as his corporal residence is in heaven; again, seeing they do not affirm (it were intolerable if they should) that Christ doth personally administer the external regiment of outward actions in the Church, but by the secret inward influence of his grace, giveth spiritual life and the strength of ghostly motions thereunto: impossible it is, that they should so close up their eyes, as not to discern what odds there is between that kind of operation which we imply in the headship of princes, and that which agreeth to our Saviour's dominion over the Church. The headship which we give unto kings is altogether visibly exercised, and ordereth only the external frame of the Church's affairs here amongst us; so that it plainly differeth from Christ's, even in very nature and kind. To be in such sort united unto the Church as he is; to work as he worketh, either on the whole Church, or on any particular assembly, or on any one man; doth neither agree, nor hath possibility of agreeing, unto any besides him.

OPPOSITION AGAINST THE FIRST DIFFERENCE, WHEREBY, CHRIST BEING HEAD SIMPLY, PRINCES ARE SAID TO BE HEADS UNDER CHRIST

[7.] Against the first distinction or difference it is objected, that to entitle a magistrate Head of the Church, although it be under Christ, is most absurd. For Christ hath a twofold superiority; a superiority over his Church, and a superiority over kingdoms: according to the one, he "hath a superior, which is his Father; according to the other, none but immediate authority with his Father:" that is to say, of the Church he is Head and Governor only as the Son of man; Head and Governor over kingdoms only as the Son of God. In the Church, as man, he hath officers under him, which officers are ecclesiastical persons: as for the civil magistrate, his office belongeth unto kingdoms and commonwealths, neither is he therein an under or subordinate head of Christ, "considering that his authority cometh from God, simply and immediately, even as our Saviour Christ's doth."

Whereunto the sum of our answer is, first, that as Christ being Lord or Head over all, doth by virtue of that sovereignty rule all; so he hath no more a superior in governing his Church, than in exercising sovereign dominion upon the rest of the world besides. Secondly, that all authority, as well civil as ecclesiastical, is subordinate unto his. And thirdly, that the civil magistrate being termed Head, by reason of that authority in ecclesiastical affairs which it hath been already declared that themselves do in word acknowledge to be lawful; it followeth that he is an Head even subordinated of and to Christ.

For more plain explication whereof, first, unto God we acknowledge daily [Matt. vi. 13], that kingdom, power, and glory are his; that he is [1 Tim. i. 17] the immortal and the invisible King of ages, as well the future which shall be, as the present which now is. That which the Father doth work as Lord and king over all, he work not without, but by the Son, who through coeternal generation receiveth of the Father that power which the Father hath of himself. And for that cause our Saviour's words concerning his own dominion are, "To me all power both in heaven and [in] earth is given." The Father by the Son both did create, and doth guide all; wherefore Christ hath supreme dominion over the whole universal world.

Christ is God, Christ is Λόγος, the consubstantial Word of God, Christ is also that consubstantial Word made man. As God, he saith of himself, "I am Alpha and Omega, the beginning and the end: he which was, which is, and which is to come; even the very Omnipotent." [Apoc. i. 8] As the consubstantial Word of God, he had with God before the beginning of the world, that glory which as man he requesteth to have; "Father, glorify thy Son now with that glory which with thee I enjoyed before the world was." [John xvii. 5] For there is no necessity that all things spoken of Christ should agree unto him either as God or else as man; but some things as he is the consubstantial Word of God, some things as he is that Word incarnate. The works of supreme dominion which have been since the first beginning wrought by the power of the Son of God, are now most truly and properly the works of the Son of man: the Word made flesh doth sit for ever, and reign as sovereign Lord over all. Dominion belongeth unto the kingly office of Christ, as propitiation and mediation unto his priestly; instruction, unto his pastoral or prophetical office. His works of dominion are in sundry degrees or kinds, according to the different condition of them which are subject unto it: he presently doth govern, and hereafter shall judge the world, entire and whole, therefore his regal power cannot be with truth restrained unto a portion of the world only. Notwithstanding forasmuch as all do not shew and acknowledge with dutiful submission that obedience which they owe unto him; therefore such as do, their Lord he is termed by way of excellency, no otherwise than the Apostle doth term God [1 Tim. iv. 10], the Saviour generally of all, but especially of the faithful: these being brought to the obedience of faith, are every where spoken of as men translated into that kingdom, wherein whosoever is comprehended, Christ is [Heb. v. 9] the author of eternal salvation unto them; they have a high kind of ghostly fellowship [1 John i. 3] with God, and Christ, and saints; or as the Apostle in more ample manner speaketh [Heb. xii. 22–4], "Aggregated they are unto Mount Sion, and to the city of the living God, the celestial Jerusalem, and to the company of innumerable angels, and to the congregation of the first-born, which are written in heaven, and to God the judge of all, and to the spirits of just and perfect men, and to Jesus the Mediator of the New Testament." In a word, they are of that mystical body, which we term the Church of Christ. As for the rest, we find them accounted "aliens from the commonwealth of Israel, men that lay in the kingdom of darkness, and that are in this present world without God." Our Saviour's dominion is therefore over these, as over rebels; over them as dutiful subjects.

Which things being in holy Scriptures so plain, I somewhat muse at those strange positions, "that Christ in the government of the Church, and superiority over the officers of it, hath himself a superior, which is his Father; but in the government of kingdoms and commonwealths, and in the superiority which he hath over kings, no superior." Again, "that the civil magistrate cometh from God immediately, as Christ doth, and is not subordinate unto Christ." In what evangelist, apostle, or prophet is it found, that Christ, supreme governor of the Church, should be so unequal to himself, as he is supreme governor of kingdoms? The works of his providence for preservation of mankind by upholding of kingdoms, not only obedient unto, but even rebellious and obstinate against him, are such as proceed from divine power; and are not the works of his providence for safety of God's elect, by gathering, inspiring, comforting, and every way preserving his Church, such as proceed from the same power likewise? Surely, if Christ "as God and man have ordained certain means for the gathering and keeping of his Church," seeing this doth belong to the government of his Church; it must in reason follow, I think, that as God and man he worketh in church regiment, and consequently hath no more therein any superior, than in the government of commonwealths.

Again, to "be in the midst of his, wheresoever they are assembled in his name," and to be "with them till the world's end," are comforts which Christ doth perform to his Church as Lord and Governor; yea, such as he cannot perform but by that very power wherein he hath no superior.

Wherefore, unless it can be proved, that all the works of our Saviour's government in the Church are done by the mere and only force of his human nature, there is no remedy but to acknowledge it a manifest error, that Christ in the government of the world is equal unto the Father, but not in the government of the Church. Indeed, to the honour of this dominion it cannot be said that God did exalt him otherwise than only according to that human nature wherein he was made low: for as the Son of God, there could no advancement or exaltation grow unto him: and yet the dominion, whereunto he was in his human nature lifted up, is not without divine power exercised. It is by divine power, that the Son of man who sitteth in heaven, doth work as king and lord upon us which are on earth.

The exercise of his dominion over the Church militant cannot choose but cease, when there is no longer any militant Church in the world. And therefore as generals of armies when they have finished their work, are wont to yield up such commissions as were given them for that purpose, and to remain in the state of subjects and not of lords, as concerning their former authority; even so, when the end of all things is come, the Son of man, who till then reigneth, shall do the like, as touching regiment over the militant Church on earth. So that between the Son of man and his brethren, over whom he now reigneth in this their warfare, there shall be then, as touching the exercise of that regiment, no such difference; they not warfaring under him any longer, but he together with them under God receiving the joys of everlasting triumph, that so God may be all in all; all misery in all the wicked through his justice; in all the righteous, through his love, all felicity and bliss. In the meanwhile he reigneth over this world as king, and doth those things wherein none is superior unto him, whether we respect the works of his providence over kingdoms, or of his regiment over the Church.

The cause of error in this point doth seem to have been a misconceit that Christ as Mediator being inferior unto his Father doth as Mediator all works of regiment over the Church; when in truth, government doth belong to his kingly office, mediatorship to his priestly. For, as the high priest both offered sacrifice for expiation of the people's sins, and entered into the holy place, there to make intercession for them: so Christ [Heb. ix. 24. vii. 25], having finished upon the cross that part of his priestly office which wrought the propitiation for our sins, did afterwards enter into very heaven, and doth there as mediator of the New Testament appear in the sight of God for us. A like slip of judgment it is, when they hold that civil authority is from God, but not mediately through Christ, nor with any subordination unto Christ. For "there is no power," saith the Apostle, "but from God;" [Rom. xiii. 1] nor doth any thing come from God but by the hands of our Lord Jesus Christ.

They deny it not to be said of Christ in the Old Testament, "By me kings reign, and princes decree justice; by me princes rule, and the nobles, and all the judges of the earth." [Prov. viii. 15–16] In the New as much is taught, "That Christ is the Prince of the kings of the earth." [Rev. i. 5] Wherefore to the end it may more plainly appear how all authority of man is derived from God through Christ, and must by Christian men be acknowledged to be no otherwise held than of and under him; we are to note, that because whatsoever hath necessary being, the Son of God doth cause it to be, and those things without which the world cannot well continue, have necessary being in the world: a thing of so great use as government amongst men, and human dominion in government, cannot choose but be originally from him, and have reference also of subordination unto him. Touching that authority which civil magistrates have in ecclesiastical affairs, it being from God by Christ, as all other good things are, cannot choose but be held as a thing received at his hands. And because such power, as is of necessary use for the ordering of religion, wherein the essence and very being of the Church consisteth, can no otherwise flow from him, than according to that special care which he hath to guide and govern his own people: it followeth that the said authority is of and under him after a more peculiar manner, namely, in that he is Head of the Church, and not in respect of his general regency over the world. "All things," (saith the Apostle speaking unto the Church) "are yours, and ye are Christ's, and Christ is God's." [1 Cor. iii. 21–3] Kings are Christ's as saints, and kings are Christ's as kings: as saints, because they are of the Church; as kings, because they are in authority over the Church, if not collectively, yet divisively understood; that is over each particular person within that Church where they are kings. Such authority, reaching both unto all men's persons, and unto all kinds of causes also, it is not denied but that they lawfully may have and exercise; such authority it is, for which, and for no other in the world, we term them heads; such authority they have under Christ, because he in all things is Lord over all. And even of Christ it is that they have received such authority, inasmuch as of him all lawful powers are: therefore the civil magistrate is, in regard of this power, an under and subordinate head of Christ's people.

AGAINST THE SECOND DIFFERENCE, WHEREBY CHRIST IS SAID TO BE UNIVERSALLY HEAD, THE KING NO FURTHER THAN WITHIN HIS OWN DOMINIONS

[8.] It is but idle when they plead, "that although for several companies of men there may be several heads or governors, differing in the measure of their authority from the chiefest who is head of all; yet so it cannot be in the Church, for that the reason why head-magistrates appoint others for such several places is, because they cannot be present every where to perform the office of a head. But Christ is never from his body, nor from any part of it, and therefore needeth not to substitute any, which may be heads, some over one church and some over another." Indeed the consideration of man's imbecility, which maketh many hands necessary where the burden is too great for one, moved Jethro to be a persuader of Moses, that a number of heads or rulers might be instituted for discharge of that duty by parts, which in whole he saw was troublesome. Now although there be not in Christ any such defect or weakness, yet other causes there may be diverse, moe than we are able to search into, wherefore it might seem to him expedient to divide his kingdom into many portions, and to place many heads over it, that the power which each of them hath in particular with restraint, might illustrate the greatness of his unlimited authority. Besides, howsoever Christ be spiritually always united unto every part of his body, which is the Church, nevertheless we do all know, and they themselves who allege this will, I doubt not, confess also, that from every church here visible, Christ, touching visible and corporal presence, is removed as far as heaven from earth is distant. Visible government [is] a thing necessary for the Church; and it doth not appear how the exercise of visible government over such multitudes every where dispersed throughout the world should consist without sundry visible governors; whose power being the greatest in that kind so far as it reacheth, they are in consideration thereof termed so far heads. Wherefore, notwithstanding that perpetual conjunction, by virtue whereof our Saviour remaineth always spiritually united unto the parts of his mystical body; Heads endued with supreme power, extending unto a certain compass, are for the exercise of visible regiment not unnecessary.

Some other reasons there are belonging unto this branch, which seem to have been objected, rather for the exercise of men's wits in dissolving sophisms, than that the authors of them could think in likelihood thereby to strengthen their cause. For example, "If the magistrate be head of the Church within his own dominion, then is he none of the Church; for all that Church maketh the body of Christ, and every one of the Church fulfilleth the place of one member of the body. By making the magistrate therefore head, we do exclude him from being a member subject to the head, and so leave him no place in the Church." By which reason, the name of a body politic is supposed to be always taken of the inferior sort alone, excluding the principal guides and governors; contrary to all men's custom of speech. The error riseth by misconstruing of some Scripture sentences, where Christ as the head, and the Church as the body, are compared or opposed the one to the other: and because in such comparisons and oppositions, the body is taken for those only parts which are subject to the head, they imagine that whoso is head of any church, he is even thereby excluded from being a part of that church: that the magistrate can be none of the Church, if so be we make him the head of the church in his own dominions. A chief and principal part, therefore no part; this is surely a strange conclusion. A church doth indeed make the body of Christ, being wholly taken together; and every one in the same church fulfilleth the place of a member in the body, but not the place of an inferior member, he which hath supreme authority and power over all the rest. Wherefore, by making the magistrate head in his own dominions, we exclude him from being a member subject unto any other person which may visibly there rule in place of an head or governor over him; but so far are we off from leaving him by this means no place in the Church, that we grant him the chiefest place. Indeed the heads of those visible bodies, which are many, can be but parts inferior in that spiritual body which is but one; yea, they may from this be excluded clean, who notwithstanding ought to be honoured, as possessing in the other the highest rooms: but for the magistrate to be termed, one way, within his own dominions, an head, doth not bar him from being either way a part or member of the Church of God.

As little to the purpose are those other cavils: "A Church which hath the magistrate for head, is a perfect man without Christ. So that the knitting of our Saviour thereunto should be an addition of that which is too much." Again, "If the Church be the body of Christ, and of the civil magistrate, it shall have two heads, which being monstrous, is to the great dishonour of Christ and his Church." Thirdly, "If the Church be planted in a popular estate, then, forasmuch as all govern in common, and all have authority, all shall be head there, and no body at all; which is another monster." It might be feared what this birth of so many monsters might portend, but that we know how things natural enough in themselves may seem monstrous through misconceit; which error of mind is indeed a monster, and so the skilful in nature's mysteries have used to term it. The womb of monsters, if any be, is that troubled understanding, wherein, because things lie confusedly mixed together, what they are it appears not.

A Church perfect without Christ, I know not which way a man should imagine; unless there may be either Christianity without Christ, or else a Church without Christianity. If magistrates be heads of the Church, they are of necessity Christians; if Christians, then is their Head Christ.

The adding of Christ the universal Head over all unto the magistrate's particular headship, is no more superfluous in any church than in other societies. It is to be both severally each subject unto some head, and to have also a head general for them all to be subject unto. For so in armies and in civil corporations we see it fareth. A body politic in such respects is not like to a natural body; in this, more heads than one are superfluous; in that, not.

It is neither monstrous nor as much as uncomely for a church to have different heads: for if Christian churches be in number many, and every of them a body perfect by itself, Christ being Lord and Head over all; why should we judge it a thing more monstrous for one body to have two heads, than one head so many bodies? Him God hath made the supreme Head of the whole Church; the Head, not only of that mystical body which the eye of man is not able to discern, but even of every Christian politic society, of every visible Church in the world.

And whereas, lastly, it is thought so strange, that in popular states a multitude should to itself be both body and head, all this wonderment doth grow from a little oversight, in deeming that the subject wherein headship is to reside, should be evermore some one person; which thing is not necessary. For in a collective body that hath not derived as yet the principality of power into some one or few, the whole of necessity must be head over each part; otherwise it could not possibly have power to make any one certain person head; inasmuch as the very power of making a head belongeth unto headship. These supposed monsters therefore we see are no such giants, that there should need any Hercules to tame them.

OPPOSITION AGAINST THE DIFFERENCE IN KIND

[9.] The last difference which we have made between the title of head when we gave it unto Christ, and when we gave it to other governors, is, that the kind of dominion which it importeth is not the same in both. Christ is head as being the fountain of life and ghostly nutriment, the well-spring of spiritual blessings poured into the body of the Church; these heads, as being his principal instruments for the Church's outward government: He head, as founder of the house; they, as his chiefest overseers. Against this there is exception especially taken, and our purveyors are herein said to have their provision from the popish shambles: for by Pighius and Harding, to prove that Christ alone is not head of the Church, this distinction they say is brought, that according to the inward influence of grace, Christ only is head; but according to outward government the being head is a thing common with him to others.

To raise up falsehoods of old condemned, and to bring that for confirmation of any thing doubtful, which hath already been sufficiently proved an error, and is worthily so taken, this would justly deserve censuring. But shall manifest truth be therefore reproached, because men in some things convicted of manifest untruth have at any time taught or alleged it? If too much eagerness against their adversaries had not made them forget themselves, they might remember where being charged as maintainers of those very things, for which others before them have been condemned of heresy, yet lest the name of any such heretic holding the same which they do should make them odious, they stick not frankly to profess, "that they are not afraid to consent in some points with Jews and Turks." Which defence, for all that, were a very weak buckler for such as should consent with Jews and Turks, in that which they have been abhorred and hated for of the Church.

But as for this distinction of headship, spiritual and mystical in Jesus

Christ, ministerial and outward in others besides Christ; what cause is to dislike either Harding, or Pighius, or any other besides for it? That which they have been reproved for is, not because they did herein utter an untruth, but such a truth as was not sufficient to bear up the cause which they did thereby seek to maintain. By this distinction they have both truly and sufficiently proved that the name of head, importing power of dominion over the Church, might be given unto others besides Christ, without prejudice unto any part of his honour. That which they should have made manifest was, that the name of Head, importing the power of universal dominion over the whole Church of Christ militant, doth, and that by divine right, appertain unto the Pope of Rome. They did prove it lawful to grant unto others besides Christ the power of headship in a different kind from his; but they should have proved it lawful to challenge, as they did to the bishop of Rome, a power universal in that different kind. Their fault was therefore in exacting wrongfully so great power as they challenged in that kind, and not in making two kinds of power, unless some reason can be shewed for which this distinction of power should be thought erroneous and false.

[10.] A little they stir, although in vain, to prove that we cannot with truth make any such distinction of power, whereof the one kind should agree unto Christ only, and the other to be further communicated. Thus therefore they argue: "If there be no head but Christ, in respect of the spiritual government, there is no head but he in respect of the word, sacraments, and discipline, administered by those whom he hath appointed, forasmuch as that is also his spiritual government." Their meaning is, that whereas we make two kinds of power, of which two, the one being spiritual is proper unto Christ; the other men are capable of, because it is visible and external: we do amiss altogether, they think, in so distinguishing, forasmuch as the visible and external power of regiment over the Church, is only in relation unto the word, the sacraments, and discipline, administered by such as Christ hath appointed thereunto, and the exercise of this power is also his spiritual government: therefore we do but vainly imagine a visible and external power in the Church differing from his spiritual power.

Such disputes as this do somewhat resemble the wonted practising of well-willers upon their friends in the pangs of death, whose manner is even to put smoke in their nostrils, and so to fetch them again, although they know it a matter impossible to keep them living. The kind affection which the favourers of this labouring cause bear towards it will not suffer them to see it die, although by what means they should be able to make it live, they do not see. But they may see that these wrestlings will not help. Can they be ignorant how little it booteth to overcast so clear a light with some mist of ambiguity in the name of spiritual regiment?

To make things therefore so plain that henceforth a child's capacity may serve rightly to conceive our meaning: we make the spiritual regiment of Christ to be generally that whereby his Church is ruled and governed in things spiritual. Of this general we make two distinct kinds; the one invisibly exercised by Christ himself in his own person; the other outwardly administered by them whom Christ doth allow to be the rulers and guiders of his Church. Touching the former of these two kinds, we teach that Christ in regard thereof is peculiarly termed the Head of the Church of God; neither can any other creature in that sense and meaning be termed head besides him, because it importeth the conduct and government of our souls by the hand of that blessed Spirit wherewith we are sealed and marked, as being peculiarly his. Him only therefore we do acknowledge to be that Lord, which dwelleth, liveth and reigneth in our hearts; him only to be that Head, which giveth salvation and life unto his body; him only to be that fountain, from whence the influence of heavenly grace distilleth, and is derived into all parts, whether the word, or sacraments, or discipline, or whatsoever be the mean whereby it floweth. As for the power of administering those things in the Church of Christ, which power we call the power of order, it is indeed both Spiritual and His; Spiritual, because such duties properly concern the Spirit; His, because by him it was instituted. Howbeit neither spiritual, as that which is inwardly and invisibly exercised; nor his, as that which he himself in person doth exercise.

Again, that power of dominion which is indeed the point of this controversy, and doth also belong to the second kind of spiritual regiment, namely unto that regiment which is external and visible; this likewise being spiritual in regard of the matter about which it dealeth, and being his, inasmuch as he approveth whatsoever is done by it, must notwithstanding be distinguished also from that power whereby he himself in person administereth the former kind of his own spiritual regiment, because he himself in person doth not administer this. We do not, therefore, vainly imagine, but truly and rightly discern a power external and visible in the Church, exercised by men, and severed in nature from that spiritual power of Christ's own regiment, which power is termed spiritual, because it worketh secretly, inwardly, and invisibly; his, because none doth or can personally exercise it, either besides or together with him. So that him only we may name our Head, in regard of this, and yet, in regard of that other power differing from this, term others also besides him heads, without any contradiction at all.

[11.] Which thing may very well serve for answer unto that also which they further allege against the foresaid distinction, namely, "that even in the outward society and assemblies of the Church, where one or two are gathered in his name, either for hearing of the word, or for prayer, or any other church-exercise, our Saviour Christ being in the midst of them as

Mediator, must needs be there as head: and if he be there not idle, but doing the office of the head fully, it followeth that even in the outward society and meetings of the Church no mere man can be called the head of it, seeing that our Saviour Christ doing the whole office of the head himself alone, leaveth nothing to men by doing whereof they may obtain that title."

Which objection I take as being made for nothing but only to maintain argument. For they are not so far gone as to argue thus in sooth and right good earnest. "God standeth," saith the Psalmist [Ps. lxxxii. 1] "in the midst of gods;" if God be there present, he must undoubtedly be present as a God; if he be there not idle, but doing the office of a God fully, it followeth, that God himself alone doing the whole office of a God, leaveth nothing in such assemblies unto any other, by doing whereof they may obtain so high a name. The Psalmist therefore hath spoken amiss, and doth ill to call judges gods. Not so; for as God hath his office differing from theirs, and doth fully discharge it even in the very midst of them, so they are not thereby excluded from all kind of duty for which that name should be given unto them also, but in that duty for which it was given them they are encouraged religiously and carefully to order themselves. After the selfsame manner, our Lord and Saviour being in the midst of his Church as Head [is] our comfort, and not the abridgment of any one duty, for performance whereof others are termed heads in another kind than he is.

[12.] If there be of the ancient Fathers which say, "There is but one Head of the Church, Christ; and that the minister which baptizeth cannot be the head of him which is baptized, because Christ is the head of the whole Church: and that Paul could not be the head of the Churches which he planted, because Christ is Head of the whole body;" they understand the name of head in such sort as we grant that it is not appliable to any other, no not in relation to the least part of the whole Church: he which baptizeth, baptizeth into Christ: he which converteth, converteth unto Christ; he which ruleth, ruleth for Christ. The whole Church can have but one to be head as lord and owner of all: wherefore if Christ be Head in that kind, it followeth, that no other can be so else either to the whole or to any part.

Chapter 5

OF THEIR PREROGATIVE TO CALL ASSEMBLIES ABOUT THE GENERAL AFFAIRS OF THE CHURCH

[1.] The consuls of Rome Polybius affirmeth to have had a kind of regal authority, in that they might call together the senate and people whensoever it pleased them. Seeing therefore the affairs of the Church and Christian religion are public affairs, for the ordering whereof more solemn assemblies sometimes are of as great importance and use, as they are for secular affairs; it seemeth no less an act of supreme authority to call the one than the other. Wherefore amongst sundry other prerogatives of Simon's dominion over the Jews, this is reckoned as not the least, "that no man might gather any great assembly in the land without him." [1 Macc. xiv. 44] For so the manner of Jewish regiment had always been, that whether the cause for which men assembled themselves in peaceable, good, and orderly course, were ecclesiastical or civil, supreme authority should assemble them. David gathered all Israel together unto Jerusalem; when the ark was to be removed, he assembled the sons of Aaron and the Levites [1 Chr. xv. 3, 4]. Solomon did the like at such time as the temple was to be dedicated [1 Reg. viii. 1]: when the Church was to be reformed, Asa in his time did the same: the same upon like occasions done afterwards by Joas, Ezekias, Josias, and others [2 Chr. xv. 9; xxiv. 5; xxx. 1; xxxiv. 29].

[2.] The ancient imperial law forbiddeth such assemblies as the emperor's authority did not cause to be made. Before emperors became Christian, the Church had never any synod general, their greatest meetings consisted of bishops and others, the gravest in each province. As for the civil governor's authority, it suffered them only as things not regarded or accounted of, at such times as it did suffer them. So that what right a Christian king hath as touching assemblies of that kind we are not able to judge, till we come unto later times, when religion had won the hearts of the highest powers. Constantine (as Pighius doth grant) was not only the first that ever did call any general council together, but even the first that devised the calling of them for consultation about the business of God. After he had once given the example, his successors a long time followed the same; insomuch that St. Jerome, to disprove the authority of a synod which was pretended to be general, used this as a forcible argument, "Dic quis imperator hanc synodum jusserit convocari."* Their answer hereunto is no answer, which say, "that emperors did not this without conference had with bishops:" for to our purpose it is enough, if the clergy alone did it not otherwise than by the leave or appointment of their sovereign lords and kings.

Whereas therefore it is on the contrary side alleged, that Valentinian the elder being requested by Catholic bishops to grant that there might be a synod for the ordering of matters called in question by the Arians, answered, that he being one of the laity might not meddle with such affairs, and thereupon wished, that the priests and bishops, to whom the care of those things belonged, should meet and consult thereof by themselves wheresoever they thought good: we must together with the emperor's

* ["Tell me which emperor commanded this synod to be called together."]

speech weigh the occasion and the drift thereof. Valentinian and Valens, the one a Catholic, the other an Arian, were emperors together: Valens the governor of the east, Valentinian of the west empire. Valentinian therefore taking his journey from the east part into the west, and passing for that intent through Thracia, the bishops there which held the soundness of Christian belief, because they knew that Valens was their professed enemy, and therefore if the other were once departed out of those quarters, the Catholic cause was like to find small favour, moved presently Valentinian about a council to be assembled under the countenance of his authority; who by likelihood considering what inconvenience might thereby grow, inasmuch as it could not but be a mean to incense Valens the more against them, refused himself to be author of or present at any such assembly; and of this his denial gave them a colourable reason, to wit, that he was although an emperor, yet a secular person, and therefore not able in matters of so great obscurity to sit as a competent judge; but, if they which were bishops and learned men did think good to consult thereof together, they might. Whereupon when they could not obtain that which they most desired, yet that which was granted them they took, and forthwith had a council. Valentinian went on towards Rome, they remaining in consultation till Valens which accompanied him returned back; so that now there was no remedy, but either to incur a manifest contempt, or else at the hands even of Valens himself to seek approbation of that they had done. To him, therefore, they became suitors: his answer was short, "Either Arianism, or else exile, which they would;" whereupon their banishment ensued. Let reasonable men therefore now be judges, how much this example of Valentinian doth make against the authority, which we say that sovereign rulers may lawfully have as concerning synods and meetings ecclesiastical.

The clergy, in such wise gathered together, is an ecclesiastical senate, which with us, as in former times the chiefest prelate at his discretion did use to assemble, so that afterwards in such considerations as have been before specified, it seemeth more meet to annex the said prerogative unto the crown. The plot of reformed discipline not liking hereof so well, taketh order that every former assembly before it break up should itself appoint both the time and place of their after meeting again. But because I find not any thing on that side particularly alleged against us herein, a longer disputation about so plain a cause shall not need.

Chapter 6
OF THEIR POWER IN MAKING ECCLESIASTICAL LAWS

[1.] The natural subject of power civil all men confess to be the body of the commonwealth: the good or evil estate whereof dependeth so much upon the power of making laws, that in all well settled states, yea though they be monarchies, yet diligent care is evermore had that the commonwealth do not clean resign up herself and make over this power wholly into the hands of any one. For this cause William, whom we call the Conqueror, making war against England in right of his title to the crown, and knowing that as inheritor thereof he could not lawfully change the laws of the land by himself, for that the English commonwealth had not invested her kings before with the fulness of so great power; therefore he took the style and title of a conqueror. Wherefore, as they themselves cannot choose but grant that the natural subject of power to make laws civil is the commonwealth; so we affirm that in like congruity the true original subject of power also to make church-laws is the whole entire body of that church for which they are made. Equals cannot impose laws and statutes upon their equals. Therefore neither may any one man indifferently impose canons ecclesiastical upon another, nor yet one church upon another. If they go about at any time to do it, they must either shew some commission sufficient for their warrant, or else be justly condemned of presumption in the sight both of God and men. But nature itself doth abundantly authorize the Church to make laws and orders for her children that are within her. For every whole thing, being naturally of greater power than is any part thereof, that which a whole church will appoint may be with reason exacted indifferently of any within the compass of the same church, and so bind all unto strict obedience.

[2.] The greatest agents of the bishop of Rome's inordinate sovereignty strive against no one point with such earnestness as against this, that jurisdiction (and in the name of jurisdiction they also comprehend the power of dominion spiritual) should be thought originally to be the right of the whole Church; and that no person hath or can have the same, otherwise than derived from the body of the Church.

The reason wherefore they can in no wise brook this opinion is, as Friar Soto confesseth, because they which make councils above popes do all build upon this ground, and therefore even with teeth and all they that favour the papal throne must hold the contrary. Which thing they do. For, as many as draw the chariot of the pope's preeminence, the first conclusion which they contend for is: "The power of jurisdiction ecclesiastical doth not rest derived from Christ immediately into the whole body of the Church, but into the prelacy." Unto the prelacy alone it belongeth; as ours also do imagine, unto the governors of the Church alone it was first given, and doth appertain, even of very divine right, in every church established to make such laws concerning orders and ceremonies as occasion doth require.

[3.] Wherein they err, for want of observing as they should, in what manner the power whereof we speak was instituted. One thing it is to ordain a power, and another thing to bestow the same being ordained: or, to appoint the special subject of it, or the person in whom it shall rest. Nature hath appointed that there should be in a civil society power to make laws; but the consent of the people (which are that society) hath instituted the prince's person to be the subject wherein supremacy of that power shall reside. The act of instituting such power may and sometimes doth go in time before the act of conferring or bestowing it. And for bestowing it there may be order two ways taken: namely, either by appointing thereunto some certain person, one or many; or else, without any personal determination, and with appointment only of some determinate condition touching the quality of their persons (whosoever they be that shall receive the same), and for the form or manner of taking it.

Now God himself preventeth sometimes these communities, himself nominateth and appointeth sometimes the subject wherein their power shall rest, and by whom either in whole or in part it shall be exercised; which thing he did often in the commonwealth of Israel. Even so Christ having given unto his Church the power whereof we speak, what she doth by her appointed agents, that duty though they discharge, yet is it not theirs peculiarly, but hers; her power it is which they do exercise. But Christ hath sometimes prevented his Church, conferring that power and appointing it unto certain persons himself, which otherwise the Church might have done. Those persons excepted which Christ himself did immediately bestow such power upon, the rest succeeding have not received power as they did, Christ bestowing it upon their persons; but the power which Christ did institute in the Church they from the Church do receive, according to such laws and canons as Christ hath prescribed, and the light of nature or Scripture taught men to institute.

But in truth the whole body of the Church being the first original subject of all mandatory and coercive power within itself, in case a monarch of the world together with his whole kingdom under him receive Christianity, the question is whether the monarch of that commonwealth may without offence or breach of the law of God have and exercise power of dominion ecclesiastical within the compass of his own territories, in such ample sort as the kings of this land may do by the laws thereof.

[4.] The case is not like when such assemblies are gathered together by supreme authority concerning other affairs of the Church, and when they meet about the making of ecclesiastical laws or statutes. For in the one they are only to advise, in the other they are to decree. The persons which are of the one, the King doth voluntarily assemble, as being in respect of gravity fit to consult withal; them which are of the other he calleth by prescript of law, as having right to be thereunto called. Finally, the one are but themselves, and their sentence hath but the weight of their own judgment; the other represent the whole clergy, and their voices are as much as if all did give personal verdict. Now the question is, Whether the clergy alone so assembled ought to have the whole power of making ecclesiastical laws, or else consent of the laity may thereunto be made necessary, and the King's assent so necessary, that his sole denial may be of force to stay them from being laws.

WHAT LAWS MAY BE MADE FOR THE AFFAIRS OF THE CHURCH, AND TO WHOM THE POWER OF MAKING THEM APPERTAINETH

[5.] If they with whom we dispute were uniform, strong and constant in that which they say, we should not need to trouble ourselves about their persons to whom the power of making laws for the Church belongeth. For they are sometimes very vehement in contention, that from the greatest thing unto the least about the Church, all must needs be immediately from God. And to this they apply the pattern of the ancient tabernacle which God delivered unto Moses, and was therein so exact, that there was not left so much as the least pin for the wit of man to devise in the framing of it. To this they often apply that strict and severe charge which God so often gave concerning his own law, "Whatsoever I command you, take heed ye do it; thou shalt put nothing thereunto, thou shalt take nothing from it;" [Deut. iv. 2; xii. 32; Jos. i. 7] nothing, whether it be great or small. Yet sometime bethinking themselves better, they speak as acknowledging that it doth suffice to have received in such sort the principal things from God, and that for other matters the Church hath sufficient authority to make laws. Whereupon they now have made it a question, what persons they are whose right it is to take order for the Church's affairs, when the institution of any new thing therein is requisite.

Laws may be requisite to be made either concerning things that are only to be known and believed in, or else touching that which is to be done by the Church of God. The law of nature and the law of God are sufficient for declaration in both what belongeth unto each man separately, as his soul is the spouse of Christ, yea so sufficient, that they plainly and fully shew whatsoever God doth require by way of necessary introduction unto the state of everlasting bliss. But as a man liveth joined with others in common society, and belongeth unto the outward politic body of the Church, albeit the said law of nature and of scripture have in this respect also made manifest the things that are of greatest necessity; nevertheless, by reason of new occasions still arising which the Church having care of souls must needs take order for as need requireth, hereby it cometh to pass, that there is and ever will be great use even of human laws and ordinances, deducted by way of discourse as conclusions from the former divine and natural, serving for principles thereunto.

No man doubteth, but that for matters of action and practice in the affairs of God, for the manner of divine service, for order in ecclesiastical proceedings about the regiment of the Church, there may be oftentimes cause very urgent to have laws made: but the reason is not so plain wherefore human laws should appoint men what to believe. Wherefore in this we must note two things: First, that in matter of opinion, the law doth not make that to be truth which before was not, as in matters of action it causeth that to be duty which was not before, but it manifesteth only and giveth men notice of that to be truth, the contrary whereunto they ought not before to have believed. Secondly, that as opinions do cleave to the understanding, and are in heart assented unto, it is not in the power of any human law to command them, because to prescribe what men shall think belongeth only unto God. "Corde creditur, ore fit confessio," saith the Apostle [Rom. x. 10]. As opinions are either fit or inconvenient to be professed, so man's law hath to determine of them. It may for public unity's sake require men's professed assent, or prohibit contradiction to special articles, wherein, as there haply hath been controversy what is true, so the same were like to continue still, not without grievous detriment to a number of souls, except law to remedy that evil should set down a certainty which no man is to gainsay. Wherefore as in regard of divine laws, which the Church receiveth from God, we may unto every man of wisdom apply those words of Solomon, "*Conserva, fili mi, præcepta patris tui*: My son, keep thou thy father's precepts;" [Prov. vi. 20] even so concerning the statutes and ordinances which the Church itself maketh, we may add thereunto the words that follow, "*Et ne dimittas legem matris tuæ*: And forsake not thou thy mother's law."

[6.] It is undoubtedly a thing even natural, that all free and independent societies should themselves make their own laws, and that this power should belong to the whole, not to any certain part of a politic body, though haply some one part may have greater sway in that action than the rest: which thing being generally fit and expedient in the making of all laws, we see no cause why to think otherwise in laws concerning the service of God; which in all well-ordained states and commonwealths is the first thing that law hath care to provide for. When we speak of the right which naturally belongeth to a commonwealth, we speak of that which needs must belong to the Church of God. For if the commonwealth be Christian, if the people which are of it do publicly embrace the true religion, this very thing doth make it the Church, as hath been shewed. So that unless the verity and purity of religion do take from them which embrace it that power wherewith otherwise they are possessed, look what authority as touching laws for religion a commonwealth hath simply it must of necessity being Christian have the same as touching laws for Christian religion.

[7.] It will be therefore perhaps alleged, that a part of the verity of Christian religion is to hold the power of making ecclesiastical laws a thing appropriated unto the clergy in their synods; and that whatsoever is by their only voices agreed upon, it needeth no further approbation to give unto it the strength of a law: as may plainly appear by the canons of that first most venerable assembly [Acts xv. 7, 13, 23], where those things which the Apostles and James had concluded, were afterward published and imposed upon the churches of the Gentiles abroad as laws, the records thereof remaining still in the book of God for a testimony, that the power of making ecclesiastical laws belongeth to the successors of the Apostles, bishops and prelates of the Church of God.

To this we answer, that the council of Jerusalem is no argument for the power of the clergy alone to make laws. For first, there hath not been since any council of like authority to that in Jerusalem: secondly, the cause why that was of such authority came by a special accident: thirdly, the reason why other councils being not like unto that in nature, the clergy in them should have no power to make laws by themselves alone, is in truth so forcible, that except some commandment of God to the contrary can be shewed, it ought notwithstanding the foresaid example to prevail.

The decrees of the council of Jerusalem were not as the canons of other ecclesiastical assemblies, human, but very divine ordinances: for which cause the churches were far and wide commanded every where to see them kept [Acts xvi. 4], no otherwise than if Christ himself had personally on earth been the author of them.

The cause why that council was of so great authority and credit above all others which have been since, is expressed in those words of principal observation, "Unto the Holy Ghost and to us it hath seemed good:" [Acts xv. 28] which form of speech, though other councils have likewise used, yet neither could they themselves mean, nor may we so understand them, as if both were in equal sort assisted with the power of the Holy Ghost; but the later had the favour of that general assistance and presence which Christ doth promise [Matt. xvi.] unto all his, according to the quality of their several estates and callings; the former, that grace of special, miraculous, rare, and extraordinary illumination, in relation whereunto the Apostle, comparing the Old Testament and the New together, termeth [2 Cor. iii. 6] the one a Testament of the letter, for that God delivered it written in stone, the other a Testament of the Spirit, because God imprinted it in the hearts and declared it by the tongues of his chosen Apostles through the power of the Holy Ghost, framing both their conceits and speeches in more divine and incomprehensible manner. Wherefore inasmuch as the Council of Jerusalem did chance to consist of men so enlightened, it had authority greater than were meet for any other council besides to challenge, wherein no such kind of persons are.

[8.] As now the state of the Church doth stand, kings being not then that which now they are, and the clergy not now that which then they were: till it be proved that some special law of Christ hath for ever annexed unto the clergy alone the power to make ecclesiastical laws, we are to hold it a thing most consonant with equity and reason, that no ecclesiastical law be made in a Christian commonwealth, without consent as well of the laity as of the clergy, but least of all without consent of the highest power.

For of this thing no man doubteth, namely, that in all societies, companies, and corporations, what severally each shall be bound unto, it must be with all their assents ratified. Against all equity it were that a man should suffer detriment at the hands of men, for not observing that which he never did either by himself or by others, mediately or immediately, agree unto; much more that a king should constrain all others unto the strict observation of any such human ordinance as passeth without his own approbation. In this case therefore especially that vulgar axiom is of force, "Quod omnes tangit ab omnibus tractari et approbari debet."* Whereupon Pope Nicholas, although otherwise not admitting lay-persons, no not emperors themselves to be present at synods, doth notwithstanding seem to allow of their presence when matters of faith are determined, whereunto all men must stand bound: "Ubinam legistis imperatores, antecessores vestros, synodalibus conventibus interfuisse; nisi forsitan in quibus de fide tractatum est, quæ universalis est, quæ omnibus communis est, quæ non solum ad clericos, verum etiam ad laicos et omnes pertinet Christianos?"† A law, be it civil or ecclesiastical, is as a public obligation, wherein seeing that the whole standeth charged, no reason it should pass without his privity and will, whom principally the whole doth depend upon. "Sicut laici jurisdictionem clericorum perturbare, ita clerici jurisdictionem laicorum non debent imminuere," saith Innocent: "As the laity should not hinder the clergy's jurisdiction, so neither is it reason that the laity's right should be abridged by the clergy." But were it so that the clergy alone might give laws unto all the rest, forasmuch as every estate doth desire to enlarge the bounds of their own liberties, is it not easy to see how injurious this might prove unto men of other condition? Peace and justice are maintained by preserving unto every order their rights, and by keeping all estates as it were in an even balance. Which thing is no way better done, than if the king, their common parent, whose care is presumed to extend most indifferently over all, do bear the chiefest sway in the making of laws which all must be ordered by.

* ["What touches all ought to be considered and approved by all."]

† ["Where have you read that the emperors before you took part in the work of synods, except perhaps in those where there was consideration of the faith, which is universal, common to all, and which pertains not only to clerics but also to laymen and all Christians?"]

[9.] Wherefore, of them which in this point attribute most to the clergy, I would demand what evidence there is, which way it may clearly be shewed, that, in ancient kingdoms Christian, any canon devised by the clergy alone in their synods, whether provincial, national, or general, hath by mere force of their agreement taken place as a law, making all men constrainable to be obedient thereunto, without any other approbation from the king before or afterwards required in that behalf? But what speak we of ancient kingdoms, when at this day, even in the papacy itself, the very Tridentine council hath not every where as yet obtained to have in all points the strength of ecclesiastical law. Did not Philip, king of Spain, publishing that council in the Low Countries, add thereunto an express clause of special provision, that the same should in no wise prejudice, hurt, or diminish any kind of privilege which the king or his vassals aforetime had enjoyed, either touching possessory judgments of ecclesiastical livings, or concerning nominations thereunto, or belonging to whatsoever rights they had else in such affairs? If therefore the king's exception taken against some part of the canons contained in that council, were a sufficient bar to make them of none effect within his territories; it followeth that the like exception against any other part had been also of like efficacy, and so consequently that no part thereof had obtained the strength of a law, if he which excepted against a part had so done against the whole: as, what reason was there but that the same authority which limited might quite and clean have refused that council? Whoso alloweth the said act of the Catholic king for good and lawful must grant that the canons even of general councils have but the force of wise men's opinions concerning that whereof they treat till they be publicly assented unto where they are to take place as laws; and that, in giving such public assent as maketh a Christian kingdom subject unto those laws, the king's authority is the chiefest. That which an University of men, a company or corporation doth without consent of their rector, is as nothing. Except therefore we make the king's authority over the clergy less in the greatest things, than the power of the meanest governor is in all things over the college or society which is under him; how should we think it a matter decent, that the clergy should impose laws, the supreme governor's assent not asked?

[10.] Yea that which is more, the laws thus made, God himself doth in such sort authorize, that to despise them, is to despise in them him. It is a loose and licentious opinion, which the Anabaptists have embraced, holding that a Christian man's liberty is lost, and the soul which Christ hath redeemed unto himself injuriously drawn into servitude under the yoke of human power, if any law be now imposed besides the Gospel of Christ, in obedience whereunto the Spirit of God, and not the constraint of men, is to lead us, according to that of the blessed Apostle, "Such as are led by the Spirit of God, they are the sons of God," [Rom. viii. 14] and not such as live in thraldom unto men. Their judgment is therefore that the Church of Christ should admit no lawmakers but the evangelists, no courts but presbyteries, no punishments but ecclesiastical censures.

As against this sort, we are to maintain the use of human laws, and the continual necessity of making them from time to time, as long as this present world doth last; so likewise the authority of laws so made doth need much more by us to be strengthened against another sort, who, although they do not utterly condemn the making of laws in the Church, yet make they a great deal less account of them than they should do. There are which think simply of human laws, that they can in no sort touch the conscience; that to break and transgress them cannot make men in the sight of God culpable as sin doth; only when we violate such laws, we do thereby make ourselves obnoxious unto external punishment in this world, so that the magistrate may in regard of such offence committed justly correct the offender, and cause him without injury to endure such pain as the law doth appoint; but further it reacheth not. For first, the conscience is the proper court of God, the guiltiness thereof is sin, and the punishment eternal death: men are not able to make any law that shall command the heart, it is not in them to make the inward conceit a crime, or to appoint for any crime other punishment than corporal: their laws therefore can have no power over the soul, neither can the heart of man be polluted by transgressing them. St. Augustine rightly defineth sin to be that which is spoken, done or desired, not against any law, but against the law of the living God. The law of God is proposed unto men, as a glass wherein to behold the stains and spots of their sinful souls. By it they are to judge themselves, and when they find themselves to have transgressed against it, then to bewail their offences with David [Ps. li. 4], "Against thee only, O Lord, have I sinned, and done wickedly in thy sight;" that so our present tears may extinguish the flames, which otherwise we are to feel, and which God in that day shall condemn the wicked unto, when they shall render account of the evil which they have done, not by violating statute laws and canons, but by disobedience unto his law and word.

For our better instruction therefore in this point, first we must note, that the law of God himself doth require at our hands subjection. "Be ye subject," saith St. Peter [1 Pet. ii. 13]; and St. Paul [Rom. xiii. 1], "Let every soul be subject; subject all unto such powers as are set over us." For if such as are not set over us require our subjection, we by denying it are not disobedient to the law of God, or undutiful unto higher powers; because though they be such in regard of them over whom they have lawful dominion, yet having not so over us, unto us they are not such.

Subjection therefore we owe, and that by the law of God; we are in conscience bound to yield it even unto every of them that hold the seats of authority and power in relation unto us. Howbeit, not all kind of subjection unto every such kind of power. Concerning Scribes and Pharisees, our Saviour's precept was [Matt. xxiii. 3], "Whatsoever they shall tell you, do it;" was it his meaning, that if they should at any time enjoin the people to levy an army, or to sell their lands and goods for the furtherance of so great an enterprize; and in a word, that whatsoever simply it were which they did command, they ought without any exception forthwith to be obeyed? No, but "whatsoever they shall tell you," must be understood *in pertinentibus ad Cathedram*, it must be construed with limitation, and restrained unto things of that kind which did belong to their place and power. For they had not power general, absolutely given them to command in all things.

The reason why we are bound in conscience to be subject unto all such powers is, because "all powers are of God" [Rom. xiii. 1]. They are of God either instituting or permitting them. Power is then of divine institution, when either God himself doth deliver, or men by light of nature find out the kind thereof. So that the power of parents over children, and of husbands over their wives, the power of all sorts of superiors, made by consent of commonwealths within themselves, or grown from agreement amongst nations, such power is of God's own institution in respect of the kind thereof. Again, if respect be had unto those particular persons to whom the same is derived, if they either receive it immediately from God, as Moses and Aaron did; or from nature, as parents do; or from men by a natural and orderly course, as every governor appointed in any commonwealth, by the orders thereof, doth: then is not the kind of their power only of God's institution, but the derivation thereof also into their persons is from him. He hath placed them in their rooms, and doth term them his ministers; subjection therefore is due unto all such powers, inasmuch as they are of God's own institution, even then when they are of man's creation, *omni humanæ creaturæ*: which things the heathens themselves do acknowledge:

Σ κηπτοῦχος βασιλεὺς, ᾧτε Ζεὺς κῦδος ἔδωκεν

As for them that exercise power altogether against order, although the kind of power which they have may be of God, yet is their exercise thereof against God, and therefore not of God, otherwise than by permission, as all injustice is.

Touching such acts as are done by that power which is according to his institution, that God in like sort doth authorize them, and account them to be his; though it were not confessed, it might be proved undeniable. For if that be accounted our deed, which others do, whom we have appointed to be our agents, how should God but approve those deeds, even as his own, which are done by virtue of that commission and power which he hath

* "A sceptre-swaying king, to whom even Jupiter himself hath given power and commandment." Hom. Il. lib. i. [ver. 279.]

given. "Take heed," saith Jehoshaphat unto his judges, "be careful and circumspect what ye do; ye do not execute the judgments of men, but of the Lord." [2 Chron. xix. 6] The authority of Cæsar over the Jews, from whence was it? Had it any other ground than the law of nations, which maketh kingdoms, subdued by just war, to be subject unto their conquerors? By this power Cæsar exacting tribute, our Saviour confesseth it to be his right, a right which could not be withheld without injury; yea disobedience herein unto him had been rebellion against God.

Usurpers of power, whereby we do not mean them that by violence have aspired unto places of highest authority, but them that use more authority than they did ever receive in form and manner beforementioned (for so they may do, whose title unto the rooms of authority which they possess, no man can deny to be just and lawful: even as contrariwise some men's proceedings in government have been very orderly, who notwithstanding did not attain to be made governors without great violence and disorder) such usurpers therefore, as in the exercise of their power do more than they have been authorized to do, cannot in conscience bind any man unto obedience.

The subjection which we owe unto lawful powers, doth not only import that we should be under them by order of our state, but that we shew all submission towards them both by honour and obedience. He that resisteth them, resisteth God: and resisted they are, if either the authority itself which they exercise be denied, as by Anabaptists all secular jurisdiction is; or if resistance be made but only so far forth as doth touch their persons which are invested with power (for they which said, *Nolumus hunc regnare*, did not utterly exclude regiment; nor did they wish all kind of government clean removed, which would not at the first have David govern); or if that which they do by virtue of their power, namely, their laws, edicts, sentences, or other acts of jurisdiction, be not suffered to take effect, contrary to the blessed Apostle's most holy precept, "Obey them that have the oversight of you." [Heb. xiii. 17] Or if they do take effect, yet is not the will of God thereby satisfied neither, as long as that which we do is contemptuously or repiningly done, because we can do no otherwise. In such sort the Israelites in the desert obeyed Moses, and were notwithstanding deservedly plagued for disobedience. The Apostle's precept therefore is, "Be subject even for God's cause; be subject, not for fear, but for mere conscience, knowing, that he which resisteth them, purchaseth unto himself condemnation." Disobedience therefore unto laws which are made by men is not a thing of so small account as some would make it.

Howbeit, too rigorous it were, that the breach of every human law should be held a deadly sin: a mean there is between these extremities, if so be we can find it out.

POWER TO MAKE LAWS

[11.] And concerning their supreme power for making laws for all persons in all causes to be guided by, it is not to be let pass, that the head enemies of this headship are constrained to acknowledge the king endowed even with this very power, so that he may and ought to exercise the same, taking order for the Church and her affairs of what nature or kind soever, in case of necessity: as when there is no lawful ministry, which they interpret then to be (and this surely is a point very markable), whensoever the ministry is wicked. A wicked ministry no lawful ministry? And in such sort no lawful ministry, that what doth belong to them as ministers by right of their calling, the same to be annihilated in respect of their bad quality? Their wickedness in itself a deprivation of right to deal in the affairs of the Church, and a warrant for others to deal in them which are held to be of a clean other society, the members whereof have been before so peremptorily for ever excluded from power of dealing with the affairs of the Church?

They which have once throughly learned this lesson, will quickly be capable perhaps of another equivalent unto it. For if the wickedness of the ministry transfer their right unto the king; in case the king be as wicked as they, to whom then shall the right descend? There is no remedy, all must come by devolution at the length, even as the family of Brown will have it, unto the godly among the people; for confusion to the wise and to the great, the poor and the simple, some Knipperdoling with his retinue, must take the work of the Lord in hand; and the making of church laws must prove to be their right in the end. If not for love of the truth, yet for very shame of so gross absurdities, let these contentions and shifting fancies be abandoned.

The cause which moved them for a time to hold a wicked ministry no lawful ministry; and in this defect of a lawful ministry, kings authorized to make laws and orders for the affairs of the Church, till the Church be well established, is surely this: First, they see that whereas the continual dealing of the kings of Israel in the affairs of the Church doth make now very strongly against them, the burden thereof they shall in time well enough shake off, if it may be obtained that it is for kings lawful indeed to follow those holy examples, howbeit no longer than during the foresaid case of necessity, while the wickedness, and in respect thereof the unlawfulness of the ministry doth continue. Secondly, they perceive right well, that unless they should yield authority unto kings in case of such supposed necessity, the discipline they urge were clean excluded, as long as the clergy of England doth thereunto remain opposite. To open therefore a door for her entrance, there is no remedy but the tenet must be this: that now when the ministry of England is universally wicked, and, in that respect, hath lost all authority, and is become no lawful ministry, no such ministry as hath the right which otherwise should belong unto them, if they were virtuous and godly as their adversaries are; in this necessity the king may do somewhat for the church: that which we do imply in the name of headship, he may both have and exercise till they be entered which will disburden and ease him of it; till they come, the king is licensed to hold that power which we call headship. But what afterwards? In a church [well?] ordered, that which the supreme magistrate hath, is "to see that the laws of God touching his worship, and touching all matters and orders of the Church, be executed and duly observed; to see that every ecclesiastical person do that office whereunto he is appointed; to punish those that fail in their office." In a word, (that which Allen himself acknowledgeth,) unto the earthly power which God hath given him it doth belong to defend the laws of the Church, to cause them to be executed, and to punish the transgressors of the same.

On all sides therefore it is confessed, that to the king belongeth power of maintaining laws made for the church regiment, and of causing them to be observed; but principality of power in making them, which is the thing that we attribute unto kings, this both the one sort and the other do withstand.

Although not both in such sort but that still it is granted by the one that albeit ecclesiastical councils consisting of church officers did frame the laws whereby the church affairs were ordered in ancient times, yet no canon, no not of any council, had the force of a law in the Church, unless it were ratified and confirmed by the emperor being Christian. Seeing therefore it is acknowledged, that it was then the manner of the emperor to confirm the ordinances which were made by the ministers, which is as much in effect to say that the emperor had in church ordinances a voice negative—and that without his confirmation they had not the strength of public ordinances—why are we condemned as giving more unto kings than the Church did in those times, we giving them no more but that supreme power which the emperor did then exercise with much larger scope than at this day any Christian king either doth or possibly can use it over the Church?

Wherein it is, from the purpose altogether, alleged, that Constantine termeth church officers, "Overseers of things within the Church," himself, "of those without the Church": that Hilary beseecheth the emperor Constance to provide that the governors of his provinces should not presume to take upon them the judgment of ecclesiastical causes, unto whom commonwealth matters only belonged: that Ambrose affirmeth palaces to belong unto the emperor, but churches to the minister: the emperor to have authority of the common walls of the city, and not over holy things. For which cause he would never yield to have "the causes of the Church debated in the prince's consistory," but "excused himself to the emperor Valentinian, for that being convented to answer concerning church matters in a civil court, he came not:" that Augustine witnesseth, how the emperor not daring to judge of the bishops' cause, committed it unto the bishops; and was to crave pardon of the bishops, for that by the Donatists' importunity, which made no end of appealing unto him, he was, being weary of them, drawn to give sentence in a matter of theirs. All which hereupon may be inferred reacheth no further than only unto the administration of church affairs, or the determination of strifes and controversies rising about the matter of religion: it proveth that in former ages of the world it hath been judged most convenient for church officers to have the hearing of causes merely ecclesiastical, and not the emperor himself in person to give sentence of them. No one man can be sufficient for all things.

And therefore public affairs are divided, each kind in all well-ordered states allotted unto such kind of persons as reason presumeth fittest to handle them. Reason cannot presume kings ordinarily so skilful as to be personal judges meet for the common hearing and determining of church controversies; but they which are hereunto appointed, and have all their proceedings authorized by such power as may cause them to take effect. The principality of which power in making laws, whereupon all these things depend, is not by any of these allegations proved incommunicable unto kings.

OF THE AUTHORITY OF MAKING LAWS

[12.] There are which wonder that we should count any statute a law, which the high court of parliament in England hath established about the matter of church regiment; the prince and court of parliament having, as they suppose, no more lawful means to give order to the Church and clergy in these things, than they have to make laws for the hierarchies of angels in heaven: that the parliament being a mere temporal court, can neither by the law of nature, nor of God, have competent power to define of such matters; that supremacy of power in this kind cannot belong unto kings, as kings, because pagan emperors, whose princely power was notwithstanding true sovereignty, never challenged thus much over the Church: that power in this kind cannot be the right of any earthly crown, prince, or state, in that they be Christians, forasmuch as if they be Christians, they all owe subjection unto the pastors of their souls: that the prince therefore not having it himself cannot communicate it unto the parliament, and consequently cannot make laws, hear, or determine of the Church's regiment by himself, parliament, or any other court in such sort subjected unto him.

[13.] The parliament of England together with the convocation annexed thereunto, is that whereupon the very essence of all government within this kingdom doth depend; it is even the body of the whole realm; it consisteth of the king, and of all that within the land are subject unto him: for they all are there present, either in person or by such as they voluntarily have derived their very personal right unto. The parliament is a court not so merely temporal as if it might meddle with nothing but only leather and wool. Those days of Queen Mary are not yet forgotten, wherein the realm did submit itself unto the legate of Pope Julius: at which time had they been persuaded as this man seemeth now to be, had they thought that there is no more force in laws made by parliament concerning the Church's affairs, than if men should take upon them to make orders for the hierarchies of angels in heaven, they might have taken all former statutes in that kind as cancelled, and by reason of nullity abrogated in themselves. What need was there that they should bargain with the cardinal, and purchase their pardon by promise made beforehand, that what laws they had made, assented unto, or executed against the bishop of Rome's supremacy, the same they would in that present parliament effectually abrogate and repeal? Had they power to repeal laws made, and none to make laws concerning the regiment of the Church?

Again, when they had by suit obtained his confirmation for such foundation of bishoprics, cathedral churches, hospitals, colleges, and schools; for such marriages before made, for such institutions unto livings ecclesiastical, and for all such judicial processes, as having been ordered according to laws before in force, but contrary to the canons and orders of the church of Rome, were in that respect thought defective; although the cardinal in his letters of dispensation did give validity unto those acts, even *apostolicæ firmitatis robur*, "the very strength of apostolical solidity;" what had all this been without those grand authentical words, "Be it enacted by the authority of this present parliament, that all and singular articles and clauses contained in the said dispensation, shall remain and be reputed and taken to all intents and constructions in the laws of this realm, lawful, good and effectual to be alleged and pleaded in all courts ecclesiastical and temporal, for good and sufficient matter either for the plaintiff or defendant, without any allegation or objection to be made against the validity of them by pretence of any general council, canon, or decree to the contrary." Somewhat belike they thought there was in this mere temporal court, without which the pope's own mere ecclesiastical legate's dispensation had taken small effect in the Church of England; neither did they or the cardinal himself, as then, imagine any thing committed against the law of nature or of God, because they took order for the Church's affairs, and that even in the court of parliament.

The most natural and religious course in making of laws is, that the matter of them be taken from the judgment of the wisest in those things which they are to concern. In matters of God, to set down a form of public prayer, a solemn confession of the articles of Christian faith, rites and ceremonies meet for the exercise of religion; it were unnatural not to think the pastors and bishops of our souls a great deal more fit, than men of secular trades and callings: howbeit, when all which the wisdom of all sorts can do is done for devising of laws in the Church, it is the general consent of all that giveth them the form and vigour of laws, without which they could be no more unto us than the counsels of physicians to the sick: well might they seem as wholesome admonitions and instructions, but laws could they never be without consent of the whole Church, which is the only thing that bindeth each member of the Church to be guided by them. Whereunto both nature and the practice of the Church of God set down in Scripture, is found every way so fully consonant, that God himself would not impose, no not his own laws upon his people by the hand of Moses, [Exod. xix] without their free and open consent. Wherefore to define and determine even of the church's affairs by way of assent and approbation, as laws are defined of in that right of power, which doth give them the force of laws; thus to define of our own church's regiment, the parliament of England hath competent authority.

Touching the supremacy of power which our kings have in this case of making laws, it resteth principally in the strength of a negative voice; which not to give them, were to deny them that without which they were but kings by mere title, and not in exercise of dominion. Be it in states of regiment popular, aristocratical, or regal, principality resteth in that person, or those persons, unto whom is given the right of excluding any kind of law whatsoever it be before establishment. This doth belong unto kings, as kings; pagan emperors even Nero himself had not less, but much more than this in the laws of his own empire. That he challenged not any interest in giving voice in the laws of the church, I hope no man will so construe, as if the cause were conscience, and fear to encroach upon the Apostles' right.

If then it be demanded by what right from Constantine downward, the Christian emperors did so far intermeddle with the church's affairs, either we must herein condemn them utterly, as being over presumptuously bold, or else judge that by a law which is termed *Regia*, that is to say *Royal*, the people having derived into the emperor their whole power for making of laws, and by that means his edicts being made laws, what matter soever they did concern, as imperial dignity endowed them with competent authority and power to make laws for religion, so they were taught by Christianity to use their power, being Christians, unto the benefit of the Church of Christ. Was there any Christian bishop in the world which did then judge this repugnant unto the dutiful subjection which Christians do owe to the pastors of their souls? to whom, in respect of their sacred order, it is not by us, neither may be denied, that kings and princes are as much as the very meanest that liveth under them, bound in conscience to shew themselves gladly and willingly obedient, receiving the seals of salvation, the blessed sacraments, at their hands, as at the hands of our Lord Jesus Christ, with all reverence, not disdaining to be taught and admonished by them, not withholding from them as much as the least part of their due and decent honour. All which, for any thing that hath been alleged, may stand very well without resignation of supremacy of power in making laws, even laws concerning the most spiritual affairs of the Church.

Which laws being made amongst us, are not by any of us so taken or interpreted, as if they did receive their force from power which the prince doth communicate unto the parliament, or to any other court under him, but from power which the whole body of this realm being naturally possessed with, hath by free and deliberate assent derived unto him that ruleth over them, so far forth as hath been declared. So that our laws made concerning religion, do take originally their essence from the power of the whole realm and church of England, than which nothing can be more consonant unto the law of nature and the will of our Lord Jesus Christ.

[14.] To let these go, and to return to our own men; "Ecclesiastical governors," they say, "may not meddle with the making of civil laws, and of laws for the commonwealth; nor the civil magistrate, high or low, with making of orders for the Church." It seemeth unto me very strange, that those men which are in no cause more vehement and fierce, than where they plead that ecclesiastical persons may not κυριεύειν, [*be lords*], should hold that the power of making ecclesiastical laws, which thing is of all other most proper unto dominion, belongeth to none but persons ecclesiastical only. Their oversight groweth herein for want of exact observation, what it is to make a law. Tully, speaking of the law of nature, saith, "That thereof God himself was *inventor, disceptator, lator,* the deviser, the discusser, the deliverer:" wherein he plainly alludeth unto the chiefest part which then did appertain to this public action. For when laws were made, the first thing was to have them devised; the second, to sift them with as much exactness of judgment as any way might be used; the next, by solemn voice of sovereign authority to pass them, and give them the force of laws. It cannot in any reason seem otherwise than most fit, that unto ecclesiastical persons the care of devising ecclesiastical laws be committed, even as the care of civil unto them which are in those affairs most skilful. This taketh not away from ecclesiastical persons all right of giving voice with others, when civil laws are proposed for regiment of that commonwealth, whereof themselves (howsoever now the world would have them annihilate) are notwithstanding as yet a part: much less doth it cut off that part of the power of princes, whereby, as they claim, so we know no reasonable cause wherefore we may not grant them, without offence to Almighty God, so much authority in making of all manner of laws within their own dominions, that neither civil nor ecclesiastical do pass without their royal assent. In devising and discussing of laws, wisdom is specially required: but that which establisheth and maketh them, is power, even power of dominion; the chiefty whereof, amongst us, resteth in the person of the king. Is there any law of Christ's which forbiddeth kings and rulers of the earth to have such sovereign and supreme power in the making of laws, either civil or ecclesiastical? If there be, our controversy hath an end.

[15.] Christ in his church hath not appointed any such law concerning temporal power, as God did of old deliver unto the commonwealth of Israel; but leaving that to be at the world's free choice, his chiefest care was [that] the spiritual law of the Gospel might be published far and wide.

They that received the law of Christ, were for a long time people scattered in sundry kingdoms, Christianity not exempting them from the laws which they had been subject unto, saving only in such cases as those laws did enjoin that which the religion of Christ forbade. Hereupon grew their manifold persecutions throughout all places where they lived: as oft as it thus came to pass, there was no possibility that the emperors and kings under whom they lived, should meddle any whit at all with making laws for the Church. From Christ therefore having received power, who doubteth, but as they did, so they might bind themselves to such orders as seemed fittest for the maintenance of their religion, without the leave of high or low in the commonwealth; forasmuch as in religion it was divided utterly from them, and they from it?

But when the mightiest began to like of the Christian faith; by their means whole free states and kingdoms became obedient unto Christ. Now the question is, whether kings by embracing Christianity do therein receive any such law, as taketh from them the weightiest part of that sovereignty which they had even when they were heathens: whether being infidels they might do more in causes of religion, than now they can by the law of God, being true believers. For whereas in regal states, the king or supreme head of the commonwealth had before Christianity a supreme stroke in the making of laws for religion, he must by embracing Christian religion utterly thereof deprive himself and in such causes become a subject to his own subjects, having even within his own dominions them whose commandment he must obey, unless this power be placed in the hand of some foreign spiritual potentate: so that either a foreign or domestical commander on earth he must needs admit more now than before he had, and that in the chiefest things whereupon commonwealths do stand. But apparent it is unto all men which are not strangers in the doctrine of Jesus Christ, that no state in the world receiving Christianity is by any law therein contained bound to resign the power which they lawfully held before: but over what persons and in what causes soever the same hath been in force, it may so remain and continue still. That which as kings they might do in matter of religion, and did in matter of false religion, being idolaters or superstitious kings, the same they are now even in every respect as fully authorized to do in all affairs pertinent unto the state of true and Christian religion.

Chapter 7

OF THEIR POWER IN MAKING ECCLESIASTICAL GOVERNORS

Touching the advancement of prelates unto their rooms by the king; whereas it seemeth in the eyes of many a thing very strange that prelates, the officers of God's own sanctuary, than which nothing is more sacred, should be made by persons secular; there are that will not have kings be altogether of the laity, but to participate that sanctified power which God hath endued his clergy with, and that in such respect they are anointed with oil. A shift vain and needless. For as much as, if we speak properly, we cannot say kings do make, but that they only do place, bishops. For in a bishop there are these three things to be considered; the power whereby he is distinguished from other pastors; the special portion of the clergy and people over whom he is to exercise that bishoply power; and the place of his seat or throne, together with the profits, preeminences, honours thereunto belonging. The first every bishop hath by consecration; the second his election investeth him with; the third he receiveth of the king alone.

[2.] With consecration the king intermeddleth not further than only by his letters to present such an elect bishop as shall be consecrated. Seeing therefore that none but bishops do consecrate, it followeth that none but they only do give unto every bishop his being. The manner of uniting bishops as heads, unto the flock and clergy under them, hath often altered. For, if some be not deceived, this thing was sometime done even without any election at all. "At the first" (saith he to whom the name of Ambrose is given) "the first created in the college of presbyters was still the bishop. He dying, the next senior did succeed him. Sed quia cœperunt sequentes presbyteri indigni inveniri ad primatus tenendos immutata est ratio, prospiciente concilio; ut non ordo sed meritum crearet episcopum multorum sacerdotum judicio constitutum, ne indignus temere usurparet et esset multis scandalum."*

In elections at the beginning the clergy and the people both had to do, although not both after one sort. The people gave their testimony, and shewed their affection, either of desire or dislike, concerning the party which was to be chosen. But the choice was wholly in the sacred college of presbyters. Hereunto it is that those usual speeches of the ancient do commonly allude: as when Pontius concerning St. Cyprian's election saith, he was chosen "judicio Dei et populi favore," "by the judgment of God and favour of the people," the one branch alluding to the voices of the

* ["But because later presbyters began to be found unworthy of holding primacy, the principle was changed, in the light of due deliberation, so that not order but merit should make a bishop, who would be chosen by the judgment of many priests, lest someone unworthy chance to obtain the office and many be offended."]

ecclesiastical senate which with religious sincerity choose him, the other to the people's affection, who earnestly desired to have him chosen their bishop.

Again, Leo: "No reason doth grant that they should be reckoned amongst bishops, whom neither clergy hath elected nor laity coveted." In like sort Honorius: "Let him only be established bishop in the see of Rome whom Divine judgment and universal consent hath chosen."

[3.] That difference, which is between the form of electing bishops at this day with us, and that which was usual in former ages, riseth from the ground of that right which the kings of this land do claim in furnishing the place where bishops, elected and consecrated, are to reside as bishops. For considering the huge charges which the ancient famous princes of this land have been at, as well in erecting episcopal sees, as also in endowing them with ample possessions; sure of their religious magnificence and bounty we cannot think but to have been most deservedly honoured with those royal prerogatives, [of] taking the benefit which groweth out of them in their vacancy, and of advancing alone unto such dignities what persons they judge most fit for the same. A thing over and besides even therefore the more reasonable; for that, as the king most justly hath preeminence to make lords temporal which are not such by right of birth, so the like preeminence of bestowing where pleaseth him the honour of spiritual nobility also, cannot seem hard, bishops being peers of the realm, and by law itself so reckoned.

Now, whether we grant so much unto kings in this respect, or in the former consideration whereupon the laws have annexed it unto the crown, it must of necessity being granted, both make void whatsoever interest the people aforetime hath had towards the choice of their own bishop, and also restrain the very act of canonical election usually made by the dean and chapter, as with us in such sort it doth, that they neither can proceed unto any election till leave be granted, nor elect any person but that is named unto them. If they might do the one, it would be in them to defeat the king of his profits; if the other, then were the king's preeminences of granting those dignities nothing. And therefore, were it not for certain canons requiring canonical election to be before consecration, I see no cause but that the king's letters patents alone might suffice well enough to that purpose, as by law they do in case those electors should happen not to satisfy the king's pleasure. Their election is now but a matter of form: it is the king's mere grant which placeth, and the bishop's consecration which maketh, bishops.

[4.] Neither do the kings of this land use herein any other than such prerogatives as foreign nations have been accustomed unto.

About the year of our Lord 425, pope Boniface solicited most earnestly the emperor Honorius to take some order that the bishops of Rome might be created without ambitious seeking of the place. A needless petition, if so be the emperor had no right at all in the placing of bishops there. But from the days of Justinian the emperor, about the year 553, Onuphrius himself doth grant that no man was bishop in the see of Rome whom first the emperor by his letters patents did not license to be consecrated. Till in Benedict's time it pleased the emperor to forego that right; which afterwards was restored to Charles with augmentation, and continued in his successors till such time as Hildebrand took it from Henry IV, and ever since the cardinals have held it as at this day.

Had not the right of giving them belonged to the emperors of Rome within the compass of their dominions, what needed Pope Leo the Fourth to trouble Lotharius and Lodowick with those his letters, whereby, having done them to understand that the church called Reatina was without a bishop, he maketh suit that one Colonus might have the room, or, if that were otherwise disposed of, his next request was, "May it please your clemencies to grant unto him the church of Tusculum now likewise void; that by our episcopal authority he being after consecrated may be to Almighty God and your highness therefore thankful."

[5.] Touching other bishopricks, extant there is a very short but a plain discourse, written almost 500 years since, by occasion of that miserable contention raised between the emperor Henry IVth and Pope Hildebrand, named otherwise Gregory the VIIth, not, as Platina would bear men in hand, for that the bishop of Rome would not brook the emperor's simoniacal dealings, but because the right, which Christian kings and emperors had to invest bishops, hindered so much his ambitious designments, that nothing could detain him from attempting to wrest it violently out of their hands.

This treatise I mention, for that it shortly comprehendeth not only the fore-alleged right of the emperor of Rome acknowledged by six several popes, even with bitter execration against whomsoever of their successors that should by word or deed at any time go about to infringe the same, but also further these other specialties appertaining thereunto: first, that the bishops likewise of Spain, England, Scotland, Hungary, had by ancient institution always been invested by their kings, without opposition or disturbance. Secondly, that such was their royal interest, partly for that they were founders of bishopricks, partly because they undertook the defence of them against all ravenous oppressions and wrongs, partly in as much that it was not safe that rooms of so great power and consequence in their estate should without their appointment be held by any under them. And therefore that bishops even then did homage and took their oaths of fealty unto the kings which invested them. Thirdly, that what solemnity or ceremony kings do use in this action it skilleth not, as namely whether they do it by word, or by precept set down in writing, or by delivery of a staff and a ring, or by any other means whatsoever, only that use and custom would, to avoid all offence, be kept. Some base canonists there are, which contend that neither kings nor emperors had ever any right hereunto, saving only by the pope's either grant or toleration. Whereupon not to spend any further labour, we leave their folly to be controlled by men of more ingenuity and judgment even among themselves, Duarenus, Papon, Choppinus, Ægidius, Magister, Arnulphus Rusæus, Costlius, Philippus Probus, and the rest, by whom the right of Christian kings and princes herein is maintained to be such as the bishop of Rome cannot lawfully either withdraw or abridge or hinder.

But of this thing there is with us no question, although with them there be. The laws and customs of the realm approving such regalities, in case no reason thereof did appear, yet are they hereby abundantly warranted unto us, except some law of God or nature to the contrary could be shewed. How much more, when they have been every where thought so reasonable that Christian kings throughout the world use and exercise, if not altogether, yet surely with very little odds the same. So far that Gregory the Tenth forbidding such regalities to be newly begun where they were not in former times, if any do claim those rights from the first foundation of churches, or by ancient custom, of them he only requireth that neither they nor their agents damnify the Church of God by using the said prerogatives.

[6.] Now as there is no doubt but the church of England by this means is much eased of some inconveniences, so likewise a special care there is requisite to be had, that other evils no less dangerous may not grow. By the history of former times it doth appear, that when the freedom of elections was most large, men's dealings and proceedings therein were not the least faulty.

Of the people St. Jerome complaineth that their judgments many times went much awry, and that in allowing of their bishops every man favoured his own quality; every one's desire was, not so much to be under the regiment of good and virtuous men, as of them which were like himself. What man is there whom it doth not exceedingly grieve to read the tumults, tragedies, and schisms, which were raised by occasion of the clergy at such time as, diverse of them standing for some one place, there was not any kind of practice, though never so unhonest or vile, left unassayed whereby men might supplant their competitors and the one side foil the other. Sidonius, speaking of a bishoprick void in his time, "The decease of the former bishop," saith he, "was an alarum to such as would labour for the room: whereupon the people, forthwith betaking themselves unto parts, storm on each side: few there are that make suit for the advancement of any other man; many who not only offer, but enforce themselves. All things light, variable, counterfeit: what should I say? I see not any thing plain and open but impudence only."

In the church of Constantinople about the election of St. Chrysostom, by reason that some strove mightly for him and some for Nectarius, the troubles growing had not been small, but that Arcadius the emperor interposed himself: even as at Rome the emperor Valentinian, whose forces were hardly able to establish Damasus bishop, and to compose the strife between him and his competitor Ursicinus, about whose election the blood of a hundred and thirty-seven was already shed. Where things did not break out into so manifest and open flames, yet between them which obtained the place and such as before withstood their promotion, that secret heart burning often grew, which could not afterwards be easily slaked. Insomuch that Pontius doth note it as a rare point of virtue in Cyprian, that whereas some were against his election, he notwithstanding dealt ever after in most friendly manner with them, all men wondering that so good a memory was so easily able to forget.

[7.] These and other the like hurts accustomed to grow from ancient elections we do not feel. Howbeit, lest the Church in more hidden sort should sustain even as grievous detriment by that order which is now of force, we are most humbly to crave at the hands of our sovereign kings and governors, the highest patrons which this church of Christ hath on earth, that it would please them to be advertised thus much.

Albeit these things which have been sometimes done by any sort may afterwards appertain unto others, and so the kind of agents vary as occasions daily growing shall require; yet sundry unremovable and unchangeable burthens of duty there are annexed unto every kind of public action, which burthens in this case princes must know themselves to stand now charged with in God's sight no less than the people and the clergy, when the power of electing their prelates did rest fully and wholly in them. A fault it had been if they should in choice have preferred any whom desert of most holy life and the gift of divine wisdom did not commend; a fault, if they had permitted long the rooms of the principal pastors of God to continue void; not to preserve the church patrimony as good to each successor as any predecessor did enjoy the same, had been in them a most odious and grievous fault. Simply good and evil do not lose their nature: that which was, is the one or the other, whatsoever the subject of either be. The faults mentioned are in kings by so much greater, for that in what churches they exercise those regalities whereof we do now entreat, the same churches they have received into their special care and custody, with no less effectual obligation of conscience than the tutor standeth bound in for the person and state of that pupil whom he hath solemnly taken upon him to protect and keep. All power is given unto edification, none to the overthrow and destruction of the Church.

Concerning therefore the [fourth] branch of spiritual dominion thus much may suffice; seeing that they with whom we contend do not directly oppose themselves against regalities, but only so far forth as generally they hold that no church-dignity should be granted without consent of the common people, and that there ought not to be in the Church of Christ any episcopal rooms for princes to use their regalities in. Of both which questions we have sufficiently spoken before.

Chapter 8

OF THEIR POWER IN JUDGEMENT ECCLESIASTICAL

Touching the king's supereminent authority in commanding, and in the judging of causes ecclesiastical; first, to explain therein our meaning, it hath been taken as if we did hold, that kings may prescribe what themselves think good to be done in the service of God; how the word shall be taught, how sacraments administered: that kings may personally sit in the consistory where bishops do, hearing and determining what causes soever do appertain unto the courts: that kings and queens in their own proper persons are by judicial sentence to decide the questions which rise about matter of faith and Christian religion: that kings may excommunicate: finally, that kings may do whatsoever is incident unto the office and duty of an ecclesiastical judge. Which opinion because we count as absurd as they who have fathered the same upon us, we do them to wit that thus our meaning is, and no otherwise: There is not within this realm any ecclesiastical officer, that may by the authority of his own place command universally throughout the king's dominions; but they of his people whom one may command, are to another's commandment unsubject: only the king's royal power is of so large compass, that no man commanded by him according to order of law, can plead himself to be without the bounds and limits of that authority; I say, according to order of law, because with us the highest have thereunto so tied themselves, that otherwise than so they take not upon them to command any.

[2.] And, that kings should be in such sort supreme commanders over all men, we hold it requisite, as well for the ordering of spiritual as of civil affairs; inasmuch as without universal authority in this kind, they should not be able when need serves to do as virtuous kings have done. Joas, purposing to renew the house of the Lord, assembled the Priests and Levites, and when they were together, gave them their charge, saying, "Go out unto the cities of Judah, and gather of all Israel money to repair the house of your God from year to year, and haste the things: but the Levites hasted not. Therefore the king called Jehoiada, the chief, and said unto him, Why hast thou not required of the Levites to bring in out of Judah and Jerusalem, the tax of Moses, the servant of the Lord, and of the congregation of Israel, for the tabernacle of the testimony? For wicked Athaliah and her children brake up the house of God, and all the things that were dedicated for the house of the Lord did they bestow upon Baalim. Therefore the king commanded, and they made a chest, and set it at the gate of the house of the Lord without; and they made a proclamation through Judah and Jerusalem, to bring unto the Lord the tax of Moses the servant of God, laid upon Israel in the wilderness." [2 Chron. xxiv. 5–9] Could either he have done this, or after him Ezechias the like concerning the celebration of the passover [2 Chron. xxx. 6], but that all sorts of men in all things did owe unto those their sovereign rulers the same obedience which sometime Joshua had them by solemn vow and promise bound unto? [Josh. i. 18] "Whosoever shall rebel against thy commandments, and will not obey thy words in all that thou commandest him, let him be put to death; only be strong and of a good courage."

[3.] Furthermore, judgment ecclesiastical we say is necessary for decision of controversies rising between man and man, and for correction of faults committed in the affairs of God; unto the due execution whereof there are three things necessary, *laws, judges, and a supreme governor of judgments.*

What courts there shall be, and what causes shall belong to each court, and what judges shall determine of every cause, and what order in all judgments shall be kept; of these things the laws have sufficiently disposed: so that his duty which sitteth in every such court is to judge, not of, but after, the said laws: "Imprimis illud observare debet judex, ne aliter judicet quam legibus, aut constitutionibus, aut moribus proditum est."* Which laws (for we mean the positive laws of our own realm concerning ecclesiastical affairs) if they otherwise dispose of any such thing than according to the law of reason and of God, we must both acknowledge them to be amiss, and endeavour to have them reformed: but touching that point what may be objected shall after appear.

Our judges in causes ecclesiastical are either ordinary or commissionary: ordinary, those whom we term Ordinaries; and such by the laws of the land are none but prelates only, whose power to do that which they do is in themselves, and belongeth unto the nature of their ecclesiastical calling. In spiritual causes, a lay person may be no ordinary; a commissionary judge there is no let but that he may be: and that our laws do evermore serve the ordinary judgment of spiritual causes unto spiritual persons, such as are termed Ordinaries, no man which knoweth any thing in the practice of this realm can easily be ignorant.

[4.] Now, besides them which are authorized to judge in several territories, is required an universal power which reacheth over all, importing supreme authority of government over all courts, all judges, all causes; the operation of which power is as well to strengthen, maintain and uphold

* ["A judge ought principally to take care lest he judge otherwise than as the laws, constitutions, or established customs permit."]

particular jurisdictions, which haply might else be of small effect; as also to remedy that which they are not able to help, and to redress that wherein they at any time do otherwise than they ought to do. This power being sometime in the bishop of Rome, who by sinister practices had drawn it into his hands, was for just considerations by public consent annexed unto the king's royal seat and crown. From thence the authors of reformation would translate it into their national assemblies and synods; which synods are the only help that they think lawful to use against such evils in the Church as particular jurisdictions are not sufficient to redress. In which case our laws have provided that the king's supereminent authority and power shall serve. As namely, when the whole ecclesiastical state, or the principal persons therein, do need visitation and reformation; when, in any part of the Church, errors, heresies, schisms, abuses, offences, contempts, enormities, are grown, which men in their several jurisdictions either do not or cannot help: whatsoever any spiritual authority or power (such as legates from the see of Rome did sometimes exercise) hath done or might heretofore have done for the remedy of those evils in lawful sort (that is to say, without violation of the law of God or nature in the deed done), as much in every degree our laws have fully granted that the king for ever may do, not only by setting ecclesiastical synods on work, that the thing may be their act and the king their motioner unto it, (for so much perhaps the masters of reformation will grant;) but by commissionaries few or many, who having the king's letters patents, may in the virtue thereof execute the premises as agents in the right, not of their own peculiar and ordinary but of his supereminent power.

[5.] When men are wronged by inferior judges, or have any just cause to take exception against them, their way for redress is to make their appeal. An appeal is a present delivery of him which maketh it out of the hands of their power and jurisdiction from whence it is made. Pope Alexander having sometime the king of England at the advantage, caused him, amongst other things, to agree, that as many of his subjects as would, might appeal to the court of Rome. "And thus," saith one,* "that whereunto a mean person at this day would scorn to submit himself, so great a king was content to be subject. Notwithstanding even when the pope," saith he, "had so great authority amongst princes which were far off, the Romans he could not frame to obedience, nor was able to obtain that himself might abide at Rome, though promising not to meddle with other than ecclesiastical affairs." So much are things that terrify more feared by such as behold them aloof off than at hand.

Reformers I doubt not in some cases will admit appeals made unto their synods; even as the church of Rome doth allow of them so they be made to the bishop of Rome. As for that kind of appeal which the English laws

* Machiavel. Hist. Florent. lib. i.

do approve, from the judge of any particular court unto the king, as the only supreme governor on earth, who by his delegates may give a final definitive sentence, from which no further appeal can be made; will their platform allow of this? Surely, forasmuch as in that estate which they all dream of, the whole Church must be divided into parishes, of which none can have greater or less authority and power than another; again, the king himself must be but as a common member in the body of his own parish, and the causes of that only parish must be by the officers thereof determinable; in case the king had so much preferment, as to be made one of those officers (for otherwise by their positions he were not to meddle any more than the meanest amongst the subjects with the judgment of any ecclesiastical cause), how is it possible they should allow of appeals to be made from any other abroad to the king?

[6.] To receive appeals from all other judges, belongeth unto the highest in power over all; and to be in power over all, as touching the judgment of ecclesiastical causes, this as they think belongeth only unto synods. Whereas therefore with us, kings do exercise over all kinds of persons and causes, power both of voluntary and litigious jurisdiction; so that according to the one they visit, reform, and command; according to the other, they judge universally, doing both in far other sort than such as have ordinary spiritual power: oppugned herein we are by some colourable shew of argument, as if to grant thus much unto any secular person it were unreasonable. "For sith it is," say they, "apparent out of the Chronicles, that judgment in church matters pertaineth unto God; seeing likewise it is evident out of the Apostle, that the high priest is set over those matters in God's behalf; it must needs follow that the principality or direction of the judgment of them is by God's ordinance appertaining unto the [high] priest, and consequently to the ministry of the Church: and if it be by God's ordinance appertaining unto them, how can it be translated from them unto the civil magistrate?" Which argument, briefly drawn into form, lieth thus: That which belongeth unto God, may not be translated unto any other than whom he hath appointed to have it in his behalf: but principality of judgment in church matters appertaineth unto God, which hath appointed the high priest, and consequently the ministry of the Church alone, to have it in [his] behalf; therefore, it may not from them be translated to the civil magistrate. The first of which three propositions we grant; as also in the second that branch which ascribeth unto God principality in the church matters. But that either he did appoint none but only the high priest to exercise the said principality for him; or that the ministry of the Church may in reason from thence be concluded to have alone the same principality by his appointment: these two points we deny utterly.

For concerning the high priest, there is first no such ordinance of God to be found. "Every high priest," saith the Apostle, "is taken from among men, and is ordained for men in things pertaining to God:" [Heb. v. 1] whereupon it may well be gathered, that the priest was indeed ordained of God to have power in things pertaining unto God. For the Apostle doth there mention the power of offering gifts and sacrifices for sins; which kind of power was not only given of God unto priests, but restrained unto priests only. The power of jurisdiction and ruling authority, this also God gave them, but not them alone. For it is held, as all men know, that others of the laity were herein joined by the law with them. But concerning principality in church affairs (for of this our question is, and of no other) the priests neither had it alone, nor at all; but (as hath been already shewed) principality in spiritual affairs was the royal prerogative of kings.

Again, though it were so, that God had appointed the high priest to have the said principality of government in those matters; yet how can they who allege this, enforce thereby that consequently the ministry of the Church, and no other, ought to have the same, when they are so far off from allowing as much to the ministry of the Gospel, as the priesthood of the Law had by God's appointment, that we but collecting thereout a difference in authority and jurisdiction amongst the Clergy, to be for the polity of the Church not inconvenient, they forthwith think to close up our mouths by answering, "That the Jewish high priests had authority above the rest, only in that they prefigured the sovereignty of Jesus Christ; as for the ministers of the Gospel, it is," they say, "altogether unlawful to give them as much as the least title, any syllable that any way may sound towards principality." And of the regency which may be granted, they hold others even of the laity no less capable than pastors themselves. How shall these things cleave together?

[7.] The truth is, that they have some reason to think it not all of the fittest for kings to sit as ordinary judges in matters of faith and religion. An ordinary judge must be of that quality which in a supreme judge is not necessary: because the person of the one is charged with that which the other's authority dischargeth, without employing personally himself herein. It is an error to think that the king's authority can have no force or power in the doing of that which himself may not personally do. For first, impossible it is, that at one and the same time the king in person should order so many and so different affairs, as by his power every where present are wont to be ordered both in peace and at war, at home and abroad. Again, the king, in regard of his nonage or minority, may be unable to perform that thing wherein years of discretion are requisite for personal action; and yet his authority even then be of force. For which cause we say, that the king's authority dieth not, but is, and worketh, always alike. Sundry considerations there may be, effectual to withhold the king's person from being a doer of that which his power must notwithstanding give force unto. Even in civil affairs, where nothing doth either more concern the duty, or better beseem the majesty of kings, than personally to administer justice unto their people, as most famous princes have done: yet, if it be in case of felony or treason, the learned of the laws of this realm do plainly affirm, that well may the king commit his authority unto another to judge between him and the offender; but the king being himself here a party, he cannot personally sit to give judgment.

As therefore the person of the king may, for just consideration, even where the cause is civil, be notwithstanding withdrawn from occupying the seat of judgment, and others under his authority be fit, he unfit himself to judge; so the considerations for which it were haply not convenient for kings to sit and give sentence in spiritual courts, where causes ecclesiastical are usually debated, can be no bar to that force and efficacy which their sovereign power hath over those very consistories, and for which, we hold without any exception that all courts are the king's. All men are not for all things sufficient; and therefore public affairs being divided, such persons must be authorized judges in each kind, as common reason may presume to be most fit: which cannot of kings and princes ordinarily be presumed in causes merely ecclesiastical; so that even common sense doth rather adjudge this burden unto other men. We see it hereby a thing necessary, to put a difference, as well between that ordinary jurisdiction which belongeth to the clergy alone, and that commissionary wherein others are for just consideration appointed to join with them; as also between both these jurisdictions, and a third, whereby the king hath a transcendent authority, and that in all causes, over both. Why this may not lawfully be granted unto him, there is no reason.

[8.] A time there was when kings were not capable of any such power, as namely, while they professed themselves open adversaries unto Christ and Christianity. A time there followed, when they, being capable, took sometimes more sometimes less to themselves, as seemed best in their own eyes, because no certainty touching their right was as yet determined. The bishops, who alone were before accustomed to have the ordering of such affairs, saw very just cause of grief, when the highest, favouring heresy, withstood by the strength of sovereign authority religious proceedings. Whereupon they oftentimes, against this new unresistible power, pleaded that use and custom which had been to the contrary; namely, that the affairs of the Church should be dealt in by the clergy, and by no other: unto which purpose, the sentences that then were uttered in defence of unabolished orders and laws, against such as did of their own heads contrary thereunto, are now altogether impertinently brought in opposition against them who use but the power which laws have given them, unless men can shew that there is in those laws some manifest iniquity or injustice.

Whereas therefore against the force judicial and imperial, which supreme authority hath, it is alleged, how Constantine termeth church-officers, "Overseers of things within the Church," himself, "of those without the Church:" how Augustine witnesseth, that the emperor not daring to judge of the bishops' cause, committed it unto the bishops; and was to crave pardon of the bishops, for that by the Donatists' importunity, which made no end of appealing unto him, he was (being weary of them) drawn to give sentence in a matter of theirs: how Hilary beseecheth the emperor Constance to provide that the governors of his provinces should not presume to take upon them the judgment of ecclesiastical causes, to whom commonwealth matters only belonged: how Ambrose affirmeth, that palaces belong unto the emperor, churches to the minister; that the emperor hath authority over the common walls of the city, and not in holy things; for which cause he never would yield to have "the causes of the Church debated in the prince's consistory," but "excused himself to the emperor Valentinian, for that being convented to answer concerning church matters in a civil court, he came not." Besides these testimonies of antiquity which Mr. Cartwright bringeth forth, Dr. Stapleton, who likewise citeth them one by one to the same purpose, hath augmented the number of them by adding other of the like nature: namely, how Hosius the bishop of Corduba answered the emperor, saying, "God hath committed to thee empire; with those things that belong to the Church he hath put us in trust." How Leontius bishop of Tripolis also told the selfsame emperor as much: "I wonder how thou, which art called unto one thing, takest upon thee to deal in another. For being placed in military and politic affairs, in things that belong unto bishops alone thou wilt bear rule." We may by these testimonies drawn from antiquity, if we list to consider them, discern how requisite it is that authority should always follow received laws in the manner of proceeding. For inasmuch as there was at the first no certain law, determining what force the principal civil magistrate's authority should be of, how far it should reach, and what order it should observe; but Christian emperors from time to time did what themselves thought most reasonable in those affairs; by this mean it cometh to pass that they in their practice vary, and are not uniform.

Virtuous emperors, such as Constantine the Great was, made conscience to swerve unnecessarily from the customs which had been used in the Church, even when it lived under infidels. Constantine, of reverence to bishops and their spiritual authority, rather abstained from that which himself might lawfully do, than was willing to claim a power not fit or decent for him to exercise. The order which had been before, he ratified, exhorting bishops to look to the Church, and promising that he would do the office of a bishop over the commonwealth: which very Constantine did not thereby so renounce all authority in judging of spiritual causes, but that sometime he took, as St. Augustine witnesseth, even personal cognition of them; howbeit whether as purposing to give therein judicially any sentence, I stand in doubt. For if the other, of whom St. Augustine elsewhere speaketh, did in such sort judge, surely there was cause why he should excuse it as a thing not usually done. Otherwise there is no let, but that any such great person may hear those causes to and fro debated, and deliver in the end his own opinion of them, declaring on which side himself doth judge that the truth is. But this kind of sentence bindeth no side to stand thereunto; it is a sentence of private persuasion, and not of solemn jurisdiction, albeit a king or an emperor pronounce it.

Again, on the contrary part, when governors infected with heresy were possessed of the highest power, they thought they might use it as pleased themselves, to further by all means therewith that opinion which they desired should prevail; they not respecting at all what was meet, presumed to command and judge all men in all causes, without either care of orderly proceeding, or regard to such laws and customs as the Church had been wont to observe. So that the one sort feared to do even that which they might; and that which the other ought not they boldly presumed upon; the one sort modestly excused themselves where they scarce needed; the other, though doing that which was inexcusable, bare it out with main power, not enduring to be told by any man how far they roved beyond their bounds. So great odds between them whom before we mentioned, and such as the younger Valentinian, by whom St. Ambrose being commanded to yield up one of the churches under him unto the Arians, whereas they which were sent on his message alleged, that the emperor did but use his own right, forasmuch as all things were in his power: the answer which the holy bishop gave them was, "That the Church is the house of God, and that those things which be God's are not to be yielded up, and disposed of at the emperor's will and pleasure; his palaces he might grant unto whomsoever, but God's own habitations not so." A cause why many times emperors did more by their absolute authority than could very well stand with reason, was the over great importunity of heretics, who being enemies to peace and quietness, cannot otherwise than by violent means be supported.

[9.] In this respect therefore we must needs think the state of our own church much better settled than theirs was; because our laws have with far more certainty prescribed bounds unto each kind of power. All decisions of things doubtful, and corrections of things amiss, are proceeded in by order of law, what person soever he be unto whom the administration of judgment belongeth. It is neither permitted unto prelate nor prince to judge or determine at their own discretion, but law hath prescribed what both shall do. What power the king hath he hath it by law, the bounds and limits of it are known; the entire community giveth general order by law how all things publicly are to be done, and the king as the head thereof, the highest in authority over all, causeth according to the same law every particular to be framed and ordered thereby. The whole body politic maketh laws, which laws give power unto the king, and the king having bound himself to use according unto law that power, it so falleth out, that the execution of the one is accomplished by the other in most religious and peaceable sort. There is no cause given unto any to make supplication, as Hilary did, that civil governors, to whom commonwealth-matters only belong, might not presume to take upon them the judgment of ecclesiastical causes. If the cause be spiritual, secular courts do not meddle with it: we need not excuse ourselves with Ambrose, but boldly and lawfully we may refuse to answer before any civil judge in a matter which is not civil, so that we do not mistake the nature either of the cause or of the court, as we easily may do both, without some better direction than can be had by the rules of this new-found discipline. But of this most certain we are, that our laws do neither suffer a spiritual court to entertain those causes which by law are civil, nor yet if the matter be indeed spiritual, a mere civil court to give judgment of it.

Touching supreme power therefore to command all men, in all manner of causes of judgment to be highest, let thus much suffice as well for declaration of our own meaning, as for defence of the truth therein.

Chapter 9

OF THEIR EXEMPTION FROM JUDICIAL KINDS OF PUNISHMENT BY THE CLERGY

The last thing of all which concerns the king's supremacy is, whether thereby he may be exempted from being subject to that judicial power which ecclesiastical consistories have over men. It seemeth, first, in most men's judgments to be requisite that on earth there should not be any alive altogether without standing in awe of some by whom they may be controlled and bridled.

The good estate of a commonwealth within itself is thought on nothing to depend more than upon these two special affections, fear and love: fear in the highest governor himself; and love, in the subjects that live under him. The subject's love for the most part continueth as long as the righteousness of kings doth last; in whom virtue decayeth not as long as they fear to do that which may alienate the loving hearts of their subjects from them. Fear to do evil groweth from the harm which evildoers are to suffer. If therefore private men, which know the danger they are subject unto, being malefactors, do notwithstanding so boldly adventure upon heinous crimes, only because they know it is possible for some transgressor sometimes to escape the danger of law: in the mighty upon earth, (which are not always so virtuous and holy that their own good minds will bridle them,) what may we look for, considering the frailty of man's nature, if the world do once hold it for a maxim that kings ought to live in no subjection: that, how grievous disorders soever they fall into, none may have coercive power over them? Yet so it is that this we must necessarily admit, as a number of right well learned men are persuaded.

[2.] Let us therefore set down first, what there is which may induce men so to think; and then consider their several inventions or ways, who judge it a thing necessary, even for kings themselves, to be punishable, and that by men. The question itself we will not determine. The reasons of each opinion being opened, it shall be best for the wise to judge which of them is likeliest to be true. Our purpose being not to oppugn any save only that which reformers hold; and of the rest, rather to inquire than to give sentence. Inducements leading men to think the highest magistrate should not be judged of any, saving God alone, are specially these.

First, as there could be in natural bodies no motion of any thing, unless there were some which moveth all things and continueth unmoveable; even so in politic societies there must be some unpunishable, or else no man shall suffer punishment. For sith punishments proceed always from superiors, to whom the administration of justice belongeth, which administration must have necessarily a fountain that deriveth it to all others, and receiveth it not from any; because otherwise the course of justice should go infinitely in a circle, every superior having his superior without end, which cannot be: therefore a well-spring it followeth there is, and a supreme head of justice, whereunto all are subject, but itself in subjection to none. Which kind of preeminence if some ought to have in a kingdom, who but the king should have it? Kings therefore no man can have lawfully power and authority to judge. If private men offend, there is the magistrate over them, which judgeth. If magistrates, they have their prince. If princes, there is Heaven, a tribunal, before which they shall appear: on earth they are not accountable to any.

Which thing likewise the very original of kingdoms doth shew . . .

Unto the prince. The name of Head of the Church of England, to give to the prince, they count it injurious unto Christ.

What authority they leave to princes.

The cause of this doubt is a conceit that the Church and Commonweal in respect of regiment must needs be always two distinct bodies, so that the head of the one cannot be the head of the other also. Their reason frivolous, that because Christ is properly termed the Head of the Church, therefore the prince may not be called the Head of this Church under Christ. What the name of Headship doth import being attributed unto Christ; that his headship over all churches doth not exclude the authority of governors placed as heads over each particular church for the visible regiment thereof. That a Christian prince within his dominions hath supreme power, authority, and headship, over all governors, and that in causes of whatsoever kind, no less if they belong to the Church of Christ than if they merely concern the temporal and civil State.

Their minds, I doubt not, are far from treason. Howbeit, in the days of Henry VIII to have held that which now is maintained concerning the prince's power, had then been adjudged a capital offence. Out of the principles which the learneder sort of them deliver, the simpler may draw, as some have done, that by just execution of law hath cost them their lives. A hard case, and to them small comfort which have taught these silly persons such doctrine as being unsaid they have notwithstanding suffered death.

The church governors' jurisdiction to be held immediately from God without dependency on the prince.

They whose "callings are not only inclusively, but also expressly in the Word;" they that have not their authority "by human institution, but by divine ordinance;" they that "hold their jurisdiction" as from God, not "as from men" (which pastors, doctors, elders and deacons do): "their places ought to be in this commonwealth whether her Majesty and our State will or no."

The urging of that principle, what belongeth unto all, all should give voice in, and therefore no church officer without the people.

Their taking away the prince's prerogative in pardoning certain offendors.

Their claiming coercive authority over the prince.

[3.] "His second point, whereby he would make us odious, is, that we think the prince may be subject to excommunication; that is, that he is a brother [Deut. xvii. 15; Matt. xviii. 15], that he is not without but within the Church [1 Cor. v. 12, 13]. If this be dangerous, why is it printed and allowed in the famous writings of Bishop Jewel: 'In that the high priest doth his office when he excommunicates and cuts off a dead member from the body, so far forth the prince, be he never so mighty, is inferior to him. Yea not only to a bishop, but to a simple priest?' Why is it suffered which Mr. Nowell hath written, 'The prince ought patiently to abide excommunication at the bishop's hands?' Why are not the worthy examples of emperors rased out of the histories, seeing they have been subject to his censure?"

The Jews were forbidden to choose an alien king over them; inasmuch as there is not any thing more natural than that the head and the body subject thereunto should always, if it were possible, be linked in that bond of nearness also which birth and breeding as it were in the bowels of one common mother usually causeth. Which being true did not greatly need to be alleged for proof that kings are in the Church of God of the same spiritual fraternity with their subjects: a thing not denied nor doubted of.

Indeed the king is a brother; but such a brother as unto whom all the rest of the brethren are subject. He is a sheaf of the Lord's field as the rest are; howbeit, a sheaf which is so far raised up above the rest [Gen. xxxvii. 7] that they all owe reverence unto it. The king is a brother which hath dominion over all his brethren. A strange conclusion to gather hereby, that therefore some of his brethren ought to have the authority of correcting him. We read that God did say unto David, "If Solomon thy son forget my laws, I will punish his transgressions with a rod." But that he gave commission unto any of Solomon's brethren to chastise Solomon, we do not read.

It is a thing very much alleged, that the church of the Jews had the sword of excommunication. Is any man able to allege where the same was ever drawn forth against the king? Yet how many of their kings how notoriously spotted?

Our Saviour's words are, "If thy brother offend thee." And St. Paul's, "Do ye not judge them that are within?" Both which speeches are but indefinite. So that neither the one nor the other is any let but some brother there may be whose person is exempt from being subject to any such kind of proceeding: some within, yet not therefore under, the jurisdiction of any other. Sentences, indefinitely uttered, must sometimes universally be understood: but not where the subject or matter spoken of doth in particulars admit that difference which may in reason seclude any part from society with the residue of that whole, whereunto one common thing is attributed. As in this case it clearly fareth where the difference between kings and others of the Church is a reason sufficient to separate the one from the other in that which is spoken of brethren, albeit the name of brethren itself do agree to both. Neither doth our Saviour nor the Apostle speak in more general sort of ecclesiastical punishments than Moses in his law doth of civil: "If there be found men or the man amongst you that hath served other gods." [Deut. xvii. 2] Again, "The man that committeth adultery." The punishment of both which transgressions being death, what man soever did offend therein, why was not Manasses for the one, for the other why not David accordingly executed? "Rex judicat, non judicatur," saith one. The king is appointed a judge of all men that live under him; but not any of them his judge.

The king is not subject unto laws; that is to say, the punishment which breach of laws doth bring upon inferiors taketh not hold on the king's person; although the general laws which all mankind is bound unto do tie no less the king than others, but rather more. For the grievousness of sin is aggravated by the greatness of him that committeth it: for which cause it also maketh him by so much the more obnoxious unto Divine revenge, by how much the less he feareth human.

[4.] Touching Bishop Jewel's opinion hereof, there is not in the place alleged any one word or syllable against the king's prerogative royal to be free from the coercive power of all spiritual, both persons and courts, within the compass of his own dominions. "In that," saith he, "the priest doeth his office, in that he openeth God's word, or declareth his threats, or rebuketh sin, or excommunicateth and cutteth off a dead member from the body; so far forth the prince, be he never so mighty, is inferior unto him. But in this respect the prince is inferior not only to the pope or bishop, but also to any other simple priest." He disputeth earnestly against that supremacy which the bishop of Rome did challenge over his sovereign lord the emperor: and by many allegations he laboureth to shew that popes have been always subject unto his supreme dominion, not he to theirs; he supreme judge over them, not they over him. Now whereas it was objected, that within the Church, when the priest doth execute his office, the very prince is inferior to him; so much being granted by Mr. Jewel, he addeth that this doth no more prove the pope than the simplest priest in the Church to be lord and head over kings. For although it doth hereby appear that in those things which belong to his priestly office the pope may do that which kings are not licensed to meddle with; in which respect it cannot be denied but that the emperor himself hath not only less power than the chiefest bishop, but even less than the meanest priest within his empire, and is consequently every priest's inferior that way: nevertheless, sith this appertaineth nothing at all to judicial authority and power, how doth this prove kings and emperors to be by way of subjection inferior to the pope as to their ecclesiastical judge? Impertinently therefore is the answer, which to such effect that admirable prelate maketh, brought by way of evidence to shew that in his opinion the king may not be exempted from the coercive authority and power of his own Clergy, but ought for his faults to be as punishable in their courts as any other subject under him.

[5.] The excommunication, which good Mr. Nowell thinketh that princes ought patiently to suffer at the bishop's hands, is no other than that which we also grant may be exercised on such occasions and in such manner as those two alleged examples out of antiquity do enforce.

"It is reported," saith Eusebius, "that one of the Philips which succeeded Gordian, came, being a Christian, to join with the rest of the people in prayer, the last festival day of Easter. At which time he which governed the Church there whither the emperor did resort, would in no case admit him, unless he first made confession, and were contented afterwards to stay his time in the place appointed for penitents," (according to the manner of Church discipline in those days, whereof we have spoken in the fifth [sixth?] book sufficiently); "because he was known to be many ways faulty. To this he readily condescended, making manifest by his deeds his true and religious affection to Godwards."

Another example there is, of the emperor Theodosius, who understanding that violence in the city of Thessalonica had been offered unto certain magistrates, sent in great rage a band of men; and, without any examination had to know where the fault was, slew mel-pell both guilty and innocent, to the number of 7000. It chanced afterwards, that the emperor coming to Milan, and intending to go to the Church as his accustomed manner was, St. Ambrose the bishop of that city, who before had heard of the emperor's so cruel and bloody an act, met him before the gate of the church, and in this wise forbade him to enter: "Emperor, it seemeth that how great the slaughter is which thyself hast made thou weighest not; nor, as I think, when wrath was settled did reason ever call to account what thou hadst committed. Peradventure thine imperial royalty hindreth the acknowledgment of thy sin; and thy power is a let to reason. Notwithstanding know thou shouldst what our nature is, how frail a thing and how fading; and that the first original from whence we have all sprung was the very dust whereunto we must slide again. Neither is it meet that being inveigled with the show of thy glistering robes thou shouldst forget the imbecility of that flesh which is covered therewith. Thy subjects (O Emperor) are in nature thy colleagues: yea even in her service thou art also joined as a fellow with them. For there is one Lord and Emperor, the Maker of this whole assembly of all things. With what eyes therefore wilt thou look upon the habitation of that common Lord? With what feet wilt thou tread upon that sacred floor? How wilt thou stretch forth those hands from which the blood as yet of unrighteous slaughter doth distil? The body of our Lord all holy how wilt thou take into such hands? How wilt thou put his honourable blood unto that mouth, the wrathful word whereof hath caused against all order of law the pouring out of so much blood? Depart therefore, and go not about by after deeds to add to thy former iniquity. Receive that bond wherewith from heaven the Lord of all doth give consent that thou shouldst be tied; a bond which is medicinable, and procureth health." Hereunto the king submitted himself; (for being brought up in religion he knew very well what belonged unto priests, what unto kings;) and with sobbing tears returned to the court again. Some eight months after, came the feast of our Saviour's Nativity; but yet the king sat still at home, mourning and emptying the lake of tears: which when Rufinus beheld, being at that time commander over the king's house, and by reason of usual access the bolder to speak; he came and asked the cause of those tears. To whom the king, with bitter grief and tears more abundantly gushing out, answered, "Thou, O Ruffin, dalliest, for mine evils thou feelest not: I mourn and bewail mine own wretchedness, considering that servants and beggars go freely to the house of God, and there present themselves before their Lord: whereas both from thence and from heaven also I am excluded. For in my mind I carry that voice of our Lord which saith with express terms, 'Whomsoever ye shall bind on earth, he in heaven shall be bound also.'" The rest of the history, which concerneth the manner of the emperor's admission after so earnest repentance, needeth not to be here set down.

It now remaineth to be examined whether these alleged examples prove that which they should do, yea or no. The thing which they ought to confirm is, that no less Christian kings than other persons under them ought to be subject to the selfsame coercive authority of Church-governors, and for the same kinds of transgressions, to receive at their hands the same spiritual censure of excommunication judicially inflicted by way of punishment. But in the aforesaid examples, whether we consider the offence itself of the excommunicate, or the persons excommunicating, or the manner of their proceeding; which three comprehend the whole substance of that which was done; it doth not by any of these appear that kings in suchwise should be subject. For, concerning the offences of men, there is no breach of Christian charity, whether it be by deed or by word; no excess, no lightness of speech or behaviour; no fault for which a man in the course of his life is openly noted as blameable; but the same being unamended through admonition ought, (as they say,) with the spiritual censure of excommunication to be punished. Wherefore unless they can shew, that in some such ordinary transgression, kings and princes, upon contempt of the Church's more mild censure, have been like other men in ancient times excommunicated, what should hinder any man to think but that the rare and unwonted crimes of those two emperors did cause their bishops to try what unusual remedy would work in so desperate diseases? Which opinion is also made more probable, inasmuch as the very histories, which have recorded them, propose them for strange and admirable patterns; the bishops, of boldness; the emperors, of meekness and humility. They wonder at the one, for adventuring to do it unto emperors; at the other, for taking it in so good part at the hands of bishops. What greater argument that all which was herein done proceeded from extraordinary zeal on both sides, and not from a settled judicial authority which the one was known to have over the other by a common received order in the Church. For at such things who would wonder?

Furthermore, if ye consider their persons, whose acts these excommunications were; he which is said to have excommunicated Philip emperor of Rome was Babylas the bishop of Antioch: and he which Theodosius emperor of Constantinople, Ambrose the bishop of Milan. Neither of which two bishops (as I suppose) was ordinary unto either of the two emperors. And therefore they both were incompetent judges, and such as had no authority to punish whom they excommunicated: except we will grant the emperor to have been so much the more subject than his subjects, that whereas the meanest of them was under but some one diocesan, any that would might be judge over him. But the manner of proceeding doth as yet more plainly evict that these examples make less than nothing for proof that ecclesiastical governors had at that time judicial authority to excommunicate emperors and kings. For what form of judgment was there observed, when neither judges nor parties judged did once dream of any such matter; till the one by chance repaired unto the place where the others were, and at that very instant suffered a sudden repulse; not only besides their own expectation, but also without any purpose beforehand in them who gave it? Judicial punishment hath at the leastwise sentence going always before execution, whereas all which we read of here is, that the guilty being met in the way were presently turned back, and not admitted to be partakers of those holy things whereof they were famously known unworthy.

[6.] I therefore conclude, that these excommunications have neither the nature of judicial punishments, nor the force of sufficient arguments to prove that ecclesiastical judges should have authority to call their own sovereign to appear before them into their consistories, there to examine, to judge, and by excommunication to punish them, if so be they be found culpable.

But concerning excommunication, such as is only a dutiful, religious, and holy refusal to admit notorious transgressors in so extreme degree unto the blessed communion of saints, especially the mysteries of the Body and Blood of Christ, till their humbled penitent minds be made manifest: this we grant every king bound to abide at the hands of any minister of God wheresoever through the world. As for judicial authority to punish malefactors, if the king be as the kings of Israel were, and as every of ours is, a supreme Lord, than whom none under God is by way of ruling authority and power higher, where he reigneth, how should any man there have the high place of a judge over him? He must be more than thine equal that hath a chastising power over thee: so far is it off that any under thee should be thy judge. Wherefore, sith the kings of England are within their own dominions the most high, and can have no peer, how is it possible that any, either civil or ecclesiastical person under them should have over them coercive power, when such power would make that person so far forth his superior's superior, ruler, and judge? It cannot therefore stand with the nature of such sovereign regiment that any subject should have power to exercise on kings so highly authorized the greatest censure of excommunication, according to the platform of Reformed Discipline: but if this ought to take place, the other is necessarily to give place. For which cause, till better reason be brought, to prove that kings cannot lawfully be exempted from subjection unto ecclesiastical courts, we must and do affirm their said exemption lawful.

A. S. McGRADE was born in Brooklyn, New York, and studied at the Universities of Chicago, Texas, Yale and Cambridge. He is now Professor in the Philosophy Department of the University of Connecticut. In the last year he has been engaged in research at the University of Tubingen as a Humboldt Fellow.

BRIAN VICKERS was educated at St Marylebone Grammar School and Trinity College, Cambridge, where he took his B.A. and Ph.D. He taught at Cambridge for ten years, and is now Professor of English Literature at the University of Zurich.